Jack Burd's
Civil War
Source Book
3rd Edition: 1998

Rockbridge Publishing Company
Berryville, Virginia

Published by
Rockbridge Publishing Company
PO Box 351
Berryville, VA 22611

(800) 473-3943
(540) 955-4126 (fax)
cwpub@visuallink.com

Cover photo © 1997 by Julio Zangroniz
The 1st Pennsylvania Light Artillery (foreground) starts the cannonade that opened
the Battle of the Cornfield at the 135th anniversary program of the battle of Antietam
outside of Hagerstown, Maryland, September 1997.

ISBN 1 883522-20-X
ISSN 1091-1618

Contents

Dear Readers,

We've been working hard for the past year to top the wildly popular 2nd Edition of the Civil War Source Book. Many readers contacted us with suggested new listings, which have been included. Tracey Barger combed Civil War publications and scoured the Internet gathering new information. The result is a directory almost **TWICE** the size of the previous edition—just under 3,000 entries!

We scratched our heads and tried to figure out how to list the entries so you can find what you're looking for. Our solution was to list some entries in more than one category in what we hope you will agree is a logical manner, but even so, some multi-faceted businesses were a bit tricky. Our suggestion is to take a little time to look over the table of contents, then skim through the Source Book itself and see what's what. Like learning to shop in a new store, you'll soon know on which "aisle" to look to satisfy your needs.

The Internet section has exploded, as has use of the net itself. Many businesses and organizations now maintain their own websites. Those URLs (and e-mail addresses) will be found with the business listing. Many listings in the Internet section of the Source Book are good places to start for general information.

We appreciate the interest of our readers and appreciate your suggestions. (The name of the business/organization is in **boldface** type this year, so it's easier to spot what you're looking for ... thanks to a reader suggestion.) We're revising constantly as we look toward the next edition. Let us know what you'd like to see here—we'll make every effort to make it so.

Sincerely,

Jack

Jack Burd

20TH MAINE, INC.
207-865-4340
207-865-9575 Fax
Patricia Hodgdon
49 West St
Freeport ME 04032-1127
Specialized bookstore devoted to Civil War
with new & old books, art, music, videos,
antiques & much more.

ALPHAEUS H. ALBERT
PO Box 5266
Clinton NJ 08809-0266
Identifies buttons, Confederate/U.S., state
seals, Republic of Texas. 3,000+ buttons.

ALTUS INTERNATIONAL, LTD.
612-922-6948
5609 Interlachen Cir
Edina MN 55436
Civil War chess set - wooden, hand-carved,
painted, lacquered. Historically accurate.
Board is plate glass with beveled edges; ea.
player stands 6-1/2" tall.

AMERICA'S COVERED BRIDGES
PO Box 516
Lightfoot VA 23090-0516
22-piece collection of replicas, incl. "Old
Humpback Bridge," covered bridge saved
from destruction by negotiated agreement
between Union & Confederate forces. $45 ea.
Write for complete list.

AMERICAN HISTORICAL FOUNDATION
800-368-8080 • 804-353-1812
804-359-4895 Fax
http://www.ahfrichmond.com
1142 W Grace St
Richmond VA 23220-3613
Firing reproductions of Lee's 1851 Navy
Revolver (limited). Colt's 34d Model Dragoon
Revolvers, Jackson LeMat, JEB Stuart Le
Mat, Lee/Grant Henry Rifles, etc.

AMERICAN MILITARY ANTIQUES
410-465-6827
Courtney B. Wilson & Assoc.
8398 Court Ave
Ellicott City MD 21043-4514
Appraisers & dealers in fine 19th-c. military
Americana. Civil War memorabilia, books,
photos, swords, forearms, relics. Buys/sells.

AMERICANA SOUVENIRS & GIFTS
http://www.americanagifts.com
302 York St
Gettysburg PA 17325

Most complete line of Civil War souvenirs &
memorabilia for both USA & CSA. Cannons,
bullets, patches, toys, books, flags, videos,
documents, insignias, & much more. (See ad
page 242)

AMES INSTRUMENT COMPANY
PO Box 651
Ames NY 13317-0651
Signalman's compass - 2" solid brass with
level & "slit and window" sights in lined walnut
box, $90.50 ppd.

DALE C. ANDERSON CO.
4 W Confederate Ave
Gettysburg PA 17325
Firearms, edged weapons, uniforms,
accoutrements, & 1000s of other objects - all
periods & significant events, 1776-1945;
emphasis on Civil War era. Our 37th year.
Bi-monthly, photo-illus. militaria catalog -
$12/yr.

ANDERSONVILLE ANTIQUES
912-924-2558 • 912-924-1044
Peggy & Fred Sheppard
PO Box 26
Andersonville GA 31711
Authentic Civil War guns, swords, buttons,
documents; books on the Civil War.

ANTIQUE AMERICANA
PO Box 19
Abington MA 02351-0019
Colonial American & Civil War documents,
books, autographs, maps. Reasonably priced.

THE ANTIQUE CENTER OF GETTYSBURG
717-337-3669
7 Lincoln Sq
Gettysburg PA 17325-2205
100 showcases of quality antiques &
collectibles, including large selection of Civil
War memorabilia, artifacts, weapons &
medical supplies. In historic Wills House on
the square in Gettysburg.

ANTIQUE EDGE
PO Box 2958
Fort Dearborn MI 48124
Buys/sells Civil War antiques, curios, & relics.

ARROWHEAD FORGE
605-938-4814
RR 1 Box 25
Wilmot SD 57279-9718
Tools, fire irons, candleholders, grills, eating
utensils, tomahawks, much more. Catalog -$3.

ARSENAL ARTIFACTS, INC.
800-483-1861
486 W Main St
Sylva NC 28779
Limited edition prints by Bob Graham, John Warr, Mort Kunstler, John Paul Strain & others. Large selection of dug artifacts. Specialize in artillery.

ARTCAST
770-270-9659
PO Box 28561
Atlanta GA 30358-0561
1861 reproduction West Point class ring. Original reproductions of May & June class (only year with 2 graduations.) Sterling - $59.95; gold - $169.95.

ATLANTA ARSENAL
5750 Pebblebrook Trl
Gainesville GA 30506-6595
Reproduction Confederate painted canvas accoutrements, copy from originals, incl. cartridge boxes, cap boxes, bayonet scabbards, slings, belts. Free price list.

THE BAG MAN
615-859-9658
Patrick Strickland
588 Dividing Ridge Rd
Goodlettsville TN 37072
Best possible reproductions. Knapsacks - $50 & up; S&K copper or tin canteens - $39 & $55.

BALLANTYNES OF WALKERBURN (USA)
888-269-8720 • 910-323-4872
910-323-0214 Fax
bowusa@aol.com
Tracey Lindsay
PO Box 35001
Fayetteville NC 28303-0001
Fine quality, 8" hand-painted porcelain resin statues. Ask about our collectors club. Free catalog.

BARTLETT'S COLLECTIBLES
PO Box 545
Mechanicsburg PA 17055-0545
Civil War trading cards; superb photography, educational, collectible. Free sample card & catalog.

BELL CONSULTING, INC.
352-753-0219
Ted & Pat Bell
PO Box 579
Lady Lake FL 32158-0579

Antique handguns, Bowie knives, cartridge belts & holsters, rifles, deringers, swords. Buy/sell/trade. Catalog - send #10 SASE.

BELLINGER'S MILITARY ANTIQUES
770-992-5574
Bill Bellinger
PO Box 76371-SB
Atlanta GA 30358-1371
FULL-TIME DEALER of antique firearms, edged weapons, belt plates, leather goods, books & miscellaneous from the 17th-19th century. Civil War a specialty. Catalog - $3; 4 issues - $10 (overseas - $20).

BENCKENDORF PIPES
515-255-0838
PO Box 30062
Des Moines IA 50310-3330
Finest reproduction & collectible pipes & smoking accoutrements. Free catalog.

D. BIGDA ANTIQUES
803-722-0248
http://bmark.com/bigda.antiques
dbigda@awod.com
178 King St
Charleston SC 29401-2212
Matching period & modern sterling silverware. Many patterns in stock. Tea sets, perfume bottles, etc.

BLACKSWORD ARMOURY, INC.
352-495-9967
11717 SW 99th Ave
Gainesville FL 32608-5800
Replicas of historical weapons & armor from ancient to Civil War. Catalog - $3.

BLUE/GREY MILITARIA
860-749-3407
PO Box 296
Somers CT 06071-0296
GAR, Regimental & Veteran Association reunion ribbons & badges. Collections & single items bought. Catalog/list -$1.

BORDER STATES LEATHERWORKS
501-361-2642
501-361-2851 Fax
1158 Apple Blossom Ln
Springdale AR 72762-9762
Civil War collectibles, original weapons & equipment. Reproduction cavalry saddles & equipment. Custom hand-forged bits.

MIKE BRACKIN
203-647-8620
PO Box 23
Manchester CT 06045-0023
Large assortment of Civil War & Indian War autographs, accoutrements, memorabilia, insignia, medals, buttons, GAR, documents, photos & books. Catalog - $6/yr for 5 issues.

THE BRADFORD EXCHANGE
9345 N Milwaukee Ave
Niles IL 60714-1393
The Heart of Plate Collecting. Limited edition collector's plates featuring historic events.

BRITISH COLLECTIBLES LTD.
1727 Wilshire Blvd
Santa Monica CA 90403-5509
Authentic collectibles for serious collectors, 1800s-WWII. Catalog - $15.

KEN BROWN
614-498-8379
17261 Sligo Rd
Kimbolton OH 43749
Quality, handmade, reproduction cavalry tack, equipment & accoutrements. Free brochure.

WALTER BUDD
3109 Eubanks Rd
Durham NC 27707-3622
Finest selection of US military antiques, firearms, swords, uniforms, head gear, cavalry equipment, McClellan saddles, mess gear, horse-drawn army wagons & rolling stock, etc. Subscription rate - $5 for 8 issues.

BUFFALO ROBE TRADING POST
520-457-2322
George Henry
9 N 5th St
PO Box 741
Tombstone AZ 85638-0741
Civil War, local history, American Indian, western lawmen & outlaws. Gift shop, artifacts, video & audio tapes. Historian in attendance.

THE BUGLE CALL
630-350-1116
630-350-1606 Fax
http://www.infinitiv.com/BugleCall
Robert C. Trownsell
1241 N Ellis St
Bensenville IL 60106-1118
Fine military antiques. Shoulder straps a specialty.

RICH BURNHAM
310-832-3252
PO Box 4056
Torrance CA 90510
Union & Confederate dug & non-dug buttons. Many rare. Large list - $2.

STANLEY BUTCHER
4 Washington Ave
Andover MA 01810-1724
Buys Confederate generals' autographs, letters, & other Civil War documents.

CALDWELL & CO. COLLECTIBLES
765-482-6280
civilwr@in-motion.net
816 Pleasant St
Lebanon IN 46052
Edged weapons, firearms, Civil War items & general antiques. Buy/sell. Free catalog.

KEITH CANGELOSI
4201 Frenchman St
New Orleans LA 70122
Civil War military antiques. Longarms, carbines, handguns, edged weapons. List - $2.

CAROLINA COLLECTORS CIVIL WAR RELICS
http://www.collectorsnet.com/ccrelics/index.htm
Rick Burton or Warren Vestal
PO Box 1177
Kernersville NC 27285-1177
Dug & non-dug relics from battlefields & camp sites. Photo-illus. catalog.

THE CARRIAGE HOUSE
918-367-6425
PO Box 8
Slick OK 74071-0008
Wooden wheels for cannon, old auto, carriage & decor.

CAT'S MEOW VILLAGE
717-359-8608 • 717-359-7411
1295 Frederick Pike
Littlestown PA 17340
Historic Gettysburg series, collectable painted wooden buildings; includes Jenny Wade House, Lee's Headquarters, Meade's Headquarters, Pa. Monument, Lutheran Seminary Chapel, several others.

THE CAVALRY SHOP
804-266-0898
T.E. Johnson, Jr.
9700 Royerton Dr
Richmond VA 23228-1218

Civil War leather goods, buckles; horsegear.
Catalog - $2. (See ad page 233)

CEDAR CREEK RELIC SHOP
540-869-5207
Rex & Mary Bailey
PO Box 232
Middletown VA 22645-0232
Largest selection of authentic Civil War relics
in the Shenandoah Valley. Next to battlefield.
Catalog - $6 for 4 issues/yr.

CIVIL WAR "THINGS 'N FRAMES"
615-952-3672
http://www.i285.com/civil/index.html
sonny@viponline.com
Sonny Collins
PO Box 422
Kingston Springs TN 37082-0422
Forrest, Davis, Mosby & Stuart prints &
notecards from original museum pieces
painted from life. Antique medical equipment
& Civil War artifacts.

CIVIL WAR ANTIQUES
419-878-8355 • 419-882-5547
David W. Taylor
PO Box 87
Sylvania OH 43560-0087
Pedigreed Civil War antiques, guns, swords,
uniforms, buckles, flags, drums, letters,
diaries, etc. Bought/sold. Catalog - $10.

CIVIL WAR ANTIQUITIES
614-363-1862
http://www.civilwarantiquities.com
Todd Rittenhouse, Prop.
PO Box 1411
Delaware OH 43015-1411
Quality CW items. Guns, swords, letters,
currency, books, prints. Buy/sell/trade. Full
service custom framing & matting; specializing
in conservation framing. Shop located at
13-1/2 N Sandusky St., Delaware, Ohio.
Catalog - $5.

**CIVIL WAR BULLET COLLECTOR
NEWSLETTER**
oma00077@mail.wvnet.edu
Chuck Haislip
66 W Main St Apt 3
White Sulphur Springs WV 24986
Newsletter with classified section distributed
by Civil War Bullet Collector Association.
$10/yr. for 6 issues.

CIVIL WAR CATALOG
Bob & Pat Bartosz
PO Box 226

Wenonah NJ 08090-0226
Attention Civil War Collectors - $3 for next 3
issues. Letters, documents, slave papers,
hires, etc. Historical documents, ephemera.

CIVIL WAR EMPORIUM, INC.
408 Mill St
Occoquan VA 22125
From harmonicas to working cannons.
Working repros. Decorator models.
Consignments welcome. Buy/sell.

CIVIL WAR TABLE
716-632-4603
Michael Valentic
52 Mill St
Williamsville NY
Buy/sell. Free appraisal.

STAN CLARK MILITARY BOOKS
717-337-1728
717-337-0581 Fax
915 Fairview Ave
Gettysburg PA 17325-2906
Buys/sells Civil War books, ltd. edition prints,
autographs, letters, documents, postcards,
soldiers' items; special interest in U.S. Marine
Corps items.

CLARK'S GUN SHOP, INC.
540-439-8988
10016 James Madison Hwy
Warrenton VA 20186-7820
Retailer of books, Civil War relics, Kepis,
flags, buttons, Confederate souvenirs, original
Confederate money & state notes, CW prints.

COLLECTING THE CIVIL WAR
800-440-8478
PO Box 18844
Denver CO 80218-0844
2 videotapes - "Collecting the Union Soldier"
vol. 1, & "... Confederate Soldier" vol. 2.
Expert descriptions, close-up color
photography. 100s of items. $19.95 ea.; set
$29.95. Add $4 S&H.

COLLECTOR'S ARMOURY
800-544-3456 x515 • 703-684-6111
703-683-5486 Fax
James W. Hernly
PO Box 59, Dept CWB
Alexandria VA 22313-0059
Full line of "non-firing" reproduction pistols,
rifles, cannons, Civil War swords, knives,
bayonets, canteens, cap boxes, bugles &
flags. Free catalog. (See ad page 242)

COLLECTORS HERITAGE, INC.
PO Box 355
Bernardsville NJ 07924-0355
Reproduction museum-quality military swords,
knives, & bayonets. Catalog - $5 (ref.).

COLLECTORS' ANTIQUITIES, INC.
60 Manor Rd Ste 2000
Staten Island NY 10310-2626
American military antiques & memorabilia.
Catalog - $12 for 3 issues. $15 overseas.

COLUMBUS ARMORY
706-327-1424 Phone & Fax
David S. Brady
1104 Broadway
Columbus GA 31901-2429
Complete Civil War store featuring books,
relics, art, muskets & supplies. Buy/sell/trade.
Free price list. (See ad page 236)

DAVID CONDON, INC.
540-687-5642 • 800-364-8416 Orders only
540-687-5649 Fax
PO Box 7
Middleburg VA 20118-0007
Dealing in fine antique firearms since 1957.
Store located at 109 E Washington St (Route
50), Middleburg, Va.

CONFEDERATE ARTS
8301 Alvord St Dept. C
Mc Lean VA 22102-1736
Great Seal of the Confederacy minted in
exact detail in solid bronze. Limited ed. -
$69.95.

THE CONFEDERATE MBR NEWSLETTER
770-270-0542
Peter Bertram, Editor
PO Box 451421
Atlanta GA 31145-9421
6-pg illustrated newsletter cataloging UCV,
SCV Reunion Medals, badges & ribbons.
$12/yr. ($17 outside USA), 4 issues. Free
sample copy - large SASE.

**CONFEDERATE STATES MILITARY
ANTIQUES**
504-387-5044
http://www.collectorsnet.com/jjackson/index.htm
jjackson@aollectorsnet.com
2905 Government St
Baton Rouge LA 70806
Civil War relics & memorabilia; metal detector
sales.

CRANE MERCANTILE & MFG. CO.
314-231-4163
1212 Allen Ave
Saint Louis MO 63104-3914
Purveyor of finest cavalry saddle hardware.
Iron frame coat strap buckles. McClellan
saddle kit, tree & all hardware. Brochure - $2.

CSA
PO Box 570060
Whitestone NY 11357-0060
Confederate passports. Accurate, historical
might-have-beens. $4.

RON DACUS
800-868-0339
719 Turkey Trl
Fortson GA 31808
"General Order #9: Lee's Farewell to the
Confederacy" displayed in 18"x22" solid
wood, gold-trimmed frame. $99.95 + $10 S&H.

DALESAND
PO Box 513
Norge VA 23127-0513
Civil War bullets excavated from battlefield
areas. 2 for $9. (1 Union & 1 Confederate).

DEAD HORSE FORGE
1220 Price Station Rd
Church Hill MD 21623-1315
All types of knives, Hawks & other ironware,
powder horns & gourd canteens. Brochure -
send SASE.

DER DIENST
PO Box 221
Lowell MI 49331-0221
Confederate officer's hat insignia, exact
full-size repros -$21.50. More than 400
authentic metal & badge replicas. Catalog -
$5 (free w/ order).

DR. K. DIETRICH
PO Box 994
Stockbridge MA 01262-0994
Buy/sell Civil War memorabilia, soldiers'
letters, weapons & accoutrements, images.
Listing - 2 stamps.

DIXIE DEPOT
706-265-7533 • 706-265-3952 Fax
http://www.ilinks.net/~dixiegeneral
Dixie_Depot@stc.net
John Black
PO Box 1448
72 Keith Evans Rd
Dawsonville GA 30534

Pro-Southern educational products: video/ audio tapes, new/old books, bumper stickers, flags, wearables, lapel pins, exclusive Great Seal items. More than 600 items! Catalog. (See ad page 235)

DIXIE LEATHER WORKS
502-442-1058
800-888-5183 Orders only
502-448-1049 Fax
PO Box 8221
Paducah KY 42002-8221
Military & civilian museum-quality repros. 60+ hard-to-find leather items. Documents, maps, printed labels & stationery. Swords, firearms, & hats. Handmade chairs, desks; leather medical cases & bottle roll-up kits. Photo-illus. catalog - $6.

THE DIXIE SUTLER
PO Box 5162
Mobile AL 36605
Civil War-period supplies & collectibles for the reenactor or collector.

DOBI PUBLISHING
716-372-8687
1662 Haskell Pkwy
Olean NY 14760
New edition of *Directory of Buyers* - lists 1000s of collectors & dealers who are anxious to buy. $14.95 + $3 S&H.

R. STEPHEN DORSEY ANTIQUE MILITARIA
541-937-3348
PO Box 263
Eugene OR 97440-0263
Largest western dealer in pre- & post-Civil War, Civil War, & post-1900 U.S. militaria. Guns, accoutrements, edged weapons, etc. Catalog - $8 for 4 issues.

DRUM & MUSKET
906-842-3549
RR 1 Box 95A
Republic MI 49879-9758
Buys/sells/trades Civil War memorabilia by appointment, or send for free catalog.

DRUMMER BOY AMERICAN MILITARIA
717-296-7611
Christian Hill Rd
RR 4 Box 7198
Milford PA 18337-9702
Civil War repro goods: uniforms, buttons, leather goods, insignia, firearms, tinware, canteens, flags, books, blankets, sabers, etc. Catalog - $1.

EARLY AMERICAN HISTORY AUCTIONS
619-459-4159 • 800-473-5686
619-459-4373 Fax
http://www.cts.com/browse/ean
PO Box 3341
La Jolia CA 92038
Mail bid auctions every two months; approx. 1,000 lots in each. Historic Americana & Civil War-related material. Always buying collections & accepting important consign- ments. Catalog - $36/yr. for 6 issues. Free on Internet.

THE EARLY AMERICAN HISTORY SHOPPE
603-772-7973
225 Water St
Exeter NH 03833-2417
Books (antiquarian & in-print), ephemera, prints, antique memorabilia & collectibles, T-shirts, CD-Rom, flags, games, tapes, maps, mugs, miniatures, genealogies & more. Specialize in the Civil War. Free catalogs.

AN EARLY ELEGANCE
717-338-9311
39 N Washington St
Gettysburg PA 17325-1128
American-made items & authentic repro- ductions. CW-era writing box, fabrics. Gifts at reasonable prices. Product guide - business- size SASE. Fabric swatch book - $2.50.

GEORGE ESKER
PO Box 100
La Place LA 70069-0100
Civil War memorabilia (especially Confederate), currency, images, relics, bullets, buttons, projectiles, documents. Catalog - $9 for 3 issues.

PETER EVANS PIPES
305-361-5589
285 W Mashta Dr • Dept F
Key Biscayne FL 33149-2419
Custom-made period pipes, reproductions, clays, quality pipe accessories. For smokers, reenactors, collectors, historians. Free brochure.

EXCELSIOR PRESS
516-475-7069 • 516-874-2489 Fax
Don Roberts
PO Box 926
Bellport NY 11713-0926
Civil War Cabinet Cards. Color art prints of 24 famous regiments include period battle maps & regimental histories. Boxed set - $23.95 + $3.50 S&H (30-day money-back guarantee). Catalog/brochure - $1 (ref. w/ purchase).

FEDERAL HILL ANTIQUITIES
410-584-8185 / 8329
14 Glen Lyon Ct
Phoenix MD 21131-1212
Purveyors of fine autographs & collectibles.
Letters & documents, photos, relics &
artifacts, ephemera. Buy/sell/trade.

FIELDS OF GLORY
800-517-3382 Orders • 717-337-2837
717-337-9315 Fax
http://www.collectorsnet.com/fog/index.htm
foglory@cvn.net
55 York St
Gettysburg PA 17325-2302
Best in Civil War memorabilia. Visit our store.
Catalog -$10 for 12 issues.

N. FLAYDERMAN & CO., INC.
305-761-8855
PO Box 2446
Fort Lauderdale FL 33303-2446
Antique guns, swords, & knives. Nautical,
western & military collectibles from
Revolutionary through Spanish-American
wars. Catalog - $15.

THE FLINTLOCK ROOM
201-543-1861
201-543-1865 Fax
http://www.flintlockroom.com
6 Hilltop Rd
Mendham NJ 07945
Collectibles for Connoisseurs - classic
firearms, fine cigars, military figurines, prints &
militaria, Victorian miniatures.

TIM FORTIER
15 Ramblewood Dr
Newbury NH 03255-6109
Confederate passports. Lifelike document
allows safe passage. Customs information,
Southern institutions, photo page,
entries/departures, etc. $4.

FOUR WINDS TRADING COMPANY
1010 California Dr
Columbia SC 29205-4219
Buys/sells Civil War art & memorabilia. Open
& ltd. ed. prints. Catalog - $4.

FRENCH'S STORE & TRADING COMPANY
717-530-5037
PO Box 454
Shippensburg PA 17257-0454
Authentic Civil War reproductions of trade
goods, 17th-19th century. Cavalry & leather
goods & saddles. Catalog - $1.

FRONTIER SADDLE
941-322-2560
Gabriel Libraty
5530 Juel Gill Rd
Myakka City FL 34251
Replica saddles of the Old West & military;
from mountain man to Civil War to classic
Western saddles. Free catalog.

GALVANIZED YANKEE
540-373-1886
10611 Heather Greens Cir
Spotsylvania VA 22553-1717
Military collectibles from the Civil War.
Catalog - $10 domestic/$20 overseas.

**GETTYSBURG CIVIL WAR & ANTIQUE
CENTER**
717-337-1085
705 Old Harrisburg Pk
N Gettysburg Plaza
Gettysburg PA 17325
Multi-dealer complex in heart of antique
country. Civil War memorabilia, military art,
antiques & fine collectibles. Open 7 days/wk.
Free parking.

JOHN S. GIMESH, MD
910-484-2212
PO Box 53788
Fayetteville NC 28305-3788
Authentic Civil War-era medical, surgical,
dental & apothecary items; Civil War-era
medical texts. Buy/sell.

CARL GIORDANO, TINSMITH
330-336-7270
tinsnip@newreach.net
PO Box 74
Wadsworth OH 44282-0074
18th- & 19th-century reproductions. Hand-
wrought, custom work. Brochure - send SASE.

WILL GORGES CIVIL WAR MILITARIA
919-636-3039
919-637-1862 Fax
http://www.collectorsnet.com/gorges/index.htm
rebel!@abaco.coastalnet.com
2100 Trent Blvd
New Bern NC 28560-5326
Largest active inventory of authentic items in
the Southeast. Fine quality uniforms &
weapons our specialty. Buy/sell/appraise/
broker. Catalog - $10.

GREAT CIRCLE FORGE
PO Box 9040
Lexington OH 44904-9040

Hand-forged ironwork: tent stakes, tripods, potted plant stands, coat racks, decorative hooks, trammel hooks, & more. Catalog - $1.50.

GREAT WAR OF THE CONFEDERACY
704-739-5862
704-739-1809 Fax
http://www.civilwarmall.com/gwotc.htm
243 Oak Grove Rd
Kings Mountain NC 28086
Civil War memorabilia & collectibles, including historic Confederate art.

W.D. GRISSOM, SR.
medals@cei.net
PO Box 59
Cabot AR 72023-0059
Medals, documents, related items. Regimental research, reasonable price. Specialist for US & foreign military medals. Catalog - $1 (ref.).

GWYN'S COLLECTIBLES & BOOKS
717-957-4141
717-957-9208 Fax
Gwyn L. Irwin
211 Front St
Marysville PA 17053-1413
Civil War books. Roster of soldiers in the "War of the Rebellion" from Monroe County, New York. 26 pp., 3 columns - $12 ppd.

THE HAMILTON COLLECTION
4810 Executive Park Ct
PO Box 44051
Jacksonville FL 32231-4051
Collectible plates, featuring Civil War Generals.

THE HAVERSACK DEPOT
210-620-5192
1236 River Acres Dr
New Braunfels TX 78130
Museum-quality products at reasonable prices, incl. US haversack, CS cartridge box sling & CS leather belt with Ga. frame brass buckle. Satisfaction guaranteed.

HEART OF HISTORY & VARIABLE HEART
540-234-9031 (mall)
John & Miriam Heatwole, Dick Swanson
Simonetti's Antique Center
Rt 11, off exit 235 on I-81
Weyerrs Cave VA 24486
One of the best Civil War shops in the Shenandoah Valley - museum-quality photos & artifacts, wrought iron, pharmaceutical relics, buttons, books, documents, much more.

DENNIS HEATH
919-569-8781
RR 1 Box 55A
Deep Run NC 28525-9703
Civil War weapons, relics, accoutrements. Catalog - $7/yr.

HERITAGE CLASSICS
800-357-8548 • 718-218-8587
543 Bedford Ave # 163
Brooklyn NY 11211
Wood Collector's plate, laser-cut inlay of Lincoln & others - $34.95 ea. + $4.95/order S&H.

HERITAGE STUDIO
540-659-1070 • 540-374-1872
606 Caroline St
Fredericksburg VA 22401
Donna J. Neary's *Even to Hell Itself* - $130. *A Terrible Gale* - $150. *Till Death Do Us Part* - $125. *Do Your Duty, Boys* - $175. *Edge of the Storm* - $150.

THE HISTORIAN'S GALLERY
770-522-8383 • 770-522-8388 Fax
http://www.nr-net.com/history/
history@atl.mindspring.com
3232 Cobb Pkwy Ste 207
Atlanta GA 30339
Brokers & dealers in maps, autographs, selected relics.

HISTORIC FRAMING & COLLECTIBLES
410-465-0549
Joe Parr
8344 Main St • Ellicott City MD 21043-4653
Civil War weaponry & assorted items. Military art by all major artists, including aviation & WWII. True conservation-quality framing.

HISTORICAL COLLECTIBLE AUCTIONS
910-570-2803 • 910-570-2748 Fax
Holzman-Caren Associates
PO Box 975
Burlington NC 27215-0975
Semi-annual auctions of Civil War collectibles. Consignments encouraged. Catalog - $18; next 3 for $45.

HISTORICAL DOCUMENTS INTL., INC.
603-472-7040 • 603-472-8773 Fax
PO Box 10488
Bedford NH 03110-0488
Museum quality historical documents originally signed by many of the most famous individuals in history: Washington, Lee, Lincoln, Edison, Twain, Churchill, etc.

HISTORICAL MILITARY ART & COLLECTIBLES
PO Box 1806
Lafayette CA 94549-8006
Collector books, limited edition military art, & military & political collectibles, including medals, flags, badges, pins, & patches. Free catalog.

THE HISTORICAL SHOP
504-467-2532 • 504-464-7552 Fax
Yvonne & Cary Delery
PO Box 73244
Metairie LA 70033-3244
Photos, documents, autographs, CSA currency, letters, slavery ads & items, relics, framed displays & other collectibles. Buys/sells. Illus. catalogs - $8/yr.

HISTORICAL SUPPLY CO.
802-464-0535
PO Box 12
Wilmington VT 05363-0012
Authentic brass camp candlesticks perfect for 19th-century impression. Set of 2 - $12.95 + $3 S&H.

THE HISTORY WORKS
800-717-7359
vjackson@select.net
2788 Loker Ave W
Carlsbad CA 92008-6612
Reproductions of Muster Roll forms, stationery, art, & Regimental Action Reviews. Call/write for complete details. Free catalog.

HISTORY-MAKERS
4040 E 82nd St Dept 44
Indianapolis IN 46250-4209
Historic letters & documents signed by the greatest history makers who ever lived. Free report.

PETER HLINKA
718-409-6407
Historical Americana
PO Box 310
New York NY 10028-0017
Military & civilian decorations, medals, award certificates, insignia items, books, & other Americana collectibles. Free catalog.

THE HORSE SOLDIER
717-334-0347
717-334-5016 Fax
http://www.bmark.com/horsesoldier.antiques
hsoldier@cvn.net
PO Box 184
Cashtown PA 17310-0184

Buy, sell & appraise Civil War military antiques: firearms, edged weapons, photographs, documents, battlefield relics & more! Unconditionally guaranteed. Soldier research service available. Semi-annual catalog - $10/yr.

HUGHES
717-326-1045 • 717-326-7606 Fax
timhu@sunlink.net
PO Box 3636
Williamsport PA 17701-8636
Newspapers; rare, historic - 1600s-1880s. Extensive catalog of genuine issues - $2.

THE INDIAN SHOP
606-441-0773
Von Hilliard • PO Box 246
Independence KY 41051-0246
Authentic Civil War newspapers - $10 ea. Indian relics. Catalog - $5 (ref.).

J & B, INC.
910-674-2999
520 Hwy 62 E • Pleasant Garden NC 27313
Fine quality, hand-painted resin Civil War figurines. List -$1 (ref.).

J.J.B. LTD.
PO Box 507 • Shamokin PA 17872-0507
Civil War print/calendar of the year 1861. Day-to-day events. 20"x17-1/2" - $29.95.

JACQUES NOEL JACOBSEN, JR.
718-981-0973
60 Manor Rd • Staten Island NY 10310-2626
Antiques & military collectibles, insignia, weapons, medals, uniforms, Kepis, relics, photos, paintings, & band instruments. Catalog - $12 for 3 issues. $15 overseas.

JEBCO CLOCKS
800-635-3226
301 Industry Dr • Carlisle OH 45005-6309
Leading manufacturer of collectibles. Artwork by Kunstler & Gnatek now available on plaques or limited ed. clocks. Clocks - 11"x23", $69.95 ppd. Plaques - 11"x14", $44.95 ppd.

THE JEWELER'S DAUGHTER
301-733-3200 • 301-733-5076 Fax
24 W Washington St
Hagerstown MD 21740-4804
1860 VMI (Virginia Military Institute) class ring. Repro from original museum piece. 10K gold, wax seal style, "Let Virginia Choose" - $259.95.

JOHN'S RELICS
803-549-7751
John Steele
227 Robertson Blvd
Walterboro SC 29488-2752
Civil War & colonial relics, arms
accoutrements, veteran memorabilia,
newspapers, books, CW tokens, photography,
buttons & related memorabilia. Catalog - $1
(ref. w/ purchase).

JPL ANTIQUES
914-896-6006
211 Main St
Fishkill NY 12524-2209
CSA currency, bonds, documents, letters,
CDVs, newspapers, accoutrements,
CSA/Union imprints. Price list - $1.

KAWARTHA MARKETING COMPANY
705-639-2572
705-639-1809 Fax
RR 1 Station W
Norwood Ontario, KOL 2VO Canada
Firearms, cannons, knives, helmets,
bayonets, daggers, swords, surplus, uniforms,
etc. Including originals that have seen battle.
Catalog - $4 (ref. w/ order).

J. E. KELLY & CO.
9 Langdon St
Montpelier VT 05602-2903
Recruiting posters of famous Civil War
regiments reproduced from rare, mint-
condition originals, 18"x24" - $12.95 ea. 1st
U.S. Sharpshooters, 1st Penn. Cavalry, 5th
N.Y., Lincoln's Assassin Wanted poster.

KENNESAW MOUNTAIN MILITARY ANTIQUES
770-424-5225
770-424-0434 Fax
CANNONBALL@aol.com.
1810 Old Highway 41
Kennesaw GA 30152-4430
Civil War relics & complete list of books
available. New, reprints, & reference books.
Catalog subscription - $10.

KEYA GALLERY
212-366-9742 • 800-906-KEYA Orders only
http://www.KeyaGallery.com
Key15@aol.com
110 W 25th St Gallery 304A
New York NY 10001-7401
Excavated relics - bullets, tokens, buckles,
buttons, insignia, & more. Catalog.

KINGSTON MILITARY ANTIQUES
770-336-9354
Jerelhook@aol.com
Jere Hook
PO Box 217
Kingston GA 30145-0217
Buy/sell/trade pre-1898 militaria, mostly Civil
War. By appt. only. Catalog - 32¢.

L & G EARLY ARMS
2049 Clermont Laurel Rd
New Richmond OH 45157-9557
Authentic Civil War guns. Free list w/
business-size SASE.

LAGRANGE
3601 Vanderwood Dr
Memphis TN 38128-3417
Shiloh bullets. Authentic Civil War bullets
excavated in the vicinity of Shiloh Battlefield. 3
for $10.

PHILLIP B. LAMB, LTD.
504-899-4710 • 800-391-0115 Orders
504-891-6826 Fax
http://www.LambRarities.com
lambcsa@aol.com
PO Box 15850
2727 Prytania St
New Orleans LA 70175-5850
Buy/sell Confederate memorabilia; CDVs,
currency, documents, photos, art, bonds,
slave items, swords, buttons, bullets,
autographs, & much more. (See ad page 234)

DEBORAH LAMBERT
1945 Lorraine Ave
Mc Lean VA 22101-5331
Slavery documents, CW newspapers, prints,
letters, autographs, battle maps. List - $1.

LAWRENCE OF DALTON
706-226-8894
4773 Tammy Dr NE
Dalton GA 30721-6936
Civil War bullets, projectiles, buttons, buckles,
plates, bayonets, bottles, hat pins, dug relics.
Growing into one of South's largest mail order
dealers. Buy/sell. 4 mail order lists - $4.

LEE-GRANT, INC.
800-350-5234
Harry A. Lillie
RR 4 Box 102
Appomattox VA 24522-8916
Limited ed. prints. Dug & undug artifacts from
in & around Appomattox, Va. Flags of all sorts.

LEGENDARY ARMS, INC.
800-528-2767 • 908-788-7330
908-788-8522 Fax
PO Box 479
Three Bridges NJ 08887-0479
Museum-quality, authentic duplication. Finest repros: swords, knives, battle axe, & bugle, uniforms of the Civil War.

LEXINGTON HISTORICAL SHOP
540-463-2615
Bob Lurate
PO Box 1428
Lexington VA 24450-1428
Civil War memorabilia. Buy/sell books, relics, flags, currency, ephemera. Appraisals. Visit shop Mon-Sat 10-6, College Square Shopping Center, Route 11N, Lexington, Va.

LOGAN CREEK DESIGNS
800-944-5684 • 540-944-5555
540-944-3504 Fax
10347 Lindell Rd
Abingdon VA 24210-8985
Stonewall Jackson's field desk, handmade. Licensed through VMI Museum. Solid cherry, limited ed. Cherry table - perfect complement to desk. Desk - $1,863; table -$350 + S&H. Color brochure.

LOOK BACK IN TIME
803-986-9097
803-986-9297 Fax
PO Box 572
Port Royal SC 29935-0572
Civil War newspapers, engravings, books, relics, & much more. Want lists welcome. Free catalog.

LOST MOUNTAIN RELICS
800 Wyntuck Dr
Kennesaw GA 30152
Battlefield bullet set - 3 dropped minies in display case, $12 ppd. Illus. relic list - 3 stamps.

M.J.M. COLLECTIBLES
879 W Park Ave # 244
Ocean NJ 07712
Reproduced copy of Lee's death certificate, suitable for framing. $10.

ROBERT J. MADISON
PO Box 582
Claymont DE 19703-0582
Civil War collectors' watches in color. Gold-plated case, black leather band, quartz movement. Select Grant, Lee or Jackson. $40 ea. + $5 S&H.

MAGIC TOWN
800-878-4276
49 Steinwehr Ave
Gettysburg PA 17325
Bradford Exchange plates - Battles ... & Gallant Men of the Civil War. Michael Garman sculptures at great prices!

JOSEPH L. MARTIN
770-428-1966
PO Box 603 • Smyrna GA 30081-0603
Buying, selling, trading fine Civil War swords, guns, uniforms, flags, etc. Over 35 yrs of experience in dealing military items. Competent appraisals available.

MATUSZEK'S
847-253-4685
Frank Matuszek • 126 E Wing St # 210
Arlington Heights IL 60004-6064
Civil War & Indian War firearms, swords, uniforms & other collectibles. Sample catalog - $2. Mention the Civil War Source Book!

MC GOWAN BOOK CO.
919-403-1503 • 800-449-8406
919-403-1706 Fax
R. Douglas Sanders
39 Kimberly Dr
Durham NC 27707-5418
Always buying. Highest prices paid for fine & rare Civil War books, autographs, documents, photographs, etc. Catalog subs. - $3. (See ad page 243)

MEEHAN MILITARY POSTERS
212-634-5683
PO Box 477
New York NY 10028-0018
Genuine war posters. Catalog - $10 (ref.).

MILES OF HISTORY
423-337-2540
http://www.collectorsnet.com/miles
huskey@usit.net
Miles Huskey
PO Box 599
Sweetwater TN 37874-0599
Buy/sell/trade Civil War items. Images, buttons, weapons, documents, personal items, & authentic period jewelry available through internet auction on website.

MILITARY BOOK CATALOG
PO Box 4470
Cave Creek AZ 85327-4470
Military history, medals, uniforms, weapons, collectibles. More than 1,000 titles. Catalog - $2. Medals catalog - $1.

THE MILITARY COLLECTION
PO Box 830970M
Miami FL 33283-0970
Helmets, uniforms, field gear, awards,
medals, flags, weapons, swords, photos, etc.
Catalog - $8.

MORGAN'S CIVIL WAR MEMORABILIA
7864 Pullbridge Ct
West Chester OH 45069-1687
Buys/sells/trades buttons, relics, documents,
weapons. Catalog - free w/ SASE.

MTM RELICS
32 Edgehill Rd
Birmingham AL 35209
Fine Civil War relics, reasonably priced.
Catalogs - $6/yr.

MULLINS ANTIQUES
320 Davis Ave
Elkins WV ‾26241
Reproduction Civil War state medals - $20 ea.

MUSEUM OF AMERICAN CAVALRY
540-740-3959
Peter & Jane Comtois
298 Old Cross Rd
New Market VA 22844-9511
History of the Horse Soldier from colonial
times through Vietnam & modern times. Gift
shop with books, flags, weapons, relics, other
items. Formerly Indian Hollow Antiques.

MUSEUM REPLICAS LIMITED
PO Box 840
Conyers GA 30207-0840
Reproductions of authentic museum quality,
historically accurate replicas of weapons &
period battle wear. Catalog - $1.

SUSAN A. NASH
304-876-3772
PO Box 1011
Shepherdstown WV 25443-1011
Paper conservation. Specialist in historic
documents, photographs, prints, drawings,
maps, letters, broadsides. Cleaning, mending,
deacidification, museum matting. By appt.

NESHANIC DEPOT
610-847-5627
610-847-8618 Fax
283 Durham Rd
PO Box 367
Ottsville PA 18942-0367
Historic artifacts, muzzleloading guns &
supplies, originals, reproductions, & historic
flags.

NEW MARKET BATTLEFIELD MILITARY MUSEUM
540-740-8065
540-740-3663 Fax
John Bracken
9500 Collins Dr
PO Box 1131
New Market VA 22844-1131
Comprehensive museum shop featuring CW
relics, flags, uniforms, bullets, buttons,
swords, muskets, currency, personal items,
memorabilia, etc. More than 1200 book titles.
Open Mar. 15-Dec. 1.

NMC ENTERPRISES
800-591-2999 (24 hrs.)
913 18th St Ste 2
Santa Monica CA 90403
Civil War blackpowder accessories; fine,
hand-crafted leather. Holsters, belts, pouches,
bags, buckles. Free catalog.

THE NOBEL COLLECTION
800-806-6253
PO Box 3444
Merrifield VA 22116-3444
Historic reproductions & collectible swords.
From King Arthur to Samurai. Free catalog.

NORTH & SOUTH RECREATIONS
603-629-7192
122 Laura Ln
Hampstead NH 03841-2331
Civil War-era antique reproductions including
uniform corps badges & lapel pins, ladies'
scroll brooch & pennant corps badge, pipes,
etc. Catalog - $1.

NORTH SOUTH TRADERS CIVIL WAR
540-67-CIVIL
540-672-7283 Fax
nstcw@msn.com
PO Box 631
Orange VA 22960-0370
Illustrated, bi-annual *Civil War Collectors'
Price Guide* -$25 + $3 S&H. Bi-monthly
magazine, heavily illustrated -$25/yr.

OHIO SILVER
301-834-5389
PO Box 124
Brunswick MD 21716-0124
Silver bullet key chains & necklaces. Minie
bullet replicas (.575 cal.) on key ring or
sterling silver chain.

THE OLD PAPERPHILES
401-624-9420 • 401-624-4204 Fax
PO Box 135 • Tiverton RI 02878-0135

Offering 100s of accurately described paper collectibles. Great variety, wide price range. Autographs, documents, books. Catalog - $8 for next 10.

OLD SOUTH MILITARY ANTIQUES
919-523-7181
Dennis Heath
403A E Newbern Rd
Kinston NC 28501
Full line of Civil War muskets, swords, accoutrements & artifacts at reasonable prices. Shop open Mon-Sat. Catalog - $7/yr.

OLDE AMERICAN COLLECTIBLES, INC.
13 Nathalie Ct
Peekskill NY 10566
Semi-annual auctions, mail/telephone. Collections purchased outright or accepted on consignment. Fully illus. catalog - $20 for 2-issue subscription.

ORIGINAL FRAMEWORKS
800-654-1861 • 540-953-1655
civilwar@nrv.net
Jay Rainey
Gables Shopping Center
1300 S Main St
Blacksburg VA 24060-5526
All Civil War artists at discount; signatures, documents, 19th-century steel engravings, relics. Will find any artwork. Always looking to purchase. Also at 4 E Washington St, Lexington, Va. (See ad page 232)

PALMETTO HISTORICAL WORKS
803-699-6746
Tim Bradshaw
120 Branch Hill Dr
Elgin SC 29045-9383
Civil War researcher. Union & Confederate letters, 6th East Tenn VI muster roll, tintypes.

PECARD ANTIQUE LEATHER CARE
541-937-3348
R.S. Dorsey
PO Box 263
Eugene OR 97440-0263
Finest antique leather care. Moisturizes, softens, preserves - absolutely safely. Colorless, odorless, long-lasting. 6 oz. tub - $9.50 ppd. 16 oz. tub - $17 ppd. 32 oz. tub - $28 ppd.

ALEX PECK
217-348-1009 • PO Box 710
Charleston IL 61920-0710
Medical antiques. Surgery, military, other fields. Buy/sell. Send SASE for info.

PEMBROKE INK
PO Box 445
Chesterfield VA 23832-0445
For the discriminating collector. Dealer of documents & rare books. Extensive list.

PERRYVILLE CIVIL WAR RELICS & MUSEUM
Ken Hamilton & Dr. Craig Knox
302 Buell St • Perryville KY 40468
Authentic Civil War artifacts & collectibles, 1861-1865. Guns, swords, photographs, belt buckles, buttons, dug relics, etc.

THE PICKET POST
540-371-7703
Tim Garrett & Bill Henderson
602 Caroline St.
Fredericksburg VA 22401-5902
Civil War military antiques: canteens, buttons, swords, guns, images, buckles, uniforms. Buys/sells. Photo-illus. catalog - $10 for 3 issues.

PICTURE THAT ANTIQUES & COLLECTIBLES
414-361-0255 • 414-361-2992 Fax
107 W Huron St
Berlin WI 54923
Large selection of tintypes, CDVs, ambrotypes & cabinet cards of Civil War soldiers & civilians. Books.

THE POWDER HORN GUN SHOP, INC.
540-687-6628 • 540-687-6431 Fax
Robert M. Daly, Pres.
200 W Washington St
PO Box 1001 • Middleburg VA 20118-1001
Buy/sell. Dealers in antique firearms & militaria, Revolutionary War-WWII. Civil War a specialty. Catalog -$20 for 6 issues.

THE PROFESSIONAL TREASURE HUNTERS HISTORICAL SOCIETY
603-357-0607 • 800-447-6014 (New England)
603-352-1147 Fax
George Streeter
14 Vernon St
Keene NH 03431-3440
Info. about treasure hunting in US. Metal detecting info. Treasure club activities in US. Newsletter - *Treasure Hunter's Gazette*.

R & L PUBLISHING
28 Vesey St Ste 2116C
New York NY 10007-2906
Bottles of Old New York and *New York City's Buried Past* dealing with Civil War & Rev. War bottles. $22.95 & $27.95 ppd.

STEVEN S. RAAB AUTOGRAPHS
800-977-8333 • 610-446-4514 Fax
http://www.raabautographs.com
raab@netaxs,com
PO Box 471 • Ardmore PA 19003-0471
Serious collectors, respected dealers. Top
dollars paid for collection & quality individual
autographs, documents, manuscripts, signed
photos, & interesting letters. Catalog sample -
$5; $15/yr.

RAPINE BULLET MANUFACTURING CO.
215-679-5413
9503 Landis Ln
East Greenville PA 18041-2541
Civil War bullet molds. Catalog - $2.

M.S. RAU ANTIQUES
800-544-9440 • 504-523-5660
504-566-0057 Fax
http://www.bmark.com/rau.antiques
sjtl@aol.com
630 Royal St
New Orleans LA 70130-2116
Authentic Civil War Surgery Kits incl.
amputation kit, post-mortem kit, & neuro-
surgeon's kit - the real things! Catalog - $5.

THE RAVEN'S DEN
860-623-9470
Chet Mulka
PO Box 178
East Windsor CT 06088-0178
Repro Civil War box plates & medals. Buy/sell
Civil War relics. Catalog - $2 (ref.).

REB ACRES
540-377-2057
rebacres@cfw.com
57 Steeles Fort Rd
Raphine VA 24472-2503
Specializing in Civil War artifacts. Priced right
for beginning collectors. Comprehensive,
32-pg catalog -send 3 first-class stamps.

J. REB'S CIVIL WAR RELIC GALLERY
706-377-2057
513 Battlefield Pkwy
Fort Oglethorpe GA 30742-3848
Located near Chickamauga Battlefield. Fine
quality Civil War artifacts. Excavated &
non-exc. Art gallery houses one of finest CW
collections. Authorized metal detector dealer.
Buy/sell. Catalog - $10/yr.

REBEL STAND
PO Box 4972
Falls Church VA 22044

Hand-lettered reproduction of authentic
Confederate Officer's Commission/
Appointment - $25 ea. Include name, officer
rank, & CS unit desired on your frameable
document with order.

RED CLAY RELICS
770-445-8631
Ray McMahan
PO Box 420
Dallas GA 30132-0420
Buckles, buttons, bullets, shells.
Buy/sell/trade. Inventory list - send SASE.

RICHIE'S ARTIFACTS OF THE WEST
719-783-9028 Phone & Fax
PO Box 627
Westcliffe CO 81252-0627
Replicas of old carbon knives. 31 models.
Perfect for reenactors. Reasonably priced -
$6.95 & up.

RICHMOND ARSENAL
804-272-4570 Phone & Fax
7605 Midlothian Tpke
Richmond VA 23235-5223
100% authentic Civil War antiques, from
common bullets & buttons to museum quality
weapons, accoutrements, uniforms, drums &
flags. Photo-illus. catalog - $10 for 3 issues.

RICHMONVILLE TINWARE
800-501-1675 • 541-678-1675
PO Box 407
21328 Highway 99E
Aurora OR 97002-0407
Highest quality, historically correct tinware
obtainable. Custom orders welcome. Catalog
- $3.

ROCHESTER CHESS CENTER
800-ON-CHESS
Civil War chess sets. Grant & Lee 5" tall!
Choose from various styles.

MIKE RUSSELL
401 Virginia Ave
Herndon VA 20170-5437
Quarterly catalog of Victorian artifacts & relics,
emphasis on obsolete currency, bottles &
pipes - $2. *The Collector's Guide to Clay
Tobacco Pipes, Vol. I* - $20.45 ppd.

S & S FIREARMS
718-497-1100
718-497-1105 Fax
7411 Myrtle Ave
Glendale NY 11385-7433

Military Americana. Antique gun parts, carbines, Enfield, buttons, insignia, books, equipment, appendages, headdress, etc. Reenactor supplies. Original & reproduction. Photo-illus. catalog - $3.

SCENIC EFFECTS, INC.
510-235-1955 • 510-235-9901 Fax
Wendy Schuldt
PO Box 332
Point Richmond CA 94807-0332
Ltd. ed. of historically accurate buildings, ea. handmade. Some include figures & are hand-painted; unpainted available. Catalog/listing - send SASE.

SCHOOLHOUSE ANTIQUES
717-334-4564
Gettysburg PA 17325
Antique guns, relics, swords, uniforms, souvenirs. Close to battlefield - 5 mi. on Business Rt. 15 South.

CARL SCIORTINO MILITARIA
PO Box 29809 • Richmond VA 23242-0809
700-item catalog of Civil War militaria - $2 (ref.). Military books - 600 titles. Catalog - $2 (ref.).

SCOTT'S ANTIQUES & CIVIL WAR RELICS
717-624-2088
121 Lincoln Way E
New Oxford PA 17350-1210
Buy/sell Civil War antiques & relics. Come in & see the shop.

SCS PUBLICATIONS
PO Box 3832
Fairfax VA 22038-3832
Civil War Artifacts: A Guide for the Historian. More than 1700 items pictured, common to very rare. Data includes history, issuance, etc. 240 pp. $39.95.

EDWARD SEMMELROTH
517-278-2214
415 Fleming Rd
Tekonsha MI 49092
Antique iron sales, restoration & reproductions, incl. 1820s-1870s style kitchen cookstove. Custom casting & restoration in any medal; no job too big or small.

SHARPSBURG ARSENAL
301-432-7700
301-432-7440 Fax
101 W Main St
PO Box 568
Sharpsburg MD 21782-0568

Purveyors of fine Civil War militaria; firearms, edged weapons, buttons, bullets, leather accoutrements, battlefield relics, books, flags, personal & camp items, paper, letters, framed prints. Buy/sell.

SHILOH'S CIVIL WAR RELICS
901-689-4114
901-926-3637 Fax
http://www.shilohrelics.com
relics@shilohrelics.com
4730 Highway 22
Shiloh TN 38376
Authentic Civil War artifacts. Something for every level of collecting. Catalog - $5 for 4 issues.

SHIPS & SOLDIERS
603-742-1886
PO Box 912
Dover NH 03820-0912
Antique-toy-style toy soldiers, boats, etc. Brochure - $2.

R.J. SIMARD
PO Box 514
Bristol RI 02809-0514
Custom-made ornamental 6" Civil War dolls made to your specifications. $10 ea. (send detailed description or snapshot). Civil War drum pins, enameled red, white & blue - $10 ea. Catalog - $2 (deductible).

SOUTHERN ENCAMPMENTS
504-751-0757
tcld04@premier.net
Tim Rochester
16380 S Fulwar Skipwith Rd
Baton Rouge LA 70810
Civil War antiques; autographs, buttons, documents, period glass, insignia, letters, projectiles, books & more. Photo-illus. catalog - $2.50.

SOUTHERN GUN WORKS
757-934-1423
757-925-1177 Fax
109 Cherry St
Suffolk VA 23434
Civil War prints, autographed military books, memorabilia. Art by Troiani, Spaulding, Kunstler, Gallon, others.

SOUTHERN YANKEE VETERANS MEMORABILIA
409-264-1865 Dan Reed
409-852-2822 Mike Carter
Buy/sell/trade GAR & UCV relics, postcards, Civil War books. Catalogs - $10 (3 issues/yr.).

SPITZ MOUNTAIN ENTERPRISES
Steven Spitz
3013 S Washington St
Naperville IL 60540
Great generals & legendary heroes. Wooden
military collectibles. Hand-carved & crafted.
Authentically detailed. Grant, Lee, Jackson,
Custer, Stuart, many more. $49.95 ea. Color
brochure. Catalog - $2.50 (ref.).

DEAN SPROWL
210-816-2590
Boerne TX
Civil War Collector specializing in Civil War
images, dug relics & forts of Texas artifacts.

STARS & BARS MILITARY ANTIQUES
540-972-1863
9832 Plank Rd • Spotsylvania VA 22553-4243
Civil War militaria: edged weapons, uniforms,
accoutrements, medals, weaponry, prints, etc.
On Chancellorsville battlefield, est. 1976.

STONEMAN TREASURERS
PO Box 15309
Philadelphia PA 19111
Musket & trapdoor Springfield parts.
Affordable historical collectibles, incl.
bayonets, swords, tools, relics, etc. 6-pg. list -
$1 + stamp.

STONEWALL ENTERPRISES
800-856-6071 • 706-321-0020 Fax
Kim Hightower
205 Hickory Chase
Carrollton GA 30117-3522
Ltd. ed., museum-quality bronze sculptures
representing the battles of the Civil War by
world-renowned sculptor, Eric H. Baret, MD.
Call for free brochure.

SUMTER MILITARY ANTIQUES & MUSEUM
803-577-7766
803-856-4629 Fax
http://www.collectorsnet.com/sumter/index.html
54 Broad St
Charleston SC 29401
Authentic artifacts from the Civil War. List -
$10/yr.

SUTLERS WAGON
Stamatelos Bros, Prop.
PO Box 390005
Cambridge MA 02139-0001
Fine quality American military items,
1775-1900. Civil War uniforms, headgear,
accoutrements, buckles, tack, photos, swords,
documents. Buy/sell.

SWORD & SABER
717-334-0205
2159 Baltimore Pike
Gettysburg PA 17325-7015
Specializing in original Confederate & Union
documents, framed items, relics, weapons &
swords. 5 illus. catalogs -$10.

T5 ENTERPRISES
208-788-3348
Larry & Wende Thornton
4 Freedom Loop • Bellevue ID 83313
Buy/sell/trade U.S. cavalry & horse-related
equipment (1833-1943).

TEXANA RELICS
PO Box 717 • Boerne TX 78006-0717
Trans-Mississippi Civil War relics & images.
Photo-illus. catalog - three 32¢ stamps.

THOROUGHBRED FIGURES
3833 Buckhorn Pl
Virginia Beach VA 23456-4927
Ship models (1/600 scale) - antiques,
assembled on walnut base. Send SASE for
more info.

TIME TRAVELERS ANTIQUES
717-337-0011
312 Baltimore St • Gettysburg PA 17325
Fine general line of quality Americana,
collectibles & decorative arts in ca.1901
Victorian house. Costumed Civil War walking
tours of Old Baltimore Street sites.

TL SPECIALTIES
RR 4 Box 336B • Wynantskill NY 12198
Civil War clocks & plaques. Reproduced prints
from *Leslies* and *Harpers* magazines of
1860s. Walnut/burnt wood stain. Free
brochure - SASE.

TRADEMARK MILITARIA
2800 NW 10th St.
Oklahoma City OK 73107-5314
Dealers of historical military artifacts &
memorabilia. Trade/sell/appraise. Catalog - $5
for 3.

TRANS-MISSISSIPPI MILITARIA
972-517-8111 Phone & Fax
http://www.collectorsnet.com/transmiss/index.html
charlucv@flash.net
Charles Brecheisen
1004 Simon Dr • Plano TX 75025-2501
UCV, GAR, Civil War & Indian War period
relics, books & diaries, papers, letters, covers
& records, medical instruments. Always
buying. Catalogs - $10 (min. 3 large lists).

TWIN OAKS SADDLERY
407-790-2461
11580 46th Pl N
Royal Palm Beach FL 33411
American-made Civil War goods/
reproductions. Cartridge box plates, carbine
box, cap box, sword belts, sashes, holsters,
saddlebags, saddles & parts, belts & buckles,
tinware. Catalog - $2.

U.S. GAMES SYSTEMS, INC.
203-353-8400 • 203-353-8431 Fax
USGames@aol.com
Lee Stockwell
179 Ludlow St • Stamford CT 06902-6900
Heavily illustrated, informative & entertaining
CW playing cards & card games. Facsimile
decks of cards originally published in the
1860s. Award-winning Civil War series.
Catalog - $2. (See ad page 232)

UNCLE DAVEY'S AMERICANA
904-730-8932 Phone & Fax
http://www.collectorsnet.com/uncledv/index.htm
uncledv@southeast.net
6140 Saint Augustine Rd
Jacksonville FL 32217
Original Civil War collectibles - full range of
items for collector & historian. Catalog.

THE UNION DRUMMER BOY
610-825-6280 • 717-334-2350
http://www.uniondb.com
civilwar@uniondb.com
Bill & Brendan Synnamon, Prop.
420 Flourtown Rd
Lafayette Hill PA 19444-1002
Specializing in authentic Civil War artifacts.
Shop located at 34 York St., Gettysburg, PA
17325. Catalog - $6 for 3 issues.

VALHALLA ANTIQUES & COLLECTIBLES
9792 Edmonds Way Ste 255
Edmonds WA 98020-5940
Visit the 508 Main St, Edmonds, Washington,
location for the largest & best Civil War
selection in the Northwest.

VILLAGE TINSMITHING WORKS
330-325-9101
Bill & Judy Hoover
PO Box 189 • Randolph OH 44265-0189
Quality reproduction & period items. Lead-free
solder on potable items. More than 80 items.
Custom orders. Catalog - free w/ long SASE.

VIRGINIA STEREOSCOPIC EMPORIUM
PO Box 1718
Stafford VA 22555-1718

Civil War Stereoscopic cards. Beautiful 3D
image when viewed through stereo viewer.
Set of 6 cards - $19.95 + S&H. Catalog - $2.

THE VOLUNTEERS
207-384-1911
19 York Woods Rd
South Berwick ME 03908-2156
Civil War militaria & antiques. Good selection,
many items. Also a shop at RR1 Box 3428,
Sanbornville, NH 03872 - Tel. 603-473-8345.
Free lists.

**WAR BETWEEN THE STATES
MEMORABILIA**
717-337-2853
Len Rosa
PO Box 3965
Gettysburg PA 17325-0965
Buy/sell soldiers' letters, envelopes,
documents, CDVs, photos, autographs,
newspapers, badges, ribbons, relics, framed
display items, currency, & more. Estab. 1978.
Illus. catalogs - $10/yr for 5 issues. Active
buyers receive future subscriptions free.

WARPATH MILITARY COLLECTIBLES
910-425-7000
Ed Hicks
3805 Cumberland Rd
Fayetteville NC 28306
United Confederate Veterans Southern Cross
of Honor. WWI, WWII crosses of military
service. Sell/trade.

WATSON ENTERPRISES
PO Box 392
North Pembroke MA 02358-0392
Letter from Sullivan Ballou to wife Sarah,
1861, as heard on Civil War series on TV.
Reproduced on yellow, blue, or gray
parchment. $12.95.

WILDMAN'S CIVIL WAR SURPLUS
770-422-1785
2879 S Main St • Kennesaw GA 30144-5624
Rare & antique guns, books, & other Civil War
collectibles. Price list - $2. (See ad page 233)

**WISCONSIN VETERANS MUSEUM &
STORE**
608-264-6086 • 608-266-1680
http://badger.state.wi.us/agencies/dva/museum/
wvmmain. html
30 W Mifflin St • Madison WI 53703-2558
Authentic reproduction tinware from originals
in our collection. Coffeepot, tin cups,
canteens, etc. Blankets. Museum - 2 main
galleries & various displays.

—

CRAIG WOFFORD ANTIQUES
2101 Harrison Ave
Orlando FL 32804-5467
Civil War memorabilia bought/sold,
appraisals; specializing in autographs, letters,
documents, diaries, photographs. Identifies
items, soldiers groupings. Est. 1975.

WORLD EXONUMIA
815-226-0771
Rich Hartzog
PO Box 4143BWX
Rockford IL 61110-0643
Civil War & sutler tokens, medals, slave tags,
Civil War dogtags, corps badges, sutler paper,
GAR reunion badges, etc. Buy/sell; mail bid
sales. Publisher of *Sutler Paper Money*. (See
ad pg 231)

YANK & REB TRADER
614-366-2479
PO Box 4704 • Newark OH 43055
Civil War artifacts. Buy/sell. Large inventory of
reference books not available in bookstores.
Catalog - $5 for 6 issues (ref. w/ purchase).

YANKEE FORAGER
517-263-3925
137 Park St • Adrian MI 49221-2528
Civil War specialty books, documents, photos,
relics, & more. Catalog - $2.

YE OLDE POST OFFICE
334-928-0108
17070 Scenic Hwy 98
PO Box 9
Point Clear AL 36564-0009
Dealer in antique & military collectibles, guns,
swords, uniforms, books, etc.

YESTERDAY'S NEWS, USA
612-721-5526
5344 34th Ave S
Minneapolis MN 55417-2167
Civil War autographs, books, documents,
images, militaria, & identified items. 19th &
20th-c. newspapers & magazines. Catalogs.

YESTERYEAR
615-893-3470
Larry W. Hicklen
3511 Old Nashville Hwy
Murfreesboro TN 37129-3094
Quality dug & non-dug Civil War artifacts of all
types. Buckles, buttons, swords, guns, paper,
leather, etc. Mail order subscription - $5/yr.

ALABAMA DEPT. OF ARCHIVES & HISTORY
334-242-4363 • 334-242-4435
http://www.asc.edu/archives/agis.html
624 Washington Ave
Montgomery AL 36130-0100

ALASKA STATE ARCHIVES
907-465-2275
141 Willoughby Ave Pouch C
Juneau AK 99801-1720

ARIZONA STATE LIBRARY
602-542-4035
Dept. of Library, Archives & Public Records
State Capitol
1700 W Washington St
Phoenix AZ 85007-2812

ARKANSAS HISTORY COMMISSION
501-682-6900
1 Capitol Mall
Little Rock AR 72201-1049

CALIFORNIA OFFICE OF THE SECRETARY OF THE STATE
916-653-7715
California State Archives
1020 O St Rm 138
Sacramento CA 95814-5704

COLORADO DEPT. OF ADMINISTRATION
303-866-2055
Division of State Archives & Public Records
1313 Sherman St • Denver CO 80203-2236

CONNECTICUT STATE LIBRARY
860-566-3690
http://www.cslnet.ctstateu.edu/handg.htm
History & Genealogy Unit
231 Capitol Ave
Hartford CT 06106-1548

DELAWARE PUBLIC ARCHIVES
302-739-5318 • 302-739-3021
302-739-2578 Fax
http://del-aware.lib.de.us/archives
archives@state.de.us
Hall of Records • Dover DE 19901

FLORIDA STATE ARCHIVES
904-487-2073
R.A. Gray Bldg • 500 S Bronough St
Tallahassee FL 32399-6504

GEORGIA DEPT. OF ARCHIVES & HISTORY
404-656-2393
330 Capitol Ave SE
Atlanta GA 30334-1500

HAWAII DEPT. OF ACCOUNTING & GENERAL SERVICES
808-586-0329
Archives Division
Iolani Palace Grounds
Honolulu HI 96813

IDAHO STATE HISTORICAL SOCIETY
208-334-3356
Div. of Manuscripts & ID State Archives
610 Julia Davis Dr
Boise ID 83702-7646

ILLINOIS OFFICE OF THE SECT. OF STATE
217-782-4682
217-524-3930 Fax
Archives Division
Norton Bldg
Springfield IL 62756-0001

INDIANA STATE ARCHIVES
317-232-3660
http://www.ai.org/icpr/archives
140 N Senate Ave
Indianapolis IN 46204

STATE HISTORICAL SOCIETY OF IOWA
515-281-3007
State Archives
Capitol Complex
Des Moines IA 50319-0001

KANSAS STATE HISTORICAL SOCIETY
913-272-8681 x117
http://history.cc.ukans.edu/heritage/kshs/
kshs1.html
Library & Archives Division
6425 SW 6th Ave
Topeka KS 66615-1099

KENTUCKY DEPT FOR LIBRARIES & ARCHIVES
502-875-7000
300 Coffee Tree Rd
PO Box 537
Frankfort KY 40602-0537

LOUISIANA STATE ARCHIVES
504-922-1200
504-922-1209 Research Library
3851 Essen Ln
Baton Rouge LA 70809

MAINE STATE ARCHIVES
207-287-5795
84 State House Sta
Augusta ME 04333-0084

MARYLAND STATE ARCHIVES
410-974-3914 • 410-974-3916
Hall of Records Bldg
350 Rowe Blvd
Annapolis MD 21401-1686

MASSACHUSETTS STATE ARCHIVES
617-727-2816
220 Morrissey Blvd
Boston MA 02125-3314

MICHIGAN DEPT. OF STATE
517-373-1408
Michigan Historical Center
State Archives Unit
717 W Allegan St
Lansing MI 48918-1837

MINNESOTA HISTORICAL SOCIETY
612-296-6980
Research Center
345 Kellog Blvd W
Saint Paul MN 55102

MISSISSIPPI DEPT. OF ARCHIVES & HISTORY
601-359-6876
601-359-6964 Fax
100 S State St
PO Box 571
Jackson MS 39205-0571

MISSOURI STATE ARCHIVES
314-751-3280
600 W Main St
PO Box 778
Jefferson City MO 65102-0778

MONTANA HISTORICAL SOCIETY
406-444-4774
Division of Archives & Manuscripts
225 N Roberts St
Helena MT 59620-1201
Photographs, library, genealogy resources.

NATIONAL ARCHIVES & RECORDS ADMIN.
202-501-5400 • 202-501-5410
http://www.nara.gov
inquire@arch2.nara.gov
7th St & Pennsylvania Ave
Washington DC 20408

NEBRASKA STATE HISTORICAL SOCIETY
402-471-4771
State Archives Division
1500 R St
PO Box 82554
Lincoln NE 68501

NEVADA STATE LIBRARY & ARCHIVES
702-687-8317
Division of Archives & Records
101 S Fall St
Carson City NV 89710

NEW HAMPSHIRE DEPT. OF STATE
603-271-2236
Division of Records Mgmt.
71 S Fruit St
Concord NH 03301-2410

NEW JERSEY STATE ARCHIVES & RECORDS MGMT.
609-292-6260 • 609-530-3200
Bureau of Archives & Records Preservation
State Library Bldg
185 W State St Ste CN307
Trenton NJ 08625-0307

NEW MEXICO STATE RECORDS CENTER & ARCHIVES
505-827-7332 • 505-841-4399
Historical Services Division
404 Montezuma Ave
Santa Fe NM 87501-2502

NEW YORK STATE ARCHIVES
518-474-8955
11D40 Cultural Ctr
Albany NY 12230-0001

NORTH CAROLINA STATE ARCHIVES
919-733-3952
919-733-1354 Fax
109 E Jones St
Raleigh NC 27601-2806

NORTH DAKOTA STATE ARCHIVES & HISTORICAL RESEARCH LIBRARY
701-224-2668
North Dakota Heritage Ctr
Bismarck ND 58505

THE OHIO HISTORICAL SOCIETY
614-297-2510
http://winslo.ohio.gov/ohswww/ohshome.html
Gary J. Arnold, Bibliographer & Ref. Spec.
Archives-Library Division
1982 Velma Ave
Columbus OH 43211

OKLAHOMA DEPT. OF LIBRARIES
405-521-2502 • 405-522-5209
Archives & Records Division
200 NE 18th St
Oklahoma City OK 73105-3298

OREGON SECT. OF STATE
503-373-0701 x1
http://arcweb.sos.state.or.us
reference.archives@state.or.us
Archives Division
Oregon State Archives & Records Ctr
800 Summer St NE
Salem OR 97310

PENNSYLVANIA STATE ARCHIVES
717-783-3281
PO Box 1026
3rd & Forster Sts
Harrisburg PA 17108-1026

**RHODE ISLAND STATE ARCHIVES
DIVISION**
401-277-2353
State House Room 43
Smith St • Providence RI 02903

**SOUTH CAROLINA DEPT. OF ARCHIVES &
HISTORY**
803-734-8577 • 803-734-7918
http://www.scdah.sc.edu/homepage.htm
PO Box 11669 • Columbia SC 29211-1669

**SOUTH DAKOTA STATE HISTORICAL
SOCIETY**
605-773-3804 • 605-773-6041 Fax
http://www.state.sd.us/state/executive/deca/
            cultural/archiv es.htm
State Archives
900 Governors Dr
Pierre SD 57501-2217

TENNESSEE STATE LIBRARY & ARCHIVES
615-741-2764
referenc@mail.state.tn.us
403 7th Ave N
Nashville TN 37219-1409

TEXAS STATE LIBRARY
512-463-5463
Archives Division
1201 Brazos St / Capitol Station
PO Box 12927
Austin TX 78711-2927

**UTAH STATE ARCHIVES & RECORDS
SERVICE**
801-538-3012
State Capitol Rm B-4
Salt Lake City UT 84114

VERMONT AGENCY OF ADMINISTRATION
802-828-2794
Public Records Division
Drawer 33
Montpelier VT 05633-7601

**VIRGINIA STATE LIBRARY & ARCHIVES
DIVISION**
804-786-2306
804-371-2617 Fax
11th St at Capitol Square
Richmond VA 23219-3419

**WASHINGTON OFFICE OF THE SECT. OF
THE STATE**
206-753-5485
Division of Archives & Records Mgmt
PO Box 9000
Olympia WA 98504

**WEST VIRGINIA DEPT. OF CULTURE &
HISTORY**
304-558-0230
Archives & History Section
The Cultural Ctr
1900 Kanawha Blvd E
Charleston WV 25305-0300

**STATE HISTORICAL SOCIETY OF
WISCONSIN**
608-264-6460
Archives Division
816 State St
Madison WI 53706

WYOMING STATE ARCHIVES
307-777-7826
http://commerce.state.wy.us/cr/archives/
Barrett Bldg
Cheyenne WY 82002-0001

THE 1861 COMPANY
5718 SE Crain Hwy Ste 1861
Upper Marlboro MD 20772-4102

20TH MAINE, INC.
207-865-4340 • 207-865-9575 Fax
Patricia Hodgdon
49 West St
Freeport ME 04032-1127
Specialized bookstore devoted to Civil War
with new & old books, art, music, videos,
antiques & much more.

A & K HISTORICAL ART
800-286-3084
AandKart@aol.com
PO Box 6521
Hamden CT 06517-0521
Large inventory of Civil War art - Troiani,
Kunstler, Strain, many more. New &
secondary market.

ACCENTS & PRINTS
231 Winslow St
Fayetteville NC 28301-5515
Specializing in Civil War arts & prints,
featuring artists such as Rick Reeves.

ALLEN'S CREATIONS, INC.
800-669-2731 • 864-654-3594
864-653-4568 Fax
http://www.allenscreations.com
aci@innova.net
R. Trent Allen
PO Box 452
Clemson SC 29633-0452
Frame & art gallery. One of the nation's
largest Civil War print collections. Troiani,
Kunstler, Stivers, Gallon & more. More than
500 prints in stock.

ALLEN'S FRAMEWORKS & GALLERY
919-438-3799
RR 8 Box 386
Henderson NC 27536-9808
Kunstler, Strain, Phillips, Pernell, Spaulding,
Sieve, Troiani, Redlin, Van Gilder, etc.

**AMERICAN ANTIQUES &
ARCHITECTURALS**
Sue Phillips
3863 Old Shell Rd
Mobile AL 36608
Civil War reproduction prints.

AMERICAN ART & ANTIQUES, INC.
800-242-1994
PO Box 1994
Staunton VA 24402-1994

Limited ed. prints by Rick Reeves & other
artists; sculptures, memorabilia. Visit our
gallery, 5312 R.E. Lee Highway, in heart of
the Shenandoah Valley, Civil War country.

AMERICAN EPIC STUDIO
717-337-1814
ka-epic@cvn.net
PO Box 3994
241 N Stratton St
Gettysburg PA 17325-0994
Sculptures by Karl Anderson.

AMERICAN FRAME SHOPPE
717-334-2924
717-334-5549 Fax
39 Queen St
Gettysburg PA 17325-2809
Military, contemporary, & wildlife. Stivers,
Gnatek, Troiani, Harvey, Kunstler, Phillips,
Kidd, Reeves, Landry, Doolittle, Hirato, Lamb,
Wilson, Strain, etc.

AMERICAN MASTERS GALLERY
800-547-9232
5222 Rolling Rd
Burke VA 22015-1654
Civil War prints - buy/sell/trade. All major Civil
War artists. Authorized dealer of Strain works.
Locator service, limited ed. original art,
framing, corporate accounts.

**AMERICAN PUBLISHING GROUP & PRINT
GALLERY**
800-448-1863
PO Box 4477
Gettysburg PA 17325-4477
Publishers of Mort Kunstler's fine art prints,
America's most collected historical artist.

AMERICANA GALLERY
800-892-6119 • 541-895-2678
541-895-3679 Fax
83647 N Pacific Hwy
Creswell OR 97426-9712
Don Prechtel's limited edition prints.

AMERICAST
800-360-5772
http://www.AmericastUSA.com
AmcastUSA@aol.com
121 24th Ave NW
Norman OK 73069-6320
Limited edition hand-painted figurines (5,000)
of great military leaders. $195.

AMIRIAN'S FINE ART & FRAMING
919-735-9128
118 E Walnut St • Goldsboro NC 27530-3649

THE ANCIENT PAGE
290 Macon Ave
Asheville NC 28804-3711
Featuring Chilmark sculptures.

ANTIETAM GALLERY
301-432-5868
17320 Shepherdstown Pike
Sharpsburg MD 21782-1626
Distinctively framed & displayed prints by
Troiani, Kunstler, Gallon, Stivers, Gnatek,
Rocco & others.

ARCHIVE ARTS
760-723-2119 Phone & Fax
http://www.archivearts.com
George@primemail.com
PO Box 2455 • Fallbrook CA 92088-2455
Clip art, 62 editions for Mac & PC; 8 Civil War
editions. More than 450 CW images -
$25/edition or CD with 3600 images - $99.
Free catalog.

ARMISTEAD CIVIL WAR COLLECTIONS
310-280-3507 • 310-472-6081 Fax
8306 Wilshire Blvd Ste 684
Beverly Hills CA 90211-2382
Authentic 19th-century CW map engravings -
extremely rare. Civil War-related art.

ARSENAL ARTIFACTS, INC.
800-483-1861
486 W Main St • Sylva NC 28779
Limited edition prints by Bob Graham, John
Warr, Mort Kunstler, John Paul Strain &
others. Large selection of dug artifacts.
Specialize in artillery.

ARSENAL GALLERY
1716 Owen Dr • Fayetteville NC 28304
Gallery featuring the artwork of Dale Gallon.

ART & FRAME CLASSICS
404-270-0542
Northlake Square • 4135 Lavista Rd Ste 220
Tucker GA 30084-5325
Specializing in Civil War, military art prints.
Over 45 artists in stock, bronzes, Russ
Norgan artillery pieces, etc. Free listing -
SASE.

ART RECOLLECTIONS
800-278-7746
703-525-2805 Fax
109 N Fairfax St
Alexandria VA 22314-3223
Prints by Paul McGehee. Color catalog - $5
(free w/ purchase).

ART TO GO
888-ART-TO-GO
Ltd. ed. prints at wholesale prices, incl. *Hope
of the Confederacy* by G. Harvey.

**BACK IN TIME PORTRAIT & FINE ART
STUDIO**
800-484-1163 x2119 • 770-631-6533
P. Hardin
PO Box 181
Tyrone GA 30290-0181
"Go Back in Time." Your photo converted into
B/W or full color portrait as CW soldier,
mountain man, etc. Any era. Oil, pencil,
acrylic. Start at $75.

BALLANTYNES OF WALKERBURN (USA)
888-269-8720 • 910-323-4872
910-323-0214 Fax
bowusa@aol.com
Tracey Lindsay
PO Box 35001
Fayetteville NC 28303-0001
Fine quality, 8" hand-painted porcelain resin
statues. Ask about our collectors club. Free
catalog.

BARWICK PUBLISHING
423-984-3581
PO Box 5355 • Maryville TN 37802-5355
Black & white charcoal, full-figure ltd. ed.
portraits of Jackson, Lee, Stuart, Grant,
Sherman & Custer by the late George I.
Parrish, Jr. $35/$50 A/P.

BATTLEFLAGS OF THE CONFEDERACY
800-639-2957
Steve Bishop • Franklin TN 37068
Print designed to honor all those who fought
for Dixie & banners they followed. 10 flags
featured.

BLUE MOON IMAGES
18 Washington St Ste 210
Canton MA 02021
Set of 8 Civil War watercolor notecards - 4
scenes. $8.95 ea. set + $2.50 S&H.

BOHEMIAN BRIGADE BOOKSHOP
423-694-8227
423-531-1846 Fax
Ed Archer
7347 Middlebrook Pike
Knoxville TN 37909-3108
Specializing in 1st edition & out-of-print Civil
War books, hard-to-find CW titles & popular
reprints. Also, CW prints. Collection
assistance. Catalog - $3.

BONNIE'S GIFT WORLD OF PRODUCTS
800-650-5350 • 619-789-6485
619-789-1551 Fax
Bgwhp@aol.com
Keith Bonney
117 Los Banditos Dr
PO Box 1978
Ramona CA 92065-1978
Complete line of 54mm soldiers & sets as well as sculptures, casting molds, kits, corgi vehicles, ships, prints, etc. Catalog - $3.

BOOKMARK
414-646-4499
414-646-4427 Fax
PO Box 335
Delafield WI 53018-0335
Mort Kuntsler's *Legends in Gray* calendars & notecards. $12.95 + $5 S&H. Catalog - $2.

BOXER GALLERY & FRAME CO.
330-494-2348 Phone & Fax
PO Box 2362
North Canton OH 44720-0362
Prints by Troiani, Kunstler, Strain. Mounted officers (15"H) & other Gettysburg figures (9"H) in full color. Free list of swords, bayonets, belts, buckles, insignia.

BROUTHERS & KEEFE "CHAMPION" HOUSE
315 E 86th St
New York NY 10028-4714
Ltd. ed. framed reprints of the original 1890 H. Ellis & Co.'s *Recruit*. Cigarette-Pack-Cards highlighting Lee, Grant, Sheridan, etc. $31.23 ppd. ea.

BUCKLEY MARTIN GALLERY
4617 Montrose Blvd
Houston TX 77006-6101
Limited edition prints by P. Buckley Moss. Subjects include children of the Civil War.

BUDGET FRAMER
888-343-7263
Larry Skaff - Photography
940 North Ave
Grand Junction CO 81501
Civil War living history fine art prints & photography. Catalog - $1 (ref. w/ order).

BUTTERFIELD & BUTTERFIELD
213-850-7500 x286 • 800-223-2854 x525
Greg Shaw
7601 Sunset Blvd
Los Angeles CA 90046
Fine art auctioneers & appraisers since 1865. Call for more info. or to order catalog.

DOUG BYRUM/CUSTOM ART
614-459-2622
Creative Illustration & Graphic Design
5413 Bennington Woods Ct
Columbus OH 43220-2221
Historical & reenactor portraits, battle scenes, home-front life. CW photos rendered as custom color art, contemporary art. Commissions accepted, fees based on B&W/color, size, media/subject matter. Prints available.

C & C MILITARY FINE ART
703-904-9320
703-904-9718 Fax
PO Box 3514
Reston VA 20195-1514
Original oil paintings by Mark Churms, oil & pencil sketches. More than 750 military fine art prints by Cranston Fine Arts available. 5 vol. color catalog - $65.

CALDWELL STUDIOS
618-747-2655
RR 2 Box 160
Tamms IL 62988
Professional reproductions of regimental flags constructed & hand-painted. Reasonable prices. Reenactment tested. Call Zac for free information.

CANON PRINTS
800-303-6086 • 412-746-1573
James Sulkowski
PO Box 45
Canonsburg PA 15317-0045
Limited edition prints.

CARDINAL PRINTS
414-784-8348
414-7884-7994 Fax
Best prices on Gallon, Harvey, Kunstler, Rocco, & Troiani prints. Free list.

CHICKAMAUGA BRONZE & MARBLE, INC.
PO Box 595
Chickamauga GA 30707-0595
Legends of History Series sculptures. Confederate generals Jackson, Forrest, Stuart & Lee. 16½", cold-cast bronze, patina finish. Ltd. ed. $600 ea.

CIVIL WAR "THINGS 'N FRAMES"
615-952-3672
http://www.i285.com/civil/index.html
sonny@viponline.com
Sonny Collins
PO Box 422
Kingston Springs TN 37082-0422

Forrest, Davis, Mosby & Stuart prints & notecards from original museum pieces which were painted from life. Also, antique medical equipment & Civil War artifacts.

CIVIL WAR ANTIQUITIES
614-363-1862
http://www.civilwarantiquities.com
Todd Rittenhouse, Prop.
PO Box 1411
Delaware OH 43015-1411
Quality CW items. Guns, swords, letters, currency, books, prints. Buy/sell/trade. Full service custom framing & matting; specializing in conservation framing. Shop located at 13-1/2 N Sandusky St., Delaware, Ohio. Catalog - $5.

CIVIL WAR ART CENTER
912-929-3018
Warner Robins GA

CLARK ART
919-756-3937
646 E Arlington Blvd
Greenville NC 27858-5837
Framed & unframed prints.

CLASSIC AVIATION ART
770-419-2678
770-419-3882 Fax
http://www.warart.com
444 Manget St Ste 800
Marietta GA 30060
Recognized leader in aviation & Civil War art. New & secondary market Kunstler, Stivers & Strain prints. Buy/sell/trade. Sign website guestbook for weekly updates. Free extensive list.

CLASSIC PORTRAITS MILITARY FINE ARTS
800-677-3257 Orders & Fax
410-747-8780
Michael H. Sullivan
4 Marshs Victory Ct
Baltimore MD 21228-2425
Museum-quality oil paintings & prints of Civil War figures. Custom painted portraits by leading artists from photos. Oils from $225. Prints from $30. Free catalog.

CLUB'S COLLECTIBLES
10029 243rd Pl SW
Edmonds WA 98020-5751
Museum-quality framed prints, produced from archive negatives, & authentic Confederate currency mounted & framed. Many generals.

COLLECTOR HISTORICAL PRINTS, INC.
813-877-9334
PO Box 18661
Tampa FL 33679-8661
Limited edition prints by Reeves & others. Free catalog.

THE COLLECTOR'S ART GALLERY
919-977-0883 • 919-443-4737
1200 Browntown Rd
Rocky Mount NC 27804-9213
Huge selection of Kunstler, Prechtel, Troiani, Cole, Gallon, Strain, DeMott, Stivers, Rocco, Griffing.

COLUMBUS ARMORY
706-327-1424 Phone & Fax
David S. Brady
1104 Broadway
Columbus GA 31901-2429
Complete Civil War store featuring books, relics, art, muskets & supplies. Buy/sell/trade. Free price list. (See ad page 236)

CONFEDERATE LEGENDS
703-616-5759
PO Box 2565
Leesburg VA 20177-7764
All the Confederate legends in one magnificent portrait: Davis, Lee, A.P. Hill, Hood, Johnston, Jackson, Stuart, Longstreet, etc.

JAMES H. COOKE & SON, INC.
201-327-1482
PO Box 403
Allendale NJ 07401-0403
Civil War prints, new & secondary market. Price list.

COTTON & CO.
800-994-5366
4 Penny Ct
Hendersonville NC 28739
Tapestries picturing Lee, with Lt. Col. Marshal, leaving McLean House at Appomattox CH. Choose wall hanging ($39.95) or afghan throw ($45). Machine washable 100% cotton.

COUNTRYSIDE PRINTS, INC.
35 W Prospect Ave
Washington PA 15301-6346
Ltd. ed. Civil War art.

COVERED BRIDGE GALLERY
68 S Washington St
Waynesburg PA 15370-2036
Offering America's high-quality collectible artists such as Rick Reeves.

CREATIVE FRAMING
814-266-3477
http://www.citipage.com/minimall/creativeframing
106 College Park Plz • Johnstown PA 15904
Art prints of U.S. history. Kunstler, Stivers,
Troiani, Griffing & Buxton. 24-hr. gallery.

CSA GALLERIES, INC.
800-256-1861 • 803-744-1003
http://www.csagalleries.com
2401 Mall Dr Unit A4
North Charleston SC 29406-6539
Confederate prints by Kunstler, Troiani,
Strain, Gallon, Stivers, Reeves, Gnatek,
Rocco, Nance, etc.

CYPRESS SHADOWS
1060 E County Line Rd Ste 9
Ridgeland MS 39157-1937
Featuring the works of John P. Strain. Write or
call for complete listing of all works/artists
available.

DECK THE WALLS
2000 Riverchase Galleria Ste 180
Birmingham AL 35244-2319
Rick Reeves, limited edition historical prints.

DECOYS & WILDLIFE
47 Ridge Rd • Frenchtown NJ 08825-4100
Specializing in Civil War arts & prints.
Featuring artists such as Rick Reeves. Call for
other listings.

DESIGN TOSCANO
800-525-1733 xA711
17 E Campbell St
Arlington Heights IL 60005-1472
The Lincoln Life Mask, Hands & Draped Bust
by Leonard Wells Volk. Replicas of the
original works in iron, bronze green, & bronze.
Free catalog.

DOMINICK'S ART WORLD
610-759-9121
224 Nazareth Pike • Trolley Station Mall
Bethlehem PA 18017
Gallery featuring prints by Jeremy Scott.

DON'T KNOW MUCH ABOUT HISTORY
800-531-9173
http://members.aol.com/p20IL/index.html
P20IL@aol.com • Phil Lauricella, President
316 Franklin St
Geneva IL 60134-2639
200+ prints by well-known artists such as
Kunstler, Rocco, Troiani & Stivers. Carry 300+
CW titles on our bookshelves & will research
out-of-print or rare items. Free catalog.

EAGLES NEST/ITP
PO Box 6087
Frazier Park CA 93222-6087
Grant & Lee bust sculptures on alabaster.
3-7/16"x6"x1-1/4". Hand-painted with brief
biography. $25 ea. ppd.

ECLIPSE
PO Box 773 • Cleburne TX 76033-0773
Civil War Series starting with Lincoln &
McClellan, cold cast in bronze - 13" tall, ltd.
ed. priced from $295.

ELEGANZA, LTD
206-283-0609
Magnolia Village • 3217 W Smith # 471
Seattle WA 98199
Busts of famous people. Lincoln bronze
patinated bonded stone, 12-3/4" on alabaster
base - $169 ppd. Washington, Jefferson,
Franklin, Plato, etc. 120-pg color catalog of
museum repros - $6.

EXCELSIOR PRESS
516-475-7069 • 516-874-2489 Fax
Don Roberts
PO Box 926
Bellport NY 11713-0926
Civil War Cabinet Cards. Color art prints of 24
famous regiments include period battle maps
& regimental histories. Boxed set - $23.95 +
$3.50 S&H (30-day money-back guarantee).
Catalog/brochure - $1 (ref. w/ purchase).

FARNSWORTH HOUSE MILITARY GALLERY
717-334-8838 • 717-334-5862 Fax
FARNHAUS@mail.cvn.net
Loring H. Shultz
401 Baltimore St
Gettysburg PA 17325-2623
Large selection of Don Troiani art -
Gettysburg's exclusive dealer for over 10 yrs.
New, used & rare books on Civil & Indian
wars. Buy/sell/trade. Catalog - $2. (See ad
page 241)

FISH CREEK MILITARY PRINTS
204-765-4925 • 800-260-0268
Box 535
SHILO, MB R0K 2A0 CANADA
Dealer of Cranston Fine Arts limited edition
prints.

FOUR WINDS STUDIO
366 Summit Ave
Ligonier PA 15658-1427
Classic art of the Civil War.

FOUR WINDS TRADING COMPANY
1010 California Dr
Columbia SC 29205-4219
Buys/sells Civil War art & memorabilia. Open & ltd. ed. prints. Catalog - $4.

FOX INTERNATIONAL, INC.
800-767-8851
PO Box 80037 • Portland OR 97280-0037
Limited ed. bronze casting of Lincoln, by Nano Lopez, 19.5"x12"x8" - $1,950. Also available in bonded marble - $695.

FRAME GALLERY OF STATESVILLE
704-873-6097 Phone & Fax
Carol Chappell
110 W Broad St
Statesville NC 28677-5256
Framed & unframed prints. Offering Mort Kuntsler & Troiani prints, Civil War accessories, encapsulation services utilizing current archival technology. Books.

FRAME MAKER
15 Wade Hampton Blvd
Greenville SC 29609-5656
John Paul Strain's works are featured.

FRAMED EXPRESSIONS
1618 Lincoln Way
Mc Keesport PA 15131-1714
Offering America's high-quality collectible artists such as Rick Reeves.

FRAMING FOX ART GALLERY
800-237-6077
148 Main St
PO Box 679
Lebanon NJ 08833-0679
Troiani, Kunstler, Strain, Gallon, Reeves, Rocco & all others. Inventory of more than 1,000 prints. One of America's largest Civil War art galleries. Custom picture framing.

FREDERICKSBURG HISTORICAL PRINTS
540-373-1861 • 888-FHP-9499 Orders only
540-371-9197 Fax
829 Caroline St
Fredericksburg VA 22401-5805
All major Civil War artists. Oils, prints, sculptures, engravings, montages, memory boxes, books, custom framing. Layaway plans.

FRUDAKIS STUDIO
215-884-9433
2355 Mount Carmel Ave
Glenside PA 19038-4103
Life-size Abraham Lincoln half-round bust suitable for hanging on wall. Call for details.

THE GALLERY
800-842-4278 • 908-730-8605
Bob Brinkerhoff
1 Alan Ln
Pittstown NJ 08867-4211
Civil War prints - Kunstler, Troiani, Gallon, Strain, Stivers & more. New & hard-to-find prints. 100s in stock - many at issue price. Layaway available. Visa/MC accepted. (See ad page 229)

GALLERY SOUTH
864-461-9038
PO Box 425 • Chesnee SC 29323-0425
Prints by Robert W. Wilson S/N - $125. Artist's proofs - $175 for *The Final Farewell*, R.E. Lee at Stonewall Jackson's Gravesite.

DALE GALLON HISTORICAL ART
717-334-0430
9 Steinwehr Ave • Gettysburg PA 17325-2811
More than 75 limited edition prints of Civil War scenes. (See ad page 237)

GETTYSBURG CIVIL WAR & ANTIQUE CENTER
717-337-1085
705 Old Harrisburg Pk • N Gettysburg Plaza
Gettysburg PA 17325
Multi-dealer complex in heart of antique country. Civil War memorabilia, military art, antiques & fine collectibles. Open 7 days/wk. Free parking.

GETTYSBURG FRAME SHOP & GALLERY
717-337-2796 • 717-337-2481 Fax
Paul Selmer
25 Chambersburg St
Gettysburg PA 17325-1102
Limited prints by most noted Civil War artists. Originials by Rocco, Reeves, Gnatek, Bender, Umble, Wikoff, Prechtel, Forquer. Civil War books. Catalog - $1. (See ad page 229)

THE GETTYSBURG GIFT CENTER
800-887-7775 • 717-334-6245
297 Steinwehr Ave
Gettysburg PA 17325-2815
In the lobby of the National Civil War Wax Museum. Pewter sculptures of the Civil War by Barnum. For a complete listing and more info., write, call, or stop in.

GETTYSBURG HISTORICAL PRINTS
717-334-3800 • 888-GHP-2515 Orders only
717-334-7562 Fax
ghprints@erols.com
219 Steinwehr Ave
Gettysburg PA 17325-2801

America's oldest military art gallery. Civil War art of most popularly collected historic artists; prints & originals. Montages, memory boxes, sculptures. Custom framing; lay-away plans.

GETTYSBURG MILITARY PUBLISHING
800-900-1862
1 White Oak Trl • Gettysburg PA 17325
Limited edition fine art prints by John Paul Strain.

GNATEK STUDIOS
202-363-6803
6642 Barnaby St NW
Washington DC 20015-2357
Michael Gnatek's latest offerings.

CRAIGIE GORDON STUDIO
717-657-8628 • 717-657-5073 Fax
279 Linglestown Rd
Harrisburg PA 17110
Your Civil War art alternative. Representing Don Troiani & Dale Gallon. Call for listings of many other prints.

GRAY STONE PRESS
615-327-9497 • 800-251-2664
615-320-1389 Fax
205 Louise Ave
Nashville TN 37203-1896
Limited ed. collector art prints by David Wright & various other artists. Large variety of artwork available. Free catalog.

GREAT WAR OF THE CONFEDERACY
704-739-5862
704-739-1809 Fax
http://www.civilwarmall.com/gwotc.htm
243 Oak Grove Rd
Kings Mountain NC 28086
Civil War memorabilia & collectibles, including historic Confederate art.

GREEN FLAG PRODUCTIONS
800-739-6464
PO Box 7757
Greenwich CT 06836-7757
Art series celebrating the Irish Brigade, by Bradley Schmehl.

GREENPOINT GALLERY
704-844-8026
http://www.greenpointart.com
Rob Miller
908 W John St
Matthews NC 28105
Charlotte's largest selection of Civil War & aviation art. New issue & secondary market prints. Custom framing.

GREYSTONE'S HISTORY EMPORIUM & GALLERY
717-338-0631 • 717-338-0851 Fax
http://www.GreystoneOnline.com
461 Baltimore St
Gettysburg PA 17325-2623
Producers of CW Journal have created a store, gallery & museum. Military miniatures, books, videos, collectibles, art, exhibits, story theatre. Unique merchandise.

HALLOWED GROUND PRINTS
800-576-7409 • 919-872-7111
http://www.jps.com/hgp
PO Box 61322
Raleigh NC 27661-1322
Limited edition prints by Jeremy L. Scott.

NESTA HARPER
PO Box 44
Aldie VA 20105-0044
19th-century engravings of Civil War leaders & battle scenes. Hand-tinted & signed by artist. 9x12 - $11.95 ea. + $3.60 S&H. Price list - send SASE.

HEDGEROW GALLERY
800-433-4376
Civil War prints - Kuntsler, Strain, Summers, Casteel & others.

HENDRICKSEN STUDIO
800-313-7701
Unit 4B The Shipyard
8 Western Ave Ste 18
Kennebunk ME 04043-2878

HERITAGE EMBROIDERY
402-488-7913
402-488-8167 Fax
http://WWW.CivilWarMall.com/Image.htm
Heritage@navix.net
Tom & Dorothy Rivett
PO Box 22424
Lincoln NE 68542-2424
Exclusive Mort Kunstler art images embroidered on quality American-made garments. Personalization available for reenactors, round tables, museums & galleries. Visit our online catalog.

HERITAGE STUDIO
540-659-1070 • 540-374-1872
606 Caroline St
Fredericksburg VA 22401
Donna J. Neary's Even to Hell Itself - $130. A Terrible Gale - $150. Till Death Do Us Part - $125. Do Your Duty, Boys - $175. Edge of the Storm - $150.

HERITAGE WEST PUBLISHING
800-303-6629
2501 S Mason Rd
Katy TX 77450-5936

HISTORIC FRAMING & COLLECTIBLES
410-465-0549
Joe Parr
8344 Main St • Ellicott City MD 21043-4653
Civil War weaponry & assorted items. Military
art by all major artists, including aviation &
WWII. True conservation-quality framing.

HISTORIC MIDWAY MUSEUM STORE
606-846-4214
PO Box 4592
124 E Main St
Midway KY 40347
Morgan at Midway - 5"x7" print by KY artist
Jim Hoffman; matted.

HISTORICAL ART PRINTS
203-262-6680
HAPRINTS@aol.com
PO Box 660
Southbury CT 06488-0660
Limited edition Civil War & military art prints
by one of America's most respected military
artists, Don Troiani. Contact for more info.

HISTORICAL HOUSE PRESS
615-297-4357
2805 Westmoreland Dr
Nashville TN 37212-4714

HISTORICAL IMPRESSIONS
888-603-0100
970-256-0157 Fax
lskaf@iti2.net
PO Box 60323
Grand Junction CO 81506-0323
PC & Mac standard & multimedia Civil War
screensavers for Union, South or mixed
versions. Limited ed. art, posters, bookmarks,
magnets, postcards. Dealer inquiries
welcome. Catalog. (See ad page 233)

**HISTORICAL MILITARY ART &
COLLECTIBLES**
PO Box 1806
Lafayette CA 94549-8006
Collector books, limited edition military art, &
military & political collectibles, including
medals, flags, badges, pins, & patches. Free
catalog.

HISTORICAL MILITARY GALLERIES
219-534-4858
Civil War art prints by Troiani, Gallon, etc.

HISTORICAL PAINTINGS & SCULPTURE
817-478-3926 Phone & Fax
105420.2351@compuserve.com
Ron Moore
326 Spring Branch Ln
Kennedale TX 76060
Carefully researched & visually compelling
fine art. Strong narrative style.

HISTORICAL PRINTS, INC.
800-882-8864
PO Box 18661
Tampa FL 33679-8661
Limited edition art.

HISTORICAL SCULPTURES
518-622-3508
PO Box 141
Cairo NY 12413-0141
Ron Tunison sculptures in cold cast and hot
bronzes. Free brochure.

HISTORY UNLIMITED
540-459-3921
1374 Jadwin Rd
Maurertown VA 22644-2404
Trilogy to honor Chamberlain by Gary
Casteel. Cold-cast, hot-cast, or cold-cast
hand-painted bronzes. $975 to $3,500 each.
Exquisite detail.

THE HOLLOW LOG
800-927-0718
4 Clarksville Hwy • Cornelia GA 30531
Prints by John P. Strain. Call or write for
listing of all art available.

HOSPITAL HILL HISTORICAL
800-335-8571
145 Presidents Land • Quincy MA 02169
Distributors of *Timeless Spirit*, sepia portrait of
Lee after the war. 11"x17" - $75.

HRM & COMPANY, INC.
800-511-3864
http://www.apex-ephemera.com
hrmco@praxis.net
PO Box 775 • Silver Springs FL 34489-0775
Civil War engravings - more than 1,000
original hand-colored newspaper engravings -
$55 & up.

**MURRAY HUDSON - ANTIQUARIAN
BOOKS & MAPS**
800-748-9946 • 901-836-9057
901-836-9017 Fax
mapman@usit.net
109 S Church St • PO Box 163
Halls TN 38040-0163

Large selection of Civil War authentic maps & prints. 1300+ items (priced $25-$7,500). Also, rare Forrest bust. Catalog - $10 (ref.).

J R FRAMING
703-878-1036
4390 Kevin Walker Dr
Dumfries VA 22026-1635
Gallery featuring the work of Dale Gallon. Also at 6050 Gorgas Rd, Fort Belvoir, Va.

J.J.B. LTD.
PO Box 507
Shamokin PA 17872-0507
Civil War print/calendar of the year 1861.
Day-to-day events. 20"x17-1/2" - $29.95.

J'S GALLERY & FRAME SHOPPE
800-448-1861 • 515-448-4012
http://www.netins.net/showcase/art
406 E Broadway St
Eagle Grove IA 50533-1817
Civil War prints by Strain & others. Gallery located at 109 S Commercial, Eagle Grove, Iowa.

JEBCO CLOCKS
800-635-3226
301 Industry Dr • Carlisle OH 45005-6309
Leading manufacturer of collectibles. Artwork by Kunstler & Gnatek now available on plaques or limited ed. clocks. Clocks - 11"x23", $69.95 ppd. Plaques - 11"x14", $44.95 ppd.

TERRY JONES
610-353-2210
234 Hickory Ln • Newtown Square PA 19073
Solid cold-cast bronze and hot bronze sculptures available. Works include Stonewall Jackson, Chamberlain, Gen. John Gibbon, etc.

JUNCTION SOFTWARE
970-256-0194
751 Horizon Ct Ste 244
Grand Junction CO 81506
ArtCollector for Windows. Track your art collection, invoices, inventory, for-sale lists & much more. Living history Civil War screensavers by Historical Impressions.

K & E OUTLET
900 Conference Dr
Goodlettsville TN 37072-1909
Prints by John Paul Strain.

ERIC KAPOSTA STUDIO
800-247-3550
6109 W 34th St • Houston TX 77092-6407

Gen. R.E. Lee, 13" tall bust in cast stone with terra-cotta finish - $175. Call for details.

KATE GALLERY
652 Great Plain Ave
Needham MA 02192-3305
18th-20th century architecture, furniture & decorative art prints. Framed & unframed. Fine notecards. Illus. catalog -$2.

J. E. KELLY & CO.
9 Langdon St
Montpelier VT 05602-2903
Recruiting posters of famous Civil War regiments reproduced from rare, mint-condition originals, 18"x24" -$12.95 ea. 1st U.S. Sharpshooters, 1st Penn. Cavalry, 5th N.Y., Lincoln's Assassin Wanted poster.

KIDD HISTORIC GALLERY
100 Waterfront Dr
Colonial Heights VA 23834-2180
Henry Kidd's moving & romantic set of prints. Free color brochure.

JANE KUNSTLER
516-624-2830
PO Box 311
Oyster Bay NY 11771-0311
Kunstler Civil War artist's proofs - most prints available. Western, Native American, & other subjects.

LANG GRAPHICS
414-646-2211
PO Box 99
Delafield WI 53018-0099
Mort Kunstler's new Civil War calendar & notecards. Beautifully done, fully illustrated. $12.95 + $5 S&H. Catalog - $2.

THE LAST SQUARE
800-750-4401
http://www.lastsquare.com
questions@lastsquare.com
5944 Odana Rd
Madison WI 53719
Dedicated to military history. Gaming supplies, miniatures, books, fine prints. Call for info.

MICHAEL L. LEE
2155 Lake Park Dr SE
Smyrna GA 30080-8842
General R.E. Lee, by artist Michael L. Lee. Limited edition. 11"x14" B/W print - $35. Framed - $99.95.

LEE-GRANT, INC.
800-350-5234
Harry A. Lillie
RR 4 Box 102 • Appomattox VA 24522-8916
Limited ed. prints. Dug & undug artifacts from in & around Appomattox, Va. Flags of all sorts.

LIMITED EDITION ART
800-468-0153 Phone & Fax
1066 Lizabeth Cir
Newark OH 43056-1626
Art prints by Gallon, Duillo, Gnatek, Kidd, McGrath, Rocco, Umble, Vann.

LONE WARRIOR
800-767-3498
Olathe KS
T.M.L. Peterson, *Soldier in the Rain*, 24"x30". S/N $150; A/P $175.

MAGIC TOWN
800-878-4276
49 Steinwehr Ave
Gettysburg PA 17325
Bradford Exchange plates - Battles ... & Gallant Men of the Civil War. Michael Garman sculptures at great prices!

MAGNUM CREATION
310-659-3077
835 S Wooster Ste 315
Los Angeles CA 90035
Original sculptured soldiers, 6"-12" tall, Civil War & WWI. Certificate with ea. $39.95.

THE MARKS COLLECTION
800-849-3125
http://www.markscollection.com
1590 N Roberts Rd Ste 308
Kennesaw GA 30144-3683
Resurrection Morn - ltd. ed. 1250 - $95. *Honor in Darkest Hour* - ltd. ed. 2000 - $95.

MAYO RIVER ART & FRAME
910-427-5735
206 S Lonesome Rd
Madison NC 27025-1842
18"x24" framed, ltd. ed. print of *Lee's Flag* by Tom Butler. Includes original Civil War commemorative 1st day-issue stamped envelope. S/N - $150 ppd.

MAZE CREEK STUDIO
800-432-1581
RR 5 Box 214D
Carthage MO 64836
Cavalry Duel - hand-painted sculpture by Andy Thomas. Ltd. ed., $329.

JANET MC GRATH STUDIO
800-346-9398 • 904-697-3543
PO Box 731
Lanark Village FL 32323-0731
Lee and His Valiant Men - Longstreet, Forrest, Stuart, Jackson. Ltd. ed. S/N - $95; Artist proof - $150. $10 flat S&H.

MEADOWBROOK PUBLISHING
717-263-3282
43 S Main St
Chambersburg PA 17201-2237

MEEHAN MILITARY POSTERS
212-634-5683
PO Box 477
New York NY 10028-0018
Genuine war posters. Catalog - $10 (ref.).

MELROSE TRADING
912-742-0620
912-741-3864 Fax
PO Box 6292
Macon GA 31208
Robert E. Lee bronze sculpture with walnut frame, ltd. ed. Library of Congress 1937 copyright. $1995 ea.

MEMORIAL GRAPHICS
4461 W Flamingo Rd # 180
Las Vegas NV 89103-3703
Silk screened prints reproduced from the original headstone rubbings of Civil War greats - Lee, Stuart, Davis, etc. Free brochure.

ROD MENCH
719-380-1126
PO Box 38182
Colorado Springs CO 80937
Hand-painted horse-mounted sculptures of Lee, Jackson, Forrest, & Stuart. Catalog - $4.

DON MEREDITH'S CIVIL WAR ART
813-962-1225
PO Box 370020
Tampa FL 33697-0020
Ordinary photos turn into extraordinary CW-era portraits, with strict attention to detail. Prices vary from $75. Discounts for photos showing proper uniform, gear, pose, etc. Free color brochure.

MERENS (USA) LTD.
800-793-9365
12 Twin Lakes Dr Ste 1200
Bedford NY 10506-1609
Civil War cartoon art from original comic book panels. Each limited edition of 750 cels. - $64.90 per cel.

MILITARY ART CLASSICS
205-435-6499 Phone & Fax
Steve McCracken
PO Box 423
Jacksonville AL 36265-0423
Limited edition military prints, new &
secondary market. Civil War specialist. All
popular artists. Competitive prices; layaway.
Free price list.

THE MILITARY ART GALLERY
800-362-8567
57 Macomb Pl
Mount Clemens MI 48043
Dealer of Cranston Fine Arts limited edition
prints.

MILITARY ART SHOP
706 Edwards Dr
Harker Heights TX 76548-1340
Gallery featuring the art of Dale Gallon.

MIKE MINER'S GALLERY II
1235 Park Rd
Sevierville TN 37862-2805
Professional gallery representing most
national & regional artists. One of largest
selections of Civil War art in the nation.

MOMENTS IN HISTORY
800-328-5865
5483 Beaujolaise Ln
Fort Myers FL 33919-2703
Authentic woodcut prints of Civil War scenes
as witnessed & created by the nation's finest
artists of the period. Complete, illus. catalog.

MONUMENTS OF AMERICA
321 Baltimore St
Gettysburg PA 17325-2602
Work of sculptor Gary Casteel in
"Commanders of the Shenandoah Valley"
series.

C. W. MORGAN CO.
757-631-5393
3419 Virginia Beach Blvd Ste B14
Virginia Beach VA 23452
Series of Civil War generals & naval
commanders in 19th-century-style art.

DAN NANCE PRINTS
704-543-1115
http://www.civil-war.net/nance.html
10433 Kilmory Ter
Charlotte NC 28210-8349
The Bloody Lane (Sharpsburg, MD) by Dan
Nance - $173 (artist's proofs).

NATIONAL GLASS & MIRROR CO.
540-647-3806
205 Virginia Ave
Collinsville VA 24078-2268
Framed & unframed prints.

NATURE'S IMAGE
800-333-0395
95 8th Ave SW
Forest Lake MN 55025-1877
Civil War arts & prints. Featuring artists such
as Rick Reeves & others.

NEWFIELD PUBLICATIONS
PO Box 16613
Columbus OH 43272-2388
Set of Civil War cards. Many scenes, incl.
Battle of Gettysburg: Pickett's Charge, by
Mort Kunstler.

NEWMARK PUBLISHING, USA
800-866-5566 • 502-266-6752
11700 Commonwealth Dr Ste 900
Louisville KY 40299-6363
Featuring Robert Summer, Gary Lynn
Roberts, & Wayne Justus. Catalog - $3.50.

DAVID I. NORWOOD, ARTIST
504-344-7249
2247 Oleander
Baton Rouge LA 70806
Poster-size aerial view depicting siege of Port
Hudson in great detail. B&W - $10.

OLD GLORY GALLERIES
706-556-0677
174 N Louisville St
PO Box 1327
Harlem GA 30814-1327
Specializing in the Civil War. Kunstler, Stivers,
Strain, Gallon & others. Free catalog/price list.

**OLD GLORY GALLERY & FRAME
SHOPPE, INC.**
800-731-0060 • 817-923-5576
Robert Rubel
2966 Park Hill Dr
Fort Worth TX 76109-1143
Civil War prints. Troiani, Kunstler, Strain,
Gallon, Stivers, Reeves, Heron, Gnatek,
Freeman, Kidd, DeMott, & others. Chilmark
Civil War sculptures. Send for list.

THE OLD GUARD MILITARY ART
519-432-8410
136 Emery St, W. London
Ontario CANADA N6J 1S1
Dealer of Cranston Fine Arts limited edition
prints.

OLD SOUTH ART & FRAME
770-471-3621
2695 Emerald Dr
Jonesboro GA 30256-5231
Fine art prints by Reeves, Gallon, Gnatek,
Troiani, Kunstler, Neery, Rocco, Umble,
McGrath, Strain. Sculptures by Tunison,
Casteel, Krebs, etc.

ORANGE HISTORICAL ARTWORKS
PO Box 828
Pine Bush NY 12566-0828
Series of watercolor prints by Civil War
artist/reenactor Dianne Drewes.

ORIGINAL FRAMEWORKS
800-654-1861 • 540-953-1655
civilwar@nrv.net
Jay Rainey
Gables Shopping Center
1300 S Main St
Blacksburg VA 24060-5526
All Civil War artists at discount; signatures,
documents, 19th-century steel engravings,
relics. Will find any artwork. Always looking to
purchase. Also at 4 E Washington St,
Lexington, Va. (See ad page 232)

OSAGE PRESS
800-200-4792
PO Box 5082
Rockford IL 61125-0082
Repro of 1860 Spencer Repeating Rifle
Patent Drawings -start at $13.95. Free catalog.

P & L ENTERPRISE
301-449-5730
PO Box 518
Temple Hills MD 20757-0518
Buffalo Soldiers - ltd. ed. prints, statues,
books. Color brochure - $2.

PANIOLO ART LTD.
7325 Henderson Ct SE
Tumwater WA 98501-6832

PARAMOUNT PRESS, INC.
716-789-3001
PO Box 226
Stow NY 14785-0226
Featuring Rick Reeves prints, proofs, &
originals.

PARKER'S PICTURE FRAMING
800-648-2701
111 Erie St
Edinboro PA 16412-2208
Civil War arts & prints; featuring Rick Reeves.
Call for other listings.

PIECES OF HISTORY
602-488-1377
800-488-1316 Fax
PO Box 4470
Cave Creek AZ 85331
Civil War historical art with CW medal. Gen.
Custer or Citizen Corp of Wisconsin at South
Mountain, MD. $89.95 ea. + $5 S&H. Military
book or video catalog - $1 ea.

JOHN I. PISARCIK
1500 Annette Ave
Library PA 15129-9735
Reenactors - will draw your portrait from photo
in "Battlefield Style." Special attention paid to
details of uniforms, clothing & equipment.

DON PITCHER
PO Box 64
North Haven CT 06473-0064
Offering original wood engravings as removed
from Civil War-period newspapers. Locations,
battles, leaders, maps, etc. Free catalog/list.

PIXELCHROME PROFESSIONAL
4304 Standridge Dr
The Colony TX 75056-4033
Full color Gettysburg commemorative posters
- 11"x17". Art prints of the Penn. & Va.
monuments. Both posters -$15 + $3.95 S&H.

PORTRAIT SCULPTURE
217-422-6335
4 Ridge Ct
Decatur IL 62522
Lincoln Sculptures by John McClarey.
"Unfinished Work" - ltd. ed., 24"H bonded-
bronze - $700. Individually crafted.

THE POTOMAC GALLERY
800-882-1861 • 703-771-8085
703-771-8161 Fax
17 S King St
Leesburg VA 20175-2903
Hand-painted pewter Civil War chess set.
Limited editions by Stivers, Kunstler, Gallon,
Strain, Troiani & more. Custom framing done
on site. (See ad page 229)

PRECIOUS MEMORIES
919-639-2501
123 S Broad St
Angier NC 27501

THE PRESTON BROOKS SOCIETY
800-820-1860
PO Box 13012
James Island SC 29422-3012

Largest & best 100% Confederate Clip Art, Vol. 1. PC & MAC versions - more than 125 images on 5 disks, incl. flags, battles, soldiers, ships, weapons, stamps, forts, & much more!

THE PRINT PLACE
615-486-2929
1354 Gravel Hill Rd
Columbia TN 38401-1371
Civil War prints. Kunstler, Troiani, Strain, and others.

RAINBOW CARD CO.
800-473-5213 • 516-367-6790
516-367-3063 Fax
717 E Jericho Tpke Ste 315
Huntington Station NY 11746-7502
Official Currier & Ives "Civil War" card set. Limited edition (5,000 sets), individually serial numbered, 16 full-color cards - $14.95/set. Catalog - $1.

RAMCO FRAMING
7705C Saint Andrews Rd
Irmo SC 29063-2835
Framed & unframed prints.

J. REB'S CIVIL WAR RELIC GALLERY
706-377-2057
513 Battlefield Pkwy
Fort Oglethorpe GA 30742-3848
Located near Chickamauga Battlefield. Fine quality Civil War artifacts. Excavated & non-exc. Art gallery houses one of finest CW collections. Authorized metal detector dealer. Buy/sell. Catalog - $10/yr.

RED LANCER
PO Box 8056
Mesa AZ 85214-8056
Original 19th-century military art, rare books, Victorian-era campaign medals & helmets, toy soldiers. Catalog - $12 for 3-4 issues/yr.

RED'S MILITARY PRINTS
800-711-7337
PO Box 1071
Ringgold GA 30736-1071
Rare, historic full-color art prints - 8 Civil War, 24 Amer. Revolution. Illus. brochure - $1.

REMEMBRANCE ART
Ray Helmicki
1481 N Creek Rd
Lake View NY 14085-9516
Art gallery-quality Civil War shadow boxes in solid oak. Ltd. ed. of *Country Divided*, 30"x16" - $375. For more info, send SASE. Dealer inquiries welcome. Catalog - $3 (ref.).

RIVERDALE DECORATIVE PRODUCTS
PO Box 4959 • 1920 S Court St
Montgomery AL 36103-4959
Civil War battle scene pillows by Mort Kunstler. From $15.

ROUND TOP MINIATURES
301-330-3552
7766 Epsilon Dr
Rockville MD 20855
Painted miniatures 15mm-120mm. Custom, shadow box & museum dioramas - realistic & historically accurate; ea. is unique with custom-designed figures. Catalog - $2 (ref.).

SANDLIN & ASSOCIATES
913-432-1705
913-432-5997 Fax
6405 Metcalf # 420
Overland Park KS 66202-9802
Limited edition Civil War prints, more than 75 different types. Also available as etchings. Complete, illus. catalog - $3.50.

SCOTTISH IMAGES
800-700-0334 Orders
916-362-3474 Phone & Fax
PO Box 160133
Sacramento CA 95816-0133
Dealer for Cranston Fine Arts limited edition prints.

SCULPTURES IN CLAY
8324 Mary Ave NW
Seattle WA 98117-4240
Limited edition ceramic sculptures by Richard Bowman.

SENECA RIDGE GALLERY
412-828-0240
426 Allegheny River Blvd
Oakmont PA 15139-1725
Civil War & 18th-century art, books, videos, games, music, more!

SENECA VALLEY FINE ART GALLERIES
301-898-5786
11639 Coppermine Rd
Union Bridge MD 21791-8437
All major artists represented. Civil War prints featuring Gallon, Troiani, Strain, Stivers, Reeves, etc.

SHARPSBURG ARSENAL
301-432-7700
301-432-7440 Fax
101 W Main St
PO Box 568
Sharpsburg MD 21782-0568

Purveyors of fine Civil War militaria; firearms, edged weapons, buttons, bullets, leather accoutrements, battlefield relics, books, flags, personal & camp items, paper, letters, framed prints. Buy/sell.

SHENANDOAH FRAMING, INC.
800-368-2171
RR 7 Box 39B • Lexington VA 24450
Framed & unframed prints. Prints by Tom Gallo, Michael Gnatek, Cherrie Nute.

SILENT SENTINEL STUDIO
914-245-8903
Paul R. Martin III & Joanne F. Martin
PO Box 551
Yorktown Heights NY 10598-0551
Publishes limited edition fine art prints by Paul R. Martin III. Color pencil drawings are contemplative images featuring battlefield monuments & landscapes. Commissions & dealer inquiries welcome. Free catalog. (See ad page 241)

SIMMONS TPC
7011A Manchester Blvd Ste 165
Alexandria VA 22310-3202
Generals Grant & Lee in alabastrite sculptures. 6"x3-7/16"x1-1/4". Hand-painted (blue or gray). $25 ea. ppd.

SLAVIN'S GALLERY
800-448-9517 • 910-346-4105
http://slavin.onslowonline.net
201 Country Club Rd
Jacksonville NC 28546-6400
Finest illustrated Civil War history available. Fine art prints; original & ltd. eds. Sculptures; 1/8 & 1/4 scale model CS Artillery.

SM & S NAVAL PRINTS
410-893-8184 • 410-788-0660 Fax
PO Box 41
Forest Hill MD 21050-0041
Lithographs. Call or write for complete listing.

SOUTHERN/AMERICAN HERITAGE
PO Box 1894
Lancaster SC 29721-1894
Affordable portraits/prints. Beautiful, classic, professionally matted & framed. Lee, Jackson, Grant, Lincoln, Stuart, Forrest, etc. Gettysburg Address, Lee and Jackson's last meeting. Catalog - $4.

SOUTHERN CROSS HISTORICAL ART PRINTS
PO Box 5861
Bellingham WA 98227-5861

SOUTHERN GUN WORKS
757-934-1423
757-925-1177 Fax
109 Cherry St
Suffolk VA 23434
Civil War prints, autographed military books, memorabilia. Art by Troiani, Spaulding, Kunstler, Gallon, others.

SOUTHERN HERITAGE PRINTS
205-539-3358
George Mahoney, Jr.
PO Box 503
Huntsville AL 35804-0503
Civil War flags, memo pads, envelopes, bookmarks, paperweights, chronology chart/map, prints. *Last Charge at Brandy Station*, ltd. ed. print by C.E. Monroe, Jr. - $135 inc. S&H. Portion of proceeds goes to APCWS. (See ad page 234)

SOUTHERN HISTORICAL SHOWCASE
800-854-7832 • 615-321-0639
http://www.southernhistorical.com
southernhistorical@nashville.com
1907 Division St
Nashville TN 37203-2705
Southern military art & books, prints, original documents & autographs, photos, engravings. Artists: Prechtel, Reeves, Kunstler, Kidd, Gallon, Summers, Heron, Garner, Rocco. Catalog - $5.

SOUTHLAND HISTORICAL ART PRINTS
770-917-0177
4375 Willis St
Acworth GA 30101-5468
Art prints by Mark Lemn.

SOUTHPORT GALLERY
800-641-4901
PO Box 111405
Stamford CT 06911-1405
George Pickett, Pride of the Confederacy, by Dale Gallon. 21"x28", $199 + $5 S&H. Complete with genuine Confederate bank note.

SOUTHWEST PASSAGE
603-895-3425
8 Bow St
Portsmouth NH 03801-3802
Offering prints by Mort Kunstler.

STIVERS PUBLISHING
540-882-3855
PO Box 25
Waterford VA 20197-0025
Paintings by Don Stivers.

STONE SOUP GALLERY & SOLDIERS HAUNT INN
540-722-3976
HAUNTINN@aol.com
107 N Loudoun St
Winchester VA 22601-4717
Original etchings, antique (1800s) furniture & quilts, antique reproductions. Bed & breakfast in building built in 1760. Showcase of regional talents.

STONES RIVER PRESS, INC.
800-207-8327
316 W Lytle St Ste 106
Murfreesboro TN 37130-3641

STONEWALL ENTERPRISES
800-856-6071 • 706-321-0020 Fax
Kim Hightower
205 Hickory Chase
Carrollton GA 30117-3522
Ltd. ed., museum-quality bronze sculptures representing the battles of the Civil War by world-renowned sculptor, Eric H. Baret, MD. Call for free brochure.

STORY SLOANE'S GALLERY
713-782-5011
713-782-5048 Fax
2616 Fondren
Houston TX 77063
Generals of the Confederacy sculpture series by Edward L. Hankey. Hand-painted, crafted in fine porcelain.

STUDIO OF SUNFLOWER LANDING
901-755-2391 • 800-423-0463
http://www.civilwarart.com
stratton@civilwarart.com
Harold Stratton
162 Leif Cv
Cordova TN 38018-7327
Civil War prints of Nathan Bedford Forrest, Robert E. Lee, & Stonewall Jackson. Total of 14 prints. Brochure.

SUNSHINE STUDIO
800-628-8004
2169 Sunshine Rd
Fayetteville AR 72704-6342
Sculptor John Doty's limited editions in cold-cast bronze & hand-painted.

TAYLOR DESIGN, INC.
800-371-9452
304-876-1666 Fax
taylor@intrepid.net
PO Box 956
Harpers Ferry WV 25425-0956

Tom Taylor's mixed media technique combines intricate details with creative symbolism. *A Journey Through the Civil War*, open ed. print series, $17 ea. + S&H. Free brochure.

MARION SUE THOMPSON
501-972-0133
4300 Brenda St
Jonesboro AR 72401-8422
Sultana Disaster. Ltd. ed. prints by Marion Sue Thompson, artist. Call for more info.

TIARA GIFTS
800-457-9911
1675 Rockville Pike
Rockville MD 20852-1619
Chilmark "sold out" & nearly "sold out" sculptures. Free catalog.

TRADITION STUDIOS
540-459-5469 • 540-459-5951
Keith Rocco
PO Box 779
Woodstock VA 22664-0779
Limited ed. prints by one of the finest historical artists working today, Keith Rocco. Free color catalog.

TREASURES
800-354-6393
PO Box 126
Kiawah Island SC 29455-0126
Chilmark sculptures. Visa, MC, American Express, & checks. Call/write for complete listing.

VALLEY FRAMING STUDIO & GALLERY
800-821-7529 • 540-943-7529
http://www.pointsouth.com/valframe.htm
valframe@cfw.com
328 W Main St
Waynesboro VA 22980-4509
Most comprehensive art gallery carrying largest inventory of art & artists in Shenandoah Valley. Civil War art, ltd. ed. prints. Free info.

VALOR ART & FRAME LTD.
540-372-3376
CWFugi@aol.com
Joe Fulginiti
718 Caroline St
Fredericksburg VA 22401-5904
Civil War artwork, artifacts & books. Featuring artwork of Don Troiani. Carry all major Civil War artists. Custom museum mount framing. 15 years of service. Free catalog.

VILLAGE GALLERY & FRAME SHOPPE
800-410-3608
Main Street • PO Box 608
Pleasant Valley NY 12569-0608
Military art & sculpture. Art broker. Ltd. ed.
prints. Troiani, Kunstler, Neary, Kodera,
Phillips, Tunison, Taylor, Gnatek, Strain,
Stivers, etc.

DAVE WAGNER
619-789-5179
2027 S 10th Ave • Yuma AZ 85364-8355
A Raider's Return by new artist Dave Wagner.
1st of 4 ltd. ed. prints - $35. Proofs - $45.

WALK ON THE WILD SIDE
1245 S Cleveland-Mass. Rd
Copley OH 44321
Offering America's high-quality collectible
artists such as Rick Reeves.

WARNER LIMITED
800-371-9373
19 Seekonk Rd
Great Barrington MA 01230-1562
"Genovese: Civil War Gun series" prints. All
prints shipped flat.

WARR ART GALLERY
http://www.websun.com/warr/
Confederate-themed prints for viewing &
purchase.

WATSON ENTERPRISES
PO Box 392
North Pembroke MA 02358-0392
Letter from Sullivan Ballou to wife Sarah,
1861, as heard on Civil War series on TV.
Reproduced on yellow, blue, or gray
parchment. $12.95.

ANDREW WEISSMAN
325 Alexis Ct • Glenview IL 60025
Oil paintings by commission, replicas. Color
info. - $6.

WELL-TRAVELED IMAGES
414-574-1865
414-896-0572 Fax
http://www.globaldialog.com/~eicher/index.htm
eicher@globaldialog.com
Lynda Eicher

S60 W24160 Red Wing Dr
Waukesha WI 53186-9508
Color photos of CW battlefields, sites. Books.
Matted color prints of 10,000+ CW-related
images, also available for publication. Call or
email for catalog. See internet home page for
samples & info. on books.

WELLINGTON MILITARY ART
800-889-4978
9508 Sappington Rd
Saint Louis MO 63126-3097
Dealer of Cranston Fine Arts limited edition
prints.

GREGORY FLOYD WEST
http://www.mindspring.com/~gfwest/relee.htm
Commissioned portrait painter. View oil
painting of Lee & other works of Southern
families.

C. PHILLIP WIKOFF REPRODUCTIONS
302-239-1457
302-239-5543 Fax
PO Box 132
Rockland DE 19732-0132
Impressions of the Civil War series. *Be Strong
of Heart*, 19-1/4"x16", $85.

WRITINGS ON THE WALL
7950 Route 30
Irwin PA 15642-2725
Civil War arts & prints. Featuring artists such
as Rick Reeves.

WRM GRAPHICS
216-491-9314
http://www.wrmgraphics.com
prints@wrmgraphics.com
3667 Traver Rd
Cleveland OH 44122-5165
Finest in limited edition Civil War naval prints
by William R. McGrath. Color brochures.

REX YOUNGER ENTERPRISES
910-984-2680 • 800-528-2117
3648 Clingman Rd
Ronda NC 28670
The Last Stand - the State Capitol at
Columbia, SC, by Ron Cockerham. 21"x28",
S/N $150; A/P $200.

ABRAHAM LINCOLN BOOK SHOP
312-944-3085 • 312-944-5549 Fax
357 W Chicago Ave
Chicago IL 60610-3052
U.S. Military History, French & Indian War,
Revolution, 1812, Mexican, Civil War, Indian
Wars. Books, prints, autographs. Buy/sell.
Catalog - $5.

ANTEBELLUM COVERS
301-869-2623
888-ANTEBEL (268-3235)
301-869-2623 Fax
http://www.antebellumcovers.com
antebell@antebellumcovers.com
PO Box 3494
Gaithersburg MD 20885-3494
Civil War & 19th-century U.S. paper
collectibles incl. soldiers' letters, images,
general orders, patriotic envelopes,
autographs, slavery documents & advertising
paper; CD-ROMs of Civil War & historical
titles. Free catalog. Internet customers can be
notified by email each time auction is posted.

ANTIQUE AMERICANA
PO Box 19
Abington MA 02351-0019
Colonial American & Civil War documents,
books, autographs, maps. Reasonably priced.

AUTOGRAPH TIMES
1125 W Baseline Rd # 2-153
Mesa AZ 85210-9501
The only monthly newspaper for autograph
collectors. Sample copy - $2 S&H.

BLACKJACK TRADING COMPANY
Chuck Hanselmann
PO Box 707
Blythewood SC 29016-0707
Buyer of family Confederate paper, stamps,
letters, autographs, currency, slave
documents, slave tags, & estates.

MIKE BRACKIN
203-647-8620
PO Box 23 • Manchester CT 06045-0023
Large assortment of Civil War & Indian War
autographs, accoutrements, memorabilia,
insignia, medals, buttons, GAR, documents,
photos & books. Catalog - $6/yr for 5 issues.

STANLEY BUTCHER
4 Washington Ave
Andover MA 01810-1724
Buys Confederate generals' autographs,
letters, & other Civil War documents.

CIVIL WAR STORE
504-522-3328
212 Chartres St
New Orleans LA 70130
Mail order catalog - weapons, currency,
bonds, stamps, letters, diaries, CDVs, prints,
slave broadsides & bills of sale, autographs,
photos. Catalog - $4.

STAN CLARK MILITARY BOOKS
717-337-1728
717-337-0581 Fax
915 Fairview Ave
Gettysburg PA 17325-2906
Buys/sells Civil War books, ltd. edition prints,
autographs, letters, documents, postcards,
soldiers' items; special interest in U.S. Marine
Corps items.

COHASCO, INC.
914-476-8500
914-476-8573 Fax
E. Snyder
Postal 821 • Yonkers NY 10702
Semi-annual mail/phone auction catalogs
containing varied CW memorabilia: generals,
maps, letters, photos, ephemera, etc. Our
50th year in business. Catalog - $5.

COL. GROVER CRISWELL
352-685-2287 • 352-685-1014 Fax
PO Box 6000
Salt Springs FL 32134-6000
Buys/sells currency, stocks, bonds, money,
slavery items, autographs. 51st year of
business. *Comprehensive Catalog of
Confederate Paper Money*, hardcover, 350
pp. - $35 (ppd.). 432-pp. price list of
collectibles - $8 (ref.). Free book list.

FEDERAL HILL ANTIQUITIES
410-584-8185 / 8329
14 Glen Lyon Ct • Phoenix MD 21131-1212
Purveyors of fine autographs & collectibles.
Letters & documents, photos, relics &
artifacts, ephemera. Buy/sell/trade.

JAMES FUNKHOUSER
pres.connect@juno.com
1423 Macedonia Church Rd
Stephens City VA 22655-3710
Presidential autographs for sale. Listing - $1.

GIBSON'S CIVIL WAR COLLECTIBLES
423-323-2427 • 423-323-8123 Fax
Paul, Linda & Bryan Gibson
PO Box 948
Bristol TN 37620-0948

Autographs, CSA bonds & currency, diaries, flags, letter groups, newspapers, photos, slave items, uniforms, any other paper items.

BRIAN & MARIA GREEN, INC.
910-993-5100
910-993-1801 Fax
http://www.collectorsnet.com/bmg/index.shtml
bmgcivilwar@webtv.net
PO Box 1816J
Kernersville NC 27285-1816
Civil War autographs, letters, documents, diaries, CSA stamps, covers, currency, etc.
Catalog - $5/yr for 4 issues.

JIM HAYES
803-795-0732
PO Box 12560
Charleston SC 29422-2560
Civil War autographs. Bi-monthly list - $10/yr.

GARY HENDERSHOTT
501-224-7555
PO Box 22520
Little Rock AR 72221-2520
Autographs, photographs, imprints, flags & memorabilia of the Civil War era. Catalog - $3.

THE HISTORIAN'S GALLERY
770-522-8383
770-522-8388 Fax
http://www.nr-net.com/history/
history@atl.mindspring.com
3232 Cobb Pkwy Ste 207
Atlanta GA 30339
Brokers & dealers in maps, autographs, selected relics.

HISTORY-MAKERS
4040 E 82nd St Dept 44
Indianapolis IN 46250-4209
Historic letters & documents signed by the greatest history makers who ever lived. Free report.

HUGHES BOOKS
504-948-2427
PO Box 840237
New Orleans LA 70184-0237
Buy/sell rare books, documents, & autographs. Civil War, the South, Louisiana, New Orleans. 3 catalogs - $3.

INKWELL AUTOGRAPH GALLERY
717-337-2220
717-337-2221 Fax
777 Baltimore St
Old Gettysburg Village
Gettysburg PA 17325

Autographs bought/sold - entertainment, sports & historical. Autographs of the famous at surprisingly affordable prices. Open year-round; closed Wednesdays.

KEYA GALLERY
212-366-9742
800-906-KEYA Orders only
http://www.KeyaGallery.com
Key15@aol.com
110 W 25th St Gallery 304A
New York NY 10001-7401
Excavated relics - bullets, tokens, buckles, buttons, insignia, & more. Catalog.

KINGSTON MILITARY ANTIQUES
770-336-9354
Jerelhook@aol.com
Jere Hook
PO Box 217
Kingston GA 30145-0217
Buy/sell/trade pre-1898 militaria, mostly Civil War. By appt. only. Catalog - 32¢.

KUBIK FINE BOOKS
937-294-0253
3474 Clar Von Dr
Dayton OH 45430-1708
Buy/sell rare & out-of-print books on British, French, European, & U.S. military history. Autographs & historical fiction. 1st editions of 19th-century Civil War books. Catalog - $3.

PHILLIP B. LAMB, LTD.
504-899-4710 • 800-391-0115 Orders
504-891-6826 Fax
http://www.LambRarities.com
lambcsa@aol.com
PO Box 15850
2727 Prytania St
New Orleans LA 70175-5850
Buy/sell Confederate memorabilia; CDVs, currency, documents, photos, art, bonds, slave items, swords, buttons, bullets, autographs, & much more. (See ad page 234)

DEBORAH LAMBERT
1945 Lorraine Ave
Mc Lean VA 22101-5331
Slavery documents, CW newspapers, prints, letters, autographs, battle maps. List - $1.

HARDIE MALONEY
504-522-3328
212 Chartres St
New Orleans LA 70130-2215
Civil War store. Confederate currency, bonds, stamps, covers, CDVs, letters, diaries, documents, autographs, pistols & swords.

MC GOWAN BOOK CO.
919-403-1503 • 800-449-8406
919-403-1706 Fax
R. Douglas Sanders
39 Kimberly Dr
Durham NC 27707-5418
Always buying. Highest prices paid for fine &
rare Civil War books, autographs, documents,
photographs, etc. Catalog subs. - $3. (See ad
page 243)

MENIG'S MEMORABILIA
708-258-9487
517 S Manor Dr • Peotone IL 60468-9129
Authentic Civil War autographs, newspapers,
and documents. Free catalog.

THE MT. STERLING REBEL
606-498-5821
Terry Murphy
PO Box 481
Mount Sterling KY 40353-0481
Buy/sell since 1979 rare, out-of-print, &
previously owned Civil War books. Limited
inventory of Civil War paper items, ephemera,
autographs & images. Catalog upon request.
(See ad page 239)

NORTHERN CO. ARCHIVES/ACQUISITIONS
800-432-8777
18640 Mack Ave • PO Box 36793
Grosse Pointe Woods MI 48236-0793
Buyers of autographs, documents, photo
collections, stock certificates, letters,
contracts, etc. Lifetime member MS&D
Society. Top $ paid.

HOWARD L. NORTON
PO Box 22821
Little Rock AR 72221-2821
Buy/sell/appraise. Autographs, Civil War
items, Americana, historical documents,
photographs, coins, currency, stamps, postal
history. All transactions confidential. Catalog.

THE OLD PAPERPHILES
401-624-9420 • 401-624-4204 Fax
PO Box 135 • Tiverton RI 02878-0135
Offering 100s of accurately described paper
collectibles. Great variety, wide price range.
Autographs, documents, books. Catalog - $8
for next 10.

OLDE SOLDIER BOOKS, INC.
301-963-2929 • 301-963-9556 Fax
Warbooks@erols.com
Dave Zullo
18779 N Frederick Ave Ste B
Gaithersburg MD 20879-3158

Largest selection of rare & hard-to-find books.
Documents, letters, photographs, autographs,
manuscripts. Buy/sell. Free catalog.

ORIGINAL FRAMEWORKS
800-654-1861 • 540-953-1655
civilwar@nrv.net
Jay Rainey
Gables Shopping Center • 1300 S Main St
Blacksburg VA 24060-5526
All Civil War artists at discount; signatures,
documents, 19th-century steel engravings,
relics. Will find any artwork. Always looking to
purchase. Also at 4 E Washington St,
Lexington, Va. (See ad page 232)

PROFILES IN HISTORY
800-942-8856 • 310-859-7701
310-859-3842 Fax
345 N Maple Dr Ste 202
Beverly Hills CA 90210-3859
Autographs wanted. Also buying original
letters, documents, vintage photos,
manuscripts, & rare books (signed). Illus.
catalog - $45/yr. Sample - $10.

STEVEN S. RAAB AUTOGRAPHS
800-977-8333 • 610-446-4514 Fax
http://www.raabautographs.com
raab@netaxs,com
PO Box 471 • Ardmore PA 19003-0471
Serious collectors, respected dealers. Top
dollars paid for collection & quality individual
autographs, documents, manuscripts, signed
photos, & interesting letters. Catalog sample -
$5; $15/yr.

JOSEPH RUBINFINE
505 S Flagler Dr Ste 1301
West Palm Beach FL 33401-5923
American historical autographs.

SOUTHERN ENCAMPMENTS
504-751-0757
tcld04@premier.net
Tim Rochester
16380 S Fulwar Skipwith Rd
Baton Rouge LA 70810
Civil War antiques; autographs, buttons,
documents, period glass, insignia, letters,
projectiles, books & more. Photo-illus. catalog
- $2.50.

SOUTHERN HISTORICAL SHOWCASE
800-854-7832 • 615-321-0639
http://www.southernhistorical.com
southernhistorical@nashville.com
1907 Division St
Nashville TN 37203-2705

Southern military art & books, prints, original documents & autographs, photos, engravings. Artists: Prechtel, Reeves, Kunstler, Kidd, Gallon, Summers, Heron, Garner, Rocco. Catalog - $5.

STAMPEDE INVESTMENTS
608-254-7751
1533 River Rd
Wisconsin Dells WI 53965-9002
Large inventory of original letters & documents from the most important people in U.S. History to fit every budget. Free catalog.

THEME PRINTS, LTD.
800-CIVL WAR • 718-225-4067
PO Box 610123 • Bayside NY 11361-0123
Books, antique arms, historic documents, photographs, letters & autographs from Revolutionary era to early Hollywood. Includes Civil War memorabilia. Fully illus. catalog - $5, or $12/yr. (5 issues).

UNIVERSITY ARCHIVES
Matthew McGarry, Dir. of Advertising
1406 Overlook Dr
Mount Dora FL 32757-3769
Buy/sell. Letters, documents, clipped signatures, 1400-present. Annual subscription of $29.95 yields at least 4 of the best catalogs in the industry.

WAR BETWEEN THE STATES MEMORABILIA
717-337-2853
Len Rosa
PO Box 3965
Gettysburg PA 17325-0965
Buy/sell soldiers' letters, envelopes, documents, CDVs, photos, autographs, newspapers, badges, ribbons, relics, framed display items, currency, & more. Estab. 1978. Illus. catalogs - $10/yr for 5 issues. Active buyers receive future subscriptions free.

CRAIG WOFFORD ANTIQUES
2101 Harrison Ave
Orlando FL 32804-5467
Civil War memorabilia bought/sold, appraisals; specializing in autographs, letters, documents, diaries, photographs. Identifies items, soldiers groupings. Est. 1975.

YESTERDAY'S NEWS, USA
612-721-5526
5344 34th Ave S
Minneapolis MN 55417-2167
Civil War autographs, books, documents, images, militaria, & identified items. 19th & 20th-c. newspapers & magazines. Catalogs.

BOB ZABAWA
201-444-9653
201-444-8221 Fax
652 Ackerman Ave
Glen Rock NJ 07452
Will buy or trade for Civil War autographs of famous & lesser known generals and naval officers.

ALABAMA BUREAU OF TOURISM & TRAVEL
800-ALABAMA
334-242-4554 Fax
http://www.state.al.us
alabamat@mont.mindspring.com
Russell A. Nolen
401 Adams Ave
PO Box 4927
Montgomery AL 36103-4927
Birthplace of the most dramatic chapter in American history. Site of historic battles, parks, politics, much more. Free travel guide.

AMERICA'S NATL PARK MUSEUM STORE
215-597-2569
316 Chestnut St
Philadelphia PA 19106-2708

ANDERSONVILLE NATL HISTORIC SITE
912-924-0343
RR 49 Box 196
Andersonville GA 31711

ANTIETAM BATTLEFIELD & BOOKSTORE
301-432-4329
Parks & History Association
PO Box 692
Highway 65 N
Sharpsburg MD 21782-0692

APPOMATTOX COURT HOUSE NHP
804-352-8987
PO Box 218
Appomattox VA 24522-0218
Includes visitor center, McLean House & Clover Hill Tavern. Admission fee.

ARKANSAS POST NATL MONUMENT
501-548-2207
RR 1 Box 16
Gillett AR 72055-9707

ASSOCIATION FOR THE PRESERVATION OF CIVIL WAR SITES
888-606-1400
http://www.apcws.com
11 Public Sq Ste 200
Hagerstown MD 21740-5510
Not-for-profit membership organization that preserves Civil War sites for educational & recreational uses. Website: organizational news & membership info.

ATLANTA CYCLORAMA
404-658-7625
800C Cherokee Ave SE
Atlanta GA 30315-1440

BE BOOKS
3712 Walnut Ave Ste 8135
Altoona PA 16601-1342
National Park handbooks: Gettysburg, Antietam, Fort Sumter, Vicksburg, etc. *Artillery Through the Ages*, *Fort Pulaski*, etc. Free catalog.

BEAUVOIR
601-388-9074 • 800-570-3818
http://www.beauvoir.org
2244 Beach Blvd • Biloxi MS 39531
Last home of CSA president Jefferson Davis. Open daily 9AM-5PM (CST); closed for Thanksgiving & Christmas.

CEDAR CREEK BATTLEFIELD FOUNDATION, INC.
540-869-2064 • 540-869-1438 Fax
http://www.winchesterva.com/cedarcreek
Suzanne Lewis
PO Box 229
Middletown VA 22645-0229
Visitors Center & bookshop overlooking battlefield. October reenactment. Reference library, large CW book selection, flags, prints, maps & square foot certificates. All proceeds go to preservation of battlefield.

CENTER STATE 29
800-732-5821
"Virginia's Civil War Connection." Follow Highway 29 to sample sites rich in Civil War heritage & history. Call for free brochure.

CHANCELLORSVILLE NATL HISTORIC SITE
RR 1 Box 125P
Route 3 W
Fredericksburg VA 22407

CHICKAMAUGA / CHATTANOOGA NATL MILITARY PARK
615-821-7786
PO Box 2387
US Highway 27
Fort Oglethorpe GA 30742-2387

CHRISTMAS AT THE FORT
334-861-6992
Fort Gaines Historic Site
PO Box 97
Dauphin Island AL 36528-0097
Annual living history weekend; 1998 dates - December 5-6. Experience 1861 Christmas at the fort with Confederate soldiers — authenticity stressed. Candlelight tour, feast, dance, drills, camp life, etc.

CUMBERLAND GAP NATL HISTORIC PARK
606-248-7606
PO Box 156
Middlesboro KY 40965-0156

FORT DONELSON NATL BATTLEFIELD
615-232-5706
PO Box 434
Dover TN 37058-0434

FORT PULASKI NATL MONUMENT
912-786-5787
PO Box 30757
Highway 80E
Savannah GA 31410-0757

FORT SUMTER NATL MONUMENT
803-883-9783
1214 Middle St
Sullivans Island SC 29482-9717

FREDERICKSBURG & SPOTSYLVANIA NATL MILITARY PARK
703-373-6122
http://www.nps.gov/frsp/frspweb.htm
1011 Lafayette Blvd
Fredericksburg VA 22401-5501
Largest military park in the world.

GETTYSBURG NATL MILITARY PARK
95 Taneytown Rd Electric Map
Gettysburg PA 17325-2804

GULF ISLANDS NATL SEASHORE
904-934-8742
1400 Fort Pickens Rd Bldg 5
Pensacola Beach FL 32561-5116

JEFFERSON DAVIS STATE HISTORIC SITE
912-831-2335
912-831-2060 Fax
338 Jeff Davis Park Rd
Fitzgerald GA 31750
Confederate memorial & museum, containing relics from a Ga. battle flag to rare uniforms. Davis family's capture at this site on May 10, 1865, marked official end of the Confederacy.

KENNESAW MOUNTAIN NATL BATTLEFIELD PARK
770-422-3696
900 Kennesaw Mountain Dr
Kennesaw GA 30152

LINCOLN HOME NATL HISTORIC SITE
217-523-3421
426 S 7th St
Springfield IL 62701-1905

MANASSAS NATL BATTLEFIELD
703-754-7107
6511 Sudley Rd
Manassas VA 20109-2358

MISSOURI DIVISION OF TOURISM
800-777-0068
Convention & Visitors Bureau
Cape Girardeau MO
"Hearts of Blue & Grey" Civil War sites - Fort D, Union Monument & fountain, Confederate War memorial, CW hospital.

MONOCACY BATTLEFIELD & BOOKSTORE
301-662-3515
Parks & History Association
4801 Urbana Pike # B • Frederick MD 21704

NATCHEZ NATL HISTORIC PARK
601-446-5790
1 Melrose Montebello Pkwy
Natchez MS 39120-4715

NEW MARKET BATTLEFIELD HISTORICAL PARK
540-464-7323
PO Box 1864 • 8895 Collins Dr
New Market VA 22844-1864

NEWPORT NEWS, VA
888-493-7386
Battlefield tours, historic houses, harbor tours, museum exhibits & living history events. Free visitor guide & Civil War tour brochure.

OATLANDS PLANTATION & GIFT SHOP
703-777-3174
20850 Oatlands Plantation Ln
Leesburg VA 20175

PAMPLIN PARK CW SITE
804-861-2408
http://www.pamplinpark.org
6523 Duncan Rd
Petersburg VA 23803-7449
Battlefield where in April 1865 Grant's forces "broke through" Confederate defenses, ending longest siege in US history. Pathways along original Confederate fortifications, interactive games. Tour a plantation house.

PEA RIDGE NATL MILITARY PARK
501-451-8122
Highway 62E • Pea Ridge AR 72751

PETERSBURG NATL BATTLEFIELD PARK
804-732-3531
1539 Hickory Hill Rd
Petersburg VA 23804

RICHMOND NATL BATTLEFIELD PARK
804-226-1981
3215 E Broad St
Richmond VA 23223-7517

A.H. STEPHENS STATE HISTORIC PARK
706-456-2602
PO Box 283 • Crawfordsville GA 30631
Site of Liberty Hall, home to Vice-President of
the Confederacy Stephens; Confederate
Museum.

STONES RIVER NATL BATTLEFIELD
615-893-9501
3501 Old Nashville Hwy
Murfreesboro TN 37129-3094

STONEWALL JACKSON HEADQUARTERS MUSEUM
540-667-3242
WFCH@shentel.com
Todd Kern
415 N Braddock St
Winchester VA 22601-3921
Gen. Jackson used this home during the
winter of 1861-62 to plan his famous "Valley
Campaign."

STONEWALL JACKSON HOUSE
540-463-2552 • 540-463-4088 Fax
Michael A. Lynn
8 E Washington St.
Lexington VA 24450-2529
The Confederate general's only home with
restored garden & museum shop. Tours every
half hour Mon-Sat 9-5, Sun 1-5; last tour
begins at 4:30PM. Open until 6PM
June-August. Closed major holidays.

J.E.B. STUART BIRTHPLACE, INC.
540-251-1833
PO Box 240
Ararat VA 24053-0240
Memberships to help preserve the birthplace
of J.E.B. Stuart begin at $25.

TALLASSEE CHAMBER OF COMMERCE
334-283-5151
334-283-2940 Fax
301A King St
Tallassee AL 36708
Oversees Confederate Armory (only one to
have survived war) & Confederate Officers
Quarters (believed to be only 2 houses ever
built by CSA government).

U.S. NPS CIVIL WAR PARKS
http://www.nps.gov/Architext/AT-NPSquery.html
Provides search for all national park sites
relating to the Civil War.

VALENTINE RIVERSIDE
800-365-7272
550 E Marshall St
Richmond VA 23219-1852
Richmond's innovative history park at the falls
of the James River. Civil War tours,
sound/light show, vintage carousel, high-tech
exhibits, African-American history/tours,
archeological digs, living history.

VICKSBURG BATTLEFIELD
601-636-0583
3201 Clay St
Vicksburg MS 39180-3469

VICKSBURG CONVENTION & VISITORS BUREAU
800-221-3536
601-636-4642 Hayes Latham
http://www.vicksburg.org/cvb
PO Box 110
Vicksburg MS 39181-0110
Annual March "Run Through History" through
Vicksburg NMP. 10K race, 5K walk, 1-mile
run. Refreshments, music.

LIBRARY BINDING COMPANY
800-792-3352
2900 Franklin Ave
Waco TX 76710-7315
Professional binding service with fast delivery
for books, theses, magazines, newspapers,
paperbacks, leather editions, Bibles,
portfolios, etc. Free price list or advice.

JAMES MEYER BOOKBINDING CO.
315-258-3930 • 800-841-7797
26 E Genesee Rd
Auburn NY 13021
Professional bookbinding & restoration - our
full-time business. Leather, goldwork, edge
gilding. Prices vary.

OLDE RIDGE BOOKBINDERY
800-635-3421 • 716-244-5510
274 Goodman St N
Rochester NY 14607-1154
Book repair & rebinding done by professional.
Leather book binding, protective boxes,
custom binding our specialty.

148TH NEW YORK
George Shadman
PO Box 64
Watkins Glen NY 14891-0064
They Marched on Richmond - story of the
148th NY Volunteers & the Army of the
James. 300 pp. - $22 + $3 S&H.

ABCDEF BOOKSHOP
717-243-5802
726 N Hanover St
Carlisle PA 17013-1534

ACADEMIC BOOK CENTER
503-287-6657
503-284-8859 Fax
5600 NE Hassalo St
Portland OR 97213-3699

CHARLES S. ADAMS
304-876-3533 Phone & Fax
201 Ryan Ct
Shepherdstown WV 25443
Civil War books concerning operations in Md.,
W.Va. & the Shenandoah Valley.

AMAZON.COM BOOKS
http://www.amazon.com
Order from a list of more than a million titles,
including all of Rockbridge Publishing's fine
Civil War titles.

AMERICA'S NATL PARK MUSEUM STORE
215-597-2569
316 Chestnut St
Philadelphia PA 19106-2708

AMERICAN HISTORY CO.
540-371-6822
540-371-6897 Fax
AMHSTCO@ahoynet.com
701 Caroline St
Fredericksburg VA 22401-5903

AMERICAN OVERSEAS BOOK CO.
201-767-7600
201-784-0263 Fax
550 Walnut St
Norwood NJ 07648-1393

AMERICANA SOUVENIRS & GIFTS
http://www.americanagifts.com
302 York St
Gettysburg PA 17325
Most complete line of Civil War souvenirs &
memorabilia for both USA & CSA. Cannons,
bullets, patches, toys, books, flags, videos,
documents, insignias, & much more. (See ad
page 242)

AMHERST COUNTY HISTORICAL MUSEUM
804-946-9860
PO Box 741 • 301 S Main St
Amherst VA 24521-0741

AMIRIAN'S FINE ART & FRAMING
919-735-9128
118 E Walnut St
Goldsboro NC 27530-3649

ANDERSONVILLE ANTIQUES
912-924-2558 • 912-924-1044
Peggy & Fred Sheppard
PO Box 26
Andersonville GA 31711
Authentic Civil War guns, swords, buttons,
documents; books on the Civil War.

ANTHEIL BOOKSELLERS
516-826-3101 Phone & Fax
2177 Isabelle Ct
North Bellmore NY 11710-1599
Naval, maritime, military aviation book
catalogs. 1,500 book listings per catalog
(quarterly). Catalog (1 yr subs.) -$6.

ANTIETAM BATTLEFIELD & BOOKSTORE
301-432-4329
Parks & History Association
PO Box 692
Highway 65 N
Sharpsburg MD 21782-0692

APPALACHIAN BOOKSTORE
706-276-1992
190 Old Orchard Sq
East Ellijay GA 30539-1929

THE ARCHIVE SOCIETY
800-257-3481
717-233-0561 Fax
PO Box 940
Hicksville NY 11802-0940
Union Leaders - a library of firsthand accounts
by the men who led the Union to victory.

ARIZONA HISTORICAL SOCIETY
520-628-5774
Publications Division
949 E 2nd St
Tucson AZ 85719
*Confederate Pathway to the Pacific: Major
Sherod Hunter and Arizona Territory, CSA*, by
L. Boyd Finch. $39.95 + S&H.

THE ARMCHAIR SUTLER
919-875-0111
1500 Seminole Trl
Raleigh NC 27609-7416

ASHLAWN HIGHLAND GIFT SHOP
804-293-5539
1941 Ashlawn Highland Dr
Charlottesville VA 22902-7549

ATLANTA CYCLORAMA
404-658-7625
800C Cherokee Ave SE
Atlanta GA 30315-1440

ATLANTIC BOOKS
803-723-4751
310 King St
Charleston SC 29401-1441

B J'S BOOKS
703-347-4111
381 W Shirley Ave
Warrenton VA 20186-3113

BARBARA'S BOOKSTORE
800-327-5471
817-335-5972 Phone & Fax
215 W 8th St
Fort Worth TX 76102-6150

BARNETTE'S FAMILY TREE BOOK CO.
barnette@neosoft.com
Mic Barnette
1001 North Loop W
Houston TX 77008-1766
Guide to tracing your Civil War ancestors -
$12.50. Catalog - $1.

BATTLEZONE, LTD.
PO Box 266
Towaco NJ 07082-0266
Military patches, pins, decals, planes, books.
5,000+ items. Color catalog - $4.50 ppd. ($2
ref. w/ 1st order)

BE BOOKS
3712 Walnut Ave Ste 8135
Altoona PA 16601-1342
National Park handbooks: Gettysburg,
Antietam, Fort Sumter, Vicksburg, etc. *Artillery
Through the Ages, Fort Pulaski*, etc. Free
catalog.

BEACHVIEW BOOKS
912-638-7282
215 Mallory St
Saint Simons Island GA 31522-4716

THE BEAUFORT BOOKSTORE
803-525-1066
2127 Boundary St
Beaufort SC 29902-3827

BECK'S ANTIQUES & BOOKS
540-371-1766
708 Caroline St
Fredericksburg VA 22401-5904

BELLE & BLADE
201-328-8488
201-442-0669 Fax
124 Penn Ave
Dover NJ 07801-5335
Send for catalog of war books, videos, toys,
swords, knives, & gifts. Catalog - $3; free w/
order.

BERGMAN BOOKS
PO Box 28393
Columbus OH 43228-0393
Ohio in the War, by Whitelaw Reid. One of the
most thorough state histories to come out of
the Civil War. 2 vol., 2100 pp., hardcover.
$99.00 ppd.

THE BEST SELLER
540-463-4647
540-463-3714 Fax
29 W Nelson St
Lexington VA 24450-2033

**BLOUNT COUNTY GENEALOGICAL &
HISTORICAL SOCIETY**
ATTN: TC
PO Box 4986
Maryville TN 37802-4986
*Loyal Mountain Troopers: The 2nd and 3rd
Tenn. Vol. Cavalry in the Civil War*. Details
these largely ignored Southerners who served
the Union. $32.50 ppd.

BLUE & GRAY BOOKS & PRINTS
919-441-5311
PO Box 1835
1700 S Virginia Dare Trl
Kill Devil Hills NC 27948-1835

BLUE PEACH
540-253-5536
PO Box 375
The Plains VA 20198-0375

THE BOOK CELLAR
804-979-7788 • 804-979-7787
316 E Main St
Charlottesville VA 22902-5234

THE BOOK CENTER
301-663-1222
1305 W 7th St
Frederick MD 21702-4128

THE BOOK CENTER
301-722-2284
301-722-8344 Phone & Fax
bkcenter@netbiz.net
15 N Centre St
Cumberland MD 21502-2305

THE BOOK CHASE
540-687-6874
PO Box 2258 • 102 W Washington St
Middleburg VA 20118-2258

THE BOOK DEPOT
919-527-9663
4109 W Vernon Ave
Kinston NC 28504-9672

THE BOOK GALLERY
11400 W Huguenot Rd
Midlothian VA 23113-1193

BOOK KEEPERS, INC.
205-879-5741
2408 Canterbury Rd
Birmingham AL 35223-2384

BOOK PEOPLE
804-288-4346
536 Granite Ave
Richmond VA 23226-2148

THE BOOKERY
540-464-3377
107 W Nelson St
Lexington VA 24450-2035

BOOKMARK OF CHARLOTTE
704-377-2565
100 N Tryon St Ste 265
Charlotte NC 28202-4000

BOOKMASTERS DISTRIBUTION SERVICES
800-247-6553
1444 US Route 42 • Mansfield OH 44903
The Irish Brigade & Its Campaigns as seen
through the eyes of *New York Herald* war
correspondent David Conyngham - $27.50.

BOOKS & COMPANY
PO Box 1046
Dunkirk NY 14048-1046
Historical recipes & cooking info. from CW
era. Recipes from notable figures & soldiers.
History of some classic recipes. $7 ppd.

BOOKS OF THE SOUTH
205-854-2690
1269 Huffman Rd
Birmingham AL 35215-6314

BOOKS! BY GEORGE
205-323-6036
2424 7th Ave S
Birmingham AL 35233-3318

THE BOOKSTACK
540-885-2665
1 E Beverley St
Staunton VA 24401-4322

THE BOOKSTORE
804-384-1746
4925 Boonsboro Rd
Lynchburg VA 24503-2260

BOOKWORLD
800-444-2524
1933 Whitfield Loop
Sarasota FL 34243
Leather and Soul, 513-pg novel based on the
escape of a POW from Confederates - $21.89.

THE BOOKWORM
540-829-6209 Phone & Fax
214 N East St # A
Culpeper VA 22701-2738

BOONTON BOOKS
800-234-1862 • 201-263-4060 Fax
121 Hawkins Pl
Boonton NJ 07005-1127

BRASSEY'S
800-775-2518 • 800-428-5331
PO Box 960 • Herndon VA 20172-0960
Books on history, including *Confederate
Raider*, biography of Raphael Semmes,
commander of CSS *Alabama*.

BREEDLOVE ENTERPRISES
PO Box 538
Bolivar OH 44612-0538
Titles pertaining to women & the Civil War.

THE CANNONADE
PO Box 20601
Rochester NY 14602-0601
*Nice Boom: The Amerian Civil War Artillery
Reenactor's Handbook*, Sean McAdoo, ed.
100+ pp., including drill, living history, tactics,
NCO training & more. $10.95 + $3 S&H.

**CEDAR CREEK BATTLEFIELD
FOUNDATION, INC.**
540-869-2064 • 540-869-1438 Fax
http://www.winchesterva.com/cedarcreek
Suzanne Lewis
PO Box 229
Middletown VA 22645-0229

Visitors Center & bookshop overlooking battlefield. October reenactment. Reference library, large CW book selection, flags, prints, maps & square foot certificates. All proceeds go to preservation of battlefield.

CHAMPLIN BOOKS, INC.
PO Box 782 • Gulf Breeze FL 32562-0782
Military history, GeoPolitics, & Techno-Thrillers. All periods & conflicts. Free catalog.

CHOCTAW BOOKS
601-352-7281
926 North St • Jackson MS 39202-2614

CITADEL GIFT SHOP
803-953-5110
803-953-4802 Fax
MSC # 110 • 171 Moultrie St
Charleston SC 29409

CIVIL WAR BOOK DISCUSSION GROUP
JPHA1982@aol.com (for more info.)
Peggy Vogtsberger
Discuss Civil War books with other AOL members, every other Wed., 8 PM EST.
Keyword - CAFE BOOKA; held in Salon #2.

CIVIL WAR BOOKS ONLINE
http://members.aol.com/bookkritik/civilwar.html
Fritz Heinzen
Selection of the finest in Civil War publishing; features new & recent titles as well as the classics.

CIVIL WAR SOLDIERS MUSEUM
904-469-1900
Norman W. Haines, Jr., MD
108 S Palafox Pl • Pensacola FL 32501-5630
See artifacts from Ft. Sumter to Appomattox, one of nation's largest displayed Civil War medical collections; more than 600 book titles.
Catalog - $2.

SUSAN LOTT CLARK
PO Box 2009 • Waycross GA 31502-2009
Southern Letters & Life in the Mid-1800s.
Hardbound, 472-pg. book based on 214 war-era family letters. Cloth -$40. Leather - $50.

CLARK'S GUN SHOP, INC.
540-439-8988
10016 James Madison Hwy
Warrenton VA 20186-7820
Retailer of books, Civil War relics, Kepis, flags, buttons, Confederate souvenirs, original Confederate money & state notes, Civil War prints.

COMMAND POST
201-627-6272 • 201-627-6627 Fax
PO Box 1015
Denville NJ 07834-0615
Books & videos on the Civil War, including the role of women. Free catalog.

CONFEDERATE BOOKSHELF
PO Box 1327
Harlem GA 30814-1327
New & reprinted books on the War for Southern Independence. Free price list.

CONFEDERATE DIRECTORY
915-446-4439
David Martin
PO Box 61 • Roosevelt TX 76874-0061
Reference for vendors of Confederate currency, books, tapes, flags, stationery, memorabilia, reenactors' supplies, services, memorials, etc.; includes COMPLETE Confederate Constitution. $12 (ppd.).

CONFEDERATE MEMORIAL ASSOCIATION
202-483-5700
1322 Vermont Ave NW
Washington DC 20005-3607

THE CONFEDERATE SHOPPE
205-942-8978
928 Delcris Dr
Birmingham AL 35226-1953

CONSERVATIVE BOOK CLUB
33 Oakland Ave
Harrison NY 10528
Best books on history, politics, & other important issues together in one book club.

THE CORNER SHELF
540-825-4411
213 Southgate Shopping Ctr
Culpeper VA 22701-3833

CORTLAND COUNTY HISTORICAL SOCIETY, INC.
607-756-6071
25 Homer Ave
Cortland NY 13045-2056
Hosts Suggett House Museum & Kellogg Memorial Research Library. *A Regiment Remembered: 157th New York Volunteers* - Lt. William Saxton's diary, 157 pp. - $20 + $3.40 S&H. NYS - add 8% sales tax.

COTTON ROW BOOKSTORE
601-843-7083
333 Central Ave
Cleveland MS 38732-2647

COWLES HISTORY GROUP
http://www.thehistorynet.com
Attn: Military History Index
PO Box 3242 • Leesburg VA 20177-8111
Cross-referenced index of more than 3,000
entries, through 1000s of years of battle.
Every subject addressed in *Military History*
magazine's first decade of publication -
$24.95.

JONATHAN CREEK BOOKS
PO Box 6 • Lake Junaluska NC 28745-0006
Civil War Curiosities. Strange stories, oddities,
events & coincidences - $9.95. Other titles
available from Rutledge Hill Press.

COL. GROVER CRISWELL
352-685-2287
352-685-1014 Fax
PO Box 6000
Salt Springs FL 32134-6000
Buys/sells currency, stocks, bonds, money,
slavery items, autographs. 51st year of
business. *Comprehensive Catalog of
Confederate Paper Money*, hardcover, 350
pp. - $35 (ppd.). 432-pp. price list of
collectibles - $8 (ref.). Free book list.

CRITTENDEN SCHMITT ARCHIVES
http://www.erols.com/tyrannus/archives/
csavideo.html
PO Box 4253 / Courthouse Station
Rockville MD 20850
Technical & historical books & videotapes
relating to weapons & ammunition of all types
& eras.

CROSSROADS COUNTRY STORE
540-433-2084
Shenandoah Heritage Farmer's Market
Route 11 S • VA
Shenandoah Valley's premier Civil War store;
books, flags, music, souvenirs, crafts, gifts,
jewelry. Part of the Shenandoah Heritage
Farmer's Market. Open Mon-Sat 10am-6pm.

CROWN RIGHTS BOOKS
http://members.aol.com/crwnrts/resource.htm
PO Box 823
Sioux Falls SD 57101-0823
The Real Lincoln - reprint, 1904 expose. 288
pp., softcover - $10 ea. Free catalog.

CW BATTLES
1943 N Grimes Ste B229
Hobbs NM 88240
Handbook of 230 major Civil War battles;
when, where, who, what index. $9.95 + S&H.

D & B RUSSELL BOOKS
318-865-5198
129 Kings Hwy
Shreveport LA 71104-3402

ELIZABETH P. DARGAN
3257 Roman Mill Ct
Oakton VA 22124-2131
The Civil War Diary of Martha Abernathy, wife
of Dr. C.C. Abernathy of Pulaski, Tennessee.
$13.95 ppd.

JOHN H. DAVIS, JR.
9707 Old Georgetown Rd Apt 1423
Bethesda MD 20814-1751
Common Soldier Uncommon War, by Sidney
Morris Davis. 526 pp., hardcover - $38 ppd.

DEE GEE'S GIFTS & BOOKS
919-726-3314
508 Evans St
Morehead City NC 28557-4219

DENTON & ASSOCIATES
800-960-3003
L. M. Denton
PO Box 468 • Queenstown MD 21658-0468
*A Southern Star for Maryland: MD & the
Secession Crisis*. Attempt to set the record
straight as far as MD's role in the war.
Hardcover, 256 pp. - $26 ppd.

DER TIER SHOPPE
800-520-3808
25907 54th Avenue Ct E
Graham WA 98338-9515
Extensive collection of Civil War & related
books, including *The Killer Angels*, *N.B.
Forrest*, *All for the Union*, etc.

THE DIXIE PRESS
615-831-0776 Phone & Fax
PO Box 110783 • Nashville TN 37222-0783
Publisher, wholesaler & retailer of Southern
books & genealogy products. Free catalog.

DUBLIN BOOK CENTER
912-272-9255
Billie Tate, Mgr.
2001 Macon Rd # 29 • Dublin GA 31021
In business in central Georgia for 24 years.
Complete line of books for men, women &
children, including many Civil War titles. Will
special order.

EDISTO BOOKSTORE
803-869-1885
PO Box 420 • 547 Highway 174
Edisto Island SC 29438-0420

ELDEN EDITIONS
2111 Wilson Blvd # 550
Arlington VA 22201
*Rough Riding Scout: The Story of John W.
Mobberly, Loudoun's Own Civil War Guerilla
Hero,* by Richard E. Crouch. Softcover, 50 pp.
- $10 + $2 S&H.

FAMILY TREE BOOKSHOP
410-820-5252
410-820-5254 Fax
9B Goldsborough St
Easton MD 21601-3119

KENNETH B. FERGUSON
k4kxo@netside.com
204 Sailing Ct
Lexington SC 29072-7684
Defense of Charleston Harbor, by Capt. John
Johnson. Reprint of the classic 1890 edition of
Johnson's book. On top 100 list. $35.

FIRESIDE BOOKS
704-245-5188
2612 US Highway 74 Byp # 509
Tri-City Mall
Forest City NC 28043-6192

THE FLAG GUYS
914-562-0088 x305
http://www.flagguys.com
Flagguys@aol.com
283 Windsor Hwy Dept 305
New Windsor NY 12553-6909
Flags of all types & sizes. Books, Kepis,
accessories, swords, cassettes, CDs,
novelties. Free catalog.

FOUR SEASONS BOOKS
304-876-3486
116 W German St
Shepherdstown WV 25443

FRAME GALLERY OF STATESVILLE
704-873-6097 Phone & Fax
Carol Chappell
110 W Broad St
Statesville NC 28677-5256
Framed & unframed prints. Offering Mort
Kuntsler & Troiani prints, Civil War
accessories, encapsulation services utilizing
current archival technology. Books.

FRANKLIN BOOK CO.
215-635-5252
215-635-6155 Fax
7804 Montgomery Ave Ste 3
Elkins Park PA 19027-2698

FRANKLIN BOOKSELLERS
615-370-5737 Publisher
615-790-1349 Store
118 4th Ave S
Franklin TN 37064-2622

GALLERY 30
717-334-0335
30 York St
Gettysburg PA 17325-2369

GALLERY OF MOUNTAIN SECRETS
540-468-1900
Richard & Linda Holman
PO Box 370 • Route 250 Main St
Monterey VA 24465-0370

GARRETT PRODUCTIONS
800-870-9626
Thomas A. Garrett
185A Newberry Commons
Etters PA 17319-9362
Insight to the Battle of Gettysburg, 28-pg
book. Great for first-timers or refresher -
$10.97 ppd. *The Monuments of Gettysburg*
40-min. videotape - $32 ppd.

THE GENERAL STORE
703-261-3860
2522 Beech Ave • Buena Vista VA
24416-3014

THE GENERAL'S BOOKS
800-CIVIL WAR
522 Norton Rd • Columbus OH 43228-2617
Affiliate of *Blue & Grey* magazine. 1,000+ Civil
War titles. Fascinating & excellent reading.
Call for catalog.

GETTYSBURG FRAME SHOP & GALLERY
717-337-2796
717-337-2481 Fax
Paul Selmer
25 Chambersburg St
Gettysburg PA 17325-1102
Limited prints by most noted Civil War artists.
Originials by Rocco, Reeves, Gnatek, Bender,
Umble, Wikoff, Prechtel, Forquer. Civil War
books. Catalog - $1. (See ad page 229)

GETTYSBURG NMP BOOKSTORE
800-JULY 3 1863
717-334-1891 Fax
Robert Housch
Visitor Center - Electric Map
95 Taneytown Rd
Gettysburg PA 17325
Complete Civil War bookstore specializing in
books, tapes, CDs & videos. Free catalog.

GIVENS BOOKS
804-385-5027
2345 Lakeside Dr
Lynchburg VA 24501-6730

THE GOOD OL' REBEL
706-553-2202
10105 White House Pkwy
Woodbury GA 30293-3101

GOODSON ENTERPRISES, INC.
970-923-0063 • 303-838-1357
150A Watson Divide Rd
Snowmass CO 81654
Georgia Confederate 7000. Complete battle &
CW history of Barton & Stovell's Georgia
brigade, combined fighting force of the 40th,
41st, 42nd, 43rd, & 52nd. 150 pp. $27 + $3
S&H.

GOSPEL TRUTH/CIVIL WAR ROOM
412-238-7991
228 W Main St • Ligonier PA 15658-1130
Full-service Christian bookstore & Civil War
room. Kunstler calendars, patterns, pewter
figurines, books, videos, music, hats, accessories, shirts, Woolrich wool & much more.

GRANT COUNTY HISTORICAL SOCIETY
608-723-2287 • 608-723-4925
129 E Maple St • Lancaster WI 53813
Operates from Cunningham Museum. *Our
Boys* - 64 stories of men & boys from Grant
County, Wisc.; names of all 750 Grant Co.
soldiers who died in the war. $25 + $3 S&H.
(See ad page 239)

THE GREENHOUSE
540-364-1959
PO Box 525 • 8393 W Main St
Marshall VA 20116-0525

**GREYSTONE'S HISTORY EMPORIUM &
GALLERY**
717-338-0631
717-338-0851 Fax
http://www.GreystoneOnline.com
461 Baltimore St
Gettysburg PA 17325-2623
Producers of *CW Journal* have created a
store, gallery & museum. Military miniatures,
books, videos, collectibles, art, exhibits, story
theatre. Unique merchandise.

GUIDON BOOKS
602-945-8811
602-946-0521 Fax
7117 E Main St
Scottsdale AZ 85251-4315

EDWARD R. HAMILTON, BOOKSELLER
5265 Oak
Falls Village CT 06031-5005
Overstocks, remainders, imports & reprints.
1,000s of titles in more than 60 subject areas,
including the Civil War. $20-$40 books as low
as $1.95-$3.95. Free catalog.

HANNAH'S LETTERS
972-291-9266
560 Flower Ln
Cedar Hill TX 75104
Hannah's Letters, by Charles Finsley. 30
battlefield letters, history of 67th Ohio Inf. 101
pp., hardcover - $27 + $4 S&H.

HARPERS FERRY BOOKSTORE
304-535-6881
PO Box 197
Shenandoah St
Harpers Ferry WV 25425-0197

HEARTHSTONE BOOKSHOP
703-960-0086 • 888-960-3300 Orders
703-960-0087 Fax
http://www.hearthstonebooks.com
info@hearthstonebooks.com
Stuart Nixon
5735A Telegraph Rd
Alexandria VA 22303-1205
Genealogical books, software, CDs &
supplies, including listings on Civil War history
& research. Catalog - $2 (ref.).

HERITAGE ANTIQUES
540-788-3274
8733 Old Dumfries Rd
Catlett VA 20119-1934

HERITAGE BOOKS, INC.
800-398-7709 • 301-390-7709
http://www.heritagebooks.com
1540 Pointer Ridge Pl Ste E
Bowie MD 20716-1800
Books on history, Americana, Civil War, &
genealogy. Free catalog.

HERITAGE OF HONOR
703-751-1863
PO Box 22485
Alexandria VA 22304-9248

HISTORICAL BRIEFS, INC.
800-732-4746
Civil War Reports - most authentic reports
available, written as events unfolded &
published in *Harper's Weekly*. 232 pp. -
$24.95 + $3.75 S&H.

HISTORY BOOK CLUB
Camp Hill PA 17012-0001
"The Best History Has to Offer." Today's finest
selections in all areas of history, from ancient
to modern, available at discount prices.

HISTORY BOOK SOCIETY
PO Box 2225 • Williamsburg VA 23187
Outstanding books at unbeatable prices.
Broad selection of new titles. Free broadside
catalog.

HOOKED ON HISTORY
708-255-2340
15 N Elmhurst Ave
Mount Prospect IL 60056-2400

HOOP & HAVERSACK SUTLERY
517-643-5368
PO Box 415 • Merrill IL 48637-0415

HOWELL PRESS
804-977-4006
howellpres@aol.com
1147 River Rd Ste 2
Charlottesville VA 22901-4172
Civil War titles, as well as books on history,
transportation, cooking & gardening.

IRISH BRIGADE GIFT SHOP
504 Baltimore St • Gettysburg PA 17325
T-shirts, sweatshirts, jackets, books, flags,
recruiting posters, photos, pins, stationery,
prints, figurines & more - all relating to Irish
Civil War service. Detailed item list - send
business-size SASE.

THE JOHNS HOPKINS UNIVERSITY PRESS
800-537-5487
http://jhupress.jhu.edu/home.html
Hampden Station
Baltimore MD 21211
The Long Roll (softcover - $15.95) and *Cease
Firing* (softcover - $14.95), both by Mary
Johnston, a Civil War novelist rediscovered.

JUNIATA COUNTY HISTORICAL SOCIETY
498B Jefferson St
Mifflintown PA 17059-1424
*An Imperishable Fame: The Civil War
Experience of George F. McFarland*, by
Michael Dreese - 210 pp., $20 (ppd.).

KONECKY & KONECKY
212-807-8230
156 5th Ave Ste 823
New York NY 10010-7002
Books on America's Civil War & other periods.
Call/write for listing.

KRAINIK & WALVOORD
703-536-8045
PO Box 6206
Falls Church VA 22040-6206
A Collector's Guide to Photographic Cases.
Definitive reference on plastic ("Gutta
Percha") daguerreotype cases. Hardcover -
800 illus. & price guide - $90 ppd.

ROBERT LACOVARA
609-624-0608 Phone & Fax
2089 N Route 9
Cape May Court House NJ 08210-1163
*Cumberland County and South Jersey During
the Civil War, 9th New Jersey Regiment,
Flags and History of New Jersey Volunteers
During the Civil War* - all reprints. Other titles.

LADIES' ISLAND BOOKSTORE
803-524-0444
2 Islands Cswy
Beaufort SC 29902-1737

THE LAST SQUARE
800-750-4401
http://www.lastsquare.com
questions@lastsquare.com
5944 Odana Rd
Madison WI 53719
Dedicated to military history. Gaming
supplies, miniatures, books, fine prints. Call
for info.

GEORGE LAYMAN
55 Littleton Rd Apt 24F
Ayer MA 01432-1762
1866 Peabody Breech-Loading Rifle Catalog,
new repro. *Rolling Block Rifle* and *A Guide to
the Maynard Breech Loader*. Single shot
books.

LEGENDS
913-242-5060
Matt & Susan Matthews
703 S Main St
Ottawa KS 66067-2803

LINCOLN LETTERS
PO Box 80821
Lansing MI 48908-0821
Personal Reminiscences of Abraham Lincoln,
by Smith Stimmel. Reprint of rare book;
originally published in 1928. Ltd. quantities -
$15. (See ad page 241)

LINCOLN PARK BOOKSHOP
312-477-7087
2423 N Clark St
Chicago IL 60614-2717

LITTLE WARS
504-924-6304 • 504-924-5307 Fax
3034 College Dr
Baton Rouge LA 70808-3117

LONGSTREET HOUSE
609-448-1501
David Martin
PO Box 730 • Hightstown NJ 08520-0730
Original & reprint titles on Gettysburg & unit histories from New Jersey, New York, Pennsylvania, Delaware, & South Carolina. Free catalog.

LOUDOUN MUSEUM SHOP
703-777-8331
14 Loudoun St SW
Leesburg VA 20175-2907
Visit our shop located in restored 1767 log cabin. Unique gift items include historic maps, books & hand-crafted gifts by local artisans.

MAC MILLAN GENERAL REFERENCE
800-428-5331
201 W 103rd St
Indianapolis IN 46290-1093
The Atlas of the Civil War - puts the entire Civil War at your fingertips. At bookstores or order direct.

MAIN STREET BOOKS
703-628-1232
152 E Main St # 2-W
Abingdon VA 24210-2835

MAIN STREET BOOKS
704-892-6841
PO Box 1210 • 126 S Main St
Davidson NC 28036-1210

JOHN MAINOR
21493 Campbell Dr
Brooksville FL 34601-1408
Civil War Stories by E.H. Sutton, 1910. Firsthand account of 24th Georgia at Fredericksburg, Chancellorsville, Gettysburg, & life in POW camps. Reprints - $12 ppd.

MARY ELLEN & CO.
800-669-1860 Orders • 219-656-3000 Fax
Mary Ellen Smith
100 N Main St
North Liberty IN 46554-9200
Historical sewing patterns, Victorian boots, parasols, hats, fans, hoops, petticoats, camisoles, etc. Variety of books. Victorian gifts, wedding accessories, etc. Retail/wholesale. New Victorian gift shop - call for hours. Catalog - $3 (ref.).

MC CAIN'S BOOKS
703-740-3354
PO Box 369
9400 S Congress St
New Market VA 22844-0369

HENRY V. MC CREA
PO Box 951
Marianna FL 32447-0951
Red Dirt and Isinglass: A Wartime Biography of a Confederate Soldier - stirring account of infantryman Marion Hill Fitzpatrick's adventures with the ANV, 5/62-4/65. $34.45 ppd.

TIM MC KINNEY
RR 2 Box 300A
Fayetteville WV 25840-9570
Robert E. Lee & the 35th Star, R.E. Lee at Sewell Mountain: The West Virginia Campaign, & other titles.

MILITARY BOOK CATALOG
PO Box 4470
Cave Creek AZ 85327-4470
Military history, medals, uniforms, weapons, collectibles. More than 1,000 titles. Catalog - $2. Medals catalog - $1.

THE MILITARY BOOK CLUB
6550 E 30th St
PO Box 6357
Indianapolis IN 46206-6357
From ancient to modern history. Special deals with membership. Many Civil War titles.

MISSOURI HISTORICAL SOCIETY
PO Box 11940
Saint Louis MO 63112-0040
Civil War books. In *The Civil War in St. Louis, a Guided Tour,* Wm. C. Winter brings to life the monuments, markers, & memories of the Civil War in St. Louis. 192 pp. Paper - $22.95. Cloth - $32.95.

MONOCACY BATTLEFIELD & BOOKSTORE
301-662-3515
Parks & History Association
4801 Urbana Pike # B
Frederick MD 21704

MONTGOMERY COUNTY HISTORICAL SOCIETY
212 S Water St
Crawfordsville IN 47933
The Diary of Private Ambrose Remley & His Four Years in the Lightning Brigade - story of Wilder's mounted infantry & Spencer repeating rifle - $23.

W. M. MORRISON BOOKS
512-266-3381
morrisonbooks@worldnet.att.net
15801 La Hacienda Dr
Austin TX 78734-1431
Personal Civil War letters of Lawrence
Sullivan "Sul" Ross, CSA. - $29.50 ppd.

JIM MUNDIE, BOOKS
281-531-8639
12122 Westmere Dr
Houston TX 77077-4022

R. L. MURRAY
315-594-2019
13205 Younglove Rd
Wolcott NY 14590-9742
*The Redemption of the Harpers Ferry
Cowards: The 111th & 126th New York State
Vol. Regiments at Gettysburg.* 3rd printing -
$12.

MUSEUM OF FRONTIER CULTURE
540-332-7850
PO Box 810 • 1250 Richmond Rd
Staunton VA 24401-0810

NEW DOMINION BOOK SHOP
804-295-2552
804-295-9986 Fax
404 E Main St
Charlottesville NC 22902-5236

NEW LEAF BOOKSTORE, LTD.
540-347-7323
43 Main St
Warrenton VA 20186-3420

**NEW MARKET BATTLEFIELD MILITARY
MUSEUM**
540-740-8065 • 540-740-3663 Fax
John Bracken
9500 Collins Dr
PO Box 1131
New Market VA 22844-1131
Comprehensive museum shop featuring CW
relics, flags, uniforms, bullets, buttons,
swords, muskets, currency, personal items,
memorabilia, etc. More than 1200 book titles.
Open Mar. 15-Dec. 1.

MRS. A.C. NICHOLS
4048 Rectortown Rd
Marshall VA 20115-3241
*The Little Fork Rangers, 1861-1865: A Sketch
of Co. D, 4th Virginia Cavalry* (Culpeper's only
cavalry company) - 130 pp., hardcover - $21;
softcover - $11. Add S&H.

NORTHERN VIRGINIA DAILY
540-465-5137
Civil War Book
PO Box 69
Strasburg VA 22657-0069
Standing Ground - 18-part newspaper series
on Civil War in the Shenandoah Valley
compiled into unique new book. Softcover -
$16 ppd.

OLD HISTORICAL VIEWS
803-723-7708
188 Meeting St
Charleston SC 29401-3155

ANDREW OREN MILITARY BOOKS
414-744-3927
3156 S Kinnickinnic Ave
Milwaukee WI 53207
Civil War books. Booklist available.

P & L ENTERPRISE
301-449-5730
PO Box 518
Temple Hills MD 20757-0518
Buffalo Soldiers - ltd. ed. prints, statues,
books. Color brochure - $2.

PAGE ONE
PO Box 4232
Richmond VA 23220
Guide to Virginia Civil War - all the Civil War
trail sites.

PALMETTO BOOKWORKS
PO Box 11551
Columbia SC 28211-0551
*The Gallant Gladden: The Life and Times of
Gen. Addley Hogan Gladden,* by Edith
Anthony Purvis - $35 + $2 S&H.

PALMYRA TRADING CO.
703-984-8888
97 Franley Ln
Woodstock VA 22664-2653

PAPER TREASURES
703-740-3135
PO Box 1160
9595 S Congress St
New Market VA 22844-1160

JOHN M. PELLICANO
138-29 Jewel Ave
Flushing NY 11367-1964
*Conquer or Die: The 39th New York Volunteer
Infantry* - Garibaldi Guard, a military history.
$14.95 + $3 S&H.

PICKET POST
717-337-2984
341 Baltimore St
Gettysburg PA 17325-2602

THE PIEDMONT ENVIRONMENTAL
COUNCIL
540-347-2334
PO Box 460 • Warrenton VA 20186-0460
Hallowed Ground: Preserving America's
Heritage, by Rudy Abramson. Piedmont—
America's most historic land—is captured in
all its moods through words & pictures. $40.

PRAIRIE TRAVELER BOOKS
131 Cavalier Rd
Scottsville NY 14546-1206
Books: Western American History, fur traders,
Indian tribes, cavalry, cowboys, Custer, etc.
Free catalog.

PROVISION MEDIA
901-668-4249
7046 Broadway # 318
Lemon Grove CA 91945-1406
The Gettysburg Experience, book - $10.95.
Computer clip art. Civil War, anatomy, botany,
earth science, IBM/Mac format - $19.95.

R & R BOOKS
716-346-2577
3020 E Lake Rd
Livonia NY 14487
Books on weapons, featuring *The British*
Soldier's Firearm, *Spencer Repeating*
Firearms, *Confederate Edged Weapons*, etc.

R W BOOKS
703-257-7895
8657 Sudley Rd
Manassas VA 20110-4588

R.M.J.C., INC.
PO Box 684
Appomattox VA 24522-0684
CW-era New Testament, hardcover - $13
ppd. Choose Union (black) or Confederate
(brown). Reprinted from original. Free
quarterly, CW-related newspaper, *The*
Christian Banner, deals with Christian aspect
of the war.

MORRIS RAPHAEL
318-369-3220
1404 Bayouside Dr
New Iberia LA 70560-2824
A Gunboat Named Diana (book) - $21.95 ppd.
The Battle in the Bayou Country (5th printing)
- $21.95 ppd. Brochure.

RB BOOKS
800-497-1427 • 717-232-7944
717-238-3280 Fax
Ruth Hoover Seitz
1006 N 2nd St • Harrisburg PA 17102-3121
Gettysburg: Civil War Memories, including
color photos from renowned J. Howard Wert
Gettysburg Collection. 64 pp. $9.95 + $3
S&H. (See ad page 241)

REALLY NEAT BOOKS
540-564-0688
182 Neff Ave
Harrisonburg VA 22801-3488

RED TIE MUSIC & BOOKS
PO Box 3858
Ann Arbor MI 48106
The Civil War Fifer - songbook featuring
favorite & lesser-known melodies, lyrics,
histories & artwork - $12.95 + $2.50 S&H.
Other songbooks & collections of lyrics &
poetry.

THE RICHMOND BOOKSHOP, INC.
804-644-9970
808 W Broad St • Richmond VA 23220-3807

RICHMOND NEWSPAPERS
SUPPLEMENTARY PUBLICATIONS
800-422-4434
PO Box 85333 • Richmond VA 23293-5333
The Insider's Guide to the Civil War (Eastern
Theater), Travel Guide - $9.95.

ROANOKE VALLEY HISTORY MUSEUM
GIFT SHOP
540-342-5772
PO Box 1904 • 1 Market Sq
Roanoke VA 24008-1904

THE ROBERTS CIVIL WAR LIBRARY
800-520-3808
25907 54th Avenue Ct E
Graham WA 98338-9515
Many books dealing with the Civil War incl.
N.B. Forrest - $15; *Gen. A.P. Hill* - $14;
Landscapes of the Civil War - $40. Others.

ROYAL OAK BOOKSHOP
540-635-7070
207 S Royal Ave
Front Royal VA 22630-3205

RUFFIN FLAG COMPANY
706-456-2111 • 706-456-2112 Fax
http://www.mindspring.com/~micromgt/ruffin.htm
241 Alexander St NW
Crawfordville GA 30631-2804

Auto tags, bumper stickers, books, T-shirts, crew sweatshirts, polo shirts, regulation battle flags, etc. Jeff Davis, Dixie's Pride, N.B. Forrest, etc. Retail/wholesale. Catalog - $1.

RURAL CITIZEN BOOKSTORE, INC.
540-635-6673
http://ruralcitizen.com
rory@ruralcitizen.com
PO Box 286 • 370 Rome Beauty Dr
Markham VA 22643-0286
Specializes in books on Southern culture & heritage.

MIKE RUSSELL
401 Virginia Ave • Herndon VA 20170-5437
Quarterly catalog of Victorian artifacts & relics, emphasis on obsolete currency, bottles & pipes - $2. *The Collector's Guide to Clay Tobacco Pipes, Vol. I* - $20.45 ppd.

RUTH'S BOOKS & CARDS
703-879-9695
RR 1 Box 2-H • Dayton VA 22821-9801

SARATOGA SOLDIER SHOP & MILITARY BOOKSTORE
518-885-1497 • 518-885-0100 Fax
831 Route 67 Ste 40
Ballston Spa NY 12020
1000 54mm pewter soldiers, cavalry & artillery kits. Civil War & other eras, paints, modelers' aids, & booklist. Catalog - $6.

SATISFIED MIND
540-665-0855
11 S Loudoun St
Winchester VA 22601-4719

SAUERS HISTORY SHOP
800-510-1108
3531 Martha Custis Dr
Alexandria VA 22302-2002
Eagerly awaited research guide to Civil War material in the *National Tribune*, 1877-1884. $19.95 ppd. (In KY, $20.97).

SAVANNAH HISTORY MUSEUM
912-238-1779
303 Martin Luther King Jr Blvd
Savannah GA 31415-4217

THE SCHOLAR'S BOOKSHELF
609-395-6933 • 609-395-0755 Fax
http://www.scholarsbookshelf.com
books@scholarsbookshelf.com
110 Melrich Rd
Cranbury NJ 08512-3511

Major book catalog company that produces three 88-pp. Military History catalogs each year. Catalogs feature a substantial variety of Civil War books & videos. Free catalog.

CARL SCIORTINO MILITARIA
PO Box 29809
Richmond VA 23242-0809
700-item catalog of Civil War militaria - $2 (ref.). Military books - 600 titles. Catalog - $2 (ref.).

SEAWEED'S SHIPS OF HISTORY
800-SEA-WEED
304-652-1525 Fax
PO Box 154, Dept M
Sistersville WV 26175-0154
Histories of U.S. naval, army transports, most Coast Guard, sunken ships, etc. $8 & up.

SECOND CHANCE BOOKS
703-948-3667
HC 3 Box 224
Rochelle VA 22738-9707

SECOND CORPS BOOKSHOP
804-861-1863
209 High St
Petersburg VA 23803-3241

SENECA RIDGE GALLERY
412-828-0240
426 Allegheny River Blvd
Oakmont PA 15139-1725
Civil War & 18th-century art, books, videos, games, music, more!

SHAMROCK HILL BOOKS
770-569-1802
770-569-1801 Fax
http://members.aol.com/historybks/bookpage.htm
HISTORYBKS@aol.com
Ed O'Dwyer
12725 Bethany Rd
Alpharetta GA 30004
Books on the Civil War with specialty in Irish participation. Kepis, music & more. Email credit card accounts welcome. Catalog.

E. SHAVER, BOOKSELLER
912-234-7257
912-234-7258 Fax
326 Bull St
Savannah GA 31401-4594

THE SHENANDOAH ATTIC
540-464-8888
3 N Main St
Lexington VA 24450-2520

SHENANDOAH COUNTY LIBRARY STORE
540-984-8200
300 Stoney Creek Blvd
Edinburg VA 22824-9706

SHENANDOAH SEASONS
800-484-7745 code 0361
989 Black Bear Rd
Maurertown VA 22644-2839

SHENANDOAH TRADER
540-740-3735
trader@m-c-b.com
Ross & Mary Smith
1988 Shipwreck Dr
New Market VA 22844
Books for the collector of Civil War & earlier
periods of American militaria. Manufacturer of
quality artifact display cases of oak & walnut.
Button cases. Catalog - $1 (ref.).

WILLIAM S. SMEDLUND
770-322-0544
1666 Glen Arm Dr
Lithonia GA 30058-5513
Campfires of Georgia's Troops, 1861-65.
Encyclopedic history of 747 named Georgia
camps. Includes locations, dates, sources,
letters, maps, images. Indices, 322 pp.,
hardbound - $37 ppd.

SOLDIERS & SAILORS MEMORIAL
412-621-4253
4141 5th Ave
Pittsburgh PA 15213
Military history museum centering on Civil
War, emphasizing Allegheny County.
Uniforms, weapons, flags, GAR, more!
Maintains library; gift shop. Civil War through
Desert Storm displays.

SOLDIERS, ETC.
317-846-0156
317-573-9449 Fax
P0 Box 20276
Indianapolis IN 46220-0276
Books on the Civil War, including *The Story
the Soldiers Wouldn't Tell: Sex in the Civil
War*, and *Pulling the Temple Down.*

SOUTHERN GUN WORKS
757-934-1423
757-925-1177 Fax
109 Cherry St
Suffolk VA 23434
Civil War prints, autographed military books,
memorabilia. Art by Troiani, Spaulding,
Kunstler, Gallon, others.

SOUTHERN HISTORICAL SHOWCASE
800-854-7832 • 615-321-0639
http://www.southernhistorical.com
southernhistorical@nashville.com
1907 Division St
Nashville TN 37203-2705
Southern military art & books, prints, original
documents & autographs, photos, engravings.
Artists: Prechtel, Reeves, Kunstler, Kidd,
Gallon, Summers, Heron, Garner, Rocco.
Catalog - $5.

STARS & BARS GIFT SHOP AT BEAUVOIR
601-388-9074 • 601-388-1313
2244 Beach Blvd
Biloxi MS 39531-5002

A. MARTIN STEPAK
954-401-0780
PO Box 10088
Tampa FL 33679-0088
Book about the media's betrayal of the South.
Fascinating reading. $24.95.

STONEWALL JACKSON MUSEUM AT HUPP'S HILL
540-465-5884 • 540-465-5999
540-465-8157 Fax
Babs Melton
PO Box 31
US 11 North
Strasburg VA 22657-0031
Exhibits of Jackson's 1862 Valley Campaign
with original artifacts & hands-on
reproductions. Children's room has costumes,
Civil War camp, & discovery boxes.

TATTERED COVER BOOK STORE
303-322-7727
1628 16th St
Denver CO 80202-1162

ALBERTA TAYLOR
614-667-6087
27550 Clark Rd
Coolville OH 45723
*Hearts of Fire: ... Soldier Women of the Civil
War.* 2nd printing of this must-read details
accounts of women who went to war
disguised as men. $22.95 ppd.

L.B. TAYLOR, JR.
804-253-2636
108 Elizabeth Meriwether
Williamsburg VA 23185
Civil War Ghosts of Virginia - 232 pp.,
softcover, $12 + $3 S&H. Author gathers
legends, lore & happenings, matching them
with historical fact, vignettes & anecdotes.

TAYLORMADE WRIGHT
812-866-3295
10630 W State Rd Ste 256
Lexington IN 47138-6806
With Bowie Knives & Pistols by Dave Taylor.
Morgan's Raid in Indiana. Experience the raid
by those who lived it. 30 photos. $12 ppd.

TEMPEST BOOKS
519-736-8629 • 888-233-5666
519-736-8620 Fax
235 Dalhousie
Amherstburg, Ontario N9V 1W6 CANADA
New books for old ideas. Military, naval,
costuming, fiction, reference. Maps for
campaign planning.

THAT BOOKSTORE IN BLYTHEVILLE
501-763-3333
501-763-1125 Fax
316 W Main St
Blytheville AR 72315-3318

THEME PRINTS, LTD.
800-CIVL WAR • 718-225-4067
PO Box 610123
Bayside NY 11361-0123
Books, antique arms, historic documents,
photographs, letters & autographs from
Revolutionary era to early Hollywood.
Includes Civil War memorabilia. Fully illus.
catalog - $5, or $12/yr. (5 issues).

**CAROLE THOMPSON, FINE
PHOTOGRAPHS**
901-278-2741 • 901-726-5533 Fax
ctfp@ix.netcom.com
1515 Central Ave
Memphis TN 38104-4907
Gardner's Sketchbook of the Civil War, 100
museum quality albumen photos by
Alexander Gardner & Timothy O'Sullivan.
Buys/sells/appraises.

TIME-LIFE BOOKS
PO Box 85563
Richmond VA 23285-5563
Civil War series covering many interesting
facets of the war. Write for details.

TOOMEY'S BOOKSHOP
410-850-0831 Phone & Fax
PO Box 122
Linthicum MD 21090-0122
Baltimore During the Civil War, by Scott S.
Sheads & Daniel C. Toomey. Hardcover, 224
pp. - $24.95 + $3 S&H. Other titles.

TOTAL INFORMATION
716-254-0628 • 716-254-0209 Fax
robert%total_information@mcimail.com
844 Dewey Ave
Rochester NY 14613-1995

TSUNAMI, INC.
509-529-0813 • 509-527-3691 Fax
http://www.wwics.com/~tsunami
Tsunami@wwics.com
Charles Potts
PO Box 100 • Walla Walla WA 99362-0100
*How the South Finally Won the Civil War, &
the Political Future of the United States*. May
change the way you read American History.
440 pp. Hardcover, sewn, dust jacket - $29
ppd.

TURN OF THE PAGE
803-425-5100
1671 Springdale Dr Ste 9
Camden SC 29020-2079

VALOR ART & FRAME LTD.
540-372-3376
CWFugi@aol.com
Joe Fulginiti
718 Caroline St
Fredericksburg VA 22401-5904
Civil War artwork, artifacts & books. Featuring
artwork of Don Troiani. Carry all major Civil
War artists. Custom museum mount framing.
15 years of service. Free catalog.

VIRGINIA BORN & BRED
540-463-1832
16 W Washington St
Lexington VA 24450-2121

**VIRGINIA HISTORICAL SOCIETY MUSEUM
SHOP**
804-342-967 • 804-358-4901
PO Box 7311
428 North Blvd
Richmond VA 23221-0311

**THE VIRGINIA SHOP AT
CHARLOTTESVILLE**
1047B Emmet St N
Charlottesville VA 22903-4834

PATRICIA VOLKMANN
2842 Cherry Point Ln
Maryland Heights MO 63043-1708
Missouri: Our Civil War Heritage. Covers 76
Missouri counties in the Civil War. 492 pp.
Softcover - $25 ppd.

OPHELIA WADE
911 Osborn Ave
Kennett MO 63857
Preacher from Liberty Hill - biographical novel
of Joseph Richardson, who fought in Lee's
ANV & was imprisoned in Fort Delaware. 365
pp. - $22 ppd.

**WAYSIDE MUSEUM OF AMERICAN
HISTORY**
540-465-5884 • 540-465-5899 Fax
PO Box 440
Strasburg VA 22657-0440

WELL-TRAVELED IMAGES
414-574-1865 • 414-896-0572 Fax
http://www.globaldialog.com/~eicher/index.htm
eicher@globaldialog.com
Lynda Eicher
S60 W24160 Red Wing Dr
Waukesha WI 53186-9508
Color photos of CW battlefields, sites. Books.
Matted color prints of 10,000+ CW-related
images, also available for publication. Call or
email for catalog. See internet home page for
samples & info. on books.

WHEATON HISTORY CENTER
PO Box 373
Wheaton IL 60189-0373
*Journal of Capt. Henry Whipple Chester: 2nd
Ohio Volunteer Cavalry.* Recollections of the
War of the Rebellion. 200 pp., 97 illus.,
extensive index - $34.59 + $5 S&H.

WHITE'S ELECTRONIC, INC.
800-547-6911
1011 Pleasant Valley Rd
Sweet Home OR 97386-1098
Five different books on finding & detecting
buried treasure, gold, etc., from $4.95.

WILLETT BOOKS
PO Box 5871
Kingsport TN 37663-0871
A Union Soldier Returns South - Civil War
letters/diary of Prv. Willett, 113th OVI. Details
of battle, daily life, thoughts, photos.
Hardcover - $14.95.

THE WINCHESTER BOOK GALLERY
540-667-3444
185 N Loudoun St
Winchester VA 22601-4789

**WINCHESTER-FREDERICK CO. VISITORS
CENTER**
540-662-4135
1360 S Pleasant Valley Rd
Winchester VA 22601-4447

WISTERIA MANOR
540-722-0145
135 N Loudoun St
Winchester VA 22601-4717

GEORGE F. WITHAM
901-465-6722 Phone & Fax
155 Raspberry Cv
Eads TN 38028-3003
Catalog of Civil War Photographers -
alphabetical listing by state of more than 5900
Civil War-era photographers. Softcover -
$16.50 ppd.

WILLIAM P. ZUCCHERO BOOKS
804-974-7057
2105 Wisteria Dr
Charlottesville VA 22911-9047

20TH MAINE, INC.
207-865-4340
207-865-9575 Fax
Patricia Hodgdon
49 West St
Freeport ME 04032-1127
Specialized bookstore devoted to Civil War
with new & old books, art, music, videos,
antiques & much more.

ABRAHAM LINCOLN BOOK SHOP
312-944-3085
312-944-5549 Fax
357 W Chicago Ave
Chicago IL 60610-3052
U.S. Military History, French & Indian War,
Revolution, 1812, Mexican, Civil War, Indian
Wars. Books, prints, autographs. Buy/sell.
Catalog - $5.

AMERICAN HERITAGE
PO Box 10934
Des Moines IA 50340-0934

AMERICANA MERCANTILE
PO Box 4066
Hastings MN 55033-7066
American History books, documents, maps, &
more. Adults/children. Fun, educational
products, gifts.

THE ARMCHAIR SOURCE
706 Longbow Rd
Winston Salem NC 27104-1627
More than 1,500 titles of primary sources in
American history. Free catalog.

DR. C. E. BAKER
652 16th Ave NW
Birmingham AL 35215-5351
Books by great men. R. L. Dabney's works on
Jackson, Defense of Virginia, etc. M. E.
Bradford's, J. William Jones' works, etc. Write
for more listings.

BATTLEFIELD BOOKSTORE
800-340-8268
236 New Bridge St
Jacksonville NC 28540-4708
Civil War books - new, used & reprints.
Military books of all eras. Free catalog.

BAY STREET BOOKS
202-546-3893
1740 Bay St SE
Washington DC 20003-1646
Civil War books - out-of-print & some new
titles.

MIKE BRACKIN
203-647-8620
PO Box 23
Manchester CT 06045-0023
Large assortment of Civil War & Indian War
autographs, accoutrements, memorabilia,
insignia, medals, buttons, GAR, documents,
photos & books. Catalog - $6/yr for 5 issues.

BRANDY STATION BOOKSHELF
PO Box 1863 • Harrah OK 73045-1863
Buys/sells Civil War books.Regimental, rare &
out-of-print editions; also reprints & current
titles. Want lists welcome. Free catalog.

CAMP POPE BOOKSHOP
319-351-2407 • 319-339-5964 Fax
http://members.aol.com/ckenyoncpb
ckenyoncpb@aol.com
PO Box 2232
Iowa City IA 52244-2232
Largest selection of in-print titles, including
reprints, on trans-Mississippi theater of the
Civil War. Free catalog.

CIVIL WAR ANTIQUITIES
614-363-1862
http://www.civilwarantiquities.com
Todd Rittenhouse, Prop.
PO Box 1411 • Delaware OH 43015-1411
Quality CW items. Guns, swords, letters,
currency, books, prints. Buy/sell/trade. Full
service custom framing & matting; specializing
in conservation framing. Shop located at
13-1/2 N Sandusky St., Delaware, Ohio.
Catalog - $5.

CIVIL WAR ASSOCIATES BOOKSTORE
313-586-2916
6200 Blanchett Rd • Newport MI 48166-9723
Civil War, Custer & Indian Wars books, new &
used. Catalog.

STAN CLARK MILITARY BOOKS
717-337-1728 • 717-337-0581 Fax
915 Fairview Ave
Gettysburg PA 17325-2906
Buys/sells Civil War books, ltd. edition prints,
autographs, letters, documents, postcards,
soldiers' items; special interest in U.S. Marine
Corps items.

CLIO'S HISTORY BOOKSHOP
703-777-1815
ClioBooks@aol.com
Jason Duberman
PO Box 168 • 103 Loudoun St SW
Leesburg VA 20175-0168

Military & political history titles from ancient to modern times; Civil War a specialty. Catalog - $3.

COLUMBUS ARMORY
706-327-1424 Phone & Fax
David S. Brady
1104 Broadway
Columbus GA 31901-2429
Complete Civil War store featuring books, relics, art, muskets & supplies. Buy/sell/trade. Free price list. (See ad page 236)

THE CONFLICT BOOKSHOP
800-847-0911
EPETE1731@aol.com
213 Steinwehr Ave
Gettysburg PA 17325-2801
Latest in Civil War titles, as well as fine collection of used & rare books, audio & video tapes & other memorabilia. Free flyer.

COPPERFIELD'S/CBC BOOKNETWORK
915-590-0602
915-590-7010 Fax
booknet@ix.netcom.com
2150 Trawood Dr Ste B200
El Paso TX 79935-3322
Discount history & genealogy books. Searches for out-of-print books at no cost or obligation. Free catalog.

DIXIE DEPOT
706-265-7533
706-265-3952 Fax
http://www.ilinks.net/~dixiegeneral
Dixie_Depot@stc.net
John Black
PO Box 1448
72 Keith Evans Rd
Dawsonville GA 30534
Pro-Southern educational products: video/audio tapes, new/old books, bumper stickers, flags, wearables, lapel pins, exclusive Great Seal items. More than 600 items! Catalog. (See ad page 235)

DON'T KNOW MUCH ABOUT HISTORY
800-531-9173
http://members.aol.com/p20IL/index.html
P20IL@aol.com
Phil Lauricella, President
316 Franklin St
Geneva IL 60134-2639
More than 200 prints by well-known artists such as Kunstler, Rocco, Troiani & Stivers. Carry 300+ Civil War titles on our bookshelves & will research out-of-print or rare items. Free catalog.

DOSS BOOKS
PO Box 660194
Birmingham AL 35266-0194
Civil War books & maps. Many out-of-print or rare. List -$1.

THE EARLY AMERICAN HISTORY SHOPPE
603-772-7973
225 Water St
Exeter NH 03833-2417
Books (antiquarian & in-print), ephemera, prints, antique memorabilia & collectibles, T-shirts, CD-Rom, flags, games, tapes, maps, mugs, miniatures, genealogies & more. Specialize in the Civil War. Free catalogs.

THE EARLY WEST
800-245-5841
PO Box 9292
College Station TX 77842-9292
Books on Custer, the West, Indian Fighters, outlaws, lawmen, frontiersmen, etc. Free catalog.

EASTERN FRONT/WARFIELD BOOKS, INC.
540-338-1672 • 540-338-1910 Fax
36734 Pelham Ct
Philomont VA 20131
Great classic books of the American Civil War.

EDMONSTON PUBLISHING, INC.
315-824-1965
PO Box 38
Hamilton NY 13346-0038
While My Country Is in Danger, 12th NJ. *No Middle Ground*, Union Artillery. $22.95 ea. *Memoirs of the 149th NYV* - $35.95. *Unfurl the Flags* - $4.95. S&H -$3.50/$1.50/$1.00. Other new & used titles. Free catalog.

FARNSWORTH HOUSE MILITARY GALLERY
717-334-8838
717-334-5862 Fax
FARNHAUS@mail.cvn.net
Loring H. Shultz
401 Baltimore St
Gettysburg PA 17325-2623
Large selection of Don Troiani art - Gettysburg's exclusive dealer for over 10 yrs. New, used & rare books on Civil & Indian wars. Buy/sell/trade. Catalog - $2. (See ad page 241)

FIRST CORPS BOOKS
803-781-2709
FirstCorps@msn.com
42 Eastgrove Ct
Columbia SC 29212-2404

Specializing in material concerning South Carolina in the Civil War. 100s of Civil War titles, both out-of-print & new. Want lists accepted. Catalogs - $2/yr.

JIM FOX - BOOKS
9 Precipice Rd
Camden SC 29020-4811
South Carolina Regimental Series. Autobiographies, biographies, stories, regimental history, & all kinds of books dealing with South Carolina & the Civil War.

FRIENDS OF NEW YORK STATE NEWSPAPER PROJECT
http://www.nysl.nysed.gov/nysnp
vweiss@mail.nysed.gov
PO Box 2402
Empire State Plaza Station
Albany NY 12220
Maps & Letters from NY State's Civil War Newspapers, 1861-1863 - $22.

G W SPECIALTIES
816-356-7457
George Scheil
7311 Ditzler
Raytown MO 64133
Civilian reprints of magazines & schoolbooks from mid-1800s. Free catalog.

GAULEY RIVER BOOK COMPANY
http://www.cais.com/gauley/index.html
gauley@cais.com
37 Pidgeon Hill Dr
Sterling VA 20165-6102
Turn Them out to Die Like a Mule, by J.M. Priest. *Mosby's Confederacy, War Stories,* etc. INTERNET - check our website for listings of other books.

GWYN'S COLLECTIBLES & BOOKS
717-957-4141
717-957-9208 Fax
Gwyn L. Irwin
211 Front St
Marysville PA 17053-1413
Civil War books. Roster of soldiers in the "War of the Rebellion" from Monroe County, New York. 26 pp., 3 columns - $12 ppd.

S. A. HEARN - BOOKS
717-742-3737
Chet Hearn
PO Box 67
Potts Grove PA 17865-0067
Civil War books bought/sold. Want lists welcome. Free bi-monthly price list/catalog.

HERITAGE BOOKS
Dale Curry
313 Woodlawn Ave
Zanesville OH 43701-4939
Civil War books & gifts. Free catalog.

HIGGINSON BOOK COMPANY
508-745-7170
508-745-8025 Fax
higginsn@cove.com
148 Washington St
PO Box 778
Salem MA 01970-0778
Reprinters of regimental histories, American genealogies & local histories. Thousands of titles by mail or in our bookstore. Catalog - $4 (ref.).

HISTORY IN PRINT
800-541-7323
800-336-8334 Fax
PO Box 1295
Valparaiso IN 46384-1295
We stock the Civil War titles you want now. Order newest releases for delivery right to your door. Hundreds of new & used titles. Free catalog.

INKLINGS BOOKSHOP
804-845-BOOK
1206 Main St
Lynchburg VA 24504-1818
New & used books, out-of-print searches. Civil War, South, Literature, History, Religion, etc.

KENNESAW MOUNTAIN MILITARY ANTIQUES
770-424-5225
770-424-0434 Fax
CANNONBALL@aol.com.
1810 Old Highway 41
Kennesaw GA 30152-4430
Civil War relics & complete list of books available. New, reprints, & reference books. Catalog subscription - $10.

LOG CABIN SHOP
800-837-1082 • 330-948-1082
330-948-4307 Fax
http://www.logcabinshop.com
logcabin@logcabinshop.com
8010 Lafayette Rd
PO Box 275
Lodi OH 44254-0275
Full line of muzzleloading guns, kits, components, supplies, accessories, books, cookware, blankets, etc. 200-pp. catalog - $5.

BILL MASON BOOKS

919-247-6161
http://www.collectorsnet.com/mason/index.htm
bmasonbks@abaco.coastalnet.com
104 N 7th St
Morehead City NC 28557-3807
Rare, new, used, out-of-print Civil War,
Western Americana, military & nautical,
quality books, prints, & ephemera. Free
catalog.

AL MASON - BOOKS

860-693-2708
5 High Ledge Rd
Canton CT 06019
Civil War books - used, out-of-print, new &
rare. More than 350 listings; Confederate,
Union, general & Lincoln sections. Also,
spoken word & music records. Free catalog.

MAST LANDING BOOKS

207-865-6432
4 Flying Point Rd
Freeport ME 04032-6429
Civil War books bought/sold. Lists regularly
issued.

NEWMAN RARE BOOKS

410 S Michigan Ave
Chicago IL 60605-1302
Your source for Civil War history.

OLD FAVORITES BOOKSHOP

3055 Lauderdale Dr
Richmond VA 23233-7800
Civil War, WWII, other military books, prints &
maps. Free catalog on request. (See ad page
242)

OWENS & RAMSEY HISTORICAL BOOKSELLERS

804-272-8888
mramsey@rmond.mindspring.com
2728 Tinsley Dr
Richmond VA 23235-2448
Richmond's Civil War book headquarters.
Buy/sell/trade new, used & rare books. Free
monthly catalog.

WALLACE D. PRATT, BOOKSELLER

1801 Gough St Apt 304
San Francisco CA 94109-3345
Out-of-print, rare Civil War & other military &
naval books. Free catalog.

TOM ROFFE

PO Box 266
Leicester NY 14481-0266

New & out-of-print Civil War-era military
books. More than 200 bios, regimentals,
weapons, etc. Annual listing - SASE.

SANTA FE SALES

Edward Benrock or Marion Webb
1 Ranch Club Rd Ste 3-402-O
Silver City NM 88061
Replicas. Relive American History through us
for hard-to-find historical accessories, books,
reprints, tinware, numerous historical items.
Catalog - $3.

J. M. SANTARELLI

215-576-5358
Civil War Books & Publishing
226 Paxson Ave
Glenside PA 19038-4612
Antique, reprint & out-of-print books. Also
publishes new material. More than 300 Civil
War titles. Catalog - $2.

SECOND STORY BOOKSHOP

540-463-6264
books@rockbridge.net
Nancy Coplai
College Square Shopping Ctr
Lexington VA 24450
New, used & rare books on the Civil War. Also
offer mail order service - shipping daily!

SOUTHERN YANKEE VETERANS MEMORABILIA

409-264-1865 Dan Reed
409-852-2822 Mike Carter
Buy/sell/trade GAR & UCV relics, postcards,
Civil War books. Catalogs - $10 (3 issues/yr.).

SPARTAN BOOKS OF MAINE

800-515-3113
PO Box 1645
Presque Isle ME 04769-1645
Books from the originals by Gordan,
Longstreet, Early, & historians plus reference
works, etc.

TALL SHIPS BOOKS

319-396-2549
PO Box 8027
Cedar Rapids IA 52408-8027
Historical fiction from age of fighting sail.
Catalog - $3 (ref. w/ 1st order).

C. CLAYTON THOMPSON - BOOKSELLER

510-462-5211 Phone & Fax
http://members.aol.com/Greatbooks
Greatbooks@aol.com
1585 Poppybank Ct
Pleasanton CA 94566-8402

Civil War & military books - 1st editions.
Catalog - $5 (ref.).

TRANS-MISSISSIPPI MILITARIA
972-517-8111 Phone & Fax
http://www.collectorsnet.com/transmiss/index.html
charlucv@flash.net
Charles Brecheisen
1004 Simon Dr • Plano TX 75025-2501
UCV, GAR, Civil War & Indian War period
relics, books & diaries, papers, letters, covers
& records, medical instruments. Always
buying. Catalogs - $10 (min. 3 large lists).

TRULY UNIQUE MILITARY SURPLUS & COLLECTIBLES
800-336-5225
2619 N University St
Peoria IL 61604-2667
Featuring 2 new books - *The Story the Soldiers Wouldn't Tell: Sex in the Civil War*
and *Pulling the Temple Down: The Fire-Eaters and the Destruction of the Union.*
Other titles.

WILDMAN'S CIVIL WAR SURPLUS
770-422-1785
2879 S Main St
Kennesaw GA 30144-5624
Rare & antique guns, books, & other Civil War
collectibles. Price list - $2. (See ad page 233)

YANK & REB TRADER
614-366-2479
PO Box 4704
Newark OH 43055
Civil War artifacts. Buy/sell. Large inventory of
reference books not available in bookstores.
Catalog - $5 for 6 issues (ref. w/ purchase).

YANKEE FORAGER
517-263-3925
137 Park St
Adrian MI 49221-2528
Civil War specialty books, documents, photos,
relics, & more. Catalog - $2.

YE OLDE POST OFFICE
334-928-0108
17070 Scenic Hwy 98
PO Box 9
Point Clear AL 36564-0009
Dealer in antique & military collectibles, guns,
swords, uniforms, books, etc.

AVID READER USED & RARE BOOKS
919-933-9585
462 W Franklin St
Chapel Hill NC 27516-2313

BLACK HORSE BOOKS
409-449-5712
Jim Synnott
118 Wick Willow Dr
Montgomery TX 77356-8242
Rare & out-of-print Confederate military
history. Catalog -$3/3 issues.

BOHEMIAN BRIGADE BOOKSHOP
423-694-8227
423-531-1846 Fax
Ed Archer
7347 Middlebrook Pike
Knoxville TN 37909-3108
Specializing in 1st edition & out-of-print Civil
War books, hard-to-find CW titles & popular
reprints. Also, CW prints. Collection
assistance. Catalog - $3.

BOOK HUNTERS
PO Box 7519
North Bergen NJ 07047-0519
Virtually any book located - no matter how old
or how long out of print. Title alone is
sufficient. Please inquire.

BROADFOOT PUBLISHING COMPANY
910-686-4816
910-686-4379 Fax
http://broadfoot.wilmington.net
Tom Broadfoot
1907 Buena Vista Cir
Wilmington NC 28405-7892
Sell rare & out-of-print material, own
publications by catalog. In-print catalog - $2.
Out-of-print catalog - $5 (ref. w/ order).

C & W USED BOOKS
703-491-7323
14587 Potomac Mills Rd
Woodbridge VA 22192-6808

Q. M. DABNEY & CO.
PO Box 42026
Washington DC 20015-0626
Old & rare Civil War books. Catalog - $1.

DEEP SOUTH
PO Box 1184
Escatawpa MS 39552-1184
1863 CSA Almanac. Authentic, 98-pp.,
Constitution, CSA stats, battle diary, etc.
$7.95 ppd.

DAVID E. DOREMUS, BOOKS
617-641-3308
100 Hillside Ave
Arlington MA 02174-7269
Used & rare regimental histories, biographies,
& battle reports. Buys/sells. Catalog - $2, 8-10
issues/yr.

JOHN S. GIMESH, MD
910-484-2212 • PO Box 53788
Fayetteville NC 28305-3788
Authentic Civil War-era medical, surgical,
dental & apothecary items; Civil War-era
medical texts. Buy/sell.

HISTORICAL MILITARY ART & COLLECTIBLES
PO Box 1806
Lafayette CA 94549-8006
Collector books, limited edition military art, &
military & political collectibles, including
medals, flags, badges, pins, & patches. Free
catalog.

PETER HLINKA
718-409-6407
Historical Americana
PO Box 310 • New York NY 10028-0017
Military & civilian decorations, medals, award
certificates, insignia items, books, & other
Americana collectibles. Free catalog.

HOFFMAN RESEARCH SERVICES
412-446-3374
http://www.abebooks.com/home/hoffsrch
hoffsrch@westol.com
Ralph Hoffman
PO Box 342
Rillton PA 15678-0342
Free international book search. Professional
bookfinders since 1965; members of Interloc,
Advanced Book Exchange & Virtual Book
Shop. Please send SASE w/ mail requests.

MURRAY HUDSON - ANTIQUARIAN BOOKS & MAPS
800-748-9946 • 901-836-9057
901-836-9017 Fax
mapman@usit.net
109 S Church St • PO Box 163
Halls TN 38040-0163
Large selection of Civil War authentic maps &
prints. 1300+ items (priced $25-$7,500). Also,
rare Forrest bust. Catalog - $10 (ref.).

HUGHES BOOKS
504-948-2427
PO Box 840237
New Orleans LA 70184-0237

Buy/sell rare books, documents, & autographs. Civil War, the South, Louisiana, New Orleans. 3 catalogs - $3.

KUBIK FINE BOOKS
937-294-0253
3474 Clar Von Dr • Dayton OH 45430-1708
Buy/sell rare & out-of-print books on British, French, European, & U.S. military history. Autographs & historical fiction. 1st editions of 19th-century Civil War books. Catalog - $3.

RICHARD A. LA POSTA
860-828-0921
154 Robindale Dr
Kensington CT 06037-2054
Civil War books. Regimental histories. First editions. Search service. Buy/sell/trade. Next 2 price lists - $1.

LEXINGTON HISTORICAL SHOP
540-463-2615
Bob Lurate
PO Box 1428 " Lexington VA 24450-1428
Civil War memorabilia. Buy/sell books, relics, flags, currency, ephemera. Appraisals. Visit shop Mon-Sat 10-6, College Square Shopping Center, Route 11N, Lexington, Va.

LOOK BACK IN TIME
803-986-9097 • 803-986-9297 Fax
PO Box 572
Port Royal SC 29935-0572
Civil War newspapers, engravings, books, relics, & much more. Want lists welcome. Free catalog.

MARCHER BOOKS
6204 N Vermont Ave
Oklahoma City OK 73112-1312
Rare & out-of-print American History books. Free catalog.

MC GOWAN BOOK CO.
919-403-1503 • 800-449-8406
919-403-1706 Fax
R. Douglas Sanders
39 Kimberly Dr • Durham NC 27707-5418
Always buying. Highest prices paid for fine & rare Civil War books, autographs, documents, photographs, etc. Catalog subs. - $3. (See ad page 243)

MERIDIAN STREET USED BOOKS
317-482-4882
126 S Meridian St
Lebanon IN 46052
Buy/sell/trade used books on all subjects. Search service.

THE MILITARY BOOKMAN
212-348-1280
29 E 93rd St • New York NY 10128-0695
Military, naval & aviation history. Out-of-print & rare books. Catalog - by subscription.

THE MT. STERLING REBEL
606-498-5821
Terry Murphy
PO Box 481
Mount Sterling KY 40353-0481
Buy/sell since 1979 rare, out-of-print, & previously owned Civil War books. Limited inventory of Civil War paper items, ephemera, autographs & images. Catalog upon request. (See ad page 239)

THE OLD PAPERPHILES
401-624-9420
401-624-4204 Fax
PO Box 135
Tiverton RI 02878-0135
Offering 100s of accurately described paper collectibles. Great variety, wide price range. Autographs, documents, books. Catalog - $8 for next 10.

OLDE SOLDIER BOOKS, INC.
301-963-2929
301-963-9556 Fax
Warbooks@erols.com
Dave Zullo
18779 N Frederick Ave Ste B
Gaithersburg MD 20879-3158
Largest selection of rare & hard-to-find books. Documents, letters, photographs, autographs, manuscripts. Buy/sell. Free catalog.

OUT-OF-STATE-BOOK-SERVICE
PO Box 3253
San Clemente CA 92674-3253
Books located, out-of-print free search service. No obligation.

PEMBROKE INK
PO Box 445
Chesterfield VA 23832-0445
For the discriminating collector. Dealer of documents & rare books. Extensive list.

PROFILES IN HISTORY
800-942-8856 • 310-859-7701
310-859-3842 Fax
345 N Maple Dr Ste 202
Beverly Hills CA 90210-3859
Autographs wanted. Also buying original letters, documents, vintage photos, manuscripts, & rare books (signed). Illus. catalog - $45/yr. Sample - $10.

THE QUEEN'S SHILLING
703-779-4669
14 Loudoun St SE
Leesburg VA 20175-3011
Old, rare & antiquarian books, autographs on
military history, all periods. Catalog - $3.

RED LANCER
PO Box 8056
Mesa AZ 85214-8056
Original 19th-century military art, rare books,
Victorian-era campaign medals & helmets, toy
soldiers. Catalog - $12 for 3-4 issues/yr.

STEPHEN M. ROWE
PO Box 19671
Raleigh NC 27619
Rare & first editions.

PAUL SPERLING
160 E 38th St #25
New York NY 10016
Still looking for a book? Free search.

STAMPEDE INVESTMENTS
608-254-7751
1533 River Rd
Wisconsin Dells WI 53965-9002
Large inventory of original letters &
documents from the most important people in
U.S. History to fit every budget. Free catalog.

UHR BOOKS
207-929-5100
uhrbooks@mix-net.net
Old & rare books on women in the Civil War,
especially nurses. Free list.

BLACKJACK TRADING COMPANY
Chuck Hanselmann
PO Box 707 • Blythewood SC 29016-0707
Buyer of family Confederate paper, stamps, letters, autographs, currency, slave documents, slave tags, & estates.

BNR PRESS
800-793-0683 Orders & Fax
419-732-NOTE (6683)
http://www.dcache.net/~bnrpress
bnrpress@dcache.net
Fred Schwan
132 E 2nd St • Port Clinton OH 43452-1115
Publisher of the *Comprehensive Catalog of Confederate Paper Money* by Grover Criswell & other titles of interest to collectors. Hardcover - $35; dealer discounts. Advertising opportunities.

C & N COINS & COLLECTIBLES
908-845-0045
2301 Route 9 N • Howell Station (Track 3)
Howell NJ 07731
Buy/sell paper Americana, currency, stocks & bonds. Civil War & period images.

CALIFORNIA COIN COMPANY
800-370-COIN
PO Box 578128
Modesto CA 95357-8128
U.S. Morgan silver dollars & other rare collectible coins guaranteed to grade "very fine." Call/write for list.

CAROLINA GOLD & SILVER, INC.
8502 Two Notch Rd
Columbia SC 29223
1864 Confederate $5, $10, or $20 bills - $25 ea.

CIVIL WAR ANTIQUITIES
614-363-1862
http://www.civilwarantiquities.com
Todd Rittenhouse, Prop.
PO Box 1411
Delaware OH 43015-1411
Quality CW items. Guns, swords, letters, currency, books, prints. Buy/sell/trade. Full service custom framing & matting; specializing in conservation framing. Shop located at 13-1/2 N Sandusky St., Delaware, Ohio. Catalog - $5.

CIVIL WAR COMMEMORATIVE COINS
kaykay@injersey.com
Kathleen Ellerbusch
3587 Highway 9 Ste 512
Freehold NJ 07728

1995 Civil War Battlefield Commemorative Coins - Proof Silver Dollars. Designer of obverse - Troiani; reverse - Mercanti. Ltd. number with certificate of authenticity - $32 ppd.

CIVIL WAR STORE
504-522-3328
212 Chartres St • New Orleans LA 70130
Mail order catalog - weapons, currency, bonds, stamps, letters, diaries, CDVs, prints, slave broadsides & bills of sale, autographs, photos. Catalog - $4.

CLARK'S GUN SHOP, INC.
540-439-8988
10016 James Madison Hwy
Warrenton VA 20186-7820
Retailer of books, Civil War relics, Kepis, flags, buttons, Confederate souvenirs, original Confederate money & state notes, CW prints.

CLUB'S COLLECTIBLES
10029 243rd Pl SW
Edmonds WA 98020-5751
Museum-quality framed prints, produced from archive negatives, & authentic Confederate currency mounted & framed. Many generals.

THE CONFEDERATE TREASURY
800-632-2383 • 615-721-4155 Fax
http://www.ConfederateTreasury.com
1100 N Main St
Tennessee Ridge TN 37178
Confederate States Currency 1861-1865. Complete 70-note, full-color set of currency issued by Confederate government. Exact in detail, protected in album. $139.95.

PETER CRANE RARE COINS
721 Cheriwood Ct • Youngstown OH 44512
Fractional currency of the Civil War; coins.

COL. GROVER CRISWELL
352-685-2287
352-685-1014 Fax
PO Box 6000
Salt Springs FL 32134-6000
Buys/sells currency, stocks, bonds, money, slavery items, autographs. 51st year of business. *Comprehensive Catalog of Confederate Paper Money*, hardcover, 350 pp. - $35 (ppd). 432-pp. price list of collectibles - $8 (ref.). Free book list.

CSA CURRENCY PAGE
http://www.CSAcurrency.com
Info. on authentic Confederate currency, bonds, coins, & stamps.

CSA SILVER DOLLAR
1156 Sledge Ave
Memphis TN 38104
Ltd. ed. Nathan Bedford Forrest
commemorative coin, .999 fine silver, mirror
finish. $29.95 + $3 S&H.

GEORGE ESKER
PO Box 100
La Place LA 70069-0100
Civil War memorabilia (especially
Confederate), currency, images, relics,
bullets, buttons, projectiles, documents.
Catalog - $9 for 3 issues.

FIRST NATIONAL RESERVE
800-321-8700
409-866-7536 Fax
6520 College St
Beaumont TX 77707
Collectible coins. *Insider's Guide to U.S. Coin
Values* - 200-pg.

GIBSON'S CIVIL WAR COLLECTIBLES
423-323-2427
423-323-8123 Fax
Paul, Linda & Bryan Gibson
PO Box 948
Bristol TN 37620-0948
Autographs, CSA bonds & currency, diaries,
flags, letter groups, newspapers, photos,
slave items, uniforms, any other paper items.

GREAT AMERICAN COINS, INC.
800-622-3330
1 Odell Plz
Yonkers NY 10701-1402
Original U.S. govt.-minted "New Orleans"
Morgan silver dollars. Mint condition.
$35/coin. Write for extensive listing of other
coins.

BRIAN & MARIA GREEN, INC.
910-993-5100
910-993-1801 Fax
http://www.collectorsnet.com/bmg/index.shtml
bmgcivilwar@webtv.net
PO Box 1816J
Kernersville NC 27285-1816
Civil War autographs, letters, documents,
diaries, CSA stamps, covers, currency, etc.
Catalog - $5/yr for 4 issues.

MAJ. ARTHUR HENRICKS - PAYMASTER
http://midas.org/npo/cwar/acwa/pay.html
PayCall @aol.com or MajorAWH@aol.com
Pay Dept, USA
PO Box 61075
Sunnyvale CA 94088-1075

High quality facsimiles of Civil War notes. Mix
of 30+ notes, such as 1862 Greenbacks, CSA
& state/local notes - $3 (cash, check or
stamps). Member of ACWA.

THE HISTORICAL SHOP
504-467-2532
504-464-7552 Fax
Yvonne & Cary Delery
PO Box 73244
Metairie LA 70033-3244
Photos, documents, autographs, CSA
currency, letters, slavery ads & items, relics,
framed displays & other collectibles.
Buys/sells. Illus. catalogs - $8/yr.

INTERNATIONAL COINS & CURRENCY
800-451-4463
62 Ridge St
PO Box 218
Montpelier VT 05601-0218
Sets of CSA currency & historic U.S. mint first
issues.

JPL ANTIQUES
914-896-6006
211 Main St
Fishkill NY 12524-2209
CSA currency, bonds, documents, letters,
CDVs, newspapers, accoutrements,
CSA/Union imprints. Price list - $1.

PHILLIP B. LAMB, LTD.
504-899-4710 • 800-391-0115 Orders
504-891-6826 Fax
http://www.LambRarities.com
lambcsa@aol.com
PO Box 15850
2727 Prytania St
New Orleans LA 70175-5850
Buy/sell Confederate memorabilia; CDVs,
currency, documents, photos, art, bonds,
slave items, swords, buttons, bullets,
autographs, & much more. (See ad page 234)

LEXINGTON HISTORICAL SHOP
540-463-2615
Bob Lurate
PO Box 1428
Lexington VA 24450-1428
Civil War memorabilia. Buy/sell books, relics,
flags, currency, ephemera. Appraisals. Visit
shop Mon-Sat 10-6, College Square Shopping
Center, Route 11N, Lexington, Va.

HARDIE MALONEY
504-522-3328
212 Chartres St
New Orleans LA 70130-2215

Civil War store. Confederate currency, bonds, stamps, covers, CDVs, letters, diaries, documents, autographs, pistols & swords.

JOHN MASON ENTERPRISES
6878 Immokalee Rd
Keystone Heights FL 32656
Authentic Confederate war bond coupons, with informative history - $8.

N.F.C.C.
912-382-0554
1436 N Tift Ave
PO Box 1388
Tifton GA 31794-3538
Offering Battle of Gettysburg US Commemorative coins & 1861 Confederate half-dollar replicas. Both in .999 silver & crisply struck. From $29.95.

NATIONAL COLLECTOR'S MINT, INC.
800-936-MINT x443
4401 Connecticut Ave NW
Washington DC 20008-2322
Original US Morgan Silver Dollars - some of the last in the world. $19.40 ea. + $3 S&H. Independent distributor of US coins & currency, replicas, rarities, etc.

NOLES CONFEDERATE STATES TREASURE
PO Box 1134
Calena AL 35040-1134
Civil War coins. Robert E. Lee 1-oz. silver coin, 1st in series. $24.95 ea.

HOWARD L. NORTON
PO Box 22821
Little Rock AR 72221-2821
Buy/sell/appraise. Autographs, Civil War items, Americana, historical documents, photographs, coins, currency, stamps, postal history. All transactions confidential. Catalog.

OLD MILL COIN CO.
PO Box 425
New Boston NH 03070-0425
Copper-nickel Indian cent, 2-cent piece, 3-cent piece. All 3 - $21.95. Confederate currency - $27.95 ea. All currency dated 1861-65.

MIKE RUSSELL
401 Virginia Ave
Herndon VA 20170-5437
Quarterly catalog of Victorian artifacts & relics, emphasis on obsolete currency, bottles & pipes - $2. *The Collector's Guide to Clay Tobacco Pipes, Vol. I* - $20.45 ppd.

BRAD SAWYER
804-482-1725
PO Box 15543
Chesapeake VA 23328

HUGH SHULL
803-432-8500
803-432-9958 Fax
PO Box 761
Camden SC 29020-0761
Confederate notes, bonds, obsolete currency (1700s-1900). US paper money (prior to 1930). Buy/sell. Catalog -$3 (ref. on order). Annual subscription - $10.

STONEWALLS
810-231-2417
PO Box 218
Lakeland MI 48143-0218
Buy/sell/trade Confederate currency, U.S. coins. Genuine, collectible condition. Free price sheet.

TWO COLONELS ENTERPRISES
330-745-2888 Phone & Fax
http://www.webchamps.com/twocolonels
twocolonels@webchamps.com
Daniel P Sens
1287E Sevilla Ave
Akron OH 44314-1457
Patriotic reproduction stamps & stationery. Many designs. Union & Confederate. Genuine stamps, covers, & paper. Prices on request. Free wholesale & retail catalogs.

URE PRESS
636 Piney Forest Rd
Danville VA 24540
Confederate Treasure in Danville - documented, clues to 196,000 silver dollars buried in Danville, Va. Hardcover - $26.07 ppd.

VICTORIAN RARE COIN
617-665-9739
617-665-0922 Fax
numismat@aol.com
Andrew N. Seminerio
PO Box 151
Melrose MA 02176-0002
Civil War coinage. Specimens ranging from cents through $20 gold pieces, both circulated & uncirculated condition. Free price list of more than 4,500 different U.S. coins.

B. H. VINSON, JR.
804-794-5751
13205 Lady Ashley Rd
Midlothian VA 23113
Commemorative coins.

**WAR BETWEEN THE STATES
MEMORABILIA**
717-337-2853
Len Rosa
PO Box 3965
Gettysburg PA 17325-0965
Buy/sell soldiers' letters, envelopes,
documents, CDVs, photos, autographs,
newspapers, badges, ribbons, relics, framed
display items, currency, & more. Estab. 1978.
Illus. catalogs - $10/yr for 5 issues. Active
buyers receive future subscriptions free.

WORLD EXONUMIA
815-226-0771
Rich Hartzog
PO Box 4143BWX
Rockford IL 61110-0643
Civil War & sutler tokens, medals, slave tags,
Civil War dogtags, corps badges, sutler paper,
GAR reunion badges, etc. Buy/sell; mail bid
sales. Publisher of *Sutler Paper Money*. (See
ad pg 231)

ANTEBELLUM COVERS
888-ANTEBEL (268-3235)
301-869-2623 Phone & Fax
http://www.antebellumcovers.com
antebell@antebellumcovers.com
PO Box 3494
Gaithersburg MD 20885-3494
Civil War & 19th-century U.S. paper
collectibles incl. soldiers' letters, images,
general orders, patriotic envelopes,
autographs, slavery documents & advertising
paper; CD-ROMs of Civil War & historical
titles. Free catalog. Internet customers can be
notified by email each time auction is posted.

ARCHIVE ARTS
760-723-2119 Phone & Fax
http://www.archivearts.com
George@primemail.com
PO Box 2455
Fallbrook CA 92088-2455
Clip art, 62 editions for Mac & PC; 8 Civil War
editions. More than 450 CW images -
$25/edition or CD with 3600 images - $99.
Free catalog.

ART RESTORATION SERVICES
804-974-1726
PO Box 6701
Charlottesville VA 22906-6701
Document CW objects & their associated
stories with this unique new system. War book
- $14.95; w/ diskettes: DOS - 3.5" or 5.25" -
$39.95; Mac/Windows - $89.95. Visa/MC
accepted.

BOYD PUBLISHING CO.
800-452-4035
912-452-4020 after 6pm EST
tignall@accucomm.net
PO Box 367
Milledgeville GA 31061-0367
100s of new historical publications &
genealogical references. Computer software,
incl. *Official Record of the War of the
Rebellion* - all 127 vols. on CD-ROM, $89.95
+ $5 S&H.

BRODERBUND
39500 Stevenson Pl Ste 204
Fremont CA 94539
Family Tree Maker CD-Rom - solid starting
point for genealogical research. PC
compatible with Windows programs, 386 or
higher, 4MB RAM (8MB recommended).

CD-RAP
PO Box 3552
Richmond VA 23235-7552

"The Civil War Chronicles" - 1st in series of 6
CD-ROMs featuring a complete collection of
Harper's Weekly newspapers, 1860-1865.
Eyewitness accounts, battle sketches &
illustrations. 800+ documents. $49.99 + S&H.

COMPUTER ARCHIVE TECHNOLOGY
800-787-1355
PO Box 54 • Boyds MD 20841-0054
"Civil War Originals," CD-ROM, Vol. 1.
Electronic repro of historic publications
recounting original descriptions of the war.
Lee, Grant, etc.

CONFEDERATE DESK
812-948-5057
rebeldesk@aol.com
201 Virginia Ct
New Albany IN 47150-5076
New online research service. Most major
archives & manuscript depositories accessed
immediately. Call, write or access e-mail.

GENEALOGICAL PUBLISHING CO.
800-296-6687
1001 N Calvert St
Baltimore MD 21202-3897
Publishers of the *Index to the Roll of Honor*,
an incredible guide to the 228,639 Union dead
listed in the *Roll*'s 27 vols. 1164 pp. $75. On
CD-ROM, incl. entire Roll of Honor - $49.99.
Free catalog.

GRACE TECHNOLOGIES
800-778-6629
1476 Glenmore Ct
Apopka FL 32712-2046
Antietam/Sharpsburg - study the battlefield by
computer. Computer-based learning for
DOS-PCs, Windows -$33.95. Other subjects.

GRAFICA MULTIMEDIA, INC.
800-867-5563 • 415-358-5555
415-358-5556 Fax
http://www.graficamm.com
info@graficamm.com
Lisa Padilla
1777 Borel Pl Ste 500
San Mateo CA 94402-3514
Award-winning multimedia publishing &
production company since 1988. Interactive
solutions for business communication,
marketing, sales, & education. CD/ROM -
$49.95.

GROLIER INTERACTIVE, INC.
http://www.grolier.com
90 Sherman Tpke
Danbury CT 06816

Battle of the Ironclads - CD-ROM. Accurate, riveting simulation of the CW battle between the *Monitor* & the *Merrimac*. Multiple modes of play.

GUILD PRESS OF INDIANA
317-848-6421 • 800-913-9563 Orders
http://www.guildpress.com
435 Gradle Dr
Carmel IN 46032
The Civil War CD-Rom; *Iron Men, Iron Will*;
The Road to Glory; *Rebel Sons of Erin*; *Field
Surgeon at Gettysburg*. Other titles.

H-BAR ENTERPRISES
800-432-7702
205-622-3040 Fax
http://www.hbar.com
hbar@oakman.tds.net
1422 Davidson Loop
Oakman AL 35579-5820
Official Records - every word indexed, both reports & correspondence included. Custom CDs available - choose your books. Create own computer databases, add personal notes. Call for info. (See ad page 239)

HAFPAN PRODUCTIONS
518-346-3563
EDLE31A@prodigy.com
PO Box 9274
Niskayuna NY 12309-0274
Best selection of board & computer wargames. Free catalog.

HEARTHSTONE BOOKSHOP
703-960-0086 • 888-960-3300 Orders
703-960-0087 Fax
http://www.hearthstonebooks.com
info@hearthstonebooks.com
Stuart Nixon
5735A Telegraph Rd
Alexandria VA 22303-1205
Genealogical books, software, CDs & supplies, including listings on Civil War history & research. Catalog - $2 (ref.).

HISTORICAL IMPRESSIONS
888-603-0100
970-256-0157 Fax
lskaf@iti2.net
PO Box 60323
Grand Junction CO 81506-0323
PC & Mac standard & multimedia Civil War screensavers for Union, South or mixed versions. Limited ed. art, posters, bookmarks, magnets, postcards. Dealer inquiries welcome. Catalog. (See ad page 233)

HISTORICAL STUDIES GROUP
612-774-9405
1235 Reaney Ave
Saint Paul MN 55106
Series of regimental-level Civil War board & computer games. Accurate, realistic, detailed. Each includes 2 major battles, 2 learning scenarios & a 24-pp. historical analysis.

INFINET OP
800-816-4774
jameson@whytel.com
PO Box 934
Frisco TX 75034-0934
Screen savers for your PC. "Leaders & Generals" or "Confederate Flags" - 20+ images/disk. Windows 3.1 or 95, 486 with 4+ MB RAM rqd.

INFO CONCEPTS, INC.
800-747-1861
505-298-1528 Fax
11024 Montgomery Blvd NE Ste 284
Albuquerque NM 87111-3962
CW Regimental Info. System - computer-based information source detailing 2,550 Confederate units, 50 orders of battle, 6,000 officers' names, maps, portraits, flags, etc. $99.95 + $7 S&H. Call for info.

INTERACTIVE MAGIC
888-646-2442 (N. America) • 919-461-0722
http://www.imagicgames.com
"American Civil War: From Sumter to Appomattox" - Strategy game on 2 CDs. Face the challenge of refighting & rethinking the war. Bonus Historical Tapes CD.

ISIS INTERACTIVE
800-417-4747
7910 Woodmont Ave Ste 327
Bethesda MD 20814-3015
Interactive CDs - one for Lee, one for Grant. Meet the generals, up close & personal. $24.95 ea. + $3.95 S&H. Both - $39.95 + $3.95 S&H.

JUNCTION SOFTWARE
970-256-0194
751 Horizon Ct Ste 244
Grand Junction CO 81506
ArtCollector for Windows. Track your art collection, invoices, inventory, for-sale lists & much more. Living history Civil War screensavers by Historical Impressions.

MULTI EDUCATOR, INC.
800-866-6434 • 914-235-4340
914-235-4367 Fax
http://www.multied.com
multied@multied.cpm
Marc Schulman
244 North Ave
New Rochelle NY 10801-6405
2 CD-Rom set, Windows/Macintosh.
Featuring complete chronology of war events,
in-depth coverage of every major battle, 3,000
photos, more than 1,000 pgs of text. Print/
export all photos & text. $79.95.

THE PRESTON BROOKS SOCIETY
800-820-1860
PO Box 13012
James Island SC 29422-3012
Largest & best 100% Confederate Clip Art,
Vol. 1. PC & MAC versions - more than 125
images on 5 disks, incl. flags, battles, soldiers,
ships, weapons, stamps, forts, & much more!

PROVISION MEDIA
901-668-4249
7046 Broadway # 318
Lemon Grove CA 91945-1406
The Gettysburg Experience, book - $10.95.
Computer clip art. Civil War, anatomy, botany,
earth science, IBM/Mac format - $19.95.

RESEARCH DATABASE
http://www.civilwardata.com/acw
Don't miss the Civil War again! Visit the
largest, most in-depth, & fully searchable
research database of U.S. Civil War history.
See website for free demonstration.

SIERRA IMPRESSIONS
800-757-7707
http://www.sierra.com
"Robert E. Lee: Civil War General" -
true-to-life CD-ROM game. Relive battles,
lead troops through 7 historic engagements.
In-depth multimedia presentation,
reenactment footage, evocative illustrations.

STOKES IMAGING SERVICES
800-856-4498 • 512-458-2201
7000 Cameron Rd • Austin TX 78752
Selected Civil War photographs, 1861-1865.
Tapes CD-ROM for IBM or PC compatible -
$79.95.

STRATEGIC SIMULATIONS, INC.
800-601-PLAY
Wargame Construction Set III: Age of Rifles,
1846-1905, PC-DOS CD-ROM. Includes 3

Civil War campaigns, 25 CW scenarios.
Available in retail stores.

TALONSOFT
410-933-9191 • 800-211-6504 Orders only
http://www.talonsoft.com
Talonsoft1@aol.com
75162.373@compuserve.com
PO Box 632 • Forest Hill MD 21050-0632
"Battleground 7: Bull Run" - CD-ROM
computer game for Windows. Play
head-to-head via modem, e-mail or internet.
Also in the Battleground series: Antietam,
Gettysburg, Shiloh.

TARGET AUCTIONS
816-761-8259 Orders
http://www.usbusiness.com/target/us.htm
PO Box 17841 • Kansas City MO 64134
"Tattered Flags" - the most fun you'll ever
have fighting the Civil War! Original game for
the PC, $14.95 + $3 S&H. Other Civil War
games, stamps.

TEKNOVATION
540-548-4128
2594 Kendalwood Ln
Charlottesville VA 22911-8263
Images of the Civil War, Vol. 1. Selected Civil
War photographs 1861-1865. Interactive PC
images. Use as screensaver, with printout
capability. $24.95.

TROUBADOUR INTERACTIVE
800-497-0042
trubador@crocker.com
PO Box 12 • Northfield MA 01360-0012
Windows CD-ROM - *Fateful Lightning: A
Narrative History of the Civil War*. 40+
animated campaign & battle maps. Era songs,
video clips, modern color photos of
battlefields. $34.95 + $2 S&H.

TWELVE ROADS TO GETTYSBURG
800-832-0032 • 310-452-6722 Fax
Historically accurate, updated version of the
fully interactive CD-ROM. Experience
Gettysburg in such detail you can almost
smell the gunpowder. Works on both Mac &
PC. $24.95 + $5 S&H.

WALDEN FONT
800-519-4575
http://www.waldenfont.com
PO Box 871 • Winchester MA 01890-8171
Originial typefaces, graphics & ornaments to
create authentic fliers, newsletters & broadsides. Works with word processing & graphics
software - $39 + $2 S&H. For PC or Mac.

ZIGZAG MULTIMEDIA
800-561-2765
100 professional quality photos on CD-ROM, with extensive text history to print into your own documents & presentations. Heritage of America series, incl. Civil War Battlefields. $49.95/Cd.

BLUEGRASS CASE COMPANY
606-663-9871 • 800-668-9871
606-663-6369 Fax
272 Airport Rd
PO Box 386
Stanton KY 40380-0386
Display frames, collectors' frames, lined,
unlined, velvet or foam inserts, stands for
frames. Ideal for guns, knives, badges, all
collectibles. Call for sizes.

COLLECTORS SERVICES
419-884-1377
PO Box 742
Westerville OH 43086-0742
1/35 scale figurines, dioramas. Oak display
cases -custom sizes available.

D & M WOODCRAFTS
800-498-7820 • 716-625-8530
http://www.localnet.com/~dmgerber
dmgerber@localnet.com
5363 Oakwood Dr
North Tonawanda NY 14120-9619
Keepsake relic cases made of oak, cherry or
walnut. Comes complete with double strength
glass, brass hinges, lock & key. Brochure - $1.

R. ANDREW FULLER COMPANY
PO Box 2071
Pawtucket RI 02861-0071
Award cases: all sizes, hardwood, lined, glass
top. Free catalog.

GDR ENTERPRISES
803-889-6360
PO Box 807
Hollywood SC 29449-0807
Wooden ammunition crates; shipping
containers, chests, officer's desk, & more.
Handcrafted reproductions for military
historians since 1982. Photo-illus. catalog - $2.

PERSONAL TREASURES
770-431-1689
4980 Oakdale Rd SE
Smyrna GA 30080-7132
Wide variety of display cases from chip board
mounts to high quality hardwood finish &
polished brass hardware. Glass panel tops.
Price list - SASE.

REMEMBRANCE ART
Ray Helmicki
1481 N Creek Rd
Lake View NY 14085-9516
Art gallery-quality Civil War shadow boxes in
solid oak. Ltd. ed. of *Country Divided*, 30"x16"
- $375. For more info, send SASE. Dealer
inquiries welcome. Catalog - $3 (ref.).

SHENANDOAH TRADER
540-740-3735
trader@m-c-b.com
Ross & Mary Smith
1988 Shipwreck Dr
New Market VA 22844
Books for the collector of Civil War & earlier
periods of American militaria. Manufacturer of
quality artifact display cases of oak & walnut.
Button cases. Catalog - $1 (ref.).

VETERAN'S DISPLAY CASES
Paul Hammonds
S67W29308 Hawks Rest Ct
Mukwonago WI 53149-9015
Hardwood display cases made of either oak
or walnut. Also custom-made sword & gun
cases.

AMERICAN MILITARY UNIVERSITY
703-330-5398 • 703-330-5109 Fax
http://www.amunet.edu/
amugen@amunet.edu
9104P Manassas Dr
Manassas Park VA 20111-5211
Degree programs in military history, warfare
studies & defense management. "*Civil War
Studies*" concentration in M.A. in Military
Studies degree. 250+ courses in curriculum.
Three 15-week semesters beginning in
January, May & September.

**ASSOCIATION FOR THE PRESERVATION
OF CIVIL WAR SITES**
888-606-1400
http://www.apcws.com
11 Public Sq Ste 200
Hagerstown MD 21740-5510
Not-for-profit membership organization that
preserves Civil War sites for educational &
recreational uses. Website: organizational
news & membership info.

BLUE & GRAY EDUCATION SOCIETY
804-797-4535
416 Beck St • Norfolk VA 23503
Non-profit organization which interprets
battlefields for public visitation. North Anna is
most recent achievement. More than 600
members via tax-exempt donation. Seminars,
tours, symposiums & debates.

CAVALIER HISTORY
Winston B. Wine, Jr.
921 Selma Blvd • Staunton VA 24401-2083
Freelance cavalry historian endorsed by
J.E.B. Stuart IV; advisor, Brandy Station
Foundation; speaking engagements,
research, tours, other services of Eastern
Theatre Cavalry. (See ad page 241)

CELEBRATE HISTORY
800-748-9901
http://www.celebratehistory.com
PO Box 70332
Port Richmond CA 94807-0332
Held annually every President's Day holiday
weekend (Feb. 13-15, 1998) at South San
Francisco Conference Center. Includes
complete Civil War round table & symposium.

CIVIL WAR CONFERENCE
919-515-3184
Ann Coughlin
NC State Univ. Col. of Forest Resources
PO Box 8001 • Raleigh NC 27695

Conference featuring speakers & tours.
Hosted by NC Civil War Tourism Council &
NC State Univ. Annual event - April.

CIVIL WAR DRUM & FLAG SHOWS
830-966-3480
Nancy Clayton
PO Box 153
Utopia TX 78884-0153
Drum & flag storytelling performance for
school assemblies, history & music classes
(grades PK-college), teachers' meetings,
conventions & living history events. Brochure -
send SASE.

CIVIL WAR EDUCATION ASSOCIATION
800-298-1861
540-667-2339 Fax
21 N Loudoun St
Winchester VA 22601-4715
Non-profit organization presenting the finest
seminars, symposia, & tours. Develops
educational materials, publishes/distributes
Civil War books. Contact for extensive
calendar of events.

**CIVIL WAR EDUCATION ASSOCIATION
SYMPOSIUM**
800-298-1861 • 540-678-8598
PO Box 78
Winchester VA 22604-0078
Civil War Symposium. Special speakers.
Annual September event.

CIVIL WAR EDUCATION CENTER
308 W College Blvd
Roswell NM 88201-5165
Offering series of tests leading to certification
as an expert, senior expert & master expert in
Civil War knowledge.

THE CIVIL WAR LADY
507-825-3182 Phone & Fax
622 3rd Ave SW
Pipestone MN 56164-1529
Bi-monthly magazine about women & the Civil
War. Fashion news, feature article, reenacting
tips, etiquette, etc. $20/yr. (6 issues). Annual
August conference for women.

CIVIL WAR PRESERVATION CONFERENCE
540-786-2470
Rappahannock Valley CWRT
PO Box 7632
Fredericksburg VA 22404-7632
Conference & tours, banquet. Annual March
event.

CIVIL WAR SOCIETY
800-247-6253 • 540-955-1176
540-955-2321 Fax
cwmag@mnsinc.com
PO Box 770
Berryville VA 22611-0770
Membership includes award-winning *Civil War Magazine*, calendar, newsletters, membership cert., preservation & education activities, ancestors research guide, tours, seminars, discounts & camaraderie. Call for brochure.

CONFERENCE ON WOMEN & THE CIVIL WAR
800-473-3943
roslin@nfis.com
12728 Martin Rd
Smithsburg MD 21783
Through lectures on various topics, recognizes & honors the services performed by women for their country & its people during the 1860s.

CW ASSOCIATES
900-443-9854 x0019 ($1.29/min.)
PO Box 8545
New Haven CT 06531-0545
"The War Between the States Day by Day." Call now to hear what significant events occurred today in the CW (1861-1865). Average call - 3 min., $3.87. Must be 18 yrs. old or have parental permission.

GENTEEL ARTS ACADEMY
717-337-0283
717-337-0314 Fax
http://www.cvn.net/~cschmitt
cschmitt@cvn.net
CarolAnn Schmitt
PO Box 3014
Gettysburg PA 17325-0014
Offers workshops, lectures & seminars on period clothing, construction & fitting techniques. Classes offered frequently. Call/write for details & brochure. Free catalog.

HARRISBURG CIVIL WAR EXPOSITION & SEMINARS
717-780-2587
vlgentze@hacc01b.hacc.edu
Harrisburg Area Community College
1 HACC Dr
Harrisburg PA 17110-2903
Showcases reenactor demonstrations, living historians, historical societies' displays, merchants. Seminars feature many topics, guest speakers. Advance registration required. Annual March-April event. Call to be placed on mailing list.

HARTFORD CIVIL WAR SYMPOSIUM
800-298-1861
540-667-2339 Fax
Civil War Education Association
PO Box 78
Winchester VA 22604-0078
Annual May symposium in Hartford, Ct., with several Civil War historians.

MID-ATLANTIC CONFERENCE OF CIVIL WAR ROUND TABLES
610-262-1614
CWRT of Eastern PA
PO Box 333
Allentown PA 18105-0333
Special speakers. Annual conference - April.

MIDWEST CWRT CONFERENCE
Cincinnati CWRT
PO Box 1336
Cincinnati OH 45201-1336
Annual April conferences with several speakers, book sales, raffles, tours.

MINERVA CENTER ON WOMEN & THE MILITARY
410-437-5379
http://www.MinervaCenter.com
mouseminer@aol.com
20 Granada Rd
Pasadena MD 21122-2708
Non-profit education foundation & publisher presents the 3rd printing of *An Uncommon Soldier: The Civil War Letters of Sarah Rosetta Wakeman, alias Pvt. Lyons Wakeman*. $25.

MISSISSIPPI IN THE CIVIL WAR CONFERENCE
804-797-4535
BGES
PO Box 129
Danville VA 24543-0129
CW Symposium co-sponsored by BGES & MS Dept. of Archives & History in Jackson, MS. Guest speakers. Annual November event.

GEORGE TYLER MOORE CENTER FOR THE STUDY OF THE CIVIL WAR
304-876-5399 • 304-876-5429
304-876-5079 Fax
Shepherd College
Shepherdstown WV 25443
For continuing study/education of the most pivotal time in American History - the Civil War. Research being compiled on CW soldiers through a sophisticated database.

MULTI EDUCATOR, INC.
800-866-6434 • 914-235-4340
914-235-4367 Fax
http://www.multied.com
multied@multied.cpm
Marc Schulman
244 North Ave
New Rochelle NY 10801-6405
2 CD-Rom set, Windows/Macintosh.
Featuring complete chronology of war events,
in-depth coverage of every major battle, 3,000
photos, more than 1,000 pgs of text.
Print/export all photos & text. $79.95.

MUSEUM OF AMERICAN FINANCIAL HISTORY
212-908-4519
212-908-4601 Fax
http://www,mafh.org
mafh1@pipeline.com
26 Broadway
New York NY 10004-1703
America, Money and War: Financing the Civil War. 42-pg illus. catalog of exhibit - $14.25
ppd. Education kit with slides - $49.95 ppd.

NATIONAL CIVIL WAR ARTILLERY & INFANTRY SCHOOL
315-483-9284
Frank Cutler
6343 Kelly Rd
Sodus NY 14551-9502
Training & classes in Youngstown, NY, under
top instructors from around the country. Live &
train inside historic fort. $6 fee. Annual May
event.

NATIONAL CONGRESS OF CWRTs
501-225-3996
CWRTA
PO Box 7388
Little Rock AR 72217-7388
Speakers & tours. Annual October conference.

NATIONAL MUSEUM OF CIVIL WAR MEDICINE
301-695-1864 • 800-564-1864
301-695-6823 Fax
http://www.civilwarmed.org
LauraM@civilwarmed.org
JaNeen M. Smith, Ex. Dir.
48 E Patrick St
PO Box 470
Frederick MD 21705-0470
Center for study & interpretation of Civil War
medical history. Medical artifacts,
manuscripts, books & materials. 1861-1865.
Museum store. Memberships available.
Annual conference 1st weekend in August.

NORWICH UNIVERSITY
800-336-6794
http://www.norwich.edu
Unique, off-campus history program at
nation's first private military college. BA/MA
degrees from home. Accredited.

JOHN PELHAM HISTORICAL ASSOCIATION, INC.
757-838-1685
http://members.aol.com/JPHA1982
JPHA1982@aol.com
Peggy Vogtsberger
7 Carmel Ter
Hampton VA 23666-2807
Bi-monthly newsletter, "The Cannoneer."
Annual convention & tour of Fredericksburg;
commemorative ceremony at Kelly's Ford.
Supports preservation; active in erecting
monuments. Archives located at Jacksonville
Public Library, Jacksonville, Ala.

PENN STATE ALUMNI ASSN.
814-865-7679
Mary Jane Stout
105 Old Main
Pennsylvania State University
University Park PA 16802-1501
Penn State-sanctioned lecturers & battlefield
walking tours by leading historians/authors.
Also available over the Internet. A continuing
& distance education service.

SARASOTA CIVIL WAR SYMPOSIUM
800-298-1861
CW Education Assn.
PO Box 78
Winchester VA 22604-0078
Well-known authors & speakers on the Civil
War. Annual event: January-February.

SCHOOL OF THE PIECE
David V. Medert
600 W 5th St Apt 21
Chillicothe OH 45601-2217
School for artillery at Camp Sherman's rifle
range. Also, school of the soldier for infantry.
Modern & period camping. Annually - May.

SCHOOL OF THE SOLDIER & SWAP MEET
Steven C. Huddleston
12 Bow St
Danvers MA 01923-3520
Programs on military manual of arms,
marching maneuvers, camp life, tent setup,
period engineering, medicine, ladies' & civilian
topics. Modern facilities. Annual event - April.

SLIDE-A-FACT
PO Box 66085
Saint Petersburg FL 33736-6085
101 Civil War battles & facts listed in
chronological order in a "slide-rule" format.
Informative & fun. $6.95 ppd.

TOMAHAWK GAMES
330-539-6413
bu958@yfn.ysu.edu
Jim Schmalzried
720 Churchill Rd
Girard OH 44420-2121
"Civil War Command," more than 1,200
multiple-choice trivia questions. 52-photo ID
page, pawns, flags, objectives. Ideal for
families & teachers. $25 check or MO. 10-day
guarantee.

TRAVEL AMERICA, INC.
800-225-2553
131 Dodge St Ste 5
Beverly MA 01915-1861
Seminars & trips on such topics as the
American Revolution, the Old West, the Civil
War, American History. Contact for info.

**WEST PALM BEACH CIVIL WAR
SYMPOSIUM**
800-298-1861
540-667-2339 Fax
Civil War Education Association
PO Box 78
Winchester VA 22604
Annual February symposium with many
renowned Civil War historians.

MIKE WOSHNER
412-884-9299
mwoshner@bellatlantic.net
2306 Spokane Ave
Pittsburgh PA 15210-4414
Historical presentations on "India-rubber &
gutta-percha in the Civil War era,"
encompassing history, patents, military trials
& award-winning display of rare artifacts.

STEVEN J. WRIGHT
7644 Burholme Ave
Philadelphia PA 19111-2411
Civil War & Plains Indian Wars historian.

AMERICAN AFGHAN COMPANY
410-744-5470
1074 Craftswood Rd
Baltimore MD 21228-1312
50" x 60" cotton weave Confederate battle
flag afghan. For home, vehicle, or otherwise.
$49.95 ea. Contact for other products.

AMERICAN FLAG & GIFT
800-448-3524
805-473-0126 Fax
http://www.anyflag.com
flags@anyflag.com
John Solley
737 Manuela Way
Arroyo Grande CA 93420-6108
Discount prices on quality American-made
flags, banners & flagpoles, too! Catalog - $2
(ref. on 1st order).

ANCIENT AMERICAN ART
601-566-2778 • 601-566-4925
http://www.pointsouth.com/aaa.htm
aaart@dixie-net.com
PO Box 1745
Verona MS 38879-1745
Handmade reproductions of battle &
regimental flags of the Civil War. T-shirts $20.
Prints $25. Wholesale discounts.

C. BRENNER
540-778-1811
RR 2 Box 357
Stanley VA 22851
Authentic reproduction flags - Union &
Confederate, national colors, brigade & corps,
company, state, guidons, etc.

CALDWELL STUDIOS
618-747-2655
RR 2 Box 160
Tamms IL 62988
Professional reproductions of regimental flags
constructed & hand-painted. Reasonable
prices. Reenactment tested. Call Zac for free
information.

CATAWBA FLAG DEPOT
800-467-0082
206 N College Ave
Newton NC 28658

CAVALIER SHOPPE
800-227-5491
Rex Jarrett, Owner
PO Box 511
Bruce MS 38915-0511

Confederate flag apparel - 100% cotton.
Shirts, slacks, shorts, skirts, boxers, belts,
ties, watches, flags. Free catalog.

CIVIL WAR DRUM & FLAG SHOWS
830-966-3480
Nancy Clayton
PO Box 153
Utopia TX 78884-0153
Drum & flag storytelling performance for
school assemblies, history & music classes
(grades PK-college), teachers' meetings,
conventions & living history events. Brochure -
send SASE.

CLARK'S GUN SHOP, INC.
540-439-8988
10016 James Madison Hwy
Warrenton VA 20186-7820
Retailer of books, Civil War relics, Kepis,
flags, buttons, Confederate souvenirs, original
Confederate money & state notes, Civil War
prints.

COLLECTOR'S ARMOURY
800-544-3456 x515 • 703-684-6111
703-683-5486 Fax
James W. Hernly
PO Box 59, Dept CWB
Alexandria VA 22313-0059
Full line of "non-firing" reproduction pistols,
rifles, cannons, Civil War swords, knives,
bayonets, canteens, cap boxes, bugles &
flags. Free catalog. (See ad page 242)

THE COLONIAL CONNECTION
757-229-1499 Phone & Fax
Eric Grosfils
226 Warehams Pt
Williamsburg VA 23185-8923
Hinchliffe 25mm historically accurate flags &
military miniatures, painted or unpainted -
imported from England. Free catalog.

CONFEDERATE ENTERPRISES
800-996-8883
Flags, jackets, bumper stickers. Keep it flying!

CONFEDERATE SUPPLY CO.
PO Box 2012
Murfreesboro TN 37133-2012
Confederate flag souvenirs - bandanas,
license plates. Conf. battleflag - $15 + $2.50
S&H. Catalog - $1.

THE CORPORAL'S COLOURS
106 Haig St
Celina OH 45822-2708

Confederate Commemorative Series Battleflag T-shirts. Designs based on solid research. Portion of proceeds earmarked for flag preservation. $15. Free list.

CROSSROADS COUNTRY STORE
540-433-2084
Shenandoah Heritage Farmer's Market
Route 11 S • VA
Shenandoah Valley's premier Civil War store; books, flags, music, souvenirs, crafts, gifts, jewelry. Part of the Shenandoah Heritage Farmer's Market. Open Mon-Sat 10am-6pm.

DER DIENST
PO Box 221
Lowell MI 49331-0221
Confederate officer's hat insignia, exact full-size repros - $21.50. More than 400 authentic metal & badge replicas. Catalog - $5 (free w/ order).

DIXIE DEPOT
706-265-7533
706-265-3952 Fax
http://www.ilinks.net/~dixiegeneral
Dixie_Depot@stc.net
John Black
PO Box 1448
72 Keith Evans Rd
Dawsonville GA 30534
Pro-Southern educational products: video/audio tapes, new/old books, bumper stickers, flags, wearables, lapel pins, exclusive Great Seal items. More than 600 items! Catalog. (See ad page 235)

DRUMMER BOY AMERICAN MILITARIA
717-296-7611
Christian Hill Rd
RR 4 Box 7198
Milford PA 18337-9702
Civil War repro goods: uniforms, buttons, leather goods, insignia, firearms, tinware, canteens, flags, books, blankets, sabers, etc. Catalog - $1.

DUPAGE FLAG CO.
617-720-3294
ill13@aol.com
Steven W. Hill
20 Chester Ave
Westwood MA 02026
Museum-quality reproductions, made from unit's originals. Silk flags, hardwood staffs, cords & tassels, finials cast from originals.

THE FLAG GUYS
914-562-0088 x305
http://www.flagguys.com
Flagguys@aol.com
283 Windsor Hwy Dept 305
New Windsor NY 12553-6909
Flags of all types & sizes. Books, Kepis, accessories, swords, cassettes, CDs, novelties. Free catalog.

FRANKLIN FLAG & BANNER
800-891-5599
Many U.S. & Confederate flags.
Custom-made flags.

FRONTIER FLAGS
888-432-4324 • 307-867-2551
307-867-2523 Fax
David G. Wallace-Menard
1761 Owl Creek Rt
Thermopolis WY 82443
Makers of finely replicated historical flags specializing in silk, wool or cotton. Camp colors, company flags, regimental, guidons - all eras. Free research & quotes. Museum, movie & reenactor acclaimed. Free catalog. (See ad page 231)

GIBSON'S CIVIL WAR COLLECTIBLES
423-323-2427
423-323-8123 Fax
Paul, Linda & Bryan Gibson
PO Box 948
Bristol TN 37620-0948
Autographs, CSA bonds & currency, diaries, flags, letter groups, newspapers, photos, slave items, uniforms, any other paper items.

GRANNIE'S ATTIC SHURT HAUS
800-827-5127 • 717-337-8704
922 Johns Ave
Gettysburg PA 17325
Souvenirs, printed & embroidered T-shirts, including Gnatek color portrait shirts. Flags & accessories. 2nd shop located at 13 Steinwehr Ave., Gettysburg.

GARY HENDERSHOTT
501-224-7555
PO Box 22520
Little Rock AR 72221-2520
Autographs, photographs, imprints, flags & memorabilia of the Civil War era. Catalog - $3.

HISTORIC SPORTSWEAR
615-754-4334
611 Oakwood Ter
Mount Juliet TN 37122-2107

Beautiful silk necktie! Show your pride with Southern Banners, crafted with Southern pride of the finest silk. Free brochure & dealer list.

IRISH BRIGADE GIFT SHOP
504 Baltimore St
Gettysburg PA 17325
T-shirts, sweatshirts, jackets, books, flags, recruiting posters, photos, pins, stationery, prints, figurines & more -all relating to the Irish Civil War service. Detailed item list -send business-size SASE.

JKG HANDCRAFTS
PO Box 667
Glade Spring VA 24340-0667
Handmade Confederate battle flag quilts - $150-$350. Others flag quilts available - send SASE for descriptions.

LEE-GRANT, INC.
800-350-5234
Harry A. Lillie
RR 4 Box 102 • Appomattox VA 24522-8916
Limited ed. prints. Dug & undug artifacts from in & around Appomattox, Va. Flags of all sorts.

LEXINGTON HISTORICAL SHOP
540-463-2615
Bob Lurate
PO Box 1428
Lexington VA 24450-1428
Civil War memorabilia. Buy/sell books, relics, flags, currency, ephemera. Appraisals. Visit shop Mon-Sat 10-6, College Square Shopping Center, Route 11N, Lexington, Va.

JOSEPH L. MARTIN
770-428-1966
PO Box 603
Smyrna GA 30081-0603
Buying, selling, trading fine Civil War swords, guns, uniforms, flags, etc. Over 35 yrs of experience in dealing military items. Competent appraisals available.

THE MILITARY COLLECTION
PO Box 830970M
Miami FL 33283-0970
Helmets, uniforms, field gear, awards, medals, flags, weapons, swords, photos, etc. Catalog - $8.

MUSEUM OF AMERICAN CAVALRY
540-740-3959
Peter & Jane Comtois
298 Old Cross Rd
New Market VA 22844-9511

History of the Horse Soldier from colonial times through Vietnam & modern times. Gift shop with books, flags, weapons, relics, other items. Formerly Indian Hollow Antiques.

NESHANIC DEPOT
610-847-5627
610-847-8618 Fax
283 Durham Rd
PO Box 367
Ottsville PA 18942-0367
Historic artifacts, muzzleloading guns & supplies, originals, reproductions, & historic flags.

OLDE SOUTH, LTD.
T. R. Meetze
PO Box 11302
Columbia SC 29211-1302
Classic check design - Confederate flag background. Send void check & deposit slip with $13.95 (incl. S&H) for 200. Script lettering & personal message available.

PIEDMONT FLAG COMPANY
800-467-0082
704-466-3765 Fax
PO Box 685
Maiden NC 28650-0685
Standards & colors of the USA & CSA. 100% sewn cotton custom historical flags.

PYRAMID AMERICA
901-452-1323 • 800-737-1323
Quality USA, Texas or Confederate flags & flag apparel. Jackets, shorts, T-shirts, bandanas, backpacks, knives, framed/ unframed prints, more. Call for more info.

RBM ENTERPRISES
502-893-5057
PO Box 6374, Dept A
Louisville KY 40206-0374
Updated version of our classic necktie. Confederate battle flags with red stripes on navy or gray background -$18.50.

REGIMENTAL FLAG & BANNER
919-496-2888 • 919-496-7720 Fax
rebelflags@aol.com
1909 Seven Path Rd
Louisburg NC 27549
Flags - historical to modern. Civil War theme shirts, caps. Free catalog.

RICHMOND ARSENAL
804-272-4570 Phone & Fax
7605 Midlothian Tpke
Richmond VA 23235-5223

100% authentic Civil War antiques, from common bullets & buttons to museum quality weapons, accoutrements, uniforms, drums & flags. Photo-illus. catalog - $10 for 3 issues.

RUFFIN FLAG COMPANY
706-456-2111 • 706-456-2112 Fax
http://www.mindspring.com/~micromgt/ruffin.htm
241 Alexander St NW
Crawfordville GA 30631-2804
Auto tags, bumper stickers, books, T-shirts, crew sweatshirts, polo shirts, regulation battle flags, etc. Jeff Davis, Dixie's Pride, N.B. Forrest, etc. Retail/wholesale. Catalog - $1.

SHARON & JEFF'S WORKSHOP
914-735-2418 Phone & Fax
Jeff Rodriguez
205 Cardean Pl • Pearl River NY 10965-1828
Museum-quality, custom-made flags at reasonable prices.

SHARPSBURG ARSENAL
301-432-7700 • 301-432-7440 Fax
101 W Main St • PO Box 568
Sharpsburg MD 21782-0568
Purveyors of fine Civil War militaria; firearms, edged weapons, buttons, bullets, leather accoutrements, battlefield relics, books, flags, personal & camp items, paper, letters, framed prints. Buy/sell.

SOUTHERN HERITAGE PRINTS
205-539-3358
George Mahoney, Jr.
PO Box 503 • Huntsville AL 35804-0503
Civil War flags, memo pads, envelopes, bookmarks, paperweights, chronology chart/map, prints. *Last Charge at Brandy Station*, ltd. ed. print by C.E. Monroe, Jr. - $135 inc. S&H. Portion of proceeds goes to APCWS. (See ad page 234)

STRATFORD'S NOVELTY, LTD
803-797-8040
Kent Stratford
PO Box 1860
Goose Creek SC 29445-1860
Civil War-related novelties & gifts. Confederate flag imprinted products & merchandise. You name it—we have it in the souvenir and/or novelty line. Free list.

TARA HALL, INC.
800-205-0069 Phone & Fax
http://www.ncweb.com/biz/blackhawk
tarahall@earthlink.net
Vic Olney
PO Box 2069
Beach Haven NJ 08008-0109
Meagher's Irish Brigade, Fighting 69th, Corcoran's Irish Legion memorabilia, shirts, jackets, hats, sweaters, steins, pins, flags, books, miniatures, poster, belt buckles, NINAs, etc. Free catalog. (See ad page 232)

UNITED STATES FLAG SERVICE
800-USA-FLAG
5741 Elmer Derr Rd
Frederick MD 21703-7411
Largest historic collection of repros in the nation. All kinds & types, USA & CSA unit regiments, state & foreign country flags. Made in USA. List - $3.

VILLAGE SURPLUS
PO Box 530931
Mountain Brook AL 35253-0931
Confederate flag magnets - $5 ppd.

BASKET TREATS
2316 Delaware # 177
Buffalo NY 14216-2606
Civil War cards & American History decks.
$9.95 ea. ppd. Set - $17.76.

CHATHAM HILL GAMES, INC.
518-392-5022 • 518-392-3121 Fax
http://www.regionnet.com/colberk/chgames.html
CHGames@taconic.net
Ray Toelke
PO Box 253
Chatham NY 12037-0253
"Gettysburg, The Battlefield Game." Board
game, in full color, incorporating many events,
detailed descriptions, questions & answers of
the 3-day battle - $24.95.

COLUMBIA GAMES, INC.
800-636-3631
http://www.columbiagames.com/
questions@columbiagames.com
PO Box 3457
Blaine WA 98231-3457
"Dixie" - a tactical CW card game consisting of
collectible cards - $7.95/deck of 60 random
cards. 1 for each regiment, battery & brigade
officer at Bull Run, Shiloh, Gettysburg. Free
catalog.

R. P. DARRAH
5954 Coca Cola Blvd
Columbus GA 31909-5531
Civil War board games, master tactician level,
& kits. From $12 up. Write for details.

EDUCATIONAL MATERIALS ASSOCIATES,
804-293-GAME
PO Box 7395
Charlottesville VA 22906-7395
Civil War game with FREE poster - $12.95
ppd! From Civil War Heartland...America's #1
"family-type" map games & national
bestsellers. Ages 8-adult. Dealers welcome.
Free catalog.

FAX ATTAX, INC.
800-748-0281 Fax
http://www.ids.net/faxattax
Play major battles of the Civil War via fax or
worldwide web.

HAFPAN PRODUCTIONS
518-346-3563
EDLE31A@prodigy.com
PO Box 9274
Niskayuna NY 12309-0274
Best selection of board & computer
wargames. Free catalog.

HISTORICAL STUDIES GROUP
612-774-9405
1235 Reaney Ave • Saint Paul MN 55106
Series of regimental-level Civil War board &
computer games. Accurate, realistic, detailed.
Each includes 2 major battles, 2 learning
scenarios & a 24-pp. historical analysis.

INTERACTIVE MAGIC
888-646-2442 (N. America) • 919-461-0722
http://www.imagicgames.com
"American Civil War: From Sumter to
Appomattox" -Strategy game on 2 CDs. Face
the challenge of refighting & rethinking the
war. Bonus Historical Tapes CD.

THE JOHNNY REB GAME COMPANY
http://www.erinet.com/bp/johnreb.html
HillJhn@aol.com
7599 Chrisland Cove
Falls Church VA 22042
"Johnny Reb" is 60-page set of tactical
wargame rules that enable the refighting of
Civil War battles with miniature soldiers of any
size. Free catalog.

K & P WEAVER
Ken & Paula Weaver
PO Box 1131
Orange CT 06477-7131
Historically accurate repro men's clothing for
military or civilian impression. Custom-made
with handsewn buttonholes. Quality
accessories; cherry dominoes, checkers with
canvas board. Catalog with swatches - $1.

P.S.I.
909-652-2568 • 909-652-0497
PO Box 568
Winchester CA 92596-0568
"The Campaign of '63 Begins." Join this
sophisticated, multi-player, play-by-mail
simulation of the Gettysburg campaign.
Call/write for info.

SLIDE-A-FACT
PO Box 66085
Saint Petersburg FL 33736-6085
101 Civil War battles & facts listed in
chronological order in a "slide-rule" format.
Informative & fun. $6.95 ppd.

SPEERIT STRATEGY GAMES
800-831-1155
704-849-7777 Phone & Fax
10612 Providence Rd # 325
Charlotte NC 28277-0233
"Gettysburg: Three Days in July" - turning
point of the war is in your hands. $44.95 ppd.

STARMASTER
http://www.iboutique.com/starmaster/index.html
2500 Laurelhill Ln
Fort Worth TX 76133-8112
Playing cards featuring Civil War generals, battles, armaments & trivia. 3 decks - $18. Free catalog.

STRATEGIC SIMULATIONS, INC.
800-601-PLAY
Wargame Construction Set III: Age of Rifles, 1846-1905, PC-DOS CD-ROM. Includes 3 Civil War campaigns, 25 CW scenarios. Available in retail stores.

STUEMPFLE'S MILITARY MINIATURES
717-762-0825
13190 Scott Rd
Waynesboro PA 17268-9023
Over 200 resin kits, bunkers & conversions in 1/7s & 1/76. Leva, B P Cast, Crusader, Revell, 54mm kits, war games, etc. Catalog - $3.

TALONSOFT
410-933-9191 • 800-211-6504 Orders only
http://www.talonsoft.com
Talonsoft1@aol.com
75162.373@compuserve.com
PO Box 632
Forest Hill MD 21050-0632
"Battleground 7: Bull Run" - CD-ROM computer game for Windows. Play head-to-head via modem, e-mail or internet. Also in the Battleground series: Antietam, Gettysburg, Shiloh.

TARGET AUCTIONS
816-761-8259 Orders
http://www.usbusiness.com/target/us.htm
PO Box 17841
Kansas City MO 64134

"Tattered Flags" - the most fun you'll ever have fighting the Civil War! Original game for the PC, $14.95 + $3 S&H. Other Civil War games, stamps.

TOMAHAWK GAMES
330-539-6413
bu958@yfn.ysu.edu
Jim Schmalzried
720 Churchill Rd
Girard OH 44420-2121
"Civil War Command," more than 1,200 multiple-choice trivia questions. 52-photo ID page, pawns, flags, objectives. Ideal for families & teachers. $25 check or MO. 10-day guarantee.

TRI-J COMMUNICATIONS
PO Box 542227
Houston TX 77254-2227
Recreate famous battles with the "Phantasy Civil War Alliance." Play General & make battle plans in play-by-mail action. Win medals & other prizes. $5 for rules & free challenge.

U.S. GAMES SYSTEMS, INC.
203-353-8400
203-353-8431 Fax
USGames@aol.com
Lee Stockwell
179 Ludlow St
Stamford CT 06902-6900
Heavily illustrated, informative & entertaining CW playing cards & card games. Facsimile decks of cards originally published in the 1860s. Award-winning Civil War series. Catalog - $2. (See ad page 232)

HUDSON ALEXANDER
911 Velma Ln
Murfreesboro TN 37129-2367
Will research your soldier/unit from
Tennessee.

BARNETTE'S FAMILY TREE BOOK CO.
barnette@neosoft.com
Mic Barnette
1001 North Loop W
Houston TX 77008-1766
Guide to tracing your Civil War ancestors -
$12.50. Catalog - $1.

BATTLEFIELDS REVISITED
BattRev@aol.com
Patricia Watt
PO Box 231
New Cumberland PA 17070-0231
Research Civil War soldiers, sailors - all
nationalities. Reports, records, histories.

BLOUNT COUNTY GENEALOGICAL & HISTORICAL SOCIETY
ATTN: TC • PO Box 4986
Maryville TN 37802-4986
*Loyal Mountain Troopers: The 2nd and 3rd
Tenn. Vol. Cavalry in the Civil War*. Details
these largely ignored Southerners who served
the Union. $32.50 ppd.

BOYD PUBLISHING CO.
800-452-4035 • 912-452-4020 after 6pm EST
tignall@accucomm.net
PO Box 367
Milledgeville GA 31061-0367
100s of new historical publications &
genealogical references. Computer software,
incl. *Official Record of the War of the
Rebellion* - all 127 vols. on CD-ROM, $89.95
+ $5 S&H.

BRODERBUND
39500 Stevenson Pl Ste 204
Fremont CA 94539
Family Tree Maker CD-Rom - solid starting
point for genealogical research. PC
compatible with Windows programs, 386 or
higher, 4MB RAM (8MB recommended).

BROWN PUBLICATIONS
BrianB1578@aol.com
PO Box 25501
Little Rock AR 72221
In the Footsteps of the Blue & Gray - $24.95 +
$2 S&H. Describes CW-related research
sources in state archives, National Archives &
LDS collection. History of ea. corps &
hard-to-find technical information.

THE CIVIL WAR GARRISON
PO Box 1681
Springfield IL 62705-1681
Will research the veteran you designate &
write his personal story in the War Between
the States, or produce a Civil War plaque of
his experiences.

CIVIL WAR RESEARCH
219-483-0640
PO Box 8355 • Fort Wayne IN 46898-8355
Will research your Civil War soldier through
the official records. Provides brief report &
extracts from the official records - $34.95.

CONNECTICUT STATE LIBRARY
860-566-3690
http://www.cslnet.ctstateu.edu/handg.htm
History & Genealogy Unit
231 Capitol Ave
Hartford CT 06106-1548

DELAWARE PUBLIC ARCHIVES
302-739-5318 • 302-739-3021
302-739-2578 Fax
http://del-aware.lib.de.us/archives
archives@state.de.us
Hall of Records
Dover DE 19901

THE DIXIE PRESS
615-831-0776 Phone & Fax
PO Box 110783
Nashville TN 37222-0783
Publisher, wholesaler & retailer of Southern
books & genealogy products. Free catalog.

JOHN EMOND
PO Box 44625
Washington DC 20026-4625
Will research military & pension records at
National Archives. Reasonable fees - no
charge until found.

FLORIDA STATE ARCHIVES
904-487-2073
R.A. Gray Bldg
500 S Bronough St
Tallahassee FL 32399-6504

GENEALOGICAL PUBLISHING CO.
800-296-6687
1001 N Calvert St
Baltimore MD 21202-3897
Publishers of the *Index to the Roll of Honor*,
an incredible guide to the 228,639 Union dead
listed in the *Roll's* 27 vols. 1164 pp. $75. On
CD-ROM, incl. entire Roll of Honor - $49.99.
Free catalog.

E. GREISSER
771D E Main St
Bridgewater NJ 08807-3339
Civil War soldiers from Philadelphia & New Jersey. Pension, family & church records when available.

THE HANDLEY LIBRARY ARCHIVES
540-662-9041 x22
PO Box 58 • Winchester VA 22604-0058
Contain numerous historical documents & personal records.

HAUK DATA SERVICES
PO Box 1577
Anderson IN 46014-0577
"The Virginia Ancestor Series," indexed reports on the descendants of prominent Virginia families. Many with Civil War participants: Lee, Taylor, etc. Brochure - legal-size SASE.

HEARTHSTONE BOOKSHOP
703-960-0086 • 888-960-3300 Orders
703-960-0087 Fax
http://www.hearthstonebooks.com
info@hearthstonebooks.com
Stuart Nixon
5735A Telegraph Rd
Alexandria VA 22303-1205
Genealogical books, software, CDs & supplies, including listings on Civil War history & research. Catalog - $2 (ref.).

HEIRLINES
800-570-4049
James W. Petty, Genealogist
PO Box 893
Salt Lake City UT 84110-0893
Will help you find your ancestors & begin learning about your genealogy. Search censuses, church, court, & land records, military files, etc., in America & other countries.

HERITAGE BOOKS, INC.
800-398-7709 • 301-390-7709
http://www.heritagebooks.com
1540 Pointer Ridge Pl Ste E
Bowie MD 20716-1800
Books on history, Americana, Civil War, & genealogy. Free catalog.

HIGGINSON BOOK COMPANY
508-745-7170
508-745-8025 Fax
higginsn@cove.com
148 Washington St
PO Box 778
Salem MA 01970-0778

Reprinters of regimental histories, American genealogies & local histories. Thousands of titles by mail or in our bookstore. Catalog - $4 (ref.).

INDIANA STATE ARCHIVES
317-232-3660
http://www.ai.org/icpr/archives
140 N Senate Ave
Indianapolis IN 46204

INSTITUTE FOR CIVIL WAR RESEARCH
ICWRJohn@aol.com
7913 67th Dr
Middle Village NY 11379-2908
Histories of more than 7,500 Civil War units, Union & Confederate. Organizational data, engagement lists, maps, etc. $15/unit. Other services.

TED JONES, CIVIL WAR VETERANS
tedjones@epix.net
RR 1 Box 1317
Little Meadows PA 18830-9730
Let me find your Civil War ancestors. Write for info.

MARY LOU PRODUCTIONS
800-774-8511
PO Box 17233
Minneapolis MN 55417-0233
"Gift of Heritage" - how-to video showing you the process of creating your own family documentary, including tips on researching, organizing, & combining info. - $32.95. Call for more info.

JAMES MEJDRICH
630-668-0384
128 N Knollwood Dr
Wheaton IL 60187-4731
Will check the register of Confederate graves in Mississippi for $1/name & SASE.

MELTINGPOINT
716-875-8158
220 Delaware Ave Ste 204
Buffalo NY 14202-2107
Family crests & shields. Authentic, researched, hand-crafted jewelry & gift items relating to your family surname. Free brochure.

MERTIN RESEARCH SERVICES
888-248-7166
PO Box 1323
Summit NJ 07902-1323
Experienced genealogist will research Civil War ancestors. Pensions, service records, Union or Confederate.

NATIONAL GENEALOGICAL SOCIETY
703-525-0050 Office • 703-841-9065 Library
703-525-0052 Fax
http://www.genealogy.org/~ngs
ngslibe@wizard.net OR
76702.2417@compuserve.com
4527 17th St N
Arlington VA 22207-2399

OLD FAVORITES BOOKSHOP
3055 Lauderdale Dr
Richmond VA 23233-7800
Civil War, WWII, other military books, prints &
maps. Free catalog on request. (See ad page
242)

PHOTOGRAPHY OF YESTERYEAR
423-510-9306
cwphotogpr@aol.com
Frank or Rita Harned
1 Pryor Dr
Chattanooga TN 37421-2278
Photograph birthplaces, churches,
cemeteries, landmarks. Photograph CW
battlefields of approximate location of your
ancestor's unit. Limited unit research available
for TN, GA, KY.

PONDER BOOKS
Janice Ponder
PO Box 573
Doniphan MO 63935-0573
Publisher of books on Civil War, history &
genealogy. Trans-Mississippi region. Free
booklist.

H. J. POPOWSKI
614-276-4993
614-274-4110 Fax
PBFV68A@prodigy.com
158 N Chase Ave
Columbus OH 43204-2603
Capsule histories of any US Army unit,
1861-1865. Volunteers, regulars & USCT.
Plus sources. $10 ea.

CLAUDE V. REICH, PhD
1516 N 14th St
Reading PA 19604
Open-ended database of more than 35,000
Pa. Volunteers at the Battle of Gettysburg.

THE REPRINT COMPANY, PUBLISHERS
PO Box 5401
Spartanburg SC 29304-5401
4-volume set contains alphabetical roll of
90,000 Louisiana Confederate army
members. In-depth, many vital statistics.
Call/write.

S. SCHUMACHER
425-259-1641
103505.1733@compuserve.com
4027 Rucker Ave Ste 747
Everett WA 98201-4839
CW pension & bountyland packets
researched - $20/name. Send name, state
mustered in, wife's name, & regiment (if
known). Union soldier's burial place
researched; 200,000+ names - $10/name.
Send details & SASE.

**SOUTH CAROLINA DEPT. OF ARCHIVES &
HISTORY**
803-734-8577 • 803-734-7918
http://www.scdah.sc.edu/homepage.htm
PO Box 11669
Columbia SC 29211-1669

THE SOUTHERN ARMY ALBUM!
John Mills Bigham
4833 Arcadia Rd
Columbia SC 29206-1307
Christopher Memminger's homeplace. 4
families share Confederate oral histories &
images. Military headstones 1776+ recorded
in 3 antebellum churchyards. Lasting regional
1992 video production. $21.95.

**SOUTHERN HERITAGE PRESS, GA.
DIVISION**
PO Box 347163
Atlanta GA 30334-7163
Fine books about Southern history,
1861-1865. *In Search of Confederate
Ancestors: The Guide*. Critically acclaimed by
SCV & UDC. 112 pp., illus. - $10 + $1.50 S&H.

VERMONT AGENCY OF ADMINISTRATION
802-828-2794
Public Records Division
Drawer 33
Montpelier VT 05633-7601

GEOFF WALDEN
35197 23 Mile Rd # 4
New Baltimore MI 48047-3639
Will research your ancestor who served with
the Kentucky Infantry or Artillery for $3/name.
Capsule unit histories for $8/regt. or battery.

JAMES & KAREN WARD
9906 Warson Ct
Richmond VA 23237-3908
Virginia Confederates. Photocopies of your
ancestors' military records from the Virginia
State Archives. Send soldier's name, county
or brigade & $40.

19TH ALA. INF. REGT., ARMY OF TENN.
http://fly.hiwaay.net/~dsmart/index.html
Reenactment organization. Website provides
many links to pages of related topics.

2ND MARYLAND INFANTRY, CO. A, CSA
http://www.sutler.com/2ndMD/2ndMD.htm

5TH NEW YORK, DURYEE'S ZOUAVES
http://www.zouave.org/index.html
Enlist in the 5th NY for authentic living history
& reenacting.

6TH WISCONSIN VOLUNTEERS, CO. K
http://www.nwdc.com/~am14nysm/6wvi.html
Homepage for a unitsin the Iron Brigade.

**ALABAMA DEPT. OF ARCHIVES &
HISTORY**
http://www.asc.edu/archives/agis.html

AMAZON.COM BOOKS
http://www.amazon.com
Order from a list of more than a million titles,
including all of Rockbridge Publishing's fine
Civil War titles.

**AMERICAN BATTLEFIELD PROTECTION
PROGRAM**
http://www2.cr.nps.gov/abpp/abpp.html
U.S. government's leading battlefield
preservation program.

THE AMERICAN CIVIL WAR
http://mirkwood.ucs.indiana.edu/acw
Links to sites with many Civil War topics.

AMERICAN CIVIL WAR
http://pages.prodigy.com/NJ/schwalbe/
        schwalbe.html
Limited battlefield travelogue, links to national
groups.

**AMERICAN CIVIL WAR ACCORDING TO
SHOTGUN**
http://208.206.112.102/dweeks
Seeks to provide Civil War info. not readily
found elsewhere on the internet.

AMERICAN CIVIL WAR ASSOCIATION
http://www.acwa.org
CSA contact: AdjCSAACWA@aol.com
Union contact: FedAdjACWA@aol.com

AMERICAN CIVIL WAR HOMEPAGE
http://funnelweb.utcc.utk.edu/~hoemann/
        cwarhp.html
User-friendly general index to Civil War
websites.

**THE AMERICAN CIVIL WAR INFORMATION
ARCHIVE**
http://www.access.digex.net/~bdboyle/cw.html
Index to general-interest Civil War sites.

**AMERICAN CIVIL WAR ROUND TABLE OF
AUSTRALIA, INC.**
http://www.health.latrobe.edu.au/hs/ss/cu/
        ACWRTA/ Home/cw1page

ANTIETAM BATTLEFIELD INFO.
http://www.antietam.com
Sponsored by APCWS; info. on Antietam,
including archives.

**ANTIQUE MILITARIA & COLLECTORS
NETWORK**
http://www.collectorsnet.com/index.html
Links to services, periodicals, dealers, &
events.

**ASSOCIATION FOR THE PRESERVATION
OF CIVIL WAR SITES**
http://www.apcws.com
Organizational news & membership info.

BARRY'D TREASURE
http://www.iglou.com/btreasure
Extensive online catalog of accoutrements,
books, bullets, cartridges, dug items, other
relics & artifacts.

BATTLE OF GETTYSBURG HOMEPAGE
http://www.mindspring.com/~murphy11/getty
Strives to be the most comprehensive &
professional study of the battle of Gettysburg.

BATTLE SUMMARIES
http://www2.cr.nps.gov/abpp/battles/tvii.htm
Maintained by the Civil War Sites Advisory
Committee of the ABPP.

BEAUVOIR
http://www.beauvoir.org
Last home of CSA president Jefferson Davis.
Open daily 9AM-5PM (CST); closed for
Thanksgiving & Christmas.

THE BLUE & GRAY TRAIL
http://ngeorgia.com/travel/bgtrail.html
Civil War sites & stories from North Georgia &
Chattanooga.

**BUFFALO SOLDIERS ON THE WESTERN
FRONTIER**
http://orion.mis.net/imh/buf/buf5.html
Exhibit of the famed African-American soldiers.

CAMP CHASE GAZETTE
http://nemesis.cybergate.net/~civilwar/index.html
Sample of this publication devoted to the
coverage of Civil War reenacting.

CENSUS BUREAU
http://www.census.gov
U.S. census information.

CIVIL WAR @ CHARLESTON
http://www.awod.com/gallery/probono/cwchas/
Guide to events, local CWRT, other resources
in attempt to preserve history & heritage of
the Civil War in & around Charleston, S.C.

CIVIL WAR ARTILLERY
http://www.lib.uchicago.edu/~cjt1/artillery.html
Basic info. & suggestons for further viewing &
reading about artillery in the Civil War; focus
on field artillery.

CIVIL WAR ARTILLERY HOMEPAGE
http://www.geocities.com/Athens/1862
Includes glossary, tables, bibliography relating
to Civil War artillery.

CIVIL WAR BOOKS ONLINE
http://members.aol.com/bookkritik/civilwar.html
Selection of the finest in Civil War publishing;
features new & recent titles as well as the
classics.

CIVIL WAR CIRCUIT
http://members.tripod.com/~Chubbles/circuit/
cwc.html
Webring of Civil War sites.

CIVIL WAR FICTION
http://atl46.atl.msu.edu/atl/reh/civnovels.html
Several lists of novels concerning the war.

THE CIVIL WAR HOMEPAGE
http://www.civil-war.net
Links to Civil War pages on the internet;
calendar of events.

THE CIVIL WAR IN MINIATURE
http://serve.aeneas.net/ais/civwamin
Documented facts & interesting stories about
the Civil War.

CIVIL WAR LESSON PLAN
http://www.smplanet.com/civilwar/civilwar.html
Teaches upper elementary school students
the central issues of the Civil War.

CIVIL WAR LIST
http://www.public.usit.net/mruddy
Table of Civil War links & information.

CIVIL WAR MALL
http://www.CivilWarMall.com
Online shopping mall for Civil War
enthusiasts. Space available to Civil War
retailers.

**CIVIL WAR MASTER LINKS &
RESOURCES COLLECTION**
http://www.autonomy.com/civilwar.htm
Alphabetical listing of Civil War websites.

CIVIL WAR RESOURCES
http://homepages.dsu.edu/~jankej/civilwar/
civilwar.ht ml
Excellent link to Civil War resources on the
web. Guide to general histories, primary
sources, battlefield sites & publications.

CIVIL WAR ROUND TABLE INDEX
http://www.jerseycape.com/users/cole/
tblindex.htm
Many listings of national & international
CWRTs.

CIVIL WAR VIRTUAL ARCHIVE RING
http://www.geocities.com/Athens/Forum/1867/
cwring. html
Ring of websites with primary reference
material. "Virtual library" designed for
researchers.

CIVIL WAR WEBRINGS
http://www.geocities.com/Athens/Forum/6806/
hi_ring s.html
Lists & defines current webrings of Civil War
sites.

CIVIL WAR WOMEN
http://scriptorium.lib.duke.edu/collections/
civil-war-women. html
Manuscript sources in the Special Collections
Library at Duke University.

CONFEDERATE CIPHER WHEEL
http://members.aol.com/ubchi2/cipher.htm
Picture & history of cipher wheel used by the
South during the Civil War.

THE CONFEDERATE NETWORK
http://members.tripod.com/~jrw/index.html
Links to several sites of Southern interest,
including reenactments & merchants.

CONFEDERATE PENSION RECORDS
http://link.tsl.state.tx.us/c/compt/pension.html
Search of more than 54,000 pension records
in Texas State Archives, providing name,
pension number & county.

CONNECTICUT STATE LIBRARY
http://www.cslnet.ctstateu.edu/handg.htm

CROSSROADS OF THE CIVIL WAR
http://www.civilwarsites.com
APCWS-sponsored. Describes Civil War
attractions in & around Washington County,
MD. Day-by-day accounts of battles of
Antietam & Gettysburg.

CSA CURRENCY PAGE
http://www.CSAcurrency.com
Homepages providing info. on authentic
Confederate currency, bonds, coins, & stamps.

CSA NET
http://www.pointsouth.com
Southern heritage page with directory for
each of its several topics.

CSA ONLINE
http://www.ilinks.net/~rayder441/webzone/civil/
civil/ci vil.htm
Links to Confederate sites, list of generals,
genealogy hints, archives, live chat.

DAUGHTERS OF UNION VETERANS OF THE CIVIL WAR
http://suvcw.org/duv.htm
DUVCW@aol.com
Organization for female lineal descendants of
Union veterans.

DELAWARE PUBLIC ARCHIVES
http://del-aware.lib.de.us/archives
archives@state.de.us

DIXIE MART
http://www.pointsouth.com
Virtual Southern Mall. Links with various
merchants & services of interest to
Southerners.

DIXIELAND RING
http://www.geocities.com/BourbonStreet/2757/
index.h tml
Webring designed to bring Confederate sites
together.

DIXIENET
http://www.dixienet.org
Official national web site of the Southern
League. Several links with other sites.
Application to join can be downloaded.

E-MAIL AMERICAN CIVIL WAR
http://www.blarg.net/~dhhill/Research.html
Links to Civil War research & resource sites.

EUROPE CAMP #1612 SCV
http://serve.aeneas.net/~conam/ec1612.htm
Organization for Sons of Confederate
Veterans residing in Europe. Includes
sections on how to join & activities.

FRANKLIN COUNTY, PA, IN THE CIVIL WAR
http://www.pa.net/franklin/warcount.htm
Civil War activities in the county by area:
Chambersburg, Greencastle, Mercersburg,
Waynesboro.

FREDERICKSBURG & SPOTSYLVANIA NMP
http://www.nps.gov/frsp/frspweb.htm
Visit the largest military park in the world
without leaving home.

GENERAL OFFICERS OF THE CIVIL WAR
http://people.delphi.com/yatsuo/go_main.htm
Picture gallery of Union & Confederate
generals.

GETTYSBURG ADDRESS VISITOR'S GUIDE
http://www.gettysburgaddress.com
gbtours@mail.cvn.net
"Where History Comes Alive." The center of
everything & all within walking distance.
Package & group plans available.

GETTYSBURG DISCUSSION GROUP
http://www.arthes.com/gdg/
Discussion group focusing on Battle of
Gettysburg -scholarly & informative.

GETTYSBURG GUIDE
http://www.GettysburgGuide.com
Unofficial guide & index to anything &
everything relating to Gettysburg.

GETTYSBURG ONLINE
http://138.234.80.3/~s000057/main.html
shoffman@cvn.net
Complete tourist guide to Gettysburg,
showing B&Bs, specialty shops, activities for
kids, etc., on the Internet.

GODEY'S LADY'S BOOK
http://www.uvm.edu/~hag/godey/
Portions of & commentary on this most
famous 19th-century women's magazine.

GRAND ARMY OF THE POTOMAC
http://pages.prodigy.com/CGBD86A/garhp.htm
Homepage of the GAR - Civil War veterans
organization.

U.S.GRANT NETWORK
http://www.css.edu/mkelsey/gppg.html
usglady@excel.net
Articles, images, & other links associated with
Ulysses S. Grant.

GREAT AMERICAN HISTORY
http://www.cais.com/greatamericanhistory
Educational material on U.S. history,
especially as it pertains to the Civil War.

GREAT WAR OF THE CONFEDERACY
http://www.civilwarmall.com/gwotc.htm
Civil War memorabilia & collectibles, including
historic Confederate art.

H-NET CIVWAR
http://h-net2.msu.edu/~civwar
Online discussion list concerning Civil
War-era culture & history. Book reviews, links.

HISTORIC CARLISLE BARRACKS
http://carlisle-www.army.mil/history/history.html
Traces 200-yr. history of one of our nation's
oldest military garrisons.

HISTORY BUFF'S HOMEPAGE
http://www.historybuff.com/index.html
Devoted to newspaper press coverage of
events in U.S. history, incl. the Civil War era.

THE HISTORY CHANNEL
http://www.historychannel.com/index2.html
Homepage & index of A&E's cable History
Channel.

THE HISTORY PLACE
http://www.historyplace.com/civilwar/index.html
Timeline of major Civil War events; photos of
major players in the war.

HOWITZERS ONLINE
http://www.novagate.net/~howitzers
Designed to educate & entertain those
wishing to learn more about the 2nd
Richmond Howitzers. Includes "research
center."

ILLINOIS IN THE CIVIL WAR
http://www.outfitters.com/illinois/history/civil
Histories of Illinois companies; general history
relating to Illinois' role in the war.

IMAGES OF BATTLE
http://ils.unc.edu/civilwar/civilwar.html
Selected letters of soldiers on both sides of
the conflict; from the Southern Historical
Collection.

INDIANA IN THE CIVIL WAR
http://www.thnet.com/~liggetkw/incw/cw.htm
Details the Hoosier State's contribution to the
war effort.

INDIANA STATE ARCHIVES
http://www.ai.org/icpr/archives

INTERNET CIVIL WAR EXPO
http://www.bmark.com/cw.show
World's 1st Civil War Expo on the Internet, 24
hrs./day, 365 days/yr. Many major dealers.
One month ads available for your extra relics,
books, & other items.

JEWS IN THE CIVIL WAR
http://www.geocities.com/Athens/Forum/1867/
jewish. htm
Articles & letters from & about Jewish Civil
War participants, both Yankee & Rebel.
Includes link to genealogy database.

KANSAS STATE HISTORICAL SOCIETY
http://history.cc.ukans.edu/heritage/kshs/kshs1.
html

KENNESAW CIVIL WAR MUSEUM
http://www.ngeorgia.com/history/kcwm.html
Directions & contact info. Brief history of "the
General," famous Civil War locomotive.

**LADIES OF THE GRAND ARMY OF THE
REPUBLIC**
http://suvcw.org/lgar.htm
Organization for female descendants of Union
veterans.

**LIBRARY OF CONGRESS PHOTO
COLLECTION**
http://rs6.loc.gov/cwphome.html
Selected Civil War photos.

**LIBRARY OF CONGRESS SPECIAL
COLLECTIONS**
http://lcweb.loc.gov/spcoll/spclhome.html
Links to Library of Congress' historic photo,
law, & Jed Hotchkiss collections.

ABRAHAM LINCOLN & THE CIVIL WAR
http://sparrow.csc.vsc.edu/RREA/history
/Lincoln_and _civil_war.html
Links relating to Pres. Abraham Lincoln.

ABRAHAM LINCOLN ONLINE
http://www.netins.net/showcase/creative/
lincoln.html
Anything & everything Lincoln, including
website links, books & other resources.

MILITARY ORDER OF THE LOYAL LEGION OF THE UNITED STATES (MOLLUS)
http://suvcw.org/mollus.htm
YJNW42A@prodigy.com
Est. 1865 for direct or collateral descendants of commissioned officers of the Union army.

MUSEUM OF AMERICAN FINANCIAL HISTORY
http://www,mafh.org
mafh1@pipeline.com
America, Money and War: Financing the Civil War. 42-pg illus. catalog of exhibit - $14.25 ppd. Education kit with slides - $49.95 ppd.

NATIONAL ARCHIVES & RECORDS ADMIN.
http://www.nara.gov
inquire@arch2.nara.gov

NATIONAL CIVIL WAR ASSN.
http://ncwa.org/
Info about reenacting & living history units.

NATIONAL GENEALOGICAL SOCIETY
http://www.genealogy.org/~ngs
ngslibe@wizard.net
76702.2417@compuserve.com

NAT'L PARKS & CONSERVATION ASSN.
http://npca.org/
Provides info. regarding this non-profit organization & its dedication to preserving national parks.

NATIONAL REGISTER OF HISTORIC PLACES (NPS)
http://www.cr.nps.gov/nr/nrhome.html
Info. on how to nominate property to the National Register & benefits of registration. Lists currently registered historic properties.

NATIONAL TRUST FOR HISTORIC PRESERVATION
http://www.nthp.org
Non-profit organization committed to preserving the heritage & livability of America's communities.

NAVAL HISTORICAL CENTER
http://www.history.navy.mil
Mission statement: "To enhance the Navy's effectiveness by preserving, analyzing & interpreting its hard-earned experience & history..."

NAVY RING
http://home.att.net/~londubh/navyring.htm
Webring dedicated to reenactors of Civil War sailors & Marines.

THE OHIO HISTORICAL SOCIETY
http://winslo.ohio.gov/ohswww/ohshome.html

OHIO IN THE CIVIL WAR
http://www.infinet.com/~lstevens/a/civil.html
Info. & sources on units, prison camps, war stories, round tables, etc.

OREGON SECT. OF STATE
http://arcweb.sos.state.or.us
reference.archives@state.or.us

PAPERS OF JEFFERSON DAVIS
http://www.ruf.rice.edu/~pjdavis
Complete edition of Davis' works & papers.

POETRY & MUSIC OF THE CIVIL WAR
http://www.erols.com/kfraser/
Lyrics to poems & music of the Civil War, both Union & Confederate.

POINT LOOKOUT POW DESCENDANTS
http://members.tripod.com/~PLPOW/pointlk.htm
plpow@erols.com

REENACTOR RING
http://www.geocities.com/soho/6546/ring.html
Webring formulated to bring world of Civil War reenacting, both North & South, together.

REENACTOR'S WEB MALL
http://rampages.onramp.net/~lawsonda/mall
Links to directories of sutlers, basic 19th-century supplies, etc.

REENACTORS HOMEPAGE
http://www.cwreenactors.com
"Dedicated to the brave souls, North & South, who fought & died in the War Between the States."

RESEARCH DATABASE
http://www.civilwardata.com/acw
Don't miss the Civil War again! Visit the largest, most in-depth, & fully searchable research database of U.S. Civil War history. See website for free demonstration.

SELECTED CIVIL WAR PHOTOGRAPHS
http://rs6.loc.gov/cwphome.html
Resource providing views of 1,118 historic photos.

SONS OF CONFEDERATE VETERANS (NATL. OFFICE)
http://www.scv.org
Dedicated to preserving & defending history & principles of the Old South. Links to Civil War websites.

SONS OF UNION VETERANS
http://suvcw.org/
Organization for the descendants of Union
veterans.

**SOUTH CAROLINA DEPT. OF ARCHIVES &
HISTORY**
http://www.scdah.sc.edu/homepage.htm

**SOUTH DAKOTA STATE HISTORICAL
SOCIETY**
http://www.state.sd.us/state/executive/deca/
cultural/a rchives.htm

**STATE HISTORIC PRESERVATION
OFFICES (NPS)**
http://www2.cr.nps.gov/tps/shpolist.html
Lists state & territorial historic preservation
officers.

STONEWALL BOOKS
http://midatlantic.net/mall/bookstor/bookstor.htm
Resource for Union & Confederate Civil War
books.

SUTLERSVILLE INTERACTIVE TOWN
http://www.ncweb.com/biz/blackhawk
Civil War trading post, sutleries & gift shops.

TALONSOFT
http://www.talonsoft.com
Talonsoft1@aol.com
75162.373@compuserve.com
"Battleground 7: Bull Run" - CD-ROM
computer game for Windows. Play
head-to-head via modem, e-mail or internet.

TENNY'S CIVIL WAR PAGE
http://www.mebbs.com/tenny/civilwar.htm
Extensive links to Civil War websites.

TIME LINE OF THE CIVIL WAR
http://rs6.loc.gov/ammem/timeline.html
Time line drawn largely from the work of
Richard B. Morris.

U.S. NPS CIVIL WAR PARKS
http://www.nps.gov/Architext/AT-NPSquery.html
Provides search for all national park sites
relating to the Civil War.

UNCLE DAVEY'S AMERICANA
http://www.collectorsnet.com/uncledv/index.htm
uncledv@southeast.net
Original Civil War collectibles - full range of
items for collector & historian.

**UNITED DAUGHTERS OF THE
CONFEDERACY**
http://www.hsv.tis.net/~maxs/UDC/
hqudc@aol.com
Organization for female descendants of
Confederate veterans.

THE UNITED STATES CIVIL WAR CENTER
http://www.cwc.lsu.edu
Best comprehensive index to historic & Civil
War-related websites.

THE VALLEY CAMPAIGN CIVIL WAR SHOP
http://blue.mountain.net/vcamp
History shop with great items for you & your
history buff.

THE VALLEY OF THE SHADOW
http://jefferson.village.virginia.edu/vshadow2
Info. regarding the Shenandoah Valley in the
Civil War, gleaned from the "Valley Archive."

**VIRGINIA TECH LIBRARIES CIVIL WAR
COLLECTION**
http://scholar2.lib.vt.edu/spec/civwar/cwhp.htm
Provides descriptions & excerpts of
manuscripts from Va. Tech's archives, as well
as links to other sites.

VMI ARCHIVES & CIVIL WAR RESOURCES
http://www.vmi.edu/~archtml/cwsource.html
Full-text examples of Civil War-era collections
found in VMI's archives.

VMI ARCHIVES GUIDE TO MANUSCRIPTS
http://www.vmi.edu/~archtml/msguide2.html
Civil War collections.

WELCOME TO NORTH GEORGIA
http://ngeorgia.com
Links to people, places & events of North
Georgia's Civil War history.

WYOMING STATE ARCHIVES
http://commerce.state.wy.us/cr/archives/

BELLINGER'S MILITARY ANTIQUES
770-992-5574
Bill Bellinger
PO Box 76371-SB
Atlanta GA 30358-1371
FULL-TIME DEALER of antique firearms,
edged weapons, belt plates, leather goods,
books & miscellaneous from the 17th-19th
century. Civil War a specialty. Catalog - $3; 4
issues - $10 (overseas - $20).

BERMAN LEATHER
617-426-0870
617-357-8564 Fax
Robert S. Berman
25 Melcher St
Boston MA 02210-1516
Leather hides like Civil War era for belts,
straps, clothing, bags, even footwear. Full
catalog of hardware, tools, buckles & kits - $3
(ref.).

BORDER STATES LEATHERWORKS
501-361-2642
501-361-2851 Fax
1158 Apple Blossom Ln
Springdale AR 72762-9762
Civil War collectibles, original weapons &
equipment. Reproduction cavalry saddles &
equipment. Custom hand-forged bits.

KEN BROWN
614-498-8379
17261 Sligo Rd
Kimbolton OH 43749
Quality, handmade, reproduction cavalry tack,
equipment & accoutrements. Free brochure.

WALTER BUDD
3109 Eubanks Rd
Durham NC 27707-3622
Finest selection of US military antiques,
firearms, swords, uniforms, head gear, cavalry
equipment, McClellan saddles, mess gear,
horse-drawn army wagons & rolling stock, etc.
Subscription rate - $5 for 8 issues.

C & D JARNAGIN
601-287-4977
601-287-6033 Fax
http://www.jarnaginco.com
PO Box 1860
Corinth MS 38835-1860
Military & historical outfitters. Research,
develop, & manufacture high quality uniforms,
leather gear, footwear, & tinware for American
troops, 1750-1865. 18th-century & CW
catalogs - $3 each. (See ad page 239)

CARRICO'S LEATHERWORKS
316-922-7222
316-922-3311 Fax
David Carrico
811 5000 Rd
Edna KS 67342
Authentic reproduction Civil War cavalry
equipment & accoutrements. Saddles, bridles,
holsters, belts, etc. Free price list.

THE CAVALRY SHOP
804-266-0898
T.E. Johnson, Jr.
9700 Royerton Dr
Richmond VA 23228-1218
Civil War leather goods, buckles; horsegear.
Catalog - $2. (See ad page 233)

DIXIE GUN WORKS, INC.
800-238-6785 Orders only • 901-885-0700
901-885-0440 Fax
PO Box 130
Union City TN 38261-0130
The source for firearms, parts, shooting
supplies, leather goods, uniforms, books,
patterns & cannons. 600-pg catalog with more
than 8,000 items - $5.

DIXIE LEATHER WORKS
502-442-1058 • 800-888-5183 Orders only
502-448-1049 Fax
PO Box 8221
Paducah KY 42002-8221
Military & civilian museum-quality repros. 60+
hard-to-find leather items. Documents, maps,
printed labels & stationery. Swords, firearms,
& hats. Handmade chairs, desks; leather
medical cases & bottle roll-up kits. Photo-illus.
catalog - $6.

DRUMMER BOY AMERICAN MILITARIA
717-296-7611
Christian Hill Rd
RR 4 Box 7198
Milford PA 18337-9702
Civil War repro goods: uniforms, buttons,
leather goods, insignia, firearms, tinware,
canteens, flags, books, blankets, sabers, etc.
Catalog - $1.

FALL CREEK SUTTLERY
765-482-1861
765-482-1848 Fax
http://fcsutler.com
AJF5577@aol.com or fcsutler@aol.com
Andy Fulks
PO Box 92
Whitestown IN 46075-0092

Authentic reproduction Civil War & mid-19th-century uniforms, leather goods, weapons, shoes, tents, insignia, reference books & more. 32-pg catalog - $3. (See ad pg 242)

FRAZER BROTHERS' 17TH REGIMENT
214-696-1865
214-426-4230 Fax
5641 Yale Blvd Ste 125
Dallas TX 75206-5026
Uniforms & equipment, artillery hardware, & side arms. Civilian clothing (men only). Handmade leather goods. Large supply of tinware. Boots. American products.

FRENCH'S STORE & TRADING COMPANY
717-530-5037
PO Box 454
Shippensburg PA 17257-0454
Authentic Civil War reproductions of trade goods, 17th-19th cent. Cavalry & leather goods & saddles. Catalog - $1.

FRONTIER SADDLE
941-322-2560
Gabriel Libraty
5530 Juel Gill Rd
Myakka City FL 34251
Replica saddles of the Old West & military; from mountain man to Civil War to classic Western saddles. Free catalog.

HEARTLAND HOUSE
540-672-9267 Phone & Fax
Nick Nichols
Old Blue Ridge Tpke
Rochelle VA 22738
Troiani calls us "the *Stradivarius* of historical leather craftsmen." Full line of Victorian-era saddlery, tack & equestriana (U.S., C.S., British military, & civilian). Illus. catalog - $4 (ref.).

HILLBILLY SPORTS, INC.
410-378-4533
PO Box 70
Conowingo MD 21918-0070
Leather goods, period firearms, uniform items, camp items & much more. Catalog - $3.

J.K. LEATHER
540-955-0301
Dave Allen
RR 2 Box 3026
Berryville VA 22611
Repairs & restoration of all leather goods, esp. antique saddles & tack. Custom-made leather products. Handmade saddles.

MENDELSON'S LEATHER
501 Short St
Grants Pass OR 97527-5443
Master leather craftsman makes moccasin boots, full spectrum of custom goods you can't find anywhere else.

MERCURY SUPPLY CO.
409-327-3707
101 Lee St
Livingston TX 77351
Civil War uniforms, reproduction equipment, tents, accoutrements, leather goods, firearms military & civilian. Catalog - $2.

NAVY ARMS CO.
201-945-2500
689 Bergen Blvd
Ridgefield NJ 07657-1499
Finest in quality replica firearms. Revolvers, Sharps rifles & carbines, Enfields, leather goods.

NMC ENTERPRISES
800-591-2999 (24 hrs.)
913 18th St Ste 2
Santa Monica CA 90403
Civil War blackpowder accessories; fine, hand-crafted leather. Holsters, belts, pouches, bags, buckles. Free catalog.

OLD SUTLER JOHN
607-775-4434 Phone & Fax
Westview Station
PO Box 174
Binghamton NY 13905-0174
Full line of quality reproduction Civil War guns, bayonets, swords, uniforms, leather items, & other collectibles. Catalog - $3. (See ad page 236)

PECARD ANTIQUE LEATHER CARE
541-937-3348
R.S. Dorsey
PO Box 263
Eugene OR 97440-0263
Finest antique leather care. Moisturizes, softens, preserves - absolutely safely. Colorless, odorless, long-lasting. 6 oz. tub - $9.50 ppd. 16 oz. tub - $17 ppd. 32 oz. tub - $28 ppd.

REB'S TRADING POST
3608 Alta Vista Dr
Waco TX 76706-3741
Canvas goods, lodges, tents, flys, bags, etc. Blanket rifle sheaths, antler products, leather products, belt blanks, holsters, etc. Catalog - $1.

S & S SUTLER OF GETTYSBURG
717-677-7580 • 717-337-0438 Fax
Tim Sheads
PO Box 218 • Bendersville PA 17306-0218
Reproduction Civil War uniforms, leather
goods, insignia, tinware, & more. Free catalog.

SERVANT & CO. / CENTENNIAL GENERAL STORE
717-334-9712 • 800-GETTYS-1 Orders
717-334-7482 Fax
http://www.servantandco.com
230 Steinwehr Ave
Gettysburg PA 17325-2814
Quality Civil War uniforms & period clothing.
Patterns, Kepis, leather goods, accessories,
hats. Catalog - $6.

SHARPSBURG ARSENAL
301-432-7700
301-432-7440 Fax
101 W Main St
PO Box 568
Sharpsburg MD 21782-0568
Purveyors of fine Civil War militaria; firearms,
edged weapons, buttons, bullets, leather
accoutrements, battlefield relics, books, flags,
personal & camp items, paper, letters, framed
prints. Buy/sell.

TOM SMITH
716-337-0181
12101 New Oregon Rd
Springville NY 14141
US Cavalry Horse Equipment, 1859-1917.
Custom work. Correct hardware & leather
spec's (no harness leather). Color catalog - $7.

TWIN OAKS SADDLERY
407-790-2461
11580 46th Pl N
Royal Palm Beach FL 33411
American-made Civil War
goods/reproductions. Cartridge box plates,
carbine box, cap box, sword belts, sashes,
holsters, saddlebags, saddles & parts, belts &
buckles, tinware. Catalog - $2.

UPPER MISSISSIPPI VALLEY MERCANTILE CO
319-322-0896
319-383-5549 Fax
1607 Washington St
Davenport IA 52804-3613
Top quality goods & supplies for Civil War
reenactors; uniforms, tinware, tents, leather
goods, muskets, books, weapons, patterns,
more. 100-pp., illus. catalog - $3.

YESTERYEAR
615-893-3470
Larry W. Hicklen
3511 Old Nashville Hwy
Murfreesboro TN 37129-3094
Quality dug & non-dug Civil War artifacts of all
types. Buckles, buttons, swords, guns, paper,
leather, etc. Mail order subscription - $5/yr.

ANTIETAM OVERLOOK FARM B&B
800-878-4241
PO Box 30 • Keedysville MD 21756-0030
95 acres of tranquility with a 4-state view at
the battlefield in Sharpsburg, MD. AC suites,
private screened porches, garden tubs,
fireplaces & bath. Country-style breakfast &
hospitality.

BATTLEFIELD BED & BREAKFAST
717-334-8804
Charlie & Florence Tarbox
2264 Emmitsburg Rd
Gettysburg PA 17325-7114
Where hospitality & history come together.
Daily CW demonstrations. Each room has
theme dedicated to units which fought on
grounds; private bathrooms. Carriage rides,
weather permitting.

BECHTEL VICTORIAN MANSION B&B INN
800-550-1108 • 717-259-7760
http://www.bbonline.com/pa/bechtel
Charles E. Bechtel
400 W King St • East Berlin PA 17316
Charming restored Victorian mansion in East
Berlin National Historic District, 18 mi. east of
Gettysburg. Private baths, full candlelight
breakfasts. Perfect for Civil War, history &
architecture buffs. Brochure.

BEECHMONT INN
800-553-7009
315 Broadway
Hanover PA 17331
Elegant, ca.1834 house with 7 guest rooms &
suites, antiques, grand staircase, fireplaces,
whirlpool, A/C, private baths, gourmet
breakfast & refreshments. Quiet courtyard &
gardens. AAA/Mobil approved.

BRAFFERTON INN
717-337-3423
Sam & Jane Back
44 York St
Gettysburg PA 17325-2301
Experience the adventure & charm of historic
Gettysburg in this 1786 National Registry
home. Antiques, elaborate stenciling
throughout. 10 rooms, private baths, full
breakfasts.

BRIERFIELD B&B
717-334-8725
Nancy Rice, Prop.
240 Baltimore St
Gettysburg PA 17325-2334
Two blocks from historic Lincoln Square, 3
blocks from Natl. Park Visitors Center.

CEDAR MOUNTAIN CAMPGROUND
800-234-0968
http://www.civil-war.net/cedar.html
bemerson@hs.gemlink.com
20114 Camp Rd • Culpeper VA 22701-7404
Central to 8 battlefields. Tent sites, RV full
hook-up, fishing pond, rec room. Groups
welcome.

CLASSIC QUESTS
800-458-5394
2 Federal St • Saint Albans VT 05478-2035
Escorted tours, many with multi-night stays in
fine hotels/inns. Quality historic & scenic
tours. Escorted rail tours. Free catalog.

COTTONWOOD INN
304-725-3371 • 800-868-1188
http://www.mydestination.com/cottonwood
travels@mydestination.com
Barbara Sobol, Owner
RR 2 Box 61S
Charles Town WV 25414-9616
Antietam/Harpers Ferry area. Country setting.
Large guest rooms, private baths, TV/AC.
Fireplaces, full breakfasts. Farmhouse B&B, 6
quiet acres with stream.

COUNTRY ESCAPE B&B
800-484-3244 code 4371 • 717-338-0611
717-334-5227 Fax
Merry V. Bush
275 Old Route 30
Mc Knightstown PA 17343
Just outside Gettysburg. Rates $50-$75. Full
breakfast. Outside children's play area. Hot
tub under the stars. Call for reservations or
brochure.

DAYS INN
301-739-9050
900 Dual Hwy
Hagerstown MD 21740-5913
Conveniently located near several major
battlefields: Gettysburg, Antietam, Harpers
Ferry. Outdoor pool & playground. Full service
restaurant.

THE DOUBLEDAY INN
717-334-9119
http://www.bbonline.com/pa/doubleday
Charles & Ruth Anne Wilcox, Innkeepers
104 Doubleday Ave
Gettysburg Battlefield PA 17325-8519
Fine country inn directly on Gettysburg
Battlefield. Panoramic views from atop Oak
Ridge. CW memorabilia, antiques, central air,
full breakfast. Presentations by historians. Call
for rates & brochure.

FARNSWORTH HOUSE INN
717-334-8838
401 Baltimore St
Gettysburg PA 17325-2623
"Showplace of the Civil War." Daily house tours, fine dining. Bed & breakfast - Victorian elegance, private baths. Tavern, bookstore.

FLAHERTY HOUSE
800-217-0618
1888 Victorian B&B convenient to Gettysburg battlefield. Warm hospitality, casual elegance; hearty breakfast. Walk to 300 antique dealers. $60-$135.

FORT LEE INN
800-941-3752
http://www.Altoona.NET/fortlee/
PO Box 92
Marsteller PA 15760-0092
Journey back to the Civil War era in this secluded mountain hideaway on 100 acres of woods & farmland. Hiking & mountain biking trails, many activities, spectacular view.

GETTYSBURG HOTEL
717-337-2000 • 717-337-2075 Fax
1 Lincoln Sq
Gettysburg PA 17325-2205
Reconstructed hotel in the heart of the historic district. Call/write for more info.

HAGERSTOWN/SNUG HARBOR KOA
301-223-7571 • 800-562-7607
11759 Snug Harbor Ln
Williamsport MD 21795
Camp with us on the Conococheague Creek; fish, canoe, or just relax. 15 min. from Antietam, 30 min. from Harpers Ferry & Gettysburg. Civil War discounts!

HAMPTON INN OF FREDERICK
301-698-2500
800-HAMPTON
5311 Buckeystown Pike
Frederick MD 21701
Minutes away from noted Civil War museums & sites. Ask about the special Frederick Historian Rate.

HERITAGE MOTOR LODGE
717-334-9281
64 Steinwehr Ave
Gettysburg PA 17325
Convenient, clean, comfortable; AAA approved. Handicapped accessible rooms. Restaurant, meeting facilities; battlefield tours/package plans available. Shopping next door at Old Gettysburg Village.

HIGHPOINT
800-283-4099
215 Linton Ave • Natchez MS 39120
Large Victorian home ca.1890. Three guestrooms, private baths. Full plantation breakfast. Tour antebellum mansions & the Vicksburg battlefield.

HISTORIC CASHTOWN INN
800-367-1797 • 717-334-9722
PO Box 103 • Cashtown PA 17310-0103
Fine dining/cocktails. Four rooms, private baths, & luxury suites. Headquarters for generals A.P. Hill & Imboden. Appears in the *Gettysburg* movie.

INNS OF GETTYSBURG
800-496-2216
240 Baltimore St
Gettysburg PA 17325-2334
Gracious hospitality at 15 historic inns. Wineries, museums, tours, golf, biking, antiquing nearby. Brochure.

KEHR'S CORNER CUPBOARD
717-624-3054
New Oxford PA
Quiet, serene B&B, ca.1810. 8 mi. east of Gettysburg. Full breakfast, private baths, A/C, fireplaces, off-street parking.

KILLAHEVLIN B&B
800-847-6132 • 540-636-7335
540-636-8694 Fax
1401 N Royal Ave
Front Royal VA 22630
Located on Civil War encampment & site of Mosby's Rangers' hangings. Landmarks register. Luxurious accommodations, full breakfast, private Irish pub.

LIGHTNER FARMHOUSE B&B
717-337-9508
Gettysburg PA 17325
19 country acres just 3 miles from Cemetery Hill on Baltimore Street. Used as hospital during the battle.

THE MADISON HOUSE B&B
800-828-6422 • 804-528-1503
Dale & Irene Smith
413 Madison St
Lynchburg VA 24504-2435
Lee surrendered here. Longstreet recuperated here. Early, Dearing, Garland, Rodes buried here. Elegant accommodations. "Dedicated to Yesterday's Charm with Today's Convenience." Civil War Library. Tour packets.

MANSFIELD PLANTATION
800-355-3223
1776 Mansfield Rd
Georgetown SC 29440-9500
Historic bed & breakfast combining the best of the old & the new South. $75-$95/night, double occupancy. Guided tours for groups of 12 or more with advance registration - $6/person.

MULBERRY FARM B&B
717-334-5827
Minutes from Gettysburg battlefield; ca.1817 home in orchard country setting. Private baths, full breakfast.

OLD APPLEFORD INN
800-275-3373 • 717-337-1711
Gettysburg PA 17325
Victorian mansion, 10 guest rooms, private baths, full breakfast. AAA approved.

OLDE HARDING HOUSE INN
717-338-0151
PO Box 246
Cashtown PA 17310-0246
Built in 1803, used as tavern & inn during & after Battle of Gettysburg. Eventually became Col. Harding's home.

PIPER FARM HOUSE B&B
301-797-1862
Antietam National Battlefield
PO Box 100
Sharpsburg MD 21782-0100
Antietam National Battlefield, Sharpsburg, MD, next to Bloody Lane. Headquarters of Gen. J. Longstreet. Fully restored; period antiques. Three guest rooms, private baths.

A PLACE AWAY B&B
912-924-2558 • 912-924-1044
Peggy & Fred Sheppard
PO Box 26
Andersonville GA 31711
Bed & breakfast in historic village of Andersonville, Ga.

SELBY HOUSE
540-373-7037
226 Princess Anne St
Fredericksburg VA 22401-6039
Four spacious rooms, private bath, full breakfasts. Official tour guide for battles of Fredericksburg, Chancellorsville, Wilderness, and Spotsylvania Court House. Member of APCWS.

SKI LIBERTY HOTEL
717-642-8288 x301
Pat Custer
Carroll Valley PA
10 mi. from Gettysburg, within 1/2 hour of Antietam, Harpers Ferry & Frederick. 40 rooms. Perfect for exhibitions, receptions, reunions, & Civil War balls. Seating for up to 300 people, ample parking.

SOUTH MOUNTAIN RECREATION AREA
301-791-4767
21843 National Pike
Boonsboro MD 21713
MD State Park with camping, swimming, boating, fishing. Reservations accepted. Call about our Civil War camping package; short drive to several major CW battlefields.

STONE SOUP GALLERY & SOLDIERS HAUNT INN
540-722-3976
HAUNTINN@aol.com
107 N Loudoun St
Winchester VA 22601-4717
Original etchings, antique (1800s) furniture & quilts, antique reproductions. Bed & breakfast in building built in 1760. Showcase of regional talents.

SUNDAY'S B&B
800-221-4828
39 Broadway
Hagerstown MD 21740-4019
Minutes from Antietam. Victorian elegance. Personalized service. Full breakfasts. Afternoon tea, wine & cheese, fruit basket.

WELBOURNE
540-687-3201
Nathaniel & Sherry Morison
22314 Welbourne Farm Ln
Middleburg VA 20117-3939
Bed & breakfast - home of Col. Richard H. Dulany, 7th Va. Cavalry, where Mosby, Pelham, Stuart & von Borcke stayed! Traditional Southern breakfast & beautiful countryside.

WHITE ELEPHANT B&B INN
901-925-6410
304 Church St
Savannah TN 38372
Victorian inn, 10 miles to Shiloh battlefield.

SIDNEY ALLINSON
660 Cairndale Road
Victoria
BC V9C 3L3 Canada
MILITARY PUBLICATIONS,
INTERNATIONAL DIRECTORY helps you
contact over 600 specialist war journals
worldwide. 10th ed. - $15.

AMERICA'S CIVIL WAR
703-771-9400
AmericasCivilWar@thehistorynet.com
741 Miller Dr SE Ste D2
Leesburg VA 20175-8920
Bi-monthly magazine - $24/yr. Back issues -
$5 ea.

THE ARTILLERYMAN
800-777-1862 • 802-889-3500
802-889-5627 Fax
firetec@firetec.com attn.artilleryman
RR 1 Box 36, Monarch Hill Rd
Tunbridge VT 05077-9707
Quarterly magazine dealing with artillery,
1750-1898. Safety, places to visit, history,
workshops, & more. $18/yr. Sample - $2.

AUTOGRAPH TIMES
1125 W Baseline Rd # 2-153
Mesa AZ 85210-9501
The only monthly newspaper for autograph
collectors. Sample copy - $2 S&H.

BACKWOODSMAN MAGAZINE
719-783-9028 Phone & Fax
Lynne Richie
PO Box 627
Westcliffe CO 81252-0627
The voice of the 19th century. Features
19th-century crafts, muzzleloading,
homestead-how-to, leather projects, trapping,
etc. 1 year - $16.

BATTLE CRY
810 Gales Ave
Winston-Salem NC 27103
Multi-period reenacting publication covering
Civil War & others. $8/yr. for 4 issues.

BLUE & GRAY MAGAZINE
614-870-1861 • 800-CIVIL WAR
614-870-7881 Fax
PO Box 28685
Columbus OH 43228-0685
Excellent bi-monthly magazine covering
variety of Civil War subjects, campaigns,
profiles of famous soldiers. Interesting side
bits, etc. 1 yr - $19. 2 yrs - $35. 3 yrs -$46.

THE CITIZENS' COMPANION
614-373-1865
Camp Chase Publishing
PO Box 707 • Marietta OH 45750
Magazine for civilian side of reenacting. Info.
on clothing, behavior, living history
impressions & more. $20/yr. for 6 issues.

CIVIL WAR BULLET COLLECTOR NEWSLETTER
oma00077@mail.wvnet.edu
Chuck Haislip
66 W Main St Apt 3
White Sulphur springs WV 24986
Newsletter with classified section distributed
by Civil War Bullet Collector Association.
$10/yr. for 6 issues.

THE CIVIL WAR COURIER
800-418-1861 • 716-873-2594
716-873-0800 Fax
galprint@localnet.com
2503 Delaware Ave
Buffalo NY 14216-1712
Newspaper published 10 times/yr. Many items
of interest to Civil War buffs. 11th year of
publication. Subscriptions -$20/yr.

CIVIL WAR HISTORY
330-672-7913
330-672-3104 Fax
Sandy Clark
Kent State University Press
307 Lowry Hall / PO Box 5190
Kent OH 44242-0001
Scholarly journal featuring studies of mid-19th
century U.S. history. Book reviews. Quarterly
publication - $21/yr. individ. subs.; $32/yr.
institutional subs. & libraries. Add $6/yr. for
foreign subs.

THE CIVIL WAR LADY
507-825-3182 Phone & Fax
622 3rd Ave SW • Pipestone MN 56164-1529
Bi-monthly magazine about women & the Civil
War. Fashion news, feature article, reenacting
tips, etiquette, etc. $20/yr. (6 issues). Annual
August conference for women.

CIVIL WAR MAGAZINE
800-247-6253 • 540-955-1176
540-955-2321 Fax
cwmag@mnsinc.com
PO Box 770 • Berryville VA 22611-0770
Official magazine of the Civil War Society -
bi-monthly, full-color, devoted to Civil War
history. Scholarly, balanced representation of
people & ideas behind the war. Call for
subscription, society membership or ad info.

THE CIVIL WAR NEWS
800-777-1862 • 802-889-3500
802-889-5627 Fax
http://www.civilwarnews.com
firetec@firetec.com attn.cwn
RR 1 Box 36 • Monarch Hill Rd
Tunbridge VT 05077-9707
96+ pg current events newspaper: news,
photos, features, columns, letters,
reenactments, collecting, firearms, calendar,
book reviews, ads. 11 issues - $27. Free
sample issue. (See ad pg 238)

CIVIL WAR ROUND TABLE ASSOCIATES
501-255-3996
PO Box 7388 • Little Rock AR 72217-7388
Est. 1968; oldest national CW battlefield
preservation organization. Publishes *CWRT
Digest*, newsletter devoted to news of
contemporary activities, inspired by interest in
CW history & historic preservation. $12.50/yr.

CIVIL WAR TIMES ILLUSTRATED
800-435-9610
Cowles History Group
602 S King St Ste 300
Leesburg VA 20175-3919
Another excellent bi-monthly magazine from
Cowles covering many aspects of the Civil
War & related materials. Subscriptions -
$21/yr.

COLUMBIAD
PO Box 8200 • Harrisburg PA 17105-8200
Quarterly review of the War Between the
States. Appeals to well-informed generalists,
amateur scholars & professional historians
alike. Subs. - $34.95/yr.

CONFEDERATE DIRECTORY
915-446-4439
David Martin
PO Box 61 • Roosevelt TX 76874-0061
Reference for vendors of Confederate
currency, books, tapes, flags, stationery,
memorabilia, reenactors' supplies, services,
memorials, etc.; includes COMPLETE
Confederate Constitution. $12 (ppd.).

THE CONFEDERATE MBR NEWSLETTER
770-270-0542
Peter Bertram, Editor
PO Box 451421
Atlanta GA 31145-9421
6-pg illustrated newsletter cataloging UCV,
SCV Reunion Medals, badges & ribbons.
$12/yr. ($17 outside USA), 4 issues. Free
sample copy - large SASE.

CONFEDERATE VETERAN
8506 Braesdale Ln
Houston TX 77071-1118
Bi-monthly periodical focusing on Confederate
soldier. Articles & Southern heritage for the
unreconstructed Southerner. $14/yr.

THE CONFEDERATE YANKEE CHRONICLE
703-754-3206
Attn: Memberships
PO Box 134 • Gainesville VA 20156-0134
Discussing, debating & questioning events,
issues, & personalities of the CW.
Membership includes 12 issues -$14.95/yr.
Free sample issue.

COWLES HISTORY GROUP
http://www.thehistorynet.com
Attn: Military History Index
PO Box 3242 • Leesburg VA 20177-8111
Cross-referenced index of more than 3,000
entries, through 1000s of years of battle.
Every subject addressed in *Military History*
magazine's first decade of publication -
$24.95.

COWLES HISTORY GROUP CALENDARS
800-358-6327
PO Box 921
North Adams MA 01247-0921
1998 Civil War & Military History calendars.
Perfect gifts for history buffs - $14.95.

DEPARTMENT OF THE SOUTH, INC.
352-394-7206
PO Box 680784
Orlando FL 32868-0784
"Hilton Head Dispatch" - official newsletter for
reenactment community. Latest info. on
events, book reviews, battle reports, unit
history, life in trenches & on home front.
$17/yr. for 6 issues.

G W SPECIALTIES
816-356-7457
George Scheil
7311 Ditzler
Raytown MO 64133
Civilian reprints of magazines & schoolbooks
from mid-1800s. Free catalog.

GETTYSBURG MAGAZINE
800-648-9710
937-461-4260 Fax
http://www.morningsidebooks.com
msbooks@erinet.com
Bob Younger
PO Box 1087
Dayton OH 45401-1087

STEPHEN A. GOLDMAN HISTORICAL NEWSPAPERS
410-357-8204
SAGHNOLDNEWS@msn.com
PO Box 359 • Parkton MD 21120-0359
Historical newspapers bought/sold - 16th-20th centuries. Bound volumes or single issues. Military, political, wild west, gangsters, Civil War, many more! Extensive catalog - $2. (See ad page 238)

THE GUN REPORT
309-582-5311 • 309-582-5555 Fax
John Mullen
PO Box 38
Aledo IL 61231-0038
The new *Gun Report Index* - your guide to 35 years of collectible firearm history. 128 pp., $24.95 + $3.50 S&H.

HARRIET'S TCS
540-667-2541 • 540-722-4618 Fax
http://www.harriets.com
PO Box 1363
Winchester VA 22604-1363
185 patterns ca.1690-1945. Rentals, fabric, kits, supplies, hoops, parasols, lace. *Harriet's Then & Now* - 19th-century magazine, $6/issue. Annual subscription - $30. Color, photo-illus. catalog - $12.

HERITAGE PRESERVATION ASSOCIATION
800-86-DIXIE • 770-928-2714
770-928-2719 Fax
http://www.hpa.org
HPA@america.net
PO Box 98209
Atlanta GA 30359-1909
National non-profit organization protects & preserves history, symbols & culture of the American South. Reg. membership - $40. Call for more detailed information.

HILTON HEAD DISPATCH
407-295-7510
7214 Laurel Hill Rd
Orlando FL 32818-5233
Publication indicating where to find reenactments, shows, & book fairs dealing in history. Covering the Southeast. $15/yr. for 6 issues.

HISTORIC TRAVELER MAGAZINE
717-657-9555
102430.410@compuserve.com
6405 Flank Dr
Harrisburg PA 17112
Bi-monthly magazine guide to historic sites. Travel, routes, background, etc. $11.97/yr.

HISTORICAL BRIEFS, INC.
800-732-4746
Civil War Reports - most authentic reports available, written as events unfolded & published in *Harper's Weekly*. 232 pp. - $24.95 + $3.75 S&H.

JD PUBLISHING
PO Box 386
Crystal Lake IL 60039-0386
Monthly newsletter, *Lincoln in the 20th Century* - $5/issue.

JM COMICS
PO Box 56982
Jacksonville FL 32241-6982
First & only historically accurate Civil War comic series. "Southern Blood" takes you from Fort Sumter to Appomattox. 1 yr/12 issues - $22.50.

KENTUCKY CIVIL WAR JOURNAL
502-866-5513
PO Box 628
Russell Springs KY 42642
Monthly publication featuring the Civil War in Kentucky. Subs. - $24.

MAIL CALL JOURNAL
http://www.HistoryOnline.net
mcj@historyonline.net
PO Box 5031, Dept. B1
South Hackensack NJ 07606
Actual letters & journals written by Civil War soldiers. Excerpts from books; original essays & poetry. 6 issues/yr. - $24.95. Sample - send SASE. Free catalog.

MILITARY HISTORY MAGAZINE
703-771-9400
MilitaryHistory@thehistorynet.com
741 Miller Dr SE Ste D2
Leesburg VA 20175-8920
Excellent bi-monthly magazine covering the spectrum of military history - $24/yr. Back issues available.

MILITARY ILLUSTRATED
Wise Owl Worldwide Publication
4314 W 238th St
Torrance CA 90505-4509
Offers unrivaled reputation among military historians, enthusiasts, & modelers. Authoritative articles, research, photographs, etc. 12 issues - $80. From ancient to modern, excellent reference sources.

MILITARY IMAGES
http://www.civilwar-photos.com
milimage@csrlink.net
RR 1 Box 99A
Henryville PA 18332-9726
Estab. 1979. Publication presenting great
photographs of Yanks, Rebs & Indian
soldiers. Subscriptions - $24/yr. for 6 issues.

MUZZLE BLASTS
812-667-5131
812-667-5137 Fax
Natl. Muzzleloading Rifle Assn.
PO Box 67
Friendship IN 47021-0067
Represents all aspects of muzzleloading.
More than 25,000 members/300 charter clubs
throughout the country. Subscription with $30
membership.

NORTH SOUTH TRADERS CIVIL WAR
540-67-CIVIL
540-672-7283 Fax
nstcw@msn.com
PO Box 631
Orange VA 22960-0370
Illustrated, bi-annual *Civil War Collectors'
Price Guide* -$25 + $3 S&H. Bi-monthly
magazine, heavily illustrated -$25/yr.

OWEN & OWEN PUBLICATIONS
Jim Owen
PO Box 6745
Columbia SC 29260-6745
Publish an "American History Quarterly"
historical newsletter - with lots of Civil War
stuff. Free sample copy.

THE PROFESSIONAL TREASURE
HUNTERS HISTORICAL SOCIETY
603-357-0607 • 800-447-6014 (New England)
603-352-1147 Fax
George Streeter
14 Vernon St
Keene NH 03431-3440
Info. about treasure hunting in US. Metal
detecting info. Treasure club activities in US.
Newsletter - *Treasure Hunter's Gazette*.

R.M.J.C., INC.
PO Box 684
Appomattox VA 24522-0684
CW-period New Testament, hardcover - $13
ppd. Choose Union (black) or Confederate
(brown). Reprinted from original. Free
quarterly, CW-related newspaper, *The
Christian Banner*, deals with Christian aspect
of the war.

REBELLION CONSTITUTION
PO Box 45
Guysville OH 45735-0045
Journal on Civil War homefront life. Printed
letter press, archival paper, original wood
engravings. Sample copy - $6. Next 4 issues -
$22.

RECREATING HISTORY
http://www.recreating-history.com
PO Box 4277 • Santa Clara CA 95056
Magazine of hands-on living history. Historic
crafts, cooking & clothing from pre-medieval
to gaslight eras. 6 issues/yr.

REENACTOR'S JOURNAL
309-463-2123
309-463-2188 Fax
PO Box 1864
Varna IL 61375
For the "Who, what, where, when and how-to"
of Civil War Reenacting. 12 issues - $24.
Sample issue - $3.

DALE W. ROSE
302-239-3120 evenings
104 Tern Ct
Wilmington DE 19808
Harpers Weekly specialist. Original
engravings: Civil War through 1897. Send
want list.

SAVAS PUBLISHING CO.
800-848-6585
1475 S Bascom Ave Ste 204
Campbell CA 95008-0629
Original books. Features battles &
Ccmpaigns, unit histories, & quarterly journal -
Civil War Regiments. Free catalog.

THE SINGLE SHOT EXCHANGE MAGAZINE
803-628-5326 Phone & Fax
singleshotex@earthlink.net
Dept B
PO Box 1055
York SC 29745-1055
Monthly magazine for black powder cartridge,
silhouette & Schuetzen shooters, & antique
gun collectors. Buy/sell/trade, historical &
how-to articles. Antique & classic firearms
only - $27.50/yr. V/MC accepted.

SMOKE & FIRE CO.
800-766-5334 • 419-832-0303
419-832-5008 Fax
http://www.smoke-fire.com
dmeyers@smoke-fire.com
PO Box 166
Grand Rapids OH 43522-0166

Monthly newspaper lists upcoming living history events, all time periods. Good Civil War section. Fine articles, news & great cartoons. $18/yr. Sample - $2.

SOUTHERN PARTISAN CORP.
PO Box 11708 • Columbia SC 29211-1708
Quarterly magazine dedicated to renewing sectional consciousness among Southerners. Interesting reading from the Southern view. $18/yr.

TOY SOLDIERS & COLLECTIBLES
301-898-7686 evenings
Larry Riggles
PO Box 301 • Libertytown MD 21762-0301
Full-color quarterly magazine for plastic toy soldier collectors. Annual subscription - $18.95 ppd. Overseas & Canadian rates available. Sample copy - $5.95 ppd.

THE TRANS-MISSISSIPPI NEWS
800-204-2407 • 319-339-5964 Fax
Camp Pope Bookshop
PO Box 2232
Iowa City IA 52244

Quarterly newsletter devoted to study of Civil War west of the Mississippi River. Subs. - $15/yr.

JOHN WILLS
410-574-0771
11 Right Wing Dr
Baltimore MD 21220
Complete selection of original Civil War-dated issues of *Harper's Weekly*.

WOMEN'S HISTORY MAGAZINE
800-435-9610
PO Box 1776
Mount Morris IL 61054-0398
Magazine from Cowles History Group, focusing on women in history.

ZACH'S PUBLICATION CO.
92 Woodside Ave
Winthrop MA 02152-2901
Letters of the Civil War - quarterly publication. Letters describe camp life, battles, & engagements. Subscription -$18/yr. Also "Massachusetts During the Civil War" monthly newsletter. Subscription $6/yr.

AMERICANA MERCANTILE
PO Box 4066
Hastings MN 55033-7066
American History books, documents, maps, & more. Adults/children. Fun, educational products, gifts.

ANTIQUARIAN BOOKS & MAPS
800-748-9946
109 S Church St • PO Box 168
Halls TN 38040-0168
Largest catalog of authentic Civil War maps & graphics. More than 1300 items, including manuscript, battle plans, etc. Catalog/list - $10 (ref.).

ANTIQUE AMERICANA
PO Box 19
Abington MA 02351-0019
Colonial American & Civil War documents, books, autographs, maps. Reasonably priced.

ARMISTEAD CIVIL WAR COLLECTIONS
310-280-3507
310-472-6081 Fax
8306 Wilshire Blvd Ste 684
Beverly Hills CA 90211-2382
Authentic 19th-century CW map engravings - extremely rare. Civil War-related art.

BENNETT'S
800-825-8622
3914 Broadway St
Galveston TX 77550-3822
Hand-carved granite campaign maps of Vicksburg, Gettysburg, & Shenandoah.

CHARTIFACTS
804-272-7120
PO Box 8954
Richmond VA 23225-0654
Antique historic coast survey maps of the 1800s. Most U.S. sea ports, shores. Reprints. Illus. lists - $1. Specify area.

CIVIL WAR MAP CO.
888-745-5762
22892 Cobb House Rd
Middleburg VA 20117-3022
Reproduction map of "Battlefield of Antietam" - 17"x19". $25 (unframed) ppd.; $120 (framed) ppd. Left corner inscription - "...presented to Gen RoELee by J.E.B. Stuart."

COLLIER MAPPING
113 Mirandy Ct
Bridgewater VA 22812
Detailed maps of battles/engagements in the Shenandoah Valley. Free catalog.

DOSS BOOKS
PO Box 660194
Birmingham AL 35266-0194
Civil War books & maps. Many out-of-print or rare. List -$1.

FULCRUM PUBLISHING
303-277-1623
303-279-7111 Fax
fulcrum@concentric.net
Promotions Mgr.
350 Indiana St Ste 350
Golden CO 80401-5093
Publisher of books & calendars including *Mapping the Civil War*, collection of rare maps from the Library of Congress. Free catalog.

GETTYSBURG NMP BOOKSTORE
800-JULY 3 1863
717-334-1891 Fax
Robert Housch
Visitor Center - Electric Map
95 Taneytown Rd
Gettysburg PA 17325
Complete Civil War bookstore specializing in books, tapes, CDs & videos. Free catalog.

THE HISTORIAN'S GALLERY
770-522-8383
770-522-8388 Fax
http://www.nr-net.com/history/
history@atl.mindspring.com
3232 Cobb Pkwy Ste 207
Atlanta GA 30339
Brokers & dealers in maps, autographs, selected relics.

MURRAY HUDSON - ANTIQUARIAN BOOKS & MAPS
800-748-9946 • 901-836-9057
901-836-9017 Fax
mapman@usit.net
109 S Church St
PO Box 163
Halls TN 38040-0163
Large selection of Civil War authentic maps & prints. 1300+ items (priced $25-$7,500). Also, rare Forrest bust. Catalog - $10 (ref.).

DEBORAH LAMBERT
1945 Lorraine Ave
Mc Lean VA 22101-5331
Slavery documents, CW newspapers, prints, letters, autographs, battle maps. List - $1.

LOUDOUN MUSEUM SHOP
703-777-8331
14 Loudoun St SW
Leesburg VA 20175-2907

Visit our shop located in restored 1767 log cabin. Unique gift items include historic maps, books & hand-crafted gifts by local artisans.

MAPS OF ANTIQUITY
PO Box 569P
Montclair NJ 07042-0569
19th-century historical & decorative authentic antique maps. Catalog - $3.

MC ELFRESH MAP CO.
716-372-8801
Earl & Michiko McElfresh
309 N Union St
PO Box 565
Olean NY 14760-0565
Detailed watercolor maps showing crops, orchards, fences, farms, residences, ground cover & woodlands. Pea Ridge, Antietam, Shiloh, Gettysburg, Chancellorsville (incl. Fredericksburg & Salem Church), Manassas & Cedar Mountain. From $8.95. Free product & price list.

JOHN S. MOSBY HERITAGE AREA
540-687-6681
PO Box 1178
Middleburg VA 20118-1178
Maps of Mosby Heritage Area - $20. Audiotape driving tour "Prelude to Gettysburg" - $17. Free "Drive Through History" brochure.

SUSAN A. NASH
304-876-3772
PO Box 1011
Shepherdstown WV 25443-1011
Paper conservation. Specialist in historic documents, photographs, prints, drawings, maps, letters, broadsides. Cleaning, mending, deacidification, museum matting. By appt.

NORTHERN MAP CO.
800-314-2474
PO Box 129
Dunnellon FL 34430-0129
Maps from the Civil War. Old state, city, railroad, & county maps, 70-120 years old, & map kits. Free catalog.

OLD FAVORITES BOOKSHOP
3055 Lauderdale Dr
Richmond VA 23233-7800
Civil War, WWII, other military books, prints & maps. Free catalog on request. (See ad page 242)

DON PITCHER
PO Box 64
North Haven CT 06473-0064
Offering original wood engravings as removed from Civil War-period newspapers. Locations, battles, leaders, maps, etc. Free catalog/list.

JEFFEREY M. RIGBY, CONSERVATOR
518-828-5929 Phone & Fax
167 Route 25
Hudson NY 12534
Preservation of paper documents - letters, muster rolls, maps, broadsides, etc. Satisfaction guaranteed. AIC guidelines followed by professional associate with more than 20 yrs. experience. Free catalog.

DAVID B. ROBINSON
PO Box 35926
Richmond VA 23235-0926
Complete listing of every engagement in Virginia referenced to the Official Records. 79 pp. - $12 ppd.

TEMPEST BOOKS
519-736-8629 • 888-233-5666
519-736-8620 Fax
235 Dalhousie
Amherstburg, Ontario N9V 1W6 CANADA
New books for old ideas. Military, naval, costuming, fiction, reference. Maps for campaign planning.

TRAILHEAD GRAPHICS, INC.
800-390-5117 • 303-766-7015
303-766-7108 Fax
trlhead@dimensional.com
PO Box 472991
Aurora CO 80047-2991
Full-color, detailed Civil War battlefield maps. Show all monuments, markers & tablets; essential visitor information. Custom mapping available.

WRITE-TO-PRINT
PO Box 177
Sandy Creek NY 13145-0177
Extensive photos of men & battles. Maps showing placement of the regiments in battles, 24th, 81st, 110th, 147th, 184th NYV Infantry & 24th Cavalry, their stories - $20.

A TO Z HOBBY CENTER
718-486-5390
543 Bedford Ave Ste 163
Brooklyn NY 11211-8511
Miniatures by Marx, Timpo, MPC, etc. Painted
& unpainted. Mail order only.

MIKE ALLEN MINIATURES
816-523-0447
Mike Allen
10407 Blue Ridge Blvd Ste 524
Kansas City MO 64134-1916
54mm Civil War generals - Cleburne,
Sheridan, Polk, etc. Kits.

ALTUS INTERNATIONAL, LTD.
612-922-6948
5609 Interlachen Cir
Edina MN 55436
Civil War chess set - wooden, hand-carved,
painted, lacquered. Historically accurate.
Board is plate glass with beveled edges. Ea.
player stands 6-1/2" tall.

AMERICA'S COVERED BRIDGES
PO Box 516 • Lightfoot VA 23090-0516
22-piece collection of replicas, incl. "Old
Humpback Bridge," a covered bridge saved
from destruction by a negotiated agreement
between Union & Confederate forces. $45 ea.
Write for complete list.

AMERICAN REMEMBERS
1019 24th St
Portsmouth OH 45662-2821
54mm miniature sets mounted on oak base.
More info. - send SASE.

ARMIES IN MINIATURE
1745 Tradewinds Ln
Newport Beach CA 92660-4313
Almond, Andrea, Cheshire, Chotasahib,
Hornet, Mil-Art, Tiny Troopers, Tradition 30,
etc. Catalog - $2.

BONNIE'S GIFT WORLD OF PRODUCTS
800-650-5350 • 619-789-6485
619-789-1551 Fax • Bgwhp@aol.com
Keith Bonney
117 Los Banditos Dr
PO Box 1978 • Ramona CA 92065-1978
Complete line of 54mm soldiers & sets as well
as sculptures, casting molds, kits, corgi
vehicles, ships, prints, etc. Catalog - $3.

BUSSLER MINIATURES
PO Box 188 • Hanover MA 02339-0188
Unpainted Civil War metal soldiers. 54mm
scale shown in a 10 pp., illus. catalog - $3.

CENTRAL GEORGIA CASTING
3445 Osborne Pl
Macon GA 31204-1843
Hand-painted/unpainted miniatures. Fast
service, custom work. Reenactor miniatures
from photograph. Sample infantry figure,
brochure & $5 credit - send $5.75 for 25 mm
or $9.75 for 54 mm. Brochure only - $2.

CLASSIC TOY SOLDIERS, INC.
913-451-9458 • 413-533-5266 (Jim McGough)
913-451-2946 Fax
David Payne
11528 Canterbury Cir
Leawood KS 66211-2917
Accurate Civil War sets, Union & Confederate.
Many other items. America's leading
manufacturer & distributor of fine quality toy
soldiers. Complete list of all playsets - $2.

COASTAL ENTERPRISES
PO Box 1053 • Brick NJ 08723-0108
Create an army - molds & casting supplies.
Mold catalog -$3. Metal casting catalog - $3.
Russian figure catalog - $2.

DAVID COEN, LTD.
318-345-5450
508 McCain Dr
Monroe LA 71203
Hand-painted Civil War miniatures & historical
dioramas, museum quality. Catalog - $3 +
large SASE.

COLLECTORS SERVICES
419-884-1377
PO Box 742
Westerville OH 43086-0742
1/35 scale figurines, dioramas. Oak display
cases - custom sizes available.

THE COLONIAL CONNECTION
757-229-1499 Phone & Fax
Eric Grosfils
226 Warehams Pt
Williamsburg VA 23185-8923
Hinchliffe 25mm historically accurate flags &
military miniatures, painted or unpainted -
imported from England. Free catalog.

THE DUNKEN CO.
409-364-2020
PO Box 95
Calvert TX 77837-0095
Lead soldier molds, Civil War, WWI & II.
Cannons, ancients, fantasy, Britains, 1776,
etc. Molds $7-$15. Kits $19-$35. Include $2
S&H. Free catalog.

DUTKINS' COLLECTIBLES
609-428-9559 • 609-428-9640 Fax
http://www.dutkins.com
1019A Route 70 W
Cherry Hill NJ 08002-3530
Molds to cast 25 mm & 54 mm figures. Civil War, Indian Army, British, Zulu, etc. Catalog - $5.

F. J. AUTHENTICS
703-361-0925
9514 Country Roads Ln
Manassas VA 20112-2779
Custom, hand-painted Civil War figures. 90 mm pewter. Small diorama setting on wooden plaque. Free catalog.

ANTHONY FERRAGAM
1574 N Jerusalem Rd
Merrick NY 11566-1210
54mm metal toy soldiers. Civil War, Napoleonic, Rev. War, Zulus, Indians, Cavalry, Bengal Indians, WW II, Knights, etc.

FORPRIN ENTERPRISES, INC.
PO Box 371 • Nashua NH 03061-0371
Finest hand-painted historical miniatures from Russia. 54mm/90mm. Ancient Greeks to U.S. Civil War. Painted/unpainted. Color catalog - $3.

FRASER INTERNATIONAL
800-878-5448
5990 North Belt E # 606
Humble TX 77396
Detailed miniature sculpture of Stone Mountain memorial. Hand-crafted in Scotland, licensed by the state of Georgia. $39.50 + $4.50 S&H.

G & H STERLING INC., LTD.
8362 Pines Blvd Ste 290
Pembroke Pines FL 33024-6600
Precision molded figurines, hand-finished with antique pewter.

GHQ
800-BUY-1945
28100 Woodside Rd
Excelsior MN 55331-7951
Infantry, cavalry, artillery, siege guns, mortars, etc. 10mm by Rebellion, pewter. Free catalog.

GREYSTONE'S HISTORY EMPORIUM & GALLERY
717-338-0631 • 717-338-0851 Fax
http://www.GreystoneOnline.com
461 Baltimore St
Gettysburg PA 17325-2623

Producers of CW Journal have created a store, gallery & museum. Military miniatures, books, videos, collectibles, art, exhibits, story theatre. Unique merchandise.

HISTORICAL MINIATURES BY GEORGE GRASSE
760-944-7877 • 760-481-7550 Fax
HISTOMIN@aol.com
1573 Pacific Ranch Dr
Encinitas CA 92024-5509
Professional, hand-painted, museum-quality, military miniatures - 54mm & up. Civil War catalog - $4.

IMRIE-RISLEY MINIATURES, INC.
518-885-6054 • 518-885-0100 Fax
PO Box 89
Burnt Hills NY 12027-0089
Celebrating 50th year of model-making. 54mm pewter kits of Civil War soldiers, leaders, cavalry & artillery. Catalog -$6.

J & B, INC.
910-674-2999
520 Hwy 62 E • Pleasant Garden NC 27313
Fine quality, hand-painted resin Civil War figurines. List -$1 (ref.).

J & L MINIATURES
269 W Gates Ave
Lindenhurst NY 11757-4536
CW 54mm metal figures, painted or unpainted. Among the finest available. Free photo-illus. catalog.

MR. K PRODUCTS
Michael G. Kovacevich
Dept B
PO Box 5234
Fairlawn OH 44334-0234
CIVIL WAR SOLDIERS! 1/32 & 1/72 scale soft plastic, infantry, cavalry, artillery, accessories. Catalog - $1.

DENNIS KATALLO
323 Sioux Ln
Carol Stream IL 60188
Handpainted Civil War figures, individual pieces to dioramas. Brochure - send large SASE.

LANDMARK CREATIONS, INC.
621 NW 53rd St Ste 240
Boca Raton FL 33487-8291
Official Fort Sumter model kit. Realistic, full color. Assembles to 2.5'x2'x 8". Pre-cut & pre-scored. $14.95 + $3 S&H.

THE LAST SQUARE
800-750-4401
http://www.lastsquare.com
questions@lastsquare.com
5944 Odana Rd
Madison WI 53719
Dedicated to military history. Gaming
supplies, miniatures, books, fine prints. Call
for info.

MAGNUM CREATION
310-659-3077
835 S Wooster Ste 315
Los Angeles CA 90035
Original sculptured soldiers, 6"-12" tall, Civil
War & WWI. Certificate with ea. $39.95.

MARCH THROUGH TIMES
702-972-4022 Fax
1530 Pass Dr
Reno NV 89509
Toy soldiers, new & old. Color catalog - $5.

MARK MINIATURES
PO Box 683
Rehoboth MA 02769-0683
Miniatures from ancient times to WWI.
Military, wheeled vehicles, hand-painted
54mm metal. Catalog - $3 w/ SASE.

MICHIGAN TOY SOLDIER CO.
248-586-1022
248-398-6367 Fax
http://www.michtoy.com
otr@mich.com
Rick Berry
401 S Washington
Royal Oak MI 48067
World's best selection of Civil War toy soldiers
& figure kits. Buy/sell old toy soldiers, too! 92+
pp. catalog - $5 (ref.).

MILITARY MINIATURES
219-347-1565
The Pyles
PO Box 132
Kendallville IN 46755-0132
Hand-painted, exquisite miniatures. All wars
available; CW specialists, Indian Wars
included. List & pictures - send SASE.

MILITARY MITES
301-770-1135
301-778-6254 Fax
PO Box 2324
Rockville MD 20847-2324
Civil War action miniatures, plastic, hand-
painted, Union & Confederate. Catalog - $3.

MILITARY SHOPPE
308 Westwoods
Amherst OH 44001-2051
Bicorne miniatures, 25mm. Include Zouave in
Kepis, Union Infantry, Limbers, Louisiana
Tigers, etc. 30 figures/pack - $21. Sample/list
- $2.

MR. MINIATURE
4096 Pavia Ln
Spring Hill FL 34606-2263
Supplies wargaming needs from pre-painted
armies to painting the figures you don't have
time for. Books, rules, figures & accessories.
Catalog - $2.

MODEL EXPO, INC.
Mount Pocono Industrl Park
PO Box 1000
Tobyhanna PA 18466-1000
Video catalog of historic ship model kits.
Video & color catalog - $5.

MODELERS MART
800-223-5260
http://www.pageworld.com/modelersmart
1555 Sunshine Dr
Clearwater FL 34525
15 & 25 mm Civil War & other era metal
figures. Catalog -$5 (applicable to 1st order).

MUSKET MINIATURES, LLC
Dept. BJ
PO Box 1976
Broomfield CO 80038-1976
15mm & 22mm cast metal infantry, cavalry,
artillery, & wagons. Also, camp, hospital,
headquarters & army sets. Buildings, tents,
fortifications, & wide range of scenery &
accessories. Illus. catalog - $3 (ref.).

NORTHCOAST MINIATURES
707-443-8915
Bob & Judiann O'Connell
311 Boyle Dr
Eureka CA 95503-6403
Hand-painted 54mm metal Civil War wagons,
cannons, and figures, Victorian & Napoleonic
figures, Victorian wagons. Catalog - $1.

OZARK ARTS ASSOCIATION
OzarkArts@aol.com
PO Box 165
Rogers AR 72757-0165
Join our collectors' club to purchase
hand-crafted & painted 8" sculptures of Civil
War soldiers. Illus. brochure - $1 (ref. w/
purchase).

THE POTOMAC GALLERY
800-882-1861 • 703-771-8085
703-771-8161 Fax
17 S King St
Leesburg VA 20175-2903
Hand-painted pewter Civil War chess set.
Limited editions by Stivers, Kunstler, Gallon,
Strain, Troiani & more. Custom framing done
on site. (See ad page 229)

REGIMENTAL COLLECTIBLES
801-947-9100
PO Box 685
Sandy UT 84091-0685
CW 54mm metal miniatures. Complete line of
infantry, Zouaves, cavalry, artillery, gens.,
mortars, cannons, limbers, caissons. Various
action poses, incl. casualties. Painted &
unpainted. Catalog - $3.

ROCHESTER CHESS CENTER
800-ON-CHESS
Civil War chess sets. Grant & Lee 5" tall!
Choose from various styles.

RORY'S REGIMENTS
412-347-3153
Rory Biggins
3950 Windsor Ct
Hermitage PA 16148
54mm cast military figures, custom painted to
your branch or regiment.

ROUND TOP MINIATURES
301-330-3552
7766 Epsilon Dr
Rockville MD 20855
Painted miniatures 15mm-120mm. Custom,
shadow box & museum dioramas - realistic &
historically accurate; ea. is unique with
custom-designed figures. Catalog - $2 (ref.).

**SARATOGA SOLDIER SHOP & MILITARY
BOOKSTORE**
518-885-1497
518-885-0100 Fax
831 Route 67 Ste 40
Ballston Spa NY 12020
1000 54mm pewter soldiers, cavalry & artillery
kits. Civil War & other eras, paints, modelers'
aids, & booklist. Catalog - $6.

SCENIC EFFECTS, INC.
510-235-1955
510-235-9901 Fax
Wendy Schuldt
PO Box 332
Point Richmond CA 94807-0332

Ltd. ed. of historically accurate buildings, ea.
handmade. Some include figures & are hand-
painted; unpainted available. Catalog/listing -
send SASE.

SCOTTY'S SCALE SOLDIERS
517-892-6177
1008P Adams St • Bay City MI 48708-5812
Miniatures from more than 50 manufacturers.
6mm to 30mm catalog - $6. 54mm to 125mm
catalog - $5. Both catalogs - $10.

JACK SCRUBY'S TOY SOLDIERS
805-927-3805
789 Main St • PO Box 1658M
Cambria CA 93428-1658
54mm & 40mm traditional toy soldiers.
Tru-craft, Britains & Eriksson repros, painted
& unpainted. Catalog - $1.

SHAMROCK & THISTLE
1119 San Francisco St NE
Olympia WA 98506-4133
High-quality Civil War 54mm figures. Painted
& unpainted. Catalog - $2.

SHENANDOAH MINIATURES
011-61-3-9534-1443 Phone & Fax
Paul Clarke
12 Holywood Grove
Carnegie Vic 3163 Australia
54mm ACW metal model soldier kits.
World-wide mail order. Catalog - $7.50.

SHIPS & SOLDIERS
603-742-1886
PO Box 912
Dover NH 03820-0912
Antique-toy-style toy soldiers, boats, etc.
Brochure - $2.

R.J. SIMARD
PO Box 514
Bristol RI 02809-0514
Custom-made ornamental 6" Civil War dolls
made to your specifications. $10 ea. (send
detailed description or snapshot). Civil War
drum pins, enameled red, white & blue - $10
ea. Catalog - $2 (deductible).

SLAVIN'S GALLERY
800-448-9517 • 910-346-4105
http://slavin.onslowonline.net
201 Country Club Rd
Jacksonville NC 28546-6400
Finest illustrated Civil War history available.
Fine art prints; original & ltd. eds. Sculptures;
1/8 & 1/4 scale model CS Artillery.

SPITZ MOUNTAIN ENTERPRISES
Steven Spitz
3013 S Washington St
Naperville IL 60540
Great generals & legendary heroes. Wooden
military collectibles. Hand-carved & crafted.
Authentically detailed. Grant, Lee, Jackson,
Custer, Stuart, many more. $49.95 ea. Color
brochure. Catalog - $2.50 (ref.).

STAD'S
905 Harrison St
Allentown PA 18103-3188
Original figures by Airfix, Marx, Tim Mee,
BMC, etc. Catalog - $2 for 3 mo.

STUEMPFLE'S MILITARY MINIATURES
717-762-0825
13190 Scott Rd
Waynesboro PA 17268-9023
Over 200 resin kits, bunkers & conversions in
1/7s & 1/76. Leva, B P Cast, Crusader,
Revell, 54mm kits, war games. Catalog - $3.

TARA HALL, INC.
800-205-0069 Phone & Fax
http://www.ncweb.com/biz/blackhawk
tarahall@earthlink.net
Vic Olney
PO Box 2069
Beach Haven NJ 08008-0109
Meagher's Irish Brigade, Fighting 69th,
Corcoran's Irish Legion memorabilia, shirts,
jackets, hats, sweaters, steins, pins, flags,
books, miniatures, poster, belt buckles,
NINAs, etc. Free catalog. (See ad page 232)

THOMAS' TIN SOLDIERS
152 W 26th St Apt 36
New York NY 10001-6825
Hand-painted pewter figurines in 54mm, flag
bearers, gloss finish - $42.95 ea.

THOROUGHBRED FIGURES
3833 Buckhorn Pl
Virginia Beach VA 23456-4927
Ship models (1/600 scale) - antiques,
assembled on walnut base. Send SASE for
more info.

TOMTE TOWNE
717-337-3717
22 Baltimore St
Gettysburg PA 17325
I/R military miniatures. Full-line dollhouse &
miniature collectable shop.

THE TOY SOLDIER CO.
201-433-2370
201-433-0909 Fax
100 Riverside Dr
New York NY 10024
Largest mail order resource of old & new
plastic & lead toy soldiers. Illus., 90-pp.
catalog - $3 ea., $12/yr. (6 issues).

TOY SOLDIERS & COLLECTIBLES
301-898-7686 evenings
Larry Riggles
PO Box 301
Libertytown MD 21762-0301
Full-color quarterly magazine for plastic toy
soldier collectors. Annual subscription -
$18.95 ppd. Overseas & Canadian rates
available. Sample copy - $5.95 ppd.

TRADITION, USA
Miriam
12924 Viking Dr
Burnsville MN 55337-3524
World's largest range of figures, 25mm to
110mm. Traditional model soldiers cast in
white metal. Available in kit form or painted.
250-pg catalog - $10.

RON WALL MINIATURES
800-445-0544 • 601-388-1707
601-388-0114 Fax
http://www.RonWall.com
768 Sharon Hills Dr
Biloxi MS 39532
Est. 1975; oldest American toy soldier
company. Historically accurate, 54mm, hand-
painted, original pewter figures depicting the
Civil War era.

WARWICK MINIATURES, LTD.
603-431-7139 Phone & Fax
PO Box 1498
Portsmouth NH 03802-1498
Toy soldiers, solid cast 54mm metal, hand-
painted in historically accurate color. More
than 100 different sets from the Revolution to
Civil War to Prussian, etc. Catalog - $4.

YOST ENTERPRISES
419-869-7082
276 State Route 42
Polk OH 44866
Hand-painted pewter miniatures, Union &
Confederate, 15mm. Other time periods.
Complete list - $1 + SASE.

THE CIVIL WAR GARRISON
PO Box 1681
Springfield IL 62705-1681
Will research the veteran you designate &
write his personal story in the War Between
the States, or produce a Civil War plaque of
his experiences.

CONFEDERATE ARTS
8301 Alvord St Dept. C
Mc Lean VA 22102-1736
Great Seal of the Confederacy minted in
exact detail in solid bronze. Limited ed. -
$69.95.

ERIE LANDMARK COMPANY
800-874-7848 • 703-818-2157 Fax
4449 Brookfield Corporate Dr
Chantilly VA 20151-1692
Bronze & aluminum markers for indoor &
outdoor use. National register plaques,
custom worded. From medallions to roadside
markers. Free brochure.

NESTA HARPER
PO Box 44 • Aldie VA 20105-0044
19th-century engravings of Civil War leaders
& battle scenes. Hand-tinted & signed by
artist. 9x12 - $11.95 ea. + $3.60 S&H. Price
list - send SASE.

HRM & COMPANY, INC.
800-511-3864
http://www.apex-ephemera.com
hrmco@praxis.net
PO Box 775 • Silver Springs FL 34489-0775
Civil War engravings - more than 1,000
original hand-colored newspaper engravings -
$55 & up.

W. E. JACKSON & COMPANY
401-232-3570 Fax
PO Box 3842
North Providence RI 02911-0042
Civil War engravings, awards. Series of 3D
embossed notecards from handcut dies. Lee,
Jackson, Meade, artillery action, etc. 10 cards
& envelopes per box.

LOOK BACK IN TIME
803-986-9097 • 803-986-9297 Fax
PO Box 572 • Port Royal SC 29935-0572
Civil War newspapers, engravings, books,
relics, & much more. Want lists welcome.
Free catalog.

MOUNTAIN MAGIC IN METAL
719-486-8166
517 W Chestnut St
Leadville CO 80461
Pictures engraved on zinc plates, taken from
original photos. Lincoln, Grant, Lee ($295 ea.)
or Gettysburg Address ($375). S&H - $25.
Custom photographic engraving.

NORTHROAD & COMPANY
PO Box 554
Groton MA 01450-0554
Historical markers, house numbers,
residential & small business signs. Wooden.
Exceptional quality, reasonable prices.

ORIGINAL FRAMEWORKS
800-654-1861 • 540-953-1655
civilwar@nrv.net
Jay Rainey
Gables Shopping Center
1300 S Main St
Blacksburg VA 24060-5526
All Civil War artists at discount; signatures,
documents, 19th-century steel engravings,
relics. Will find any artwork. Always looking to
purchase. Also at 4 E Washington St,
Lexington, Va. (See ad page 232)

MICHAEL PINCUS
PO Box 839
Chesterland OH 44026-0839
Custom engraving by N-SSA Metal Engraver.
Civil War patterns, slogans, names, etc. On
your repro knives, swords. $25-$50 most
pieces.

DON PITCHER
PO Box 64
North Haven CT 06473-0064
Offering original wood engravings as removed
from Civil War-period newspapers. Locations,
battles, leaders, maps, etc. Free catalog/list.

POWDER HORNS
PO Box 397
Fletcher OH 45326-0397
Make powder horns from start to finish,
including engraving them for your use, gifts,
display, or sale - $12.95.

ALABAMA CONSTITUTION VILLAGE
205-535-6564
109 Gates Ave Se • Huntsville AL 35801-4212
19th-century living history museum. Specialty
shops.

**ALABAMA DEPT. OF ARCHIVES &
HISTORY**
334-242-4363 • 334-242-4435
http://www.asc.edu/archives/agis.html
624 Washington Ave
Montgomery AL 36130-0100

AMHERST COUNTY HISTORICAL MUSEUM
804-946-9860
PO Box 741
301 S Main St
Amherst VA 24521-0741

ATLANTA HISTORY CENTER
404-814-4000
http://www.atlhist.org
Gordon Jones
130 W Paces Ferry Rd NW
Atlanta GA 30305-1366
Turning Point - most comprehensive CW
exhibition in the Southeast. More than 1,200
objects, with photos, videos & environments,
tell story of war through eyes of soldiers &
civilians.

BALTIMORE CIVIL WAR MUSEUM
410-385-5188
410-385-5189 Fax
601 President St
Baltimore MD 21202
Occupies 1850 President Street Station of the
Philadelphia, Wilmington & Baltimore RR.
Interprets Baltimore's role in the Underground
RR, Pratt Street Riot of 1861 & the Civil War
as a whole.

BARDSTOWN CIVIL WAR MUSEUM
502-349-0291 • 502-348-5204
310 E Broadway
Bardstown KY 40004
Hundreds of authentic artifacts of the Civil
War.

**CAMP MOORE CONFEDERATE MUSEUM
& CEMETERY**
504-229-2438
70640 Camp Moore Rd
PO Box 25
Tangipahoa LA 70465
440 of Camp Moores soldiers buried in
cemetery. Museum contains artifacts from the
camp, which was destroyed by Union forces
in 1864. Walking tours offered.

CHARLES COUNTY
800-766-3386
PO Box B • La Plata MD 20646
Historic inn with visitors like John Wilkes
Booth. Dr. S.A. Mudd's house. Rolling
meadows, forests, coastline, & Maryland
seafood. Bird watching guide available.

THE CHARLESTON MUSEUM
803-722-2996
360 Meeting St • Charleston SC 29403-6297
Harbor & land tours, reenactments. Nationally
recognized speakers. Period music. Call or
write for upcoming events, exhibits, tours, &
more. Free brochure.

CIVIL WAR LIBRARY & MUSEUM
215-735-8196
215-735-3812 Fax
Steven J. Wright, Curator
1805 Pine St
Philadelphia PA 19103
America's oldest chartered Civil War
institution. 3 floors of exhibits, including
uniforms, flags, weapons, & fine art, as well
as special exhibits. Open Wed-Sun
11am-4:30pm. Small admission fee.

CIVIL WAR SOLDIERS MUSEUM
904-469-1900
Norman W. Haines, Jr., MD
108 S Palafox Pl
Pensacola FL 32501-5630
See artifacts from Ft. Sumter to Appomattox,
one of nation's largest displayed Civil War
medical collections; more than 600 book titles.
Catalog - $2.

THE CORINTH CIVIL WAR CENTER
601-287-9501
http://www.corinth.org/
civilwar@tsixroads.com
PO Box 45
Corinth MS 38835-0045
Offers 12-minute video of Corinth's role in the
Civil War. Walking/driving tour maps
available. Small gift shop.

**CORTLAND COUNTY HISTORICAL
SOCIETY, INC.**
607-756-6071
25 Homer Ave
Cortland NY 13045-2056
Hosts Suggett House Museum & Kellogg
Memorial Research Library. *A Regiment
Remembered: 157th New York Volunteers* -
Lt. William Saxton's diary, 157 pp. - $20 +
$3.40 S&H. NYS - add 8% sales tax.

DAUGHTERS OF UNION VETERANS OF THE CIVIL WAR
217-544-0616
http://suvcw.org/duv.htm
DUVCW@aol.com
503 S Walnut St
Springfield IL 62704-1932
Organization for female lineal descendants of Union veterans.

FORT DELAWARE SOCIETY
302-834-1630
PO Box 553 • 126 Sussex Ave
Delaware City DE 19706-0553
Co-sponsors reenactments, operates museum & gift shop. Involved in research & fund-raising.

FREDERICKSBURG AREA MUSEUM
540-371-3037
PO Box 922 • 907 Princess St
Fredericksburg VA 22401

FRONTIER DAYS CIVIL WAR REENACTMENT
515-573-4231
http://jsp.org/fort/
thefort@fortdodge.ia.frontiercomm.net
David Parker
Fort Museum
PO Box 1798
Fort Dodge IA 50501-1798
Annual reenactments at Fort Museum & Fort Dodge. Military ball, civilian impressions, family activities. Call for dates.

GAR MUSEUM & LIBRARY
215-289-6484
GARMUSLIB@aol.com
4278 Griscom St
Philadelphia PA 19124-3954
Museum opens 1st Sundays ea. month or by appt. GAR records, CW artifacts, extensive library. Admission - free. Inquiries welcome. Memberships - $15/yr.

THE GRAY & BLUE MUSEUM
1823 Clay St
Vicksburg MS 39180-3070
Features the world's largest collection of Civil War gunboat models.

GREYSTONE'S HISTORY EMPORIUM & GALLERY
717-338-0631
717-338-0851 Fax
http://www.GreystoneOnline.com
461 Baltimore St
Gettysburg PA 17325-2623

Producers of *CW Journal* have created a store, gallery & museum. Military miniatures, books, videos, collectibles, art, exhibits, story theatre. Unique merchandise.

HILL COLLEGE CONFEDERATE RESEARCH CENTER & MUSEUM
PO Box 619
Hillsboro TX 76645-0619
Civil War displays & exhibits; extensive collection of research material.

HISTORIC HAMPTON
800-800-2202 • 757-727-1102
http://www.hampton.va.us/tourism
710 Settlers Landing Rd
Hampton VA 23669-4035
Historic reenactments, world-class museums, Chesapeake Bay seafood, Fort Wool, Casemate Museum at Fort Monroe, new site on the Va. Civil War Trail. Minutes from Williamsburg. Free guide.

HISTORIC HUNTSVILLE DEPOT
205-535-6028
320 Church St
Huntsville AL 35801
Original 1860s train depot with Civil War exhibits & original wartime graffiti on wall. Specialty shop.

JEFFERSON DAVIS STATE HISTORIC SITE
912-831-2335 • 912-831-2060 Fax
338 Jeff Davis Park Rd
Fitzgerald GA 31750
Confederate memorial & museum, containing relics from a Ga. battle flag to rare uniforms. Davis family's capture at this site on May 10, 1865, marked official end of the Confederacy.

KATE GALLERY
652 Great Plain Ave
Needham MA 02192-3305
18th-20th century architecture, furniture & decorative art prints. Framed & unframed. Fine notecards. Illus. catalog - $2.

KENNESAW CIVIL WAR MUSEUM
http://www.ngeorgia.com/history/kcwm.html
Directions & contact info. Brief history of "the General," famous Civil War locomotive.

SGT. KIRKLAND'S MUSEUM & HISTORICAL SOCIETY, INC.
540-899-5565
540-899-7643 Fax
Civil-War@msn.com
912 Lafayette Blvd
Fredericksburg VA 22401-5617

Non-profit museum, association & press devoted to preservation of historical documents, artifacts, & texts; education; publication of meritorius books; & research & recovery of CW soldiers' records. Free catalog.

KURTZ CULTURAL CENTER
2 N Cameron St
Winchester VA 22601-4728
Welcome center for historic Winchester Civil War Information Center, Patsy Cline display, rotating exhibits. Open daily. (See ad page 229)

LOUDOUN MUSEUM SHOP
703-777-8331
14 Loudoun St SW
Leesburg VA 20175-2907
Visit our shop located in restored 1767 log cabin. Unique gift items include historic maps, books & hand-crafted gifts by local artisans.

MANASSAS MUSEUM & ASSOCIATES
703-368-1873
http://xroads.virginia.edu/~VAM/MAN/
        vamintro.html
janemriley@aol.com
PO Box 560 • 9101 Prince William St
Manassas VA 20108-0560
Non-profit organization dedicated to the support of the Manassas Museum System & its mission to preserve the rich heritage of the Northern Virginia Piedmont area.

THE MARINERS' MUSEUM
800-581-7245
100 Museum Dr • Newport News VA 23606
Chosen by NOAA as the official repository for items recovered from the *Monitor* wreck. Many other Civil War attractions less than an hour away.

MONTANA HISTORICAL SOCIETY MUSEUM
406-444-4710
225 N Roberts St • Helena MT 59620-1201

MOTTS MILITARY MUSEUM
614-836-5781
Warren Motts, Director
5761 Ebright Rd • Groveport OH 43125-9744
Civil War items & exhibits.

MUSEUM OF AMERICAN CAVALRY
540-740-3959
Peter & Jane Comtois
298 Old Cross Rd
New Market VA 22844-9511

History of the Horse Soldier from colonial times through Vietnam & modern times. Gift shop with books, flags, weapons, relics, other items. Formerly Indian Hollow Antiques.

MUSEUM OF AMERICAN FINANCIAL HISTORY
212-908-4519 • 212-908-4601 Fax
http://www,mafh.org
mafh1@pipeline.com
26 Broadway • New York NY 10004-1703
America, Money and War: Financing the Civil War. 42-pg illus. catalog of exhibit - $14.25 ppd. Education kit with slides - $49.95 ppd.

MUSEUM OF FRONTIER CULTURE
540-332-7850
PO Box 810 • 1250 Richmond Rd
Staunton VA 24401-0810

MUSEUM OF HISTORIC NATCHITOCHES
318-357-0070
840 Washington St
Natchitoches LA 71457-4728
The Forgotten March: the Red River Campaign. Video documenting the largest campaign west of the Mississippi. $22.50 ppd. (Proceeds benefit museum)

THE MUSEUM OF THE CONFEDERACY
804-649-1861 • 804-644-7150 Fax
http://www.moc.org/
Janene Charbeneau
1201 E Clay St • Richmond VA 23219-1615
Maintains most comprehensive collection of military, political & domestic artifacts & art associated with the Confederacy. Adjacent to White House of the Confederacy, restored to its CW appearance.

NATIONAL CIVIL WAR WAX MUSEUM
717-334-6245 • 717-334-9686 Fax
Tammy Myers
297 Steinwehr Ave
Gettysburg PA 17325-2815
Civil War museum appealing to young & old alike. Features causes & effects of war. Gift shop offers wide variety of CW memorabilia.

NATIONAL MUSEUM OF CIVIL WAR MEDICINE
301-695-1864 • 800-564-1864
301-695-6823 Fax
http://www.civilwarmed.org
LauraM@civilwarmed.org
JaNeen M. Smith, Ex. Dir.
48 E Patrick St
PO Box 470
Frederick MD 21705-0470

Center for study & interpretation of Civil War medical history. Medical artifacts, manuscripts, books & materials. 1861-1865. Museum store. Memberships available. Annual conference 1st weekend in August.

NEW MARKET BATTLEFIELD MILITARY MUSEUM
540-740-8065
540-740-3663 Fax
John Bracken
9500 Collins Dr
PO Box 1131
New Market VA 22844-1131
Comprehensive museum shop featuring CW relics, flags, uniforms, bullets, buttons, swords, muskets, currency, personal items, memorabilia, etc. More than 1200 book titles. Open Mar. 15-Dec. 1.

NEWPORT NEWS, VA
888-493-7386
Battlefield tours, historic houses, harbor tours, museum exhibits & living history events. Free visitor guide & Civil War tour brochure.

PAMPLIN PARK CW SITE
804-861-2408
http://www.pamplinpark.org
6523 Duncan Rd
Petersburg VA 23803-7449
Battlefield where in April 1865 Grant's forces "broke through" Confederate defenses, ending longest siege in US history. Pathways along original Confederate fortifications, interactive games. Tour a plantation house.

PEJEPSCOT HISTORICAL SOCIETY/ JOSHUA L. CHAMBERLAIN MUSEUM
207-729-6606
207-729-6012 Fax
http://www.Curtislibrary.com/pejepscot.htm
PEJEPSCOT@acornbbs.com
Erik C. Jorgenson, Dir.
159 Park Row
Brunswick ME 04011-2005
Historical Society operates the Joshua Chamberlain Museum located in Chamberlain's former home. Also maintains the most comprehensive Chamberlain research collection available anywhere. Free catalog.

PERRYVILLE CIVIL WAR RELICS & MUSEUM
Ken Hamilton & Dr. Craig Knox
302 Buell St
Perryville KY 40468

Authentic Civil War artifacts & collectibles, 1861-1865. Guns, swords, photographs, belt buckles, buttons, dug relics, etc.

ROANOKE VALLEY HISTORY MUSEUM GIFT SHOP
540-342-5772
PO Box 1904 • 1 Market Sq
Roanoke VA 24008-1904

SAVANNAH HISTORY MUSEUM
912-238-1779
303 Martin Luther King Jr Blvd
Savannah GA 31415-4217

SOLDIERS & SAILORS MEMORIAL
412-621-4253
4141 5th Ave • Pittsburgh PA 15213
Military history museum centering on Civil War, emphasizing Allegheny County. Uniforms, weapons, flags, GAR, more! Maintains library; gift shop. Civil War through Desert Storm displays.

SOLDIERS NATIONAL MUSEUM
717-334-4890 • 777 Baltimore St
Gettysburg PA 17325
Gen. Howard's headquarters during Battle of Gettysburg; later became orphanage. Exacting, detailed dioramas of major CW battles, using 5,000+ miniatures, actual headgear & weapons. Artifacts & sculptures.

SOUTH CAROLINA CONFEDERATE RELIC ROOM & MUSEUM
803-734-9813 • 803-734-9823 Fax
BMOFFAT@oir.state.sc.us
Bonnibel G. Moffat
920 Sumter St • Columbia SC 29201
SC military history from American Revolution through Desert Storm, with emphasis on Confederate era.

A.H. STEPHENS STATE HISTORIC PARK
706-456-2602
PO Box 283 • Crawfordsville GA 30631
Site of Liberty Hall, home to Vice-President of the Confederacy Stephens; Confederate Museum.

STONEWALL JACKSON HEADQUARTERS MUSEUM
540-667-3242 • WFCH@shentel.com
Todd Kern
415 N Braddock St
Winchester VA 22601-3921
Gen. Jackson used this home during the winter of 1861-62 to plan his famous "Valley Campaign."

STONEWALL JACKSON HOUSE
540-463-2552 • 540-463-4088 Fax
Michael A. Lynn
8 E Washington St.
Lexington VA 24450-2529
The Confederate general's only home with restored garden & museum shop. Tours every half hour Mon-Sat 9-5, Sun 1-5; last tour begins at 4:30PM. Open until 6PM June-August. Closed major holidays.

STONEWALL JACKSON MUSEUM AT HUPP'S HILL
540-465-5884 • 540-465-5999
540-465-8157 Fax
Babs Melton
PO Box 31 • US 11 North
Strasburg VA 22657-0031
Exhibits of Jackson's 1862 Valley Campaign with original artifacts & hands-on reproductions. Children's room has costumes, Civil War camp, & discovery boxes.

SURRATT HOUSE MUSEUM & GIFT SHOP
301-868-1121 • 301-868-8177 Fax
http://www.engr.umd.edu/~clwspoon/surratt.html
Laurie Verge, Director
PO Box 427 • 9118 Brandywine Rd
Clinton MD 20735-0427
1852 home of the Surratt family. Served also as a tavern, hostelry, post office & link in the Confederate spy network. Played role in Lincoln assassination. (See ad page 236)

UNITED STATES CAVALRY MUSEUM
PO Box 2160
Fort Riley KS 66442-0160
Relive the history of America's mounted soldiers. Fine art gallery, period & topical exhibits, dioramas, AV shows, limited edition prints, books. Gift shop, free admission. Catalog.

USS CAIRO MUSEUM
601-636-0583
3201 Clay St
Vicksburg MS 39180-3469

VALENTINE RIVERSIDE
800-365-7272
550 E Marshall St
Richmond VA 23219-1852
Richmond's innovative history park at the falls of the James River. Civil War tours, sound/light show, vintage carousel, high-tech exhibits, African-American history/tours, archeological digs, living history.

VIRGINIA HISTORICAL SOCIETY MUSEUM SHOP
804-342-9671 • 804-358-4901
PO Box 7311
428 North Blvd
Richmond VA 23221-0311

VIRGINIA WAR MUSEUM
757-247-8523
Huntington Park
9285 Warwick Blvd
Newport News VA 23607-1537
Discover America's military heritage. More than 60,000 artifacts from the Revolutionary War to Desert Storm. Galleries feature permanent exhibit on the Peninsula Campaign. Open daily - 9-5; Sunday - 1-5.

WARREN RIFLES CONFEDERATE MUSEUM
540-636-6982 • 540-635-2219
95 Chester St
Front Royal VA 22630-3368
Hours 9-4 Mon-Sat, 12-4 Sun. Open April 15-October 31. Admission fee.

WAYSIDE MUSEUM OF AMERICAN HISTORY
540-465-5884
540-465-5899 Fax
PO Box 440
Strasburg VA 22657-0440

WHEATON HISTORY CENTER
PO Box 373
Wheaton IL 60189-0373
Journal of Capt. Henry Whipple Chester: 2nd Ohio Volunteer Cavalry. Recollections of the War of the Rebellion. 200 pp., 97 illus., extensive index - $34.59 + $5 S&H.

WISCONSIN VETERANS MUSEUM & STORE
608-264-6086 • 608-266-1680
http://badger.state.wi.us/agencies/dva/museum/wvmmain. html
30 W Mifflin St
Madison WI 53703-2558
Authentic reproduction tinware from originals in our collection. Coffeepot, tin cups, canteens, etc. Blankets. Museum - 2 main galleries & various displays.

THE 2ND MARYLAND FIFES & DRUMS
PO Box 172 • Willow Hill PA 17271-0172
It's Those Marylanders Again!: Field Music of the Civil War - Cassette $10, CD $15; S&H $3. Group seen & heard in movie *Gettysburg*.

2ND SOUTH CAROLINA STRING BAND
717-337-3785
J. Ewers
1820 Old Harrisburg Rd
Gettysburg PA 17325-8119
Favorite campfire songs of the Civil War, North & South. New recording - *Southern Soldier*, $10 + $1.95 S&H.

37TH GEORGIA BAND
706-543-4559
766 Riverhill Dr • Athens GA 30606-4050
5 brass-band recordings - hymns, quicksteps, ballads, fife & drum music - all played on antique instruments in authentic 1860s style. Digital stereo on 60 min. cassettes. $13.50 ppd.

52ND TENNESSEE STRING BAND
901-685-6678
5088 Helene Rd
Memphis TN 38117
Authentic, professional 5-piece Civil War string band; variety of music for dances, balls, etc. Complete entertainment. *Voices of the Shiloh* - recent cassette.

5TH MICHIGAN REGT. BAND
http://www.mith.org
PO Box 170
Novi MI 48375-0170
Civil War field band available for reenactments, concerts, educational programs, parades, etc. Cassettes - $12 ea. ppd.; CDs - $17 ea. ppd.

97th REGIMENTAL STRING BAND
813-391-4565
PO Box 2208
Largo FL 33779-2208
Cassettes & CDs of the 80 most popular Civil War songs. Many vols. Coffee cups, T-shirts, & spoken history cassettes. Catalog - SASE.

ACLAMON MUSIC
716-654-9637
716-654-6613 Fax
singerdon@aol.com
PO Box 10098
Rochester NY 14610-0098
Battle Cry of Freedom. 20 favorite Civil War songs available on CD - $15, cassette - $10. *Grandfather's Clock* on cassette - $10.

BRIGADE BUGLER
609-589-3901
George Rabbai
PO Box 165
Pitman NJ 08071-0165
Civil War infantry bugle calls, book & cassette, $19.95 ppd. for set. *Teach Yourself How to Play the Bugle* - for all levels of buglers, incl. exercises, tonguing & lip flexibility. $8 ppd.

CAMELOT RECORDS
800-537-3839
cwsongbird@aol.com
Jan Kurtis or Susan Jacobson
6006 Barr Rd • Ferndale WA 98248-8747
Original & period Civil War music of Dave Mathews & Susan Jacobson set to spectacular reenactment footage. 3 soundtracks - cassettes $8, CDs $12; 4 videos - $15. S&H $3. Free catalog.

THE CAMP CHASE FIFES & DRUMS, INC.
PBFV68A@prodigy.com
Tom Kuhn
PO Box 461 • Groveport OH 43125-0461
150 years of US martial field music (1750-1900). 2 vols of Civil War music - $10 ea. ppd., $16 for both ppd.

DAN CHEATUM RECORDINGS
618-529-3038
616 Bakersfield Rd
Carbondale IL 62901-0641
90-min. cassettes recorded with 1850s Martin guitar, vocals, harmonica, mandolin, fiddle. Accompanying songbooks with guitar chords. Catalog.

CIVIL WAR DRUM & FLAG SHOWS
830-966-3480
Nancy Clayton
PO Box 153 • Utopia TX 78884-0153
Drum & flag storytelling performance for school assemblies, history & music classes (grades PK-college), teachers' meetings, conventions & living history events. Brochure - send SASE.

CONFEDERATE GRAY
615-320-1715
615-320-3272 Fax
Meeks Booker
PO Box 121984
Nashville TN 37212-1984
Hand-carved music boxes that play "Dixie" when opened; other tunes available. Named for great Southern leaders or battles. Refer to Source Book for 10% discount. Catalog - $2 (ref.).

DAL PRODUCTIONS, LTD.
212-496-7677
Presenting Clamma Dale, an award-winning
singing actress who has researched &
reacquaints her listeners with CW songs,
spirituals & poetry. *Unforgotten* - CD $15.98.

ELECTRIC QUILT MUSIC
http://www.equilt.com
PO Box 1314
Norcross GA 30091-1314
19-song cassette, by David Ray Skinner,
chronicles the wartime career of Conf. general
John Hunt Morgan. $10 + $2 S&H.

FIFE & DRUM TRADING CO.
378 N Lakeview Ave
Winter Garden FL 34787-2715
Authentic Civil War fife & drum tunes played
non-stop to a steady beat. Essential for
marching drills & parade use. Catalog - $3.

**HERITAGE MILITARY MUSIC
FOUNDATION, INC.**
504 S 4th St
Watertown WI 53094-4528
First Brigade Band recordings of CW music.
Cassettes & CDs. Write for complete listing.

HISTORIC IMAGES
606 Glenbrook Rd
Savannah GA 31419-2444
Confederate, minstrel music by James Lord
Pierpont, including "Strike for the South," "Our
Battle Flag." Original "Jingle Bells," etc.
Cassette - $6 ppd.

BOBBY HORTON
http://bizweb.lightspeed.net/~cwms
3430 Sage Brook Ln
Birmingham AL 35243-2046
Authentic music of the Civil War by Bobby
Horton. Cassette - $10/volume. CD - $15.
Write for list.

LOWELL JERENS
715-834-3938
639 Putnam Dr
Eau Claire WI 54701-3304
Civil War-era sheet music.

NATIVE GROUND MUSIC
800-752-2656
704-298-5607 Fax
http://www.circle.net/nativeground
banjo@circle.net
Wayne Erbsen
109 Bell Rd
Asheville NC 28805-1521

Civil War music performed in traditional style
on old-time instruments. Cassettes, CDs, &
songbooks focusing on 19th-cent. American
themes. Instruction books. Free catalog.

NORD-DISC RECORD COMPANY
517-631-4151 • 517-631-5571 Fax
W. Buechner
4407 Gladding Ct Ste 102
Midland MI 48640-3383
American Civil War, trilogy; *Flight of the
American Eagle*; *The Blue & the Gray*; & other
patriotic works - all symphony orchestra,
highest quality cassettes ($12.50 ref.) & CDs
($14.95 ref.). Catalog.

OLD DRUMS MADE NEW
301-824-5223
Tom Law
62 W Water St • Smithsburg MD 21783-1643
Authentic Civil War-style rope drums.
Men/boys - $250-$375. Old drums restored;
new drums made. Parts to fit any drum.

POPE MUSIC
800-469-4767
82 E Allendale Rd
Saddle River NJ 07458-3057
Clamma Dale, award-winning diva, sings
songs, hymns, spirituals, & poetry, both North
& South. CD or cassette.

POTOMAC THUNDER
410-549-7470
RLather@aol.com
Tom & Rosemary Lather
5081 Amantea Way • Sykesville MD 21784
Professional musicians will perform Civil War
music for reenactments, dances, weddings,
etc. Period music, fiddle & banjo tunes, &
classical music. 20+ yrs. experience;
references. (See ad page 239)

PUBLISHERS MARKETING
216 Roberts Ave
Bellmawr NJ 08031-2712
Treasury of Civil War songs. 25 of the best
songs, North & South, sung by balladeer Tom
Glazer. Cassette - $8.98, CD - $11.98 ppd.

THE REBELAIRES
912-285-8191
Dave Griffin
950 Sunset Ln
Waycross GA 31503-8030
Cassettes/CDs. *Carry the Memories On*, *For
the Cause*, and *Confederate Man*. Original
songs, old standards. $11/tape. Call for CD
prices. Ball, banquet, convention bookings.

RED DRAGON MUSIC DEN
304-267-0411
http://www.reddragonmusic.com
reddragn@reddragonmusic.com
J. T. Foultz
PO Box 1776
Martinsburg WV 25402-1776
Field drums, bagpipes, fifes, music tapes, CDs, books, & more. Free catalog.

RED TIE MUSIC & BOOKS
PO Box 3858
Ann Arbor MI 48106
The Civil War Fifer - songbook featuring favorite & lesser-known melodies, lyrics, histories & artwork - $12.95 + $2.50 S&H. Other songbooks & collections of lyrics & poetry.

RETURNING HEROES BALL
Patri & Barbara Pugliese
39 Capen St
Medford MA 02155-5824
Annual March ball featuring contra-dances, quadrilles, waltzes, polkas, & schottisches.

ROSE OF EL-A-NOY MINSTRELS
618-529-3038
Dan Cheatum
616 Bakersfield Rd
Carbondale IL 62901-0641
Authentic Historic String Band recordings, 4 vols, cassettes. Live performances & period military balls. Dan Cheatum recordings - 2 cassettes, 2 songbooks. Cassettes - $9.95 ppd. Catalog.

RSV PRODUCTS
johnson@net-info.com
Mark Johnson
PO Box 26
Hopkins MN 55343-0026
Buglers! Collections of printed music, recordings on cassette/CD, & authentic brass bugles. Free info. Try Basic Bugler package - book & cassette $9.99 ppd. Free catalog.

SHAMROCK HILL BOOKS
770-569-1802
770-569-1801 Fax
http://members.aol.com/historybks/bookpage.htm
HISTORYBKS@aol.com
Ed O'Dwyer
12725 Bethany Rd
Alpharetta GA 30004
Books on the Civil War with specialty in Irish participation. Kepis, music & more. Email credit card accounts welcome. Catalog.

SOUTHERN HORIZON
804-320-4680
minstral@aol.com
John Robison
2207 Wren's Nest Rd
Richmond VA 23235
Camp & parlor music of the Civil War, dance & vocal, 2 cassettes $10 ea. Nationally known music ensemble.

SPARX ECHO PRODUCTIONS
800-ECHOES-1
PO Box 880
Pasadena MD 21123-0880
In Spite of Reason, Pop Rock Opera, based on the life of Abraham Lincoln during the Civil War. 2 CDs & libretto -$29.95.

SPRING RIVER MUSIC
212-879-8424
Robert Trentham
Lenox Hill Station
PO Box 1408
New York NY 10021-0041
Epitaph: A Collection of Civil War Songs. Tenor Robert Trentham sings 14 heartfelt songs. CDs - $14.98 ea. + $2 S&H (ref.).

STALEY'S SUNDRIES
540-899-6464
540-373-2469 Fax
710 Caroline St
Fredericksburg VA 22401-5904
Largest collection of Civil War music anywhere. Military insignia, flags, hats, clothing, patterns, buttons, buckles, miniatures, books, magazines & gift items.

AL VASONE
PO Box 2252
Darien CT 06820-0252
Civil War songs, sung by Al Vasone. 6 cassettes - $9.50 ea.

THE WILDCAT REGIMENT BAND
167 Route 85
Home PA 15747
"Brass Band Music of the American Civil War," 70+ minutes of music, much never previously recorded. Cassette - $11.95, CD - $15.95; $1.75 S&H.

BRYAN WRIGHT
PO Box 07355
Detroit MI 48207-0355
CD, musical works dedicated to the 200,000 colored troops who fought for the restoration of the Union. "We go deal with the system." $18 ppd.

13TH VIRGINIA INFANTRY, CO. H
540-877-2483
Capt. David Melton
128 Susquehanna Trl
Winchester VA 22602
Members participate in battle reenactments, living history, camp & drill demonstrations, memorials/ceremonies/dedications & help preserve historical sites & Confederate battle flags. Recruits welcome & encouraged.

THE 17TH CONNECTICUT VOL. INFANTRY
407-295-7510
Maj. Jeff H. Grzelak
7214 Laurel Hill Rd • Orlando FL 32818-5233
Retrace the steps of the 17th Conn.; after 130 years, the regiment is once again on the march. Enlist today & see a part of U.S. history firsthand.

4TH NORTH CAROLINA REGT., CSA, INC.
410-526-4927
Stephen Bockmiller, Recruiter
101 Fitz Ct Unit 204
Reisterstown MD 21136-3327
Authentic infantry unit with members in Md., Va., & Pa. Living history emphasized. Reenactments, talks, displays, etc. Well-researched unit with uniform documentation. Registered 501.C nonprofit corporation.

5TH NEW YORK, DURYEE'S ZOUAVES
http://www.zouave.org/index.html
PO Box 1601 • Alexandria VA 22313-1601
Enlist in the 5th NY for authentic living history & reenacting.

7TH REGIMENT, TEXAS VOLUNTEER BRIGADE
303-221-3099
Capt. E. Roy Jordan
300 E Harmony Rd • Fort Collins CO 80525
Civil War gun club to promote family fun through black powder shooting & safety.

8TH REGT. NJ VOLUNTEER INFANTRY
609-654-5561 Days • 609-654-7168 Nights
Capt. Earl Aversano
226 Sunny Jim Dr • Medford NJ 08055
Honorary reactivated NJ unit which participates in reenactments & historical events throughout the eastern U.S.

ABRAHAM LINCOLN SOCIETY
2743 S Veterans Pkwy
Springfield IL 62704-6402
Abraham Lincoln enthusiasts. Free information (no obligation) - send large SASE.

AMERICAN BATTLEFIELD PROTECTION PROGRAM
202-343-3941
http://www2.cr.nps.gov/abpp/abpp.html
Natl. Park Service
PO Box 37127 • Washington DC 20013-7127
U.S. government's leading battlefield preservation program.

AMERICAN CIVIL WAR ASSOCIATION
http://www.acwa.org
CSA contact: AdjCSAACWA@aol.com ;
Union contact: FedAdjACWA@aol.com
Arthur Henricks
PO Box 61075 • Sunnyvale CA 94088-1075
Private, non-profit educational organization & reenactment society which uses living history to help the public gain better understanding of the Civil War. 350 current members. More info - send SASE.

AMERICAN FORESTS
904-765-0727
Famous & Historic Trees
8555 Plummer Rd
Jacksonville FL 32219-1628
Help preserve CW battlefields by planting a seedling from an old war-era tree. Dollar benefit to CW Trust. Complete planting kit. Free full-color Tree Selection booklet.

AMERICAN SINGLE SHOT RIFLE ASSOCIATION
709 Carolyn Dr
Delphos OH 45833-1316
Association dedicated to the shooting of old black powder cartridge rifles. Free journal & info.

ASMIC
526 Lafayette Ave
Palmerton PA 18071-1621
Oldest military collecting club in the nation. Dedicated to collection & preservation of U.S. cloth & metal military insignia. Publishes quarterly *Trading Post* & newsletter.

ASSOCIATION FOR THE PRESERVATION OF CIVIL WAR SITES
888-606-1400
http://www.apcws.com
11 Public Sq Ste 200
Hagerstown MD 21740-5510
Not-for-profit membership organization that preserves Civil War sites for educational & recreational uses. Website: organizational news & membership info.

BERKELEY COUNTY HISTORICAL SOCIETY
304-267-4713
PO Box 1624 • 126 E Race St
Martinsburg WV 25402-1624
Hosts of annual Belle Boyd Birthday Party at the Belle Boyd House.

BLOUNT COUNTY GENEALOGICAL & HISTORICAL SOCIETY
ATTN: TC
PO Box 4986 • Maryville TN 37802-4986
Loyal Mountain Troopers: The 2nd and 3rd Tenn. Vol. Cavalry in the Civil War. Details these largely ignored Southerners who served the Union. $32.50 ppd.

BLUE & GRAY EDUCATION SOCIETY
804-797-4535
416 Beck St • Norfolk VA 23503
Non-profit organization which interprets battlefields for public visitation. North Anna is most recent achievement. More than 600 members via tax-exempt donation. Seminars, tours, symposiums & debates.

CENTRAL MARYLAND HERITAGE LEAGUE
301-371-7090
PO Box 721 • Middletown MD 21769-0721
Dedicated to preserving the South Mountain battlefield area. Offering MD Campaign Afghan with scenes from South Mountain, Antietam & Harpers Ferry.

CIVIL WAR EDUCATION ASSOCIATION
800-298-1861 • 540-667-2339 Fax
21 N Loudoun St
Winchester VA 22601-4715
Non-profit organization presenting the finest seminars, symposia, & tours. Develops educational materials, publishes/distributes Civil War books. Contact for extensive calendar of events.

CIVIL WAR SOCIETY
800-247-6253 • 540-955-1176
540-955-2321 Fax
cwmag@mnsinc.com
PO Box 770 • Berryville VA 22611-0770
Membership includes award-winning *Civil War Magazine*, calendar, newsletters, membership cert., preservation & education activities, ancestors research guide, tours, seminars, discounts & camaraderie. Call for brochure.

THE CIVIL WAR TRUST
703-516-4944 • 800-CWTRUST
703-516-4947 Fax
civilwar@ari.net

Danielle McMahon
2101 Wilson Blvd Ste 1120
Arlington VA 22201
Promotes appreciation & stewardship of our nation's cultural heritage through preservation of historic CW battlefields and through related education & preservation programs. Memberships start at $25.

CONFEDERATE HERITAGE BRIGADE
540-338-7907
PO Box 1224 • Purcellville VA 20134-1224
Defend the Confederate right by joining our growing group for flag marches & commemorations. No dues.

CONFEDERATE HISTORICAL INSTITUTE
501-225-3996
PO Box 7388 • Little Rock AR 72217-7388
Est. 1979 to promote study of Confederate history. Speakers & tours, annual institute - April. Newsletter. Membership - $20/yr.

CONFEDERATE MEMORIAL ASSOCIATION
202-483-5700
1322 Vermont Ave NW
Washington DC 20005-3607

THE CONFEDERATE NAVY
8351 Roswell Rd Ste 363
Atlanta GA 30350-2810
Nation's fastest growing boat club. Membership card, official boat decal, bi-monthly newsletter, membership discounts, etc. A real boat club. $25.

CONFEDERATE SOCIETY OF AMERICA
PO Box 713
Plaquemine LA 70765-0713
"Action Arm" of the Confederate Movement. Subjects include gun control, immigration, moral breakdown, etc. Annual Membership, incl. bi-monthly newsletter - $20.

THE CORINTH CIVIL WAR CENTER
601-287-9501
http://www.corinth.org/
civilwar@tsixroads.com
PO Box 45 • Corinth MS 38835-0045
Offers 12-minute video of Corinth's role in the Civil War. Walking/driving tour maps available. Small gift shop.

CORTLAND COUNTY HISTORICAL SOCIETY, INC.
607-756-6071
25 Homer Ave
Cortland NY 13045-2056

Hosts Suggett House Museum & Kellogg Memorial Research Library. *A Regiment Remembered: 157th New York Volunteers* - Lt. William Saxton's diary, 157 pp. - $20 + $3.40 S&H. NYS - add 8% sales tax.

DAUGHTERS OF UNION VETERANS OF THE CIVIL WAR
217-544-0616
http://suvcw.org/duv.htm
DUVCW@aol.com
503 S Walnut St • Springfield IL 62704-1932
Organization for female lineal descendants of Union veterans.

DIXIANA
800-272-3589
Private Southern Pride Airline club for weekend getaways. Affordable air transportation for members only. Call for more info. on membership requirements & application.

FORT DELAWARE SOCIETY
302-834-1630
PO Box 553 • 126 Sussex Ave
Delaware City DE 19706-0553
Co-sponsors reenactments, operates museum & gift shop. Involved in research & fund-raising.

FRIENDS OF MONOCACY BATTLEFIELD
301-845-6241
FOMB@erols.com
PO Box 4101 • Frederick MD 21705-4101
Non-profit, all-volunteer organization serving as independent advocate for the battlefield & working to preserve, protect & restore the site of the "batle that saved Washington."

FRIENDS OF NEW YORK STATE NEWSPAPER PROJECT
http://www.nysl.nysed.gov/nysnp
vweiss@mail.nysed.gov
PO Box 2402 • Empire State Plaza Station
Albany NY 12220
Maps & Letters from NY State's Civil War Newspapers, 1861-1863 - $22.

FRIENDS OF THE MANASSAS NATL BATTLEFIELD PARK
703-330-1965
http://members.aol.com/manapark/friendhp.html
fit2prnt@erols.com
Karen Fojt
PO Box 141 • Catharpin VA 20143-0141
Supports the park to preserve its historic significance, cultural importance & natural values; encourages community involvement; provides a forum for community outreach.

FRIENDS OF THE NATIONAL PARKS AT GETTYSBURG
717-334-0772 • 717-334-3118
PO Box 4622 • Gettysburg PA 17325-4622
National organization with purpose of preserving & restoring Gettysburg NP land, promoting educational resources & programs, & establishing a definitive Civil War museum.

GENERAL STAFF OF THE ARMY OF THE POTOMAC
301-845-7363
Joe Shelton, Pres.
PO Box 266 • Walkersville MD 21793-0266
Personalities from Civil War past. Civil War living history group & nonprofit organization.

GENERAL STAFF OF THE CONFEDERACY
301-845-7363
Joe Shelton, Pres.
PO Box 266 • Walkersville MD 21793-0266
Personalities from Civil War past. Civil War living history group & nonprofit organization.

GETTYSBURG BATTLEFIELD PRESERVATION ASSOCIATION
717-337-0031
Dr. Walter L. Powell, Pres.
PO Box 1863
Gettysburg PA 17325
Bi-annual newsletter "Battle Lines" (for $10 annual membership). Various Civil War books & prints available for donations. Annual Civil War Book Show.

GRANT COUNTY HISTORICAL SOCIETY
608-723-2287 • 608-723-4925
129 E Maple St
Lancaster WI 53813
Operates from Cunningham Museum. *Our Boys* - 64 stories of men & boys from Grant County, Wisc.; names of all 750 Grant Co. soldiers who died in the war. $25 + $3 S&H. (See ad page 239)

U.S.GRANT NETWORK
http://www.css.edu/mkelsey/gppg.html
usglady@excel.net
Diane Meives
W3547 Playbird Rd
Sheboygan Falls WI 53085
Organization commemorating Gen. Grant. Join us to learn more about this often misunderstood Civil War hero. Quarterly newsletter - $12.

HERITAGE EMBROIDERY
402-488-7913 • 402-488-8167 Fax
http://WWW.CivilWarMall.com/Image.htm
Heritage@navix.net
Tom & Dorothy Rivett
PO Box 22424 • Lincoln NE 68542-2424
Exclusive Mort Kunstler art images
embroidered on quality American-made
garments. Personalization available for
reenactors, round tables, museums &
galleries. Visit our online catalog.

HERITAGE PRESERVATION ASSOCIATION
800-86-DIXIE • 770-928-2714
770-928-2719 Fax
http://www.hpa.org
HPA@america.net
PO Box 98209
Atlanta GA 30359-1909
National non-profit organization protects &
preserves history, symbols & culture of the
American South. Reg. membership - $40. Call
for more detailed information.

HERITAGEPAC
501-225-3996
Jerry L. Russell, Director
PO Box 7281
Little Rock AR 72217-7281
Non-profit lobbying group/action committee
devoted to battlefield preservation.

THE INDEX PROJECT, INC.
2525 N 10th St Apt 621
Arlington VA 22201
Non-profit group preparing computerized
index of 100,000 Union court-martials.

IRON BRIGADE ASSOCIATION
Milwaukee CWRT
Inst for CW Studies / Carroll College
100 N East Ave • Waukesha WI 53186
Dedicated to the memory of the Iron Brigade
in the West. Lifetime membership with lapel
pin - $5; with medal replica - $15. Send full
name, address & phone number with check.

JACKSON'S FOOT CAVALRY
804-780-3373 • 800-833-5522
B. Brenner Wood
Now mustering "F" Company, 21st Regt.,
Virginia Volunteer Cavalry. We are historians
who interpret the Civil War by authentically
portraying the common soldier.

JUNIATA COUNTY HISTORICAL SOCIETY
498B Jefferson St
Mifflintown PA 17059-1424

*An Imperishable Fame: The Civil War
Experience of George F. McFarland*, by
Michael Dreese - 210 pp., $20 (ppd.).

KENTUCKIANA ARMS COLLECTORS ASSN., INC.
PO Box 1776 • Louisville KY 40201-1776
Sponsors annual gun show in July; has
resurrected John Hunt Morgan show. 200
tables, weapons, relics, accoutrements,
displays, photos, memorabilia.

KERNSTOWN BATTLEFIELD ASSN.
540-678-8598 • 800-298-1861
jridings@mnsinc.com
http://www.kernstownbattle.org
Joanne A. Ridings
PO Box 1327 • Winchester VA 22604
Non-profit organization endeavoring to
acquire, maintain & interpret the Kernstown
Battlefield. Primary goal is acquisition of
32-acre Grim Farm.

SGT. KIRKLAND'S MUSEUM & HISTORICAL SOCIETY, INC.
540-899-5565 • 540-899-7643 Fax
Civil-War@msn.com
912 Lafayette Blvd
Fredericksburg VA 22401-5617
Non-profit museum, association & press
devoted to preservation of historical
documents, artifacts, & texts; education;
publication of meritorius books; & research &
recovery of CW soldiers' records. Free
catalog.

LADIES OF THE GRAND ARMY OF THE REPUBLIC
http://suvcw.org/lgar.htm
Mrs. Elizabeth Koch, Natl. Sect.
119 N Swarthmore Ave Apt 1-H
Ridley Park PA 19078
Organization for female descendants of Union
veterans.

LAWRENCE CIVIL WAR MEMORIAL GUARD, INC.
240 Andover St
Lawrence MA 01843
Non-profit organization dedicated to
preservation of Lawrence, Mass.'s Civil War
history, its monuments & its graves.

LITTLE BIG HORN ASSOCIATES
105 Bartlett Pl
Brooklyn NY 11229
Join with us & learn more about the life and
times of Gen. George A. Custer & his
contemporaries.

LIVING HISTORY ASSOCIATION, INC.

PO Box 1389 • Wilmington VT 05363-1389
Reenactors' Liability Insurance. Multimillion
dollar policies available, covering
reenactments, encampments, black powder,
cavalry, artillery, etc. Info - $3.

GENERAL LONGSTREET MEMORIAL FUND

919-258-6966 • 919-775-5214 Fax
thomas.ils@mhs.unc.edu
Robert C. Thomas
112 Offset Farm Rd
Sanford NC 27330-9723
Non-profit fund to erect equestrian monument
to Gen. James Longstreet at Gettysburg
National Military Park.

THE LONGSTREET SOCIETY

770-531-0100 • 770-531-7956 Fax
PO Box 191 • Gainesville GA 30503-0191
Formed to honor the life of Lt. Gen. James
Longstreet. Dedicated to preserving
landmarks & memorabilia. Currently restoring
Longstreet's old Piedmont Hotel.
Memberships accepted.

MANASSAS MUSEUM & ASSOCIATES

703-368-1873
http://xroads.virginia.edu/~VAM/MAN/
          vamintro.html
janemriley@aol.com
PO Box 560 • 9101 Prince William St
Manassas VA 20108-0560
Non-profit organization dedicated to the
support of the Manassas Museum System &
its mission to preserve the rich heritage of the
Northern Virginia Piedmont area.

MILITARY ORDER OF THE LOYAL LEGION OF THE UNITED STATES (MOLLUS)

517-694-9394
http://suvcw.org/mollus.htm
YJNW42A@prodigy.com
Keith G. Harrison
4209 Santa Clara Dr • Holt MI 48842
Founded in 1865 for direct or collateral
descendants of commissioned officers of the
Union army.

MINERVA CENTER ON WOMEN & THE MILITARY

410-437-5379
http://www.MinervaCenter.com
mouseminer@aol.com
20 Granada Rd • Pasadena MD 21122-2708
Non-profit education foundation & publisher.
3rd printing of *An Uncommon Soldier: The
Civil War Letters of Sarah Rosetta Wakeman,
alias Pvt. Lyons Wakeman.* $25.

MISSOURI HISTORICAL SOCIETY

PO Box 11940
Saint Louis MO 63112-0040
Civil War books. In *The Civil War in St. Louis,
a Guided Tour,* Wm. C. Winter brings to life
the monuments, markers, & memories of the
Civil War in St. Louis. 192 pp. Paper - $22.95.
Cloth - $32.95.

MONTGOMERY COUNTY HISTORICAL SOCIETY

212 S Water St
Crawfordsville IN 47933
*The Diary of Private Ambrose Remley & His
Four Years in the Lightning Brigade* - story of
Wilder's mounted infantry & Spencer
repeating rifle - $23.

MORGAN'S MEN ASSOC., INC.

Samuel Flora
1691 Kilkenny Dr
Lexington KY 40505
Non-profit organization seeking to perpetuate
the memory of Gen. John Hunt Morgan & his
men. Write for more information.

NATIONAL CIVIL WAR ASSN.

http://ncwa.org/
Information about reenacting & living history
units.

NATIONAL GENEALOGICAL SOCIETY

703-525-0050 Office • 703-841-9065 Library
703-525-0052 Fax
http://www.genealogy.org/~ngs
ngslibe@wizard.net
76702.2417@compuserve.com
4527 17th St N
Arlington VA 22207-2399

NATIONAL HISTORICAL SOCIETY

800-849-6148
PO Box 420334
Palm Coast FL 32142-0334
History club offering valuable benefits that
save time & money as well as support our
nation's heritage ... all designed with the
history enthusiast in mind. Division of Cowles
Media.

NATIONAL MUSEUM OF CIVIL WAR MEDICINE

301-695-1864 • 800-564-1864
301-695-6823 Fax
http://www.civilwarmed.org
LauraM@civilwarmed.org
JaNeen M. Smith, Ex. Dir.
48 E Patrick St
PO Box 470 • Frederick MD 21705-0470

Center for study & interpretation of Civil War medical history. Medical artifacts, manuscripts, books & materials. 1861-1865. Museum store. Memberships available. Annual conference 1st weekend in August.

NATIONAL MUZZLELOADING RIFLE ASSOCIATION

812-667-5131
812-667-5137 Fax
PO Box 67
Friendship IN 47021-0067
Represents all aspects of muzzleloading. More than 25,000 members/300 charter clubs throughout the country. Subscription to *Muzzle Blasts* with $30 membership.

NATIONAL TRUST FOR HISTORIC PRESERVATION

202-673-4000
800-944-6847 to join
202-673-4038 Fax
http://www.nthp.org
1785 Massachusetts Ave NW
Washington DC 20036-2117
Non-profit organization committed to preserving the heritage & livability of America's communities. Operates historic house museums, publishes monthly magazine & newsletter. Memberships welcome. Brochures.

NORTH-SOUTH SKIRMISH ASSOCIATION

http://mh004.infi.net/~nssa/
Phil Spaugy
501 N Dixie Dr
Vandalia OH 45377-2011
Team competition in high-level marksmanship with original or approved reproduction muskets, carbines, revolvers, & artillery at breakable targets in a timed match. Period regimental uniforms worn.

ORDER OF SOUTHERN GRAY, INC.

540-955-3980
540-955-4126 Fax
cwpub@visuallink.com
Katherine Tennery, President
PO Box 351
Berryville VA 22611-0351
Virginia women dedicated to preserving Southern heritage. Free brochure.

OZARK ARTS ASSOCIATION

OzarkArts@aol.com
PO Box 165
Rogers AR 72757-0165
Join our collectors' club to purchase handcrafted & painted 8" sculptures of Civil War soldiers. Illus. brochure - $1 (ref. w/ purchase).

PEJEPSCOT HISTORICAL SOCIETY/ JOSHUA L. CHAMBERLAIN MUSEUM

207-729-6606
207-729-6012 Fax
http://www.Curtislibrary.com/pejepscot.htm
PEJEPSCOT@acornbbs.com
Erik C. Jorgenson, Dir.
159 Park Row
Brunswick ME 04011-2005
Historical Society operates the Joshua Chamberlain Museum located in Chamberlain's former home. Also maintains the most comprehensive Chamberlain research collection available anywhere. Free catalog.

JOHN PELHAM HISTORICAL ASSOCIATION, INC.

757-838-1685
http://members.aol.com/JPHA1982
JPHA1982@aol.com
Peggy Vogtsberger
7 Carmel Ter
Hampton VA 23666-2807
Bi-monthly newsletter, "The Cannoneer." Annual convention & tour of Fredericksburg; commemorative ceremony at Kelly's Ford. Supports preservation; active in erecting monuments. Archives located at Jacksonville Public Library, Jacksonville, Ala.

POINT LOOKOUT POW DESCENDANTS ORGANIZATION

http://members.tripod.com/~PLPOW/pointlk.htm
plpow@erols.com
3587 Windmill Dr
Virginia Beach VA 23456-2122
Bi-monthly newsletters, medals, bumper stickers, prison grounds meetings, POW reenactors. Programs provided. For membership application - send SASE.

POTOMAC ARMS COLLECTOR'S ASSN.

301-921-9673
PO Box 1812
Wheaton MD 20915-1812
Sponsors of annual October gun show, Frederick, MD. Guns, knives, & related items. Donation - $4.

THE PROFESSIONAL TREASURE HUNTERS HISTORICAL SOCIETY

603-357-0607 • 800-447-6014 (New England)
603-352-1147 Fax
George Streeter
14 Vernon St
Keene NH 03431-3440
Info. about treasure hunting in US. Metal detecting info. Treasure club activities in US. Newsletter - *Treasure Hunter's Gazette.*

SHENANDOAH NATIONAL HISTORY ASSOCIATION
540-999-3581 • 540-999-3582
3655 US Highway 211 E
Luray VA 22835-9036

SHIP'S COMPANY, INC.
410-788-7264
Lawrence Bopp, Pres.
309 Roanoke Dr
Baltimore MD 21228
Official interpretive group of the USS *Constellation*, recruiting Federal sailors & marines for service aboard this 1855 war sloop - the last surviving warship to see Civil War action.

SONS OF CONFEDERATE VETERANS (N.C. DIVISION)
PO Box 1896
Raleigh NC 27602-1896

SONS OF CONFEDERATE VETERANS (NATL. OFFICE)
800-MY SOUTH (697-6884)
http://www.scv.org
CIC Peter W. Orlebeke
3411 Saint Cloud Cir
Dallas TX 75229-2635
Dedicated to preserving & defending history & principles of the Old South. Recruiting male descendants of those who fought in the Confederacy. Contact for membership info.

SONS OF UNION VETERANS OF THE CIVIL WAR (KENTUCKY)
Don Hackel
623 E Ormsby
Louisville KY 40203
Camps held in Louisville & Lexington, with many KY-wide area camps to follow.

SONS OF UNION VETERANS OF THE CIVIL WAR (NY STATE)
516-599-9256
James A. Grismer, Commander
313 Earle Ave
Lynbrook NY 11563-2135
Recruiting the sons of soldiers & sailors of the Union in New York State.

SONS OF UNION VETERANS OF THE CIVIL WAR (INDIANA)
153 Connie Dr
Pittsburgh PA 15214-1251
Founded by the GAR (1881). Chartered by Act of Congress (1954). Keep your heritage/ancestors' memory alive.

SONS OF UNION VETERANS OF THE CIVIL WAR (PACIFIC NORTHWEST)
John Williamson
672 Redmond Ave NE • Renton WA 98056
Gov. Isaac Stevens Camp #1 is recruiting sons of soldiers & sailors of the Union.

SONS OF UNION VETERANS OF THE CIVIL WAR (NY CITY)
718-426-8740
SVC Cliff Henke
Oliver Tilden Camp No. 26
8269 61st Dr • Middle Village NY 11379-1448
Welcome descendants of Union veterans in the NYC metropolitan area. Meet last Tuesday of month at 7th Regt. Armory, 66th & Park Aves., NYC.

SONS OF UNION VETERANS OF THE CIVIL WAR (MICHIGAN)
810-659-4999
PO Box 618 • DeWitt MI 48820-0618
Recruiting decendents of Civil War soldiers & sailors who honorably served the Union, 1861-1865.

SONS OF UNION VETERANS OF THE CIVIL WAR (CALIFORNIA BAY)
Charles L. Christian
5120 Oak Park Way
Santa Rosa CA 95409-3740
Camp #23 meets bi-monthly in Sonoma County.

J.E.B. STUART BIRTHPLACE, INC.
540-251-1833
PO Box 240 • Ararat VA 24053-0240
Memberships to help preserve the birthplace of J.E.B. Stuart begin at $25.

THE TURNER ASHBY SOCIETY
804-232-3406
Patricia Walenista
810 W 30th St • Richmond VA 23225
Organization whose mission is to honor, preserve & promote the name of Gen. Turner Ashby. Gather to study & appreciate Ashby's life & times.

UNITED DAUGHTERS OF THE CONFEDERACY
804-355-1636 • 804-353-1396 Fax
http://www.hsv.tis.net/~maxs/UDC/
hqudc@aol.com
328 North Blvd.
Richmond VA 23220-4057
Organization for female descendants of Confederate veterans. Requires proof of eligibility.

UNITED STATES CAVALRY ASSOCIATION
Mrs. Patricia S. Bright
PO Box 2325
Fort Riley KS 66442-0325
"We Remember." Proud sponsors of the US
Cavalry Museum, Memorial Research Library
& Memorial Foundation.

**WINTER WEEKEND OF THE LIVING
HISTORY SOCIETY**
612-431-4760
ekatuin@compuserve.com
Elaine M. Katuin
7624 157th St W Apt 208
Apple Valley MN 55124-9166

Weekend gala featuring mid-19th-century
dancing & civilian activities, workshops, ice
skating & sledding. Period attire requested.
Annual event - February.

MIKE WOSHNER
412-884-9299
mwoshner@bellatlantic.net
2306 Spokane Ave
Pittsburgh PA 15210-4414
Historical presentations on "India-rubber &
gutta-percha in the Civil War era,"
encompassing history, patents, military trials
& award-winning display of rare artifacts.

ABRAHAM'S LADY
609-853-6882
abraham@comten.com
Donna Abraham
1402 Saint Matthew Dr • Verga NJ 08093
Trims, notions & accessories for sewing CW
reproduction clothing; bone buttons, metal
stays, hats, jewelry, soutache. Catalog - $1.

ALICE'S COUNTRY COTTAGE
301-766-7344
1010 McCauley Ct • Hagerstown MD 21740
The "Jefferson Shirt," 100% cotton, wooden
buttons, homespun look, period design -
$24.95 + $3 S&H. Specify men's or women's.
Call for additional info.

TIM ALLEN
410-549-5145
1429 Becket Rd • Eldersburg MD 21784
Civilian slouch hats - handsewn, fully lined,
stamped with period labels, handmade to
order. Call or send SASE for more info.

ALTERYEARS
818-585-2994 • 818-432-4530 Fax
3749 E Colorado Blvd
Pasadena CA 91107
Patterns, books, supplies & accessories to
help you make your own historical clothing
from Civil War & other eras. Visit our store!
200+-pg. catalog - $5 (4th cl.); $8 (priority).

AMAZON DRY GOODS
319-322-6800 • 319-322-4138
319-322-4003 Fax
J. Burgess, Pres.
407 Brady St • Davenport IA 52801-1510
Victorian apparel & accessories. Corsets,
bonnets, hoop skirts, fans & snoods, hats,
paper dolls, flags, books, patterns, shoes &
boots. Sutlers' wholesale catalog. Retail
catalogs (pattern, shoe, & general) - all 3 for
$15.

AMERICAN STITCHES
28 Forest St • Danvers MA 01923-1571
Military & civilian clothing & accessories of the
1860s. Ladies, gentlemen, children. Custom-
made, quality reproductions.

ARTCAST
770-270-9659
PO Box 28561
Atlanta GA 30358-0561
1861 reproduction West Point class ring.
Original reproductions of the May & June
class. (Only year with 2 graduations.) Sterling
- $59.95; gold - $169.95.

AUTHENTIC REPRODUCTIONS
717-437-9174
RR 2 Box 989
Milton PA 17847-9314
Top selection of quality men, women, &
children's repro clothing & accessories at
unbeatable prices. Laidacker historical
garments. Catalog - $3.

BAINBRIDGE TRADITIONAL BOOTMAKERS
01761-471430 Phone & Fax
The Square
Timsbury, Bath, BA 3 1 HY U.K.
Handmade to measure, historically accurate
mehtods & materials. Incorporating Timefarer
footwear. Free brochure.

BERMAN LEATHER
617-426-0870
617-357-8564 Fax
Robert S. Berman
25 Melcher St
Boston MA 02210-1516
Leather hides like CW era for belts, straps,
clothing, bags, even footwear. Full catalog of
hardware, tools, buckles & kits - $3 (ref.).

BONNET BRIGADE
Pat Wullenjohn
PO Box 28
Fremont CA 94537-0028
Civil War-period clothing, equipment,
weapons, accoutrements, & camping
equipment. Catalog - $3.

C & C SUTLERY
208-388-0973 • 208-384-9523 Fax
CLOX@RMCI.NET
HC 33 Box 3330
Boise ID 83706
Full-service Civil War supplier. Uniforms, etc.

C & D JARNAGIN
601-287-4977
601-287-6033 Fax
http://www.jarnaginco.com
PO Box 1860
Corinth MS 38835-1860
Military & historical outfitters. Research,
develop, & manufacture high quality uniforms,
leather gear, footwear, & tinware for American
troops, 1750-1865. 18th-century & CW
catalogs - $3 each. (See ad page 239)

CAPS & KEPIS
302-994-6428
2665 Longfellow Dr
Wilmington DE 19808-3733

Custom-made officers' & enlisted Confederate provisionals, standard Federal, Rebel caps, extensive insignia, state buttons, haversacks, shirts, pants, coats, jackets, overcoats. Catalog - $2.

CARRICO'S LEATHERWORKS
316-922-7222 • 316-922-3311 Fax
David Carrico
811 5000 Rd
Edna KS 67342
Authentic reproduction Civil War cavalry equipment & accoutrements. Saddles, bridles, holsters, belts, etc. Free price list.

CASTLE KEEP, LTD.
630-801-1696
630-801-1910 Fax
http://www.Reenact.com
ernie@Smartgate.com
Ernest Klapmeier
83 S LaSalle St
Aurora IL 60505
Reenactor supplies; clothing & equipment to put man or woman into the field. Owner has 20 yrs. reenacting experience & understands concept of authenticity.

CAVALRY REGIMENTAL SUPPLY
806-798-8867 Fax
PO Box 64394
Lubbock TX 79464-4394
Custom, handmade, obsolete military footwear (c.1500-1943). 7 styles of Civil War boots & shoes. Catalog - $2 + SASE (ref.).

THE CAVALRY SHOP
804-266-0898
T.E. Johnson, Jr.
9700 Royerton Dr
Richmond VA 23228-1218
Civil War leather goods, buckles; horsegear. Catalog - $2. (See ad page 233)

CHILE-N-CRACKER'S
702-267-4072 Phone & Fax
Lindy Dubner, Jim Miller
PO Box 2865
Carson City NV 89702
Exclusive line of quality replica calico buttons & clothing patterns. Unique reproduction toys & sundries of mid-19th century. Dealer inquiries welcome. Brochure - send SASE. (See ad page 231)

MICHAEL D. CLARK
513-724-3167
PO Box 641
Williamsburg OH 45176-0641

Authentic key-wind watches. Completely restored. Fine running condition. Open & hunting style cases. Price list - send large SASE.

CONFEDERATE YANKEE
203-453-9900 Phone & Fax
Dennis Semrau & Terry Brettman-Semrau
PO Box 192
Guilford CT 06437-0192
Custom clothing based on originals. Reproduction fabrics used. Catalog & sample - $3. (See ad page 236)

CRESCENT CITY SUTLER
812-983-4217
17810 Highway 57
Evansville IN 47711-9318
Reproduction & original Civil War uniforms & equipment. Catalog - $3.

DINUNZIO'S SHOE REPAIR
717-273-5854
717-283-7079 Fax
118 S 8th St
Lebanon PA 17042-5213
Civil War boots repaired to authenticity, with fine workmanship giving careful attention to every detail. Est. 1916.

DIRTY BILLY'S HATS
410-775-1865 Orders
717-334-3200 Shop
7574 Middleburg Rd
Detour MD 21757
Military & civilian hats, caps & accessories; exact reproductions. Visit our shop at 430A Baltimore St, Gettysburg, Pa. Catalog - send 32¢ stamp.

DIXIE FASHIONS
804-527-2028
George Dunn • 11300 Cedar Hill Ct
Richmond VA 23233-1847
Confederate & Union exact reproduction uniforms, made to fit, museum-quality work, including all leather accessories, shell jackets, sashes, frocks, trousers, Kepis, shirts. Catalog - $3.

DIXIE GUN WORKS, INC.
800-238-6785 Orders only • 901-885-0700
901-885-0440 Fax
PO Box 130 • Union City TN 38261-0130
The source for firearms, parts, shooting supplies, leather goods, uniforms, books, patterns & cannons. 600-pg catalog with more than 8,000 items - $5.

DONNA'S STITCHES BACK IN TIME

800-808-7685
We stitch for sutlers. High-quality muslin shirts - $13.50 wholesale. Also sell retail. Price list on request.

MRS. DUBERVILLE DRESSES & MILLINERY

Celeste Burrell
Old Gettysburg Village
777 Baltimore St • Gettysburg PA 17325
Authentic, handmade period fashions.

AN EARLY ELEGANCE

717-338-9311
39 N Washington St
Gettysburg PA 17325-1128
American-made items & authentic reproductions. CW-era writing box, fabrics. Gifts at reasonable prices. Product guide - business-size SASE. Fabric swatch book - $2.50.

ELIZABETH ANN & CO.

216-632-9808
PO Box 716 • 15960 E High St
Middlefield OH 44062-0716
Top quality wool, 23 colors - $15.50/yd. + S&H. Custom tailoring. Sack coats, shell jackets, pants, officers' frocks; ladies' & children's clothing. Wool sample - send SASE.

THE EMPORIUM

417-683-2764
Ed & Maryln Peterka
RR 1 Box 363 • Ava MO 65608
Supplies for the muzzleloader & living history participant. Patterns, hosiery, ladies' straw hats. Catalog - $3 (ref.).

PETER EVANS PIPES

305-361-5589
285 W Mashta Dr • Dept F
Key Biscayne FL 33149-2419
Custom-made period pipes, reproductions, clays, quality pipe accessories. For smokers, reenactors, collectors, historians. Free brochure.

FAIR OAKS SUTLER, INC.

540-972-7744 Noon-9 PM
540-972-3256 24-hr Fax
9905 Kershaw Ct
Spotsylvania PA 22553-3768
High-quality replica Civil War uniforms, accoutrements, equipment & muskets; Kepi & bummer caps our specialty. Satisfaction guaranteed. Catalog - 2 stamps.

FAIRMOUNT SUTLERY

717-864-3335 • 717-256-3081 Daytime
Janice Hilley, Prop.
RR 1 Box 271B
Benton PA 17814-9681
Reproduction Civil War-period uniforms & civilian clothing for men & women. Catalog - free w/ SASE.

FALL CREEK SUTTLERY

765-482-1861
765-482-1848 Fax
http://fcsutler.com
AJF5577@aol.com or fcsutler@aol.com
Andy Fulks
PO Box 92
Whitestown IN 46075-0092
Authentic reproduction Civil War & mid-19th-century uniforms, leather goods, weapons, shoes, tents, insignia, reference books & more. 32-pg catalog - $3. (See ad pg 242)

FAMILY HEIRLOOM WEAVERS

717-246-2431 Phone & Fax
familyheirloom@mindspring.com
775 Meadowview Dr
Red Lion PA 17356-8608
Reproduction fabrics - historically accurate ingrain carpets & jacquard coverlets. Uniforms, shirtings, etc. Brochure & swatches - $4.

FARMHOUSE FABRICS

414-622-4884 • 414-622-5207 Fax
PO Box 188 • Pine River WI 54982-0188
Civil War dress fabric - authentic reproductions of Civil War-era cotton fabric. 10 patterns, 3 colors ea. $6.99/yd. Swatch set & catalog - $2 ppd.

FOOTWEAR

320 Dyestone Springs Rd
Hohenwald TN 38462-5565
All period footwear repaired to original condition, pegged, sewn, nailed. Soles & heels - $29.50. Boots - $48.

FRANKLY MY DEAR

777 Baltimore St
Gettysburg PA 17325
Gone with the Wind dress patterns, incl. green drapery dress, barbeque dress & burgundy dress.

FRAZER BROTHERS' 17TH REGIMENT

214-696-1865 • 214-426-4230 Fax
5641 Yale Blvd Ste 125
Dallas TX 75206-5026

Uniforms & equipment, artillery hardware, & side arms. Civilian clothing (men only). Handmade leather goods. Large supply of tinware. Boots. American products.

FREDERICKSBURG MONOGRAMMING & EMBROIDERY
540-373-3937 • 540-373-4006 Fax
604 Caroline St
Fredericksburg VA 22401-5902
Custom embroidery of favorite Civil War designs. Casual clothing, fast delivery; quantity orders/dealers welcomed. All work on-site, from artwork to finished garment.

GENTEEL ARTS ACADEMY
717-337-0283 • 717-337-0314 Fax
http://www.cvn.net/~cschmitt
cschmitt@cvn.net
CarolAnn Schmitt
PO Box 3014 • Gettysburg PA 17325-0014
Offers workshops, lectures & seminars on period clothing, construction & fitting techniques. Classes offered frequently. Call/write for details & brochure. Free catalog.

GOSPEL TRUTH/CIVIL WAR ROOM
412-238-7991
228 W Main St • Ligonier PA 15658-1130
Full-service Christian bookstore & Civil War room. Kunstler calendars, patterns, pewter figurines, books, videos, music, hats, accessories, shirts, Woolrich wool & much more.

GRAND ILLUSIONS
302-366-0300 • 302-738-1858 Fax
705 Interchange Blvd
Newark DE 19711
Manufacturers of fine Civil War uniforms & civilian clothing for men, women & children. Uniform research & manufacturer for miniseries on *Andersonville*. Catalog - $3.

THE GRAND SPECTACLE
607-732-7500 • 607-732-6045 Fax
Richard S. Buchanan, Optician
528 W Water St
Elmira NY 14905-2524
Authentic 19th-century oval spectacles with time-period cases. Free brochure.

GREY OWL INDIAN CRAFT SALES CORP.
718-341-4000
718-527-6000 Fax
Wes Cochrane
13205 Merrick Blvd
PO Box 340468
Jamaica NY 11434-0468

Green River knives, powder flasks, military buttons, buckskin, leathers, dags, strikers, books, tapes, videos, recordings, etc. 200 custom kits/4000+ items. Catalog -$3.

HARRIET'S TCS
540-667-2541 • 540-722-4618 Fax
http://www.harriets.com
PO Box 1363 • Winchester VA 22604-1363
185 patterns ca.1690-1945. Rentals, fabric, kits, supplies, hoops, parasols, lace. *Harriet's Then & Now* - 19th-century magazine, $6/issue. Annual subscription - $30. Color, photo-illus. catalog - $12.

THE HEIRLOOM EMPORIUM
216-437-8563
24 Leffingwell Dr • Orwell OH 44076
Free catalog.

HILLBILLY SPORTS, INC.
410-378-4533
PO Box 70 • Conowingo MD 21918-0070
Leather goods, period firearms, uniform items, camp items & much more. Catalog - $3.

HIS LADY & THE SOLDIER SUTLERY
517-435-3518 Summer • 352-583-4627 Winter
851 Kaypat Dr
Hope MI 48628-9615
Period hair goods & accessories for the lady & gentleman reenactor. Catalog - $2.

THE HORSE'S MOUTH HISTORICAL CLOTHIER
760-737-9548
760-737-9714 Fax
http://www.angelfire.com/biz/clothiers
costumes@pacbell.net
131 S Orange St
Escondido CA 92025-4124
Uniforms, living history, period wedding attire. Custom-made to your specifications. 45 yrs. of professional experience in design, tailoring & pattern drafting.

THE HOUSE OF TIMES PAST
864-834-0061
634 W Darby Rd
Greenville SC 29609
Period shop with authentic clothing, rifles, muzzleloading supplies & accessories for living historians & reenactors. Catalog - $2.

I. C. MERCANTILE
122 E Jewell Dr
Republic MO 65738-2202
Boots - $185. Group discount available. Additional information - send SASE.

JAMES COUNTRY MERCANTILE
816-781-9473 • 816-781-1470 Fax
JAMESCNTRY@aol.com
Del Warren or Michael Gooch
111 N Main St
Liberty MO 64068-1639
For your military & civilian reenacting needs -
weapons, accoutrements, clothing, patterns.
Illus. catalog - $6 ppd.

THE JEWELER'S DAUGHTER
301-733-3200
301-733-5076 Fax
24 W Washington St
Hagerstown MD 21740-4804
1860 VMI (Virginia Military Institute) class
ring. Repro from original museum piece. 10K
gold, wax seal style, "Let Virginia Choose" -
$259.95.

JOHNNIE O'S
401-781-0725
401-941-7932 Fax
PO Box 25083
Providence RI 02905-0596
Pocket watch chains. Ideal for reenactors.
Manufacturers of American-made watch
chains in 14 kt. gold, sterling silver, gold-filled,
layered gold. Free catalog.

K & P WEAVER
Ken & Paula Weaver
PO Box 1131
Orange CT 06477-7131
Historically accurate repro men's clothing for
military or civilian impression. Custom-made
with handsewn buttonholes. Quality
accessories; cherry dominoes, checkers with
canvas board. Catalog with swatches - $1.

KATI'S KLASSICS & SUTLERY
334-774-1254
Kathryn Nugent
RR 5 Box 78
Ozark AL 36360-9209
Ladies', men's & children's attire. Handmade
vests, ball gowns, 1800-present.

LA BONNETERIE FINE 19TH C. MILLINERY
732-928-9335
LABONNETERIE1@webtv.net
millineryone@webtv.net
http://www.webtvmagic.com/LaBonnerie.htm
Susan Pescatore
599 Hyson Rd
Jackson NJ 08527
Fine 19th c. millinery. Bonnets, hats, day caps
& headpieces specifically for the female
reenactor. Catalog -$3 (ref. w/ purchase).

LEVI LEDBETTER, SUTLER
704-485-4746 Orders
Frank Lanning, Prop.
7032 Mineral Springs Rd
Oakboro NC 28129-8855
Uniforms are our specialty. Tentage,
knapsacks, accoutrements, canteens, tinware,
blankets, buttons, buckles & brogans. Price
list - send long SASE.

W. W. LUNNSFORD
Adler@radiks.net
29601 Highway 275
Valley NE 68064
Reproduction Richmond Depot Type I, II, & III
jackets (sizes 38-46); trousers (size 28-42);
U.S. sack coat & kersys. Brochure - send
SASE.

MAGGIE DESIGNS
703-830-3640
Kathy Moffitt
13704 Springstone Dr
Cifton VA 20124-2350
Civil War scarves/panels. History on silk for
women & men. The 69th Regt. Irish Brigade
design hand-painted on 33" square
hand-rolled silk. $83.90 ppd.

HEIDI MARSH PATTERNS
3494 N Valley Rd
Greenville CA 95947-9604
Authentic patterns & how-to books of the CW
era (1855-1865) for all ages. Ballgowns,
blouses, undergarments, hoops, boning, etc.
Playing cards & other sundries; books.
Catalog - $3.

MRS. MARTIN'S MERCANTILE & MILLINERY
419-474-2093 Phone & Fax
4566 Oakhurst Dr
Sylvania OH 43560-1736
Historically correct, custom-made period
clothing from 1850-1865 for the discriminating
woman. Catalog - $4.50.

MARY ELLEN & CO.
800-669-1860 Orders
219-656-3000 Fax
Mary Ellen Smith
100 N Main St
North Liberty IN 46554-9200
Historical sewing patterns, Victorian boots,
parasols, hats, fans, hoops, petticoats,
camisoles, etc. Variety of books. Victorian
gifts, wedding accessories, etc.
Retail/wholesale. New Victorian gift shop - call
for hours. Catalog - $3 (ref.).

MC KECHNIE-LID DESIGN & RESEARCH
1146 N Central Ave # 110
Glendale CA 91202
Museum-quality 19th-century clothing at
reasonable 20th-century prices. Authentic
clothing for the discriminating woman of
fashion. Catalog - $2. (See ad page 241)

MENDELSON'S LEATHER
501 Short St • Grants Pass OR 97527-5443
Master leather craftsman makes moccasin
boots, full spectrum of custom goods you
can't find anywhere else.

MERCURY SUPPLY CO.
409-327-3707
101 Lee St
Livingston TX 77351
Civil War uniforms, reproduction equipment,
tents, accoutrements, leather goods, firearms
military & civilian. Catalog - $2.

JOSEPH MONASTRA
2332 21st St NE
Canton OH 44705-2408
Spectacles reproduced from originals,
prescription or clear poly carb. Lenses may be
added by most large vision centers. $35 ppd.

MYSTICAL MOON
207-845-2098
207-845-2023 Fax
http://www.midcoast.com/~mystical
mystical@midcoast.com
113 Liberty Rd
Washington ME 04574
Full line of 18th-19th-cent. military & civilian
clothing. Hand-stitching by request. Free price
list.

NASHVILLE DEPOT
615-833-2275
141 Neese Dr
500 Zodiac Bldg
Nashville TN 37211
Authentically reproduced carpetbag in colorful
period designs. Lined interior with pockets &
enclosed rigid bottom. Leather handles &
straps. 18"Lx18"Dx"8"W -$79.50 + $6.75 S&H.

NEEDLE & THREAD
717-334-4011
Darlene Grube
2215 Fairfield Rd
Gettysburg PA 17325-7214
Offering beautiful line of fabrics. 100% wool,
cotton, silk, linen, homespun, hooping - steel
bones, Heidi Marsh, Folkwear, Past Patterns.
Call/write. (See ad page 231)

NEW WAY BOOT SHOP
800-334-1484
120 S Keeneland Dr
Richmond KY 40475-3278
Officers' military coats, c.1862. Researched
for authenticity. Military buttons, detachable
cape, wool blend, satin lining, blue or gray -
$219.95.

NINETEENTH CENTURY MERCANTILE
508-398-1888 Phone & Fax
Barbara A. Amster
2 N Main St
South Yarmouth MA 02664-3151
Hard-to-find goods recreated in ca.1800s
fashion. Housewares, dry goods, toiletries,
remedies, hardware, fashion accessories, etc.
All presented in 19th-century mercantile
atmosphere. Hundreds of items.

PETTICOAT JUNCTION
716-549-4998
307 Lakeside Ave
Angola NY 14006-9551
100% cotton or silk underpinnings, flounced
petticoats, corset covers, 4- & 5-bone hoops,
chemise, drawers. Men's civilians & uniforms,
much more. Authenticity guaranteed. Catalog
- SASE.

QUARTERMASTER SHOP
810-367-6702
810-367-6514 Fax
5565 Griswold Rd
Kimball MI 48074-1906
Authentic reproduction men's Civil War
clothing. Union, Confederate, civilian
impressions. Large inventory & custom
tailoring. Catalog - $5.

R & K SUTLERY
217-732-8844
1015 1200th St
Lincoln IL 62656-5047
Complete line of military uniforms & civilian
clothing for both men & women; coats, pants,
skirts, blouses, dresses, etc. Top quality tents,
Officer's Wall, A-frames, dog tents & sibley.
Catalog - send SASE.

R.L. SHEP PUBLICATIONS
707-964-8662 Phone & Fax
fsbks@mcn.org
Fred Struthers
PO Box 2706
Fort Bragg CA 95437-2706
Publishes reprints of important sewing &
tailoring manuals as an aid to accurate
reproduction of period dress.

REENACTMENT EYEWARE
717-322-9849
RR 4 Box 62
Williamsport PA 17701-9551
Prescription lenses placed in your period frames by a certified optician. Frames repaired.

S & S SUTLER OF GETTYSBURG
717-677-7580 • 717-337-0438 Fax
Tim Sheads
PO Box 218
Bendersville PA 17306-0218
Reproduction Civil War uniforms, leather goods, insignia, tinware, & more. Free catalog.

SERVANT & CO. / CENTENNIAL GENERAL STORE
717-334-9712 • 800-GETTYS-1 Orders
717-334-7482 Fax
http://www.servantandco.com
230 Steinwehr Ave
Gettysburg PA 17325-2814
Quality Civil War uniforms & period clothing. Patterns, Kepis, leather goods, accessories, hats. Catalog - $6.

NANCY SHAW
716-894-2538
37 Westchester Dr
Cheektowaga NY 14225
Authentic Civil War-period design unbleached muslin shirts with gathered back, dropped shoulders, & 4 wooden buttons - $18-$20. Unbleached muslin poke bags.

SPECTACLE ACCOUTREMENTS
410-281-6069
Gregg Crockett, Optician
2918 N Rolling Rd
Baltimore MD 21244-2018
Reenactor eyewear, eyeglass prescriptions filled. Buy/sell/trade.

STALEY'S SUNDRIES
540-899-6464
540-373-2469 Fax
710 Caroline St
Fredericksburg VA 22401-5904
Largest collection of Civil War music anywhere. Military insignia, flags, hats, clothing, patterns, buttons, buckles, miniatures, books, magazines & gift items.

A STITCH IN TIME
505-847-0360
505-847-0140 Fax
PO Box 766
Mountainair NM 87036-0627

Day, camp & evening wear; ball gowns & outerwear; Scottish Highlander & Zouaves; civilian & military uniforms. Catalog.

STONY BROOK HISTORICAL UNIFORMERS
609-825-7307
Chris Sullivan
50 Porreca Dr
Millville NJ 08332
Manufacturers of Federal uniform trousers. Also supply NY State Seal buttons in stamped brass. Free catalog.

SUTLERS OF THE SIXTEEN
905-338-9427
Lorne & Nancy Weller
1359 White Oaks Blvd #906
Oakville Ontario L6H 2R8 CANADA
Period footwear, 19th-century historical clothing, pine boxes & more.

TARA HALL, INC.
800-205-0069 Phone & Fax
http://www.ncweb.com/biz/blackhawk
tarahall@earthlink.net
Vic Olney
PO Box 2069
Beach Haven NJ 08008-0109
Meagher's Irish Brigade, Fighting 69th, Corcoran's Irish Legion memorabilia, shirts, jackets, hats, sweaters, steins, pins, flags, books, miniatures, poster, belt buckles, NINAs, etc. Free catalog. (See ad page 232)

TIMELESS TEXTILES
717-930-0201
Mary Harkless
321 N Union St
Middletown PA 17057-1442
Historically correct fabric, retail & wholesale, for reenactors of all eras. Carry both civilian & military, ladies' & men's fabrics.

JAMES TOWNSEND & SON, INC.
219-594-5852
http://www.jastown.com/
PO Box 415
Pierceton IN 46562-0415
Large selections of reenactment supplies, 1740-1840. Clothing, blankets, eyeglasses, cookware, trade silver, shoes, hats, lanterns, tentage, knives, kegs, etc. Catalog -$2.

TREASURES OF THE PAST
Co. 64 H 256
Riceville TN 37330
Confederate & Union uniforms. High quality. Low prices. List - $2.

TURKEY FOOT TRADING CO.
419-832-1109
Allen & Colleen Schroll
PO Box 58
Grand Rapids OH 43522-0058
18th- & 19th-century merchandise: beads, clothing, iron work, tinware, more. Catalog.

TURTLE RUN MERCANTILE
601-638-3573
turtlemerc@aol.com
Mava Collard
714 Newit Vick Dr
Vicksburg MS 39180-8746
Exquisite, handmade hairnets of silk, fine wool, chenille, and "plain twist" from a period pattern - $15 & up + S&H. Beading & special orders welcome. Silk bonnets; cape & bonnet sets made to order. Send SASE for info.

UNIFORMS OF ANTIQUITY
501-389-6308
p.bradley@cswnet.com
122 Sweetgum Ln
Mena AR 71953-3845
Uniforms recreated for collectors, historians, & skirmishers. Catalog - $2.

UPPER MISSISSIPPI VALLEY MERCANTILE CO
319-322-0896
319-383-5549 Fax
1607 Washington St
Davenport IA 52804-3613

Top quality goods & supplies for Civil War reenactors; uniforms, tinware, tents, leather goods, muskets, books, weapons, patterns, more. 100-pp., illus. catalog - $3.

WHISKEY RUNNER
605-232-9552
PO Box 304
North Sioux City SD 57049-0304
Boots & clothing from American Colonial to the 1900 Western frontier. Catalog - $3 (ref.).

WHISTLING SWAN
814-796-6654
100% cotton muslin shirt, 1-button style. L/XL - $28 + S&H.

THE WINCHESTER SUTLER, INC.
540-888-3595
540-888-4632 Fax
270 Shadow Brook Ln
Winchester VA 22603-2071
Reproduction Civil War firearms, uniforms, camp gear, accessories, shoes, boots, hats, etc. Catalog - $4.

WOMEN'S NATION
908-726-1716 Phone & Fax
325 Avenel St
Avenel NJ 07001-1534
Fine jewelry in the Victorian style for the lady reenactor. Brooches, earrings, lockets, pendants, crosses, bracelets & rings. Free catalog.

BACK IN TIME PORTRAIT & FINE ART STUDIO
800-484-1163 x2119 • 770-631-6533
P. Hardin
PO Box 181 • Tyrone GA 30290-0181
"Go Back in Time." Your photo converted into B/W or full color portrait as CW soldier, mountain man, etc. Any era. Oil, pencil, acrylic. Start at $75.

BLACK & WHITE CUSTOM LAB, INC.
804-272-3345 • 804-744-2624
804-330-9003 Fax
MXHW21A@prodigy.com
Midlothian Festival Shopping Center
9550 Midlothian Tpke Ste 113
Richmond VA 23235
Let us preserve your treasured Civil War photos with repairs, reproductions, custom printing. Digital imaging.

MIKE BRACKIN
203-647-8620
PO Box 23 • Manchester CT 06045-0023
Large assortment of Civil War & Indian War autographs, accoutrements, memorabilia, insignia, medals, buttons, GAR, documents, photos & books. Catalog - $6/yr for 5 issues.

BUDGET FRAMER
888-343-7263
Larry Skaff - Photographry
940 North Ave • Grand Junction CO 81501
Civil War living history fine art prints & photography. Catalog - $1 (ref. w/ order).

DOUG BYRUM/CUSTOM ART
614-459-2622
Creative Illustration & Graphic Design
5413 Bennington Woods Ct
Columbus OH 43220-2221
Historical & reenactor portraits, battle scenes, home-front life. CW photos rendered as custom color art. Commissions accepted. Prints.

CONFEDERATE CALENDAR WORKS
PO Box 2084 • Austin TX 78768-2084
Illustrated with previously unpublished & researched photos of Confederate soldiers, 1861-65 events, etc. $11.95.

HENRY DEEKS
508-263-1861
PO Box 2260 • Acton MA 01720-6260
Vintage prints in carte de visite format of all participants in the Civil War era. Semi-annual catalog - offered without charge. (See ad page 242)

ELM TREE COLLECTIBLES, INC.
800-639-9886
http://www.elmtree-collectibles.com
elmtree@mindspring.com
17 Parkstone Ct
Stone Mountain GA 30087
Archival source for rare Civil War photographs. Requests taken & items located. Custom-developed 8"x10" Grant or Lee photograph $39.95 + $4 S&H ea. Immediate shipping. (See ad page 240)

FEDERAL HILL ANTIQUITIES
410-584-8185 / 8329
14 Glen Lyon Ct
Phoenix MD 21131-1212
Purveyors of fine autographs & collectibles. Letters & documents, photos, relics & artifacts, ephemera. Buy/sell/trade.

GARLAND STUDIOS
504-261-2840
9165 Sullivan Rd
Baton Rouge LA 70818
Specializes in restoring B&W photos, hand-tinting & customized B&W printing. Free estimates.

GIBSON'S CIVIL WAR COLLECTIBLES
423-323-2427
423-323-8123 Fax
Paul, Linda & Bryan Gibson
PO Box 948
Bristol TN 37620-0948
Autographs, CSA bonds & currency, diaries, flags, letter groups, newspapers, photos, slave items, uniforms, any other paper items.

DR. JOSEPH G. GOMEZ
413-533-3702
PO Box 823
Holyoke MA 01041-0823
Detailed B/W pearl finish prints from original unaltered glass plate, ca.1863.

GRAVE CONCERNS
PO Box 20094
Cincinnati OH 45220
Sell/trade photographs of burial sites of Civil War generals blue & gray, politicians, spies, notables - many hard to find. 5,000 photos on hand; send SASE & needs. Catalog - SASE.

HEART OF HISTORY & VARIABLE HEART
540-234-9031 (mall)
John & Miriam Heatwole, Dick Swanson
Simonetti's Antique Center
Rt 11, off exit 235 on I-81
Weyerrs Cave VA 24486

One of the best Civil War shops in the Shenandoah Valley - museum-quality photos & artifacts, wrought iron, pharmaceutical relics, buttons, books, documents, much more.

GARY HENDERSHOTT
501-224-7555
PO Box 22520
Little Rock AR 72221-2520
Autographs, photographs, imprints, flags & memorabilia of the Civil War era. Catalog - $3.

HISTORICAL RESOURCES PRESS
888-BOOK4US
414-469-5582 Fax
Karin K. Ramsay
7704 Castle Grn
San Antonio TX 78218-2309
Photographer ... Under Fire: The Story of George S. Cook (1819-1902). Mathew Brady's ex-partner photographed opening shots at Fort Sumter. 40 photos, limited ed. hardcover - $29.95. Brochure.

THE HISTORICAL SHOP
504-467-2532
504-464-7552 Fax
Yvonne & Cary Delery
PO Box 73244
Metairie LA 70033-3244
Photos, documents, autographs, CSA currency, letters, slavery ads & items, relics, framed displays & other collectibles. Buys/sells. Illus. catalogs - $8/yr.

THE HORSE SOLDIER
717-334-0347
717-334-5016 Fax
http://www.bmark.com/horsesoldier.antiques
hsoldier@cvn.net
PO Box 184
Cashtown PA 17310-0184
Buying, selling & appraising Civil War military antiques: firearms, edged weapons, photographs, documents, battlefield relics & more! All items unconditionally guaranteed. Soldier research service available. Semi-annual catalog - $10/yr.

IMAGES ETC.
http://www.collectorsnet.com/imagesetc/index.htm
imagesetc@collectorsnet.com
David Cress
PO Box 493
141 Circle Loop
Eden NC 27288-0493
Civil War photos - more than 40 quality images, Union & Confederate. Buy/sell/trade. Catalog - $1.

IRISH BRIGADE GIFT SHOP
504 Baltimore St • Gettysburg PA 17325
T-shirts, sweatshirts, jackets, books, flags, recruiting posters, photos, pins, stationery, prints, figurines & more -all relating to the Irish Civil War service. Detailed item list -send business-size SASE.

JACQUES NOEL JACOBSEN, JR.
718-981-0973
60 Manor Rd • Staten Island NY 10310-2626
Antiques & military collectibles, insignia, weapons, medals, uniforms, Kepis, relics, photos, paintings, & band instruments. Catalog - $12 for 3 issues. $15 overseas.

GLENN JAMES
PO Box 268 • Rancocas NJ 08073-0268
Wartime waist-up images of George E. Lowery, Co. C, 138th Pa. Volunteers, in uniform. 8"x10" repros - $15.

JOHN'S RELICS
803-549-7751
John Steele
227 Robertson Blvd
Walterboro SC 29488-2752
Civil War & colonial relics, arms accoutrements, veteran memorabilia, newspapers, books, CW tokens, photography, buttons & related memorabilia. Catalog - $1 (ref. w/ purchase).

KEYA GALLERY
212-366-9742 • 800-906-KEYA Orders only
http://www.KeyaGallery.com
Key15@aol.com
110 W 25th St Gallery 304A
New York NY 10001-7401
Excavated relics - bullets, tokens, buckles, buttons, insignia, & more. Catalog.

KRAINIK & WALVOORD
703-536-8045
PO Box 6206
Falls Church VA 22040-6206
A Collector's Guide to Photographic Cases. Definitive reference on plastic ("Gutta Percha") daguerreotype cases. Hardcover - 800 illus. & price guide - $90 ppd.

MIKE KREMAN PHOTOGRAPHS
310-837-7756
PO Box 34242
Los Angeles CA 90034-0242
Orig. limited edition platinum/palladium photo prints of Civil War sites & battle positions as they appear today -$95. Each print is titled, signed & numbered. Call for more info.

PHILLIP B. LAMB, LTD.
504-899-4710 • 800-391-0115 Orders
504-891-6826 Fax
http://www.LambRarities.com
lambcsa@aol.com
PO Box 15850 • 2727 Prytania St
New Orleans LA 70175-5850
Buy/sell; CDVs, currency, documents, photos,
art, bonds, slave items, swords, buttons,
bullets, autographs, more. (See ad page 234)

LIVING IMAGES
304-274-0153
1104 Evergreen Cir
Falling Waters WV 25419-9745
Photography by Tim Johnson. Civil War sites
with ghosted images. All photos hand-printed,
matted & signed. From $19. Free catalog.

MC GOWAN BOOK CO.
919-403-1503 • 800-449-8406
919-403-1706 Fax
R. Douglas Sanders
39 Kimberly Dr • Durham NC 27707-5418
Always buying. Highest prices for fine & rare
CW books, autographs, documents, photos,
etc. Catalog subs. - $3. (See ad page 243)

DON MEREDITH'S CIVIL WAR ART
813-962-1225
PO Box 370020 • Tampa FL 33697-0020
Ordinary photos turn into extraordinary
CW-era portraits, with strict attention to detail.
Prices vary from $75. Discounts for photos
showing proper uniform, gear, pose, etc. Free
color brochure.

THE MILITARY COLLECTION
PO Box 830970M
Miami FL 33283-0970
Helmets, uniforms, field gear, awards,
medals, flags, weapons, swords, photos, etc.
Catalog - $8.

MILITARY IMAGES
http://www.civilwar-photos.com
milimage@csrlink.net
RR 1 Box 99A
Henryville PA 18332-9726
Est. 1979. Publication presenting great
photographs of Yanks, Rebs & Indian
soldiers. Subscriptions - $24/yr. for 6 issues.

MOTTS MILITARY MUSEUM
614-836-5781
Warren Motts, Director
5761 Ebright Rd
Groveport OH 43125-9744
Civil War items & exhibits.

MOUNTAIN MAGIC IN METAL
719-486-8166
517 W Chestnut St
Leadville CO 80461
Pictures engraved on zinc plates, taken from
original photos. Lincoln, Grant, Lee ($295 ea.)
or Gettysburg Address ($375). S&H - $25.
Custom photographic engraving.

SUSAN A. NASH
304-876-3772
PO Box 1011
Shepherdstown WV 25443-1011
Paper conservation. Specialist in historic
documents, photographs, prints, drawings,
maps, letters, broadsides. Cleaning, mending,
deacidification, museum matting. By appt.

NATIONAL HERITAGE ARTS
8301 Alvord St
Mc Lean VA 22102-1736
Actual photographs, collectors' items.
Satin-finished antique prints produced from
archive negatives by noted Civil War
photographers. 11" x 14" from $16.95.

NORTH STREET STUDIO
410-392-0630
210 North St
Elkton MD 21921-5530
Framed generals: Grant, Sherman, Buford,
Chamberlain, Lee, Jackson, Stuart,
Longstreet. 8"x10" hand-printed sepia-toned
photos, double matted, walnut or silver frame.

NORTHERN CO. ARCHIVES/ACQUISITIONS
800-432-8777
18640 Mack Ave
PO Box 36793
Grosse Pointe Woods MI 48236-0793
Buyers of autographs, documents, photo
collections, stock certificates, letters,
contracts, etc. Lifetime member MS&D
Society. Top $ paid.

HOWARD L. NORTON
PO Box 22821
Little Rock AR 72221-2821
Buy/sell/appraise. Autographs, Civil War
items, Americana, historical documents,
photographs, coins, currency, stamps, postal
history. All transactions confidential. Catalog.

OLD PHOTO RESTORATION
815-227-0651
Civil War collectors - allow me to bring back
the memories. Multimedia, photocollage,
webpages.

OLDE SOLDIER BOOKS, INC.
301-963-2929
301-963-9556 Fax
Warbooks@erols.com
Dave Zullo
18779 N Frederick Ave Ste B
Gaithersburg MD 20879-3158
Largest selection of rare & hard-to-find books.
Documents, letters, photographs, autographs,
manuscripts. Buy/sell. Free catalog.

PANORAMICS
612-332-3912
James O. Phelps
PO Box 580678
Minneapolis MN 55458-0678
Panoramic, seamless battlefield photos of
Gettysburg & Antietam battlefields, with maps
& text. Free brochure.

PHOTOGRAPHY OF YESTERYEAR
423-510-9306
cwphotogpr@aol.com
Frank or Rita Harned
1 Pryor Dr
Chattanooga TN 37421-2278
Photograph birthplaces, churches,
cemeteries, landmarks. Photograph CW
battlefields of approximate location of your
ancestor's unit. Limited unit research available
for TN, GA, KY.

PICTURE THAT ANTIQUES & COLLECTIBLES
414-361-0255
414-361-2992 Fax
107 W Huron St
Berlin WI 54923
Large selection of tintypes, CDVs,
ambrotypes & cabinet cards of Civil War
soldiers & civilians. Books.

JOHN I. PISARCIK
1500 Annette Ave
Library PA 15129-9735
Reenactors - will draw your portrait from photo
in "Battlefield Style." Special attention paid to
details of uniforms, clothing & equipment.

PROFILES IN HISTORY
800-942-8856 • 310-859-7701
310-859-3842 Fax
345 N Maple Dr Ste 202
Beverly Hills CA 90210-3859
Autographs wanted. Also buying original
letters, documents, vintage photos,
manuscripts, & rare books (signed). Illus.
catalog - $45/yr. Sample - $10.

STEVEN S. RAAB AUTOGRAPHS
800-977-8333
610-446-4514 Fax
http://www.raabautographs.com
raab@netaxs,com
PO Box 471 • Ardmore PA 19003-0471
Serious collectors, respected dealers. Top
dollars paid for collection & quality individual
autographs, documents, manuscripts, signed
photos, & interesting letters. Catalog sample -
$5; $15/yr.

RIENZI PRESS
802-888-3439
Brad & Sue Limage
RR 2 Box 630 • Morrisville VT 05661-9802
"Vermont Soldiers in the Civil War" - calendar
printed annually with large prints of Vermont
brigades, CDUs, letter excerpts & battles on
corresponding dates. $10 + S&H.

RON'S PHOTOGRAPHY
419-886-4835
rburgesssr@aol.com
770 State Route 97 E
Bellville OH 44813-1230
For all your photographic needs. Reasonable
rates. Personalized service. Experienced
photo-journalist, reenactor.

SELECTED CIVIL WAR PHOTOGRAPHS
http://rs6.loc.gov/cwphome.html
Resource providing views of 1,118 historic
photos.

JOHN SICKLES
7880 Madison St • Merrillville IN 46410
Buy/sell/trade cavalry images, specializing in
Michigan Cavalry Brigade (1st, 5th, 6th, 7th
regiments) & images depicting carbines.

DALE S. SNAIR
816-747-0341
904 Deer Run Apt C
Warrensburg MO 64093
Civil War images, paper items, weapons,
accoutrements. $4 for next 4 price lists.

SOUTHERN HISTORICAL SHOWCASE
800-854-7832 • 615-321-0639
http://www.southernhistorical.com
southernhistorical@nashville.com
1907 Division St
Nashville TN 37203-2705
Southern military art & books, prints, original
documents & autographs, photos, engravings.
Artists: Prechtel, Reeves, Kunstler, Kidd,
Gallon, Summers, Heron, Garner, Rocco.
Catalog - $5.

STOKES IMAGING SERVICES
800-856-4498 • 512-458-2201
7000 Cameron Rd
Austin TX 78752
Selected Civil War photographs, 1861-1865.
Tapes CD-ROM for IBM or PC compatible -
$79.95.

SUTLERS WAGON
Stamatelos Bros, Prop.
PO Box 390005
Cambridge MA 02139-0001
Fine quality American military items,
1775-1900. Civil War uniforms, headgear,
accoutrements, buckles, tack, photos, swords,
documents. Buy/sell.

TAILORED IMAGES
804-272-3345 • 804-744-2624
804-330-9003 Fax
MXHW21A@prodigy.com
3108 Quail Hill Dr
Midlothian VA 23112
Photo restoration. Custom B&W archival
quality prints. Digital imaging. Let us preserve
your treasured Civil War photos. Repairs,
reproductions, custom printing.

TEKNOVATION
540-548-4128
2594 Kendalwood Ln
Charlottesville VA 22911-8263
Images of the Civil War, Vol. 1. Selected Civil
War photographs 1861-1865. Interactive PC
images. Use as screensaver, with printout
capability. $24.95.

THEME PRINTS, LTD.
800-CIVL WAR • 718-225-4067
PO Box 610123
Bayside NY 11361-0123
Books, antique arms, historic documents,
photographs, letters & autographs from
Revolutionary era to early Hollywood.
Includes Civil War memorabilia. Fully illus.
catalog - $5, or $12/yr. (5 issues).

CAROLE THOMPSON, FINE PHOTOGRAPHS
901-278-2741
901-726-5533 Fax
ctfp@ix.netcom.com
1515 Central Ave
Memphis TN 38104-4907
Gardner's Sketchbook of the Civil War, 100
museum quality albumen photos by
Alexander Gardner & Timothy O'Sullivan.
Buys/sells/appraises.

TIME LINE PHOTOS
717-337-0055
Old Gettysburg Village
777 Baltimore St
Gettysburg PA 17325-2600
Reenactor portraits, featuring reproduction
period backdrops. New, larger studio.

TRUE TO LIFE, INC.
800-847-6788 • 703-440-5062
7406 Alban Station Ct Ste B203
Springfield VA 22150-2310
Photo restoration, low cost, fast service. Old
or damaged images. Consultations free &
encouraged.

WAR BETWEEN THE STATES MEMORABILIA
717-337-2853
Len Rosa
PO Box 3965
Gettysburg PA 17325-0965
Buy/sell soldiers' letters, envelopes,
documents, CDVs, photos, autographs,
newspapers, badges, ribbons, relics, framed
display items, currency, & more. Estab. 1978.
Illus. catalogs - $10/yr for 5 issues. Active
buyers receive future subscriptions free.

WELL-TRAVELED IMAGES
414-574-1865
414-896-0572 Fax
http://www.globaldialog.com/~eicher/index.htm
eicher@globaldialog.com
Lynda Eicher
S60 W24160 Red Wing Dr
Waukesha WI 53186-9508
Color photos of CW battlefields, sites. Books.
Matted color prints of 10,000+ CW-related
images, also available for publication. Call or
email for catalog. See internet home page for
samples & info. on books.

GEORGE F. WITHAM
901-465-6722 Phone & Fax
155 Raspberry Cv
Eads TN 38028-3003
Catalog of Civil War Photographers -
alphabetical listing by state of more than 5900
Civil War-era photographers. Softcover -
$16.50 ppd.

CRAIG WOFFORD ANTIQUES
2101 Harrison Ave
Orlando FL 32804-5467
Civil War memorabilia bought/sold,
appraisals; specializing in autographs, letters,
documents, diaries, photographs. Identifies
items, soldiers groupings. Est. 1975.

WRITE-TO-PRINT
PO Box 177
Sandy Creek NY 13145-0177
Extensive photos of men & battles. Maps
showing placement of the regiments in
battles, 24th, 81st, 110th, 147th, 184th NYV
Infantry & 24th Cavalry, their stories - $20.

YANKEE FORAGER
517-263-3925
137 Park St
Adrian MI 49221-2528
Civil War specialty books, documents, photos,
relics, & more. Catalog - $2.

ZANGRONIZ PHOTOGRAPHY
301-924-2539
4011 Muncaster Mill Rd Ste 101
Rockville MD 20853-1426
U.S. Civil War reenactment postcards. First of
series. Images of actual events. 4 cards in
each set. 4 sets @ $1.50/set + $2 S&H. (See
ad page 230)

ZIGZAG MULTIMEDIA
800-561-2765
100 professional quality photos on CD-ROM,
with extensive text history to print into your
own documents & presentations. Heritage of
America series, incl. Civil War Battlefields.
$49.95/CD.

BLITZKRIEG PRESS
21 Meridian Cir
Newtown PA 18940-1742
Stationery, notepads, etc. For sutlers, Civil War enthusiasts; personal or business use. Any design you request or have. Send $1 for more info.

CHAMBERLAIN PRESS
355 Kingsbury Way Apt 33
Westminster MD 21157-9409
Professional desktop publisher will produce 1st-rate materials for your needs. Catalogs, calendars, certificates, manuals, newsletters, programs, special documents. Specializing in Civil War materials. Free brochure.

CIVIL WAR LABELS UNLIMITED
Paul Wilson
46 Sawmill Rd
Springfield MA 01118-1719
Personalized name/address labels, bookplates, notecards & scratch pad stationery - featuring your favorite CW personalities (more than 220 available). Illus. price list - $1.

GALLAGHER PRINTING
716-873-2434
716-873-0809 Fax
2507 Delaware Ave
Buffalo NY 14216-1792
For all your printing needs. Letterheads, envelopes, business cards, brochures, fliers, posters, etc. Call/write.

HUMMEL PRINTING
610-286-0399
PO Box 171
Geigertown PA 19523-0171
12 Civil War-theme Christmas cards (4 dif. styles) with envelopes - $8 + $1.50 S&H. Special occasion & ladies' notecards, Civil War-theme writing paper & envelopes. Catalog - $1.

MHR & SONS
7387 Bethany Ridge Rd
Guysville OH 45735
Personalized bookplates. CW theme: 50 for $14, 100 for $24. Add 10% S&H.

PATRICK A. SCHROEDER PUBLICATIONS
804-376-1865
RR 2 Box 128
Brookneal VA 24528
Civil War books - myths about Lee's surrender, Fighting Quakers, a Duryee Zouave, record of North Carolina, diary of Swedish officer. Archives research, prints, notecards, postcards available. Free catalog.

ADENIRAM PUBLICATIONS
3722 W 50th St # 328
Minneapolis MN 55410
*Brackett's Battalion: Minnesota Cavalry
1861-1866* (Bergemann). Softcover, 164 pp. -
$12.99 + $2 S&H.

AMERICAN POLITICAL BIOGRAPHY
39 Boggs Hill Rd • Newtown CT 06470-1971
Presidential biographies. Send 32-cent stamp
for monthly listing of available titles.

AYER COMPANY PUBLISHERS
603-922-5105 • 603-922-3348 Fax
Educational_Edge@msb.com
Haven Haynes
Lower Mill Rd • North Stratford NH 03590
*Black Brigade, Folks from Dixie, David
Glasgow Farragut: Admiral in the Making,
Minutes of the Proceedings of the National
Negro Convention.* More than 60 other titles.
Catalog - $24.95 on CD-ROM. 25%
restocking fee if not prepaid.

BELLE GROVE PUBLISHING CO.
800-861-1861
PO Box 483 • Kearny NJ 07032-0483
Titles include *History of the 57th
Pennsylvania, Four Years Campaigning in the
Army of the Potomac.* Videos of "lost" films
from silent movie era - *CW Cinema* Vols I-III.
Call/write for more info.

BIG SHANTY PUBLISHING CO.
PO Box 80641
Chamblee GA 30366-0641
*Ghost Trains & Depots of Georgia
(1833-1933)*, by Les R. Winn. Complete story
of all Georgia's passenger carrying railroads.
400 pp., hardcover - $65 + $4 S&H.

BLACKSMITH PUBLISHERS
800-531-2665
bcbooks@northlink.com
PO Box 1752 • Chino Valley AZ 86323-1752
Sea Officer, historical novel based on
lesser-known Civil War naval actions - $22.95
ppd. Free booklist.

JOHN F. BLAIR, PUBLISHER
800-222-9796 • 910-768-1374
910-768-9194 Fax
blairpub@aol.com
1406 Plaza Dr
Winston-Salem NC 27103-1470
*Civil War Blunders: Amusing Incidents from
the War*, by Clint Johnson; *The Lee Girls*, by
Mary Price Coulling; other regional & Civil
War titles. Catalog.

BLUE A1CORN PRESS
304-733-3917
5589 Shawnee Dr
PO Box 2684
Huntington WV 25726-0084
Book publishers: *Blood & Sacrifice, The 72nd
Indiana: Wilder's Lightning Brigade, How
Soldiers Were Made*, & many more.

BNR PRESS
800-793-0683 Orders & Fax
419-732-NOTE (6683)
http://www.dcache.net/~bnrpress
bnrpress@dcache.net
Fred Schwan
132 E 2nd St • Port Clinton OH 43452-1115
Publisher of the *Comprehensive Catalog of
Confederate Paper Money* by Grover Criswell
& other titles of interest to collectors.
Hardcover - $35; dealer discounts. Advertising
opportunities.

BOGG & LAURENCE PUBLISHING CO.
800-345-5595 • 305-866-3600
305-866-8040 Fax
1007 Kane Concourse
Bay Harbor Islands FL 33154-2105
The new *Dietz Confederate States Catalog
and Handbook*, 2nd printing. Most
comprehensive treatment of Confederate
stamps & postal history; reorganized &
expanded for easier use. Hardcover, 300 pp. -
$75.

BOYD PUBLISHING CO.
800-452-4035 • 912-452-4020 after 6pm EST
tignall@accucomm.net
PO Box 367 • Milledgeville GA 31061-0367
100s of new historical publications &
genealogical references. Computer software,
incl. *Official Record of the War of the
Rebellion* - all 127 vols. on CD-ROM, $89.95
+ $5 S&H.

BPC PUBLISHERS
PO Box 436 • Mahomet IL 61853-0436
Total War in Carolina. Story of Sherman's
1865 Carolina's campaign as told by its
participants. 125 pp. - $16.00 ppd.

BROADFOOT PUBLISHING COMPANY
910-686-4816 • 910-686-4379 Fax
http://broadfoot.wilmington.net
Tom Broadfoot
1907 Buena Vista Cir
Wilmington NC 28405-7892
Sell rare & out-of-print material, own
publications by catalog. In-print catalog - $2.
Out-of-print catalog - $5 (ref. w/ order).

BROWN PUBLICATIONS
BrianB1578@aol.com
PO Box 25501
Little Rock AR 72221
In the Footsteps of the Blue & Gray - $24.95 +
$2 S&H. Describes CW-related research
sources in state archives, National Archives &
LDS collection. History of ea. corps &
hard-to-find technical information.

BUDD PRESS
71 66th St
Glendale NY 11385
*President Lincoln's Third Largest City:
Brooklyn & the Civil War.* Fascinating reading
- $13.95 ppd.

BURD STREET PRESS
888-WHT MANE • 717-532-2237
717-532-7704 Fax
Harold Collier
PO Box 152
Shippensburg PA 17257-0152
Publisher of military history with core interest
in U.S. Civil War. Write for titles. Free catalog.

BUTTERNUT AND BLUE
410-256-9220
410-256-8423 Fax
Jim McLean
3411 Northwind Rd
Baltimore MD 21234-1250
Offer 5 to 6 comprehensive book catalogs
each year. Librarian from prestigious college
proclaimed that ours was "the best CW
catalog." Catalog - $2 ($5 outside US); free
after order.

BUTTERNUT PUBLICATIONS
304-267-0540
Susan Crites
PO Box 1851
Martinsburg WV 25402-1851
Civil War titles; ghost books.

C. W. HISTORICALS
609-854-1290 Phone & Fax
cwhist@erols.com
PO Box 113
Collingswood NJ 08108-0113
Civil War Spoken Here. Dictionary of
mispronounced people, places & things of
1860s. 216 pp. - $14 ppd. Other titles.

CAISSON PRESS
607-547-1080
81 Lake St
Cooperstown NY 13326-1038

Fields of Gray: The Battle of Griswoldville,
232 pp. *Cradled in Glory: Georgia Military
Institute, 1851-1865*, 224 pp. *Among the Best
Men the South Could Boast: The Fall of Fort
McAllister*, 160 pp. All hardcover - $25 ea.
(ppd.)

CAMP CHASE PUBLISHING
http://nemesis.cybergate.net/~civilwar
CampChase@compuserve.com
PO Box 707
Marietta OH 45750-0707
How to Get Started in Civil War Reenacting -
36-pg. handbook, written by veteran
reenactor. Great tips. $5.

CAMP POPE BOOKSHOP
319-351-2407
319-339-5964 Fax
http://members.aol.com/ckenyoncpb
ckenyoncpb@aol.com
PO Box 2232
Iowa City IA 52244-2232
Largest selection of in-print titles, including
reprints, on trans-Mississippi theater of the
Civil War. Free catalog.

CAPPER PRESS
800-678-5779 x4316
1503 SW 42nd St
Topeka KS 66609-1214
Authentic Memoirs of Civil War Soldiers.
Softcover -$6.95.

CHICKASAW BAYOU PRESS
103 Trace Harbor Rd
Madison MS 39110
*To Live and Die in Dixie: A History of the 3rd
Regiment Mississippi Infantry, CSA* - 660 pp.,
hardcover, $42.50 + $3 S&H. *Hill of Death:
The Battle of Champion Hill* -softcover, $5 +
$1.50 S&H. Ltd. eds.

STAN CLARK MILITARY BOOKS
717-337-1728
717-337-0581 Fax
915 Fairview Ave
Gettysburg PA 17325-2906
Buys/sells Civil War books, ltd. edition prints,
autographs, letters, documents, postcards,
soldiers' items; special interest in U.S. Marine
Corps items.

COBBLESTONE PUBLISHING
800-821-0115
http://www.cobblestonepub.com
custsvc@cobblestone.mv.com
7 School St
Peterborough NH 03458-1454

Two-volume Civil War Era set. Vol. I - *A House Divided*; Vol. II - *A New Nation*. $44.95/set. Forewords by Ken Burns & James McPherson. Free catalog.

COLLECTORS' LIBRARY
541-937-3348
PO Box 263 • Eugene OR 97440-0263
THE publisher for key reference books on accoutrements, guns, saddles, edged weapons, etc., for pre-Civil War, Civil War, Indian War & post-1900 period. Free illus. catalog.

COMBINED PUBLISHING
610-828-2595
http://www.dca.net/combinedbooks
combined@dca.net
1024 Fayette St • PO Box 307
Conshohocken PA 19428-0307
Titles include *Gettysburg, July 1*; *In Search of Robert E. Lee*; *Civil War Firearms*; *The Appomattox Campaign*; *The Antietam Campaign*; *The Gettysburg Campaign*, etc. Free catalog.

DA CAPO PRESS
800-321-0050
233 Spring St
New York NY 10013-1522
The Rise of U. S. Grant; My Enemy, My Brother; The Antietam and Fredericksburg; many more. From $13.95.

DETROIT BOOK PRESS
901 W Lafayette Blvd
Detroit MI 48226-3013
Michigan Regimentals facsimile hardcover reprints.

THE DIETZ PRESS
800-391-6833
804-733-3514 Fax
Wert Smith
903 Winfield Rd
Petersburg VA 23803-4747
Cornbread and Maggots, Cloak and Dagger: Union Prisoners and Spies in Civil War Richmond, by David D. Ryan - $24.95. Trials & tribulations from Union & Confederate sources.

THE DIXIE PRESS
615-831-0776 Phone & Fax
PO Box 110783
Nashville TN 37222-0783
Publisher, wholesaler & retailer of Southern books & genealogy products. Free catalog.

DOBI PUBLISHING
716-372-8687
1662 Haskell Pkwy
Olean NY 14760
New edition of *Directory of Buyers* - lists 1000s of collectors & dealers who are anxious to buy. $14.95 + $3 S&H.

DOVER PUBLICATIONS
31 E 2nd St
Mineola NY 11501
Civil War books, including *Personal Memoirs of U.S. Grant*. Many others. Free catalog.

DOWN EAST BOOKS
800-685-7962
PO Box 679
Camden ME 04843-0679
A Distant War Comes Home: Maine in the Civil War Era - Softcover, 384 pp., $21.45 ppd.

EAKIN PRESS
800-880-8642 • 512-288-1771
512-288-1813 Fax
http://www.lsjunction.com
EAKINPUB@SIG.NET
Edwin M. Eakin, Pres.
8800 Tara Ln • PO Box 90159
Austin TX 78709-0159
Battleflags of Texas in the Confederacy, 80 full-color battleflags, in-depth researched & illus. 128 pp., "coffee-table" style - $32. *Texas and Texans in the Civil War*, 464 pp., hardcover - $27.95. Catalog - $1.25 (ref.).

THE EASTON PRESS
800-367-4534
47 Richards Ave
Norwalk CT 06857
Own the finest editions of the 35 best Civil War books - the leather-bound Library of the Civil War.

EDINBOROUGH PRESS
612-415-1034
612-482-1080 Fax
edinborough@juno.com
PO Box 13790
Roseville MN 55113-2293
Our Army Nurses: Stories from Women in the Civil War, by Mary Gardner Holland - 320 pp., softcover, $19.95. Other Civil War titles. Catalog.

EDMONSTON PUBLISHING, INC.
315-824-1965
PO Box 38
Hamilton NY 13346-0038

PUBLISHERS (BOOKS)

While My Country Is in Danger, 12th NJ. *No Middle Ground*, Union Artillery. $22.95 ea. *Memoirs of the 149th NYV* - $35.95. *Unfurl the Flags* - $4.95. S&H -$3.50/$1.50/$1.00. Other new & used titles. Free catalog.

ELLIOTT & CLARK PUBLISHING
800-959-3245 • 334-265-8880 Fax
http://www.blackbeltpress.com
sales@blackbeltpress.com
PO Box 551
Montgomery AL 36101-0551
Titles include *A Guide to Civil War Washington* - $12.95, *Mapping for Stonewall: The Civil War Service of Jed Hotchkiss* - $29.95, *Fallen Soldiers: Memoir of a Civil War Casualty* - $14.95.

EPM PUBLICATIONS, INC.
703-442-7810 • 800-289-2339
703-442-0599 Fax
1003 Turkey Run Rd • McLean VA 22101
Washington's Independent Book Publisher.
Many Civil War titles. Free catalog.

FABER & FABER PUBLISHERS
53 Shore Rd
Winchester MA 01890-2821
Featuring Civil War books such as *Battlefield: Framing a Civil War Battleground*, by Peter Svenson. Clothbound - $21.95.

FIVE CEDARS PRESS
540-877-2796
Allan Tischler
841 Wardensville Grade
Winchester VA 22602-2058
The History of the Harpers Ferry Cavalry Expedition (Sept. 14 & 15, 1862) Ltd. ed. Hardcover book, illus., maps - $24.95 ppd.

FORDHAM UNIVERSITY PRESS
718-817-4782 • 800-247-6553 Orders
718-817-4785 Fax
vancott@murray.fordham.edu
Margaret Van Cott
2546 Belmont Ave • University Box L
Bronx NY 10458-5106
Scholarly books in the humanities. Two continuing Civil War series: *The Irish in the Civil War* and *The North's Civil War*. Free catalog.

FRANKLIN BOOKSELLERS
615-370-5737 Publisher
615-790-1349 Store
118 4th Ave S
Franklin TN 37064-2622

FREE PRESS
212-702-2000
866 3rd Ave
New York NY 10022-6221
A Woman of Valor: Clara Barton and the Civil War. 1994, 527 pp., illus., etc. - $27.95.

FULCRUM PUBLISHING
303-277-1623
303-279-7111 Fax
fulcrum@concentric.net
Promotions Mgr.
350 Indiana St Ste 350
Golden CO 80401-5093
Publisher of books & calendars including *Mapping the Civil War*, collection of rare maps from the Library of Congress. Free catalog.

G W SPECIALTIES
816-356-7457
George Scheil
7311 Ditzler
Raytown MO 64133
Civilian reprints of magazines & schoolbooks from mid-1800s. Free catalog.

GENEALOGICAL PUBLISHING CO.
800-296-6687
1001 N Calvert St
Baltimore MD 21202-3897
Publishers of the *Index to the Roll of Honor*, an incredible guide to the 228,639 Union dead listed in the *Roll's* 27 vols. 1164 pp. $75. On CD-ROM, incl. entire Roll of Honor - $49.99. Free catalog.

GIBBS SMITH, PUBLISHER
800-743-5439
http://www.gibbs-smith.com
info@gibbs-smith.com
PO Box 667 • Layton UT 84041-0667
Returning to the Civil War: Grand Reenactments of an Anguished Time - living history at its best in full-color photography. 96 pp., softcover - $21.95. Free catalog.

GUILD PRESS OF INDIANA
317-848-6421 • 800-913-9563 Orders
http://www.guildpress.com
435 Gradle Dr • Carmel IN 46032
The Civil War CD-Rom; *Iron Men, Iron Will*; *The Road to Glory*; *Rebel Sons of Erin*; *Field Surgeon at Gettysburg*. Other titles.

GUTS & GLORY PUBLICATIONS
3319 Dorado Pl
Carlsbad CA 92009
The Battle of Antietam and *Life in the South During the Civil War*. $20 ea. + $3 S&H.

THE HEARTHSIDE PUBLISHING CO.
301-963-0141
PO Box 2773
Staunton VA 24402
Valor in Gray: The Recipients of the Confederate Medal of Honor, by Gregg S. Clemmer. 496 pp., hardcover - $29.95 + $3 S&H.

J.W. HENRY PUBLISHING, INC.
703-404-0543 Fax
75361.755@compuserve.com
PO Box 1501
Ashburn VA 20146-1501
Corporal Si Klegg and His Pard - Col. Wilbur Hinman's classic account of the day-to-day life of the Civil War enlisted man. $34.95 + $3.50 S&H.

HIGH WATER PRESS
315 S Arrawana Ave
Tampa FL 33609-3209
Recent books by Harris Mullen - *10 Incredible Mistakes at Gettysburg* and *Confederate Generals at Gettysburg* $5.95 ea. + $1.50 S&H. Both books - $11.90; no extras.

HISTORICAL RESOURCES PRESS
888-BOOK4US
414-469-5582 Fax
Karin K. Ramsay
7704 Castle Grn
San Antonio TX 78218-2309
Photographer ... Under Fire: The Story of George S. Cook (1819-1902). Mathew Brady's ex-partner photographed opening shots at Fort Sumter. 40 photos, limited ed. hardcover - $29.95. Brochure.

H. E. HOWARD, INC.
PO Box 4161
Lynchburg VA 24502-0161
Many Civil War titles.

HOWELL PRESS
804-977-4006
howellpres@aol.com
1147 River Rd Ste 2
Charlottesville VA 22901-4172
Civil War titles, as well as books on history, transportation, cooking & gardening.

INDEPENDENT PUBLISHERS
3535 E Coast Hwy
Corona del Mar CA 92625-2404
War & Warriors series. Books, videos, audiotapes. Men, machines, strategies, battles, & politics of war. Catalog - send SASE.

INDIANA UNIVERSITY PRESS
812-855-6553 • 800-842-6796 Orders
http://www.indiana.edu/~iupress
601 N Morton St
Bloomington IN 47404-3778
The Men Stood Like Iron: How the Iron Brigade Won Its Name - hardcover, $24.95. Other titles.

JAMES RIVER PUBLICATIONS
804-220-4912
http://www.erols.com/jreb/civilwar.htm
102 Maple Ln
Williamsburg VA 23185-8106
The Chronological Tracking of the American Civil War per the Official Records, 2nd ed., fully indexed, foreword by Dr. Arthur W. Bergeron, Jr. The ultimate Civil War reference manual - $39.95.

THE JOHNS HOPKINS UNIVERSITY PRESS
800-537-5487
http://jhupress.jhu.edu/home.html
Hampden Station
Baltimore MD 21211
The Long Roll (softcover - $15.95) and *Cease Firing* (softcover - $14.95), both by Mary Johnston, a Civil War novelist rediscovered.

JOHN KALLMAN, PUBLISHERS
717-258-0919
717-258-4161 Fax
701 W North St
Carlisle PA 17013-2227
Titles include *Bull Run: Its Strategy & Tactics*, by Robert M. Johnson. 293 pp., hardcover, $29.95 ppd.

KANSAS HERITAGE PRESS
913-242-9243
PO Box 503
Ottawa KS 66067-0503
Books dealing with Kansas' heritage & the Civil War. *Rebel Invasion of Missouri and Kansas*, *The Union Indian Brigade*, *The Civil War on the Border*, etc.

KENIMAR PUBLISHING
3137 Flowers Rd S Apt C
Atlanta GA 30341-5646
The History of Stone Mountain, memorial to the valor of soldiers, sailors & women of the Confederacy. $6 ppd.

WILLIAM KENNANN PUBLICATIONS
2016 Fidler Ave
Long Beach CA 90815-2931
William Newby: A Civil War Soldier's Return.

KENNESAW MOUNTAIN PRESS, INC.
616-456-8115
75 Sheldon Blvd SE Ste 103
Grand Rapids MI 49503-4224
Melton & Pawl's Guide to CW Artillery Projectiles. Must-have pictorial handbook for collectors & researchers. Softcover - $9.95 + $3 S&H. Hardcover - $19.95.

THE KENT STATE UNIVERSITY PRESS
800-247-6553 x198
PO Box 5190 • Kent OH 44242-0001
No Sorrow Like Our Sorrow, Holding the Line, A Surgeon's Civil War, April '65, Red River Campaign, The First Day at Gettysburg, others.

SGT. KIRKLAND'S MUSEUM & HISTORICAL SOCIETY, INC.
540-899-5565 • 540-899-7643 Fax
Civil-War@msn.com
912 Lafayette Blvd
Fredericksburg VA 22401-5617
Non-profit museum, association & press devoted to preservation of historical documents, artifacts, & texts; education; publication of meritorius books; & research & recovery of CW soldiers' records. Free catalog.

LAND & LAND PUBLISHERS
504-344-1059
Ken Land
196 S 14th St • Baton Rouge LA 70802
Civil War books by William A. Spedale. *Where Bugles Called & Rifles Gleamed* - battle of Port Hudson, La. Hardcover, $17.95. *Historic Treasures of the American Civil War* - hardcover, $21.95. $2 S&H.

LENZ DESIGN & COMMUNICATIONS
404-633-0501 • 404-633-0047 Fax
Lenz_Design@msn.com
Sheila J. Lenz
2882 Delcourt Dr
Decatur GA 30033
Civil War in Georgia: An Illustrated Traveler's Guide - 116 pp., softcover, $19.95

THE LIBRARY OF AMERICA
212-308-3360 • 212-750-8352 Fax
Libamerica@aol.com
Karen Iker
14 E 60th St
New York NY 10022-1006
Independent, non-profit publisher dedicated to preserving America's most significant writing in hardcover. Over 90 vols. in print, including Grant, Sherman & Lincoln. Free catalog.

LILLIBRIDGE PUBLISHING CO.
520-775-4681
Laurence F. Lillibridge
5313 N Western Blvd
Prescott Valley AZ 86314-4255
Hard Marches, Hard Crackers, & Hard Beds - reveals a soldier's hard life in his own letters & diaries of 3 yrs. $29.95 (ppd).

LOUISIANA STATE UNIVERSITY PRESS
504-388-6666 • 504-388-6461 Fax
uppress@lsuvm.sncc.lsu.edu
Margaret Hart
PO Box 25053 • Baton Rouge LA 70894-5053
Great Civil War titles, incl. *The Battles for Spotsylvania Court House and the Road to Yellow Tavern* (Rhea) and *Collis' Zouaves* (Hagerty). Free catalog.

MADISON HOUSE PUBLISHERS, INC.
800-604-1776 Orders • 608-244-6210
608-244-7050 Fax
http://www.globaldialog.com/~mhbooks
info@mhbooks.com
PO Box 3100 • 2016 Winnebago St
Madison WI 53704
Independent scholarly press dedicated to publishing fine books of enduring significance on American history & culture. Free catalog.

MC FARLAND & CO., INC.
910-246-4460 • 800-253-2187 Orders
http://www.mcfarlandpub.com
PO Box 611 • Jefferson NC 28640-0611
Civil War books, Union & Confederate.

MC GUINN & MC GUIRE PUBLISHING
PO Box 20603 • Bradenton FL 34204-0603
In the Defense of This Flag: CW Diary of Pvt. Ormond Hupp. 309 pp. - $19.95 ppd.

MEDICAL STAFF PRESS
616-363-8655 Phone & Fax
http://www.iserv.net/~civilmed
CIVILMED@aol.com
Bradley P. Bengtson, MD
4286 Knapp Valley Ct NE
Grand Rapids MI 49505-9738
Orthopaedic Injuries of the Civil War - Softcover, $9.95 + $3 S&H; and *Photographic Atlas of Civil War Injuries* -Hardcover, $125 + $5 S&H.

MEHERRIN RIVER PRESS
919-398-3554
301 E Broad St
Murfreesboro NC 27855-1316
Gatling: A Photographic Remembrance - book on the Gatling gun - $25.

MERCER UNIVERSITY PRESS
800-637-2378 x2880 • 912-752-2264 Fax
http://www.mercer.edu/mupress
mupressorders@mercer.edu
6316 Peake Rd • Macon GA 31210-3960
The Lion of the South: Gen. Thomas C. Hindman $17.95; *Col. Burton's Spiller & Burr Revolver* $22.95; *The Forgotten "Stonewall of the West"* $32.95; *Rebel Georgia* $24.95 (HB), $15.95 (PB). *Carved in Stone* $32.95.

MERIT PRESS
1937 Robertson Rd SW
Albuquerque NM 87105-4057
Rebels on the Rio Grande, the Civil War journal of A.B. Peticolas with the Sibley Brigade in New Mexico (4th Texas Vols.). 187-pg softcover - $14.50 ppd.

MEYER PUBLISHING
800-477-5046 • 319-477-5041
319-477-5042 Fax
gfdchief@netins.net
PO Box 247 • Garrison IA 52229-0247
Iowa Valor - 250 firsthand accounts of IA troops in Civil War combat - $37.50. *Dark Days of the Rebellion* -Firsthand account, commentary of Civil War soldier in Salisbury Prison, a place worse than Andersonville - $24.95. Other titles. Free catalog.

MICHIGAN STATE UNIVERSITY PRESS
517-355-9543 • 800-678-2120 Fax
1405 S Harrison Rd Ste 25 • Manly Miles Bldg
East Lansing MI 48823-5243
Many titles. Write or call for complete list, including *The Ewing Family Civil War Letters*, *Trials and Triumphs*, *Women of the American Civil War*, etc.

MINERVA CENTER ON WOMEN & THE MILITARY
410-437-5379
http://www.MinervaCenter.com
mouseminer@aol.com
20 Granada Rd • Pasadena MD 21122-2708
Non-profit education foundation & publisher. 3rd printing of *An Uncommon Soldier: The Civil War Letters of Sarah Rosetta Wakeman, alias Pvt. Lyons Wakeman*. $25.

MISSOURI RIVER PRESS
573-446-3764
Phil Gottschalk, Pres.
1664 Highridge Cir Ste C
Columbia MO 65203-1930
In Deadly Earnest - the Missouri Brigade CSA which fought in the Vicksburg, Atlanta, & Tennessee campaigns - $30.

MONTPELIER PUBLISHING
PO Box 3384, University Station
Charlottesville VA 22903-0384
Best Little Stories from the Civil War by C. Brian Kelly, editor emeritus of *Military History* magazine, incl. "Varina: Forgotten First Lady," by Ingrid Smyer. A must-read. Softcover - $14.50 + $2.50 S&H.

MORNINGSIDE BOOKSHOP
800-648-9710 • 937-461-4260 Fax
http://www.morningsidebooks.com
msbooks@erinet.com
Bob Younger
PO Box 1087 • Dayton OH 45401-1087
Editor & publisher of Civil War books & *Gettysburg* magazine. Catalog: ours & other publishers' CW books -$4 (free w/ order).

NAVAL INSTITUTE PRESS
800-233-8764 • 410-224-3378
410-224-2406 Fax • http://www.usni.org
2062 Generals Hwy
Annapolis MD 21401-6780
Fascinating facts & references to ships, battles & prominent people in military history; many titles on Civil War ships & battles. Free catalog.

NORTH SOUTH TRADERS CIVIL WAR
540-67-CIVIL • 540-672-7283 Fax
nstcw@msn.com
PO Box 631 • Orange VA 22960-0370
Illustrated, bi-annual *Civil War Collectors' Price Guide* -$25 + $3 S&H. Bi-monthly magazine, heavily illustrated -$25/yr.

THE NUGGET PUBLISHERS
812-866-4456
2146 S Logan's Point Dr • Hanover IN 47243
Civil War books, incl. *The Alford Brothers: "We All Must Die Sooner or Later"* - 356 pp., softcover, $23.95. Other titles.

O'DONNELL PUBLICATIONS
7217 Popkins Farm Rd
Alexandria VA 22306-2448
American Military Belt Plates - 1,000+ front & back views of plates, many photos. 616 pp., hardcover - $49.95 + $4.50 S&H.

OAK HILLS PUBLISHING
moreb@pcis.net
Rick Norton
The Story of Cole Younger, by Himself - $12.95.

PALADIN PRESS
800-392-2400
http://www.paladin-press.com
pala@rmii.com
Tina Mills
PO Box 1307 • Boulder CO 80306-1307
American Swords and Sword Makers.
Definitive book for all edged weapons.
Collectors, dealers, etc. 664 pp. - $79.95.
Catalog - $2.

PARKWAY PUBLISHERS
704-265-3993 Phone & Fax
aluri@netins.net
PO Box 3678
Boone NC 28607
Across the Dark River/Clyde Ray - 56th NC
Inf. Authentic in detail. Author recreates Civil
War period in words & experiences of men &
women who lived it - $21.95 (ppd.). Free
catalog. (See ad page 236)

PEA RIDGE PRESS
M. Dunnavant
PO Box 1068
Athens AL 35612-1068
The Railroad War - Ride with N.B. Forrest on
a daring raid against Sherman's railroad
supply lines. 180 pp. - $20 (ppd).

PELICAN PUBLISHING CO.
888-5-PELICAN • 800-843-1724
http://www.pelicanpub.com
sales@pelicanpub.com
PO Box 3110
Gretna LA 70054
Offers books on the Civil War era, history, the
Confederacy, & war heroes, including the
award-winning *Weep Not for Me, Dear
Mother.* Free catalog.

PENTLAND PRESS, INC.
800-948-2786
5124 Bur Oak Cir
Raleigh NC 27612
*The Last Full Measure of Devotion: The Saga
of an Irish Freemason*, by Doby. Historical
novel; letters from Shiloh, Corinth,
Stoneman's Raid. 233 pp., softcover - 18.95.

PICTORIAL HISTORIES PUBLISHING CO.
888-WVA-PHPC
1416 Quarrier St
Charleston WV 25301
Publisher of pictorial histories & Civil War
titles, including *Last Sleep: The Battle of
Droop Mountain, Civil War Medical
Instruments* Vol. 1-3, & *Civil War in West
Virginia.* Free catalog.

PIONEER PRESS
901-885-0374 • 901-885-0440 Fax
Sherry Stribling
PO Box 684
Union City TN 38281-0684
Confederate Cannon Foundries, by
Daniel/Gunter, 114 pp., softcover - $15. Many
books on firearms.

PIONEER PUBLISHING
702-438-6565 Phone & Fax
Gloria Shepard
PO Box 43474 • Las Vegas NV 89116-0474
Private Lives of Civil War Heroes series. Vol.
1: *The Journal* - 48 pp., $5.95 + $1.50 S&H.
Vol. 2: *Once Patriots* also available.

POCAHONTAS PRESS
800-446-0467 • 540-951-0467
540-961-2847 Fax
PO Box F • Blacksburg VA 24063-1020
Montgomery White Sulphur Springs—a
history of the resort, hospital, cemeteries,
markers, and monument—describes its time
as a Confederate hospital & the nuns,
doctors, soldiers, & others who lived & worked
there.

PONDER BOOKS
Janice Ponder
PO Box 573 • Doniphan MO 63935-0573
Publisher of books on Civil War, history &
genealogy. Trans-Mississippi region. Free
booklist.

PRIDE PUBLICATIONS
888-902-5983
http://members.aol.com/pridepblsh/pride.html
PridePblsh@aol.com
PO Box 148
Radnor OH 43066-0148
The Redemption of Cpl. Nolan Giles, novel by
Jeane Heimberger Candido. 245 pp.,
softcover - $11.95 + $2 S&H.

PUBLISHERS GROUP WEST
800-788-3123
PO Box 8843 • Emeryville CA 94662-0843
Shrouds of Glory by Winston Groom. 320
pages, 30 pp. of photographs & maps by the
noted author of Forrest Gump - $23. Many
other titles.

R & L PUBLISHING
28 Vesey St Ste 2116C
New York NY 10007-2906
Bottles of Old New York and *New York City's
Buried Past* dealing with Civil War & Rev. War
bottles. $22.95 & $27.95 ppd.

R. L. SHEP PUBLICATIONS
707-964-8662 Phone & Fax
fsbks@mcn.org
Fred Struthers
PO Box 2706
Fort Bragg CA 95437-2706
Publishes reprints of important sewing &
tailoring manuals as an aid to accurate
reproduction of period dress.

RANK & FILE PUBLICATIONS
310-540-6601
310-540-1599 Fax
http://www.thirdwave.net/~rank
books@thirdwave.net
1926 S Pacific Coast Hwy Ste 228
Redondo Beach CA 90277-6146
Pickett's Charge: Eyewitness Accounts,
Paperback - $21; Hardcover - $38. *The
Damned Red Flags of the Rebellion: The
Confederate Battle Flag at Gettysburg*,
Hardcover - $41.95. Other titles. Free catalog.

RARE BOOK REPUBLISHERS
703-573-5116
703-573-5897 Fax
http://www.raredocs.com
paconose@erols.com
PO Box 3202
Merrifield VA 22116-3202
The Cook's Own Book (1832), premier
cooking reference used by families on both
sides of the Civil War. More than 2,500
recipes. Hardcover - $28.95 + $3.50 S&H.

THE REPRINT COMPANY, PUBLISHERS
PO Box 5401
Spartanburg SC 29304-5401
4-vol. set contains alphabetical roll of 90,000
Louisiana Confederate army members.
In-depth, many vital statistics. Call/write.

ROCKBRIDGE PUBLISHING CO.
800-473-3943 Orders
540-955-3980 Editorial
540-955-4126 Fax
http://www.rockbpubl.com
cwpub@visuallink.com
PO Box 351
Berryville VA 22611-0351
Our own & hard-to-find titles from other small
presses. Free catalog. (See ad pp. 244, 245)

ROKARN PUBLICATIONS
800-869-0563
PO Box 195
Nokesville VA 20182-0195
A Southern Yarn and *Brothers in Gray* by
R.W. Richards. $12.95 each.

RSG PUBLISHING
607-563-9000
217 County Highway 1
Bainbridge NY 13733-9307
Historical Addresses of the Civil War. 22nd
NYV Cavalry, 2nd Brigade, 3rd Div. Reprint of
1894 original. $20. Other titles, incl. the
History & Record of the 114th NYV Infantry.
Free catalog.

RUTLEDGE HILL PRESS
800-234-4234
211 7th Ave N • Nashville TN 37219
Civil War titles, including *Civil War Journal:
The Leaders* and *Mort Kunstler's Civil War*.
Books worth fighting for.

RYAN PLACE PUBLISHERS, INC.
800-871-0563
2525 Arapahoe Ave Ste E4-231
Boulder CO 80302-6720
Civil War Campaigns and Commanders,
unique series of books on great battles,
leaders, & failures of the Civil War. Call/write
for complete list of titles.

J.S. SANDERS & CO.
615-790-8951 • 800-350-1101 Orders
615-790-2594 Fax
PO Box 50331 • Nashville TN 37205-0331
Nashville 1864: The Dying of the Light, by
Madison Jones. Other titles.

SANDLAPPER PUBLISHING, INC.
800-849-7263
800-337-9420 Fax
PO Box 730
Orangeburg SC 29116-0730
Regional publisher of books on the history,
literature, culture & cuisine of the South, incl.
Civil War titles.

J. M. SANTARELLI
215-576-5358
Civil War Books & Publishing
226 Paxson Ave
Glenside PA 19038-4612
Antique, reprint & out-of-print books. Also
publishes new material. More than 300 Civil
War titles. Catalog - $2.

SAVAS PUBLISHING CO.
800-848-6585
1475 S Bascom Ave Ste 204
Campbell CA 95008-0629
Original books. Features battles & campaigns,
unit histories, & quarterly journal - *Civil War
Regiments*. Free catalog.

SCHOLAR OF FORTUNE PUBLICATIONS
434 Bowman Dr
Kent OH 44240-4510
Friend Alice: CW Letters of Capt. David D. Bard, 7th & 104th Regts, Ohio Vol. Inf. 1862-1864. 112 pp. - $7.95 ppd. Other titles. Brochure - send large SASE.

PATRICK A. SCHROEDER PUBLICATIONS
804-376-1865
RR 2 Box 128
Brookneal VA 24528
Civil War books - myths about Lee's surrender, Fighting Quakers, a Duryee Zouave, record of North Carolina, diary of Swedish officer. Archives research, prints, notecards, postcards available. Free catalog.

SCS PUBLICATIONS
PO Box 3832
Fairfax VA 22038-3832
Civil War Artifacts: A Guide for the Historian. More than 1700 items pictured, common to very rare. Data includes history, issuance, etc. 240 pp. $39.95.

SOUTHERN HERITAGE PRESS
615-895-5642
John McGlone, Editor
4035 Emerald Dr
Murfreesboro TN 37130
Publisher of books on Confederate history, genealogy, black Confederates, Andersonville, Pat Cleburne. Winner of John Newman Edwards Award for preserving Southern history. Free catalog. (See ad page 234)

SOUTHERN HERITAGE PRESS, GA. DIVISION
PO Box 347163
Atlanta GA 30334-7163
Fine books about Southern history, 1861-1865. *In Search of Confederate Ancestors: The Guide.* Critically acclaimed by SCV & UDC. 112 pp., illus. - $10 + $1.50 S&H.

SOUTHERN ILLINOIS UNIVERSITY PRESS
800-346-2680
800-346-2681 Fax
grpruett@siu.edu
Gordon Pruett
PO Box 3697
Carbondale IL 62902-3697
Personal Memoirs of John H. Brinton, Army Life of an Illinois Soldier, "Black Jack" *John A. Logan and Southern Illinois in the Civil War Era,* & *A History of the Ninth Regiment Illinois Volunteers,* with the Regimental Roster.

ST. MARTIN'S PRESS
800-288-2131
Publisher's Book & Audio
PO Box 070059
Staten Island NY 10307-0059
Books on the Civil War including *Mountains Touched with Fire: Chattanooga Besieged, 1863,* by Wiley Sword.

STACKPOLE BOOKS
800-732-3669
5067 Ritter Rd
Mechanicsburg PA 17055-6921
Publishers of quality Civil War books, including *Debris of Battle: The Wounded at Gettysburg* and *Portals to Hell: Military Prisons of the Civil War,* new for 1997.

STONE EAGLE PRESS
209-661-4030
PO Box 838
Madera CA 93639-0838
Manual of arms for the rifle & musket, from original text (*U.S. Infantry & Rifle Tactics, 1861*) - $10.25.

SUNFLOWER UNIVERSITY PRESS
800-258-1232
PO Box 1009
Manhattan KS 66505-1009
Since 1977, publisher of military & Western American history titles. *A Price Beyond Rubies,* Civil War novel, softcover - $25.95. *W.W. Loring: Florida's Forgotten General* - $35.95 (CL); $21.95 (PB). $2.50 S&H. Free catalog. (See ad page __)

SYRACUSE UNIVERSITY PRESS
800-365-8929
1600 Jamesville Ave
Syracuse NY 13210-4243
The Iroquois in the Civil War (Hauptman). In-depth study of Iroquois tribes in CW. Documents service records & war's impact on tribe. $34.95. Other titles.

TACITUS PUBLICATIONS
612-644-6691
612-644-2265 Fax
tacitus@gte.net
Beverly A. Rude
PO Box 14412
Saint Paul MN 55114-0412
Civil War biographies quoting original correspondence & describing where & how individuals fought. Information on historic sites dedicated to each individual. Illus. $5.95 ea. Free catalog. 30% disc. to retailers. (See ad page 234)

TEXAS A&M UNIVERSITY PRESS CONSORTIUM
800-826-8911
409-847-8752 Fax
FDL@tampress.tamu.edu
Gayla Christiansen
PO Box C
College Station TX 77843-0001
Mighty Stonewall, Make Me a Map of the Valley, Fallen Guidon, Confederate General of the Southwest. From $12.95 to $35. Also *Voices of Valor* (audio) $10.95 cassette, $17.95 CD. Free catalog.

THOMAS PUBLICATIONS
800-840-6782 • 717-334-1921
717-334-8440 Fax
Dean S. Thomas
353 Buford Ave
Gettysburg PA 17325-1138
Publishers of Civil War books. Many titles. *Ghosts of Gettysburg* series videos. Free catalog.

TRAC PRESS
313 E Strawberry Dr
Mill Valley CA 94941
Yours in Love follows daily life of Iowa foot soldier in collection of letters - 285 pp., $21.95 ppd.

TRIPHAMMER PUBLISHING
PO Box 45
Scottsville NY 14546-0045
The Beau Ideal of a Soldier and a Gentleman: The Life of Col. Patrick Henry O'Rorke from Ireland to Gettysburg - softcover, 220 pp., $22.95 + $4 S&H.

TUNSTEDE PRESS
615-385-7258
500 Elmington Ave Ste 430
Nashville TN 37205
Letters to Laura: A Confederate Surgeon's Impressions of Four Years of War - 304 pp., hardcover, $36 + $4 S&H. Only in-print letter collection written by a Confederate surgeon, Urban Grammar Owen, MD. (See ad page 244)

TWO TRAILS PUBLISHING
http://www.erspros.com/2trails
cwbklady@aol.com
7295 Houston St
Shawnee Mission KS 66227-2430
The Forgotten Men: The Missouri State Guard, 406 pp. Hardcover - $42.95; Softcover - $32.95. *Sterling Price's Lieutenants,* 362 pp. Softcover - $27.50. Catalog.

UNION PUBLISHING CO.
415 Miller Rd
Union ME 04862-3610
The 16th Maine Regiment in the War of the Rebellion, 1861-1865. Riveting reading about the famed 16th Maine Regt. at Gettysburg & their subsequent capture. $12.95 ppd.

THE UNIVERSITY OF ALABAMA PRESS
800-825-9980 • 205-348-5180
205-348-9201 Fax
http://www.uapress.ua.edu
Box 870380
University of Alabama
Tuscaloosa AL 35487-0380
Complete selection of military history titles, including the "Top 100 Classics of Civil War Literature" featuring *Attack and Die, Cracker Culture,* etc.

THE UNIVERSITY OF ARKANSAS PRESS
800-626-0090
501-575-6044 Fax
http://www.uark.edu/campus-resources/uaprinfo/public_html/
uapressinfo@cavern.uark.edu
201 N Ozark Ave
Fayetteville AR 72701-4041
Civil War in the West series: books on the trans-Mississippi & Western theaters. Portraits of Conflict series: photographic histories of individual Southern states in the Civil War. Free catalog.

UNIVERSITY OF CALIFORNIA PRESS
800-822-6657
1445 Lower Ferry Rd
Ewing NJ 08618-1424
The Frontier in American Culture, Wagner Nights, etc. Call for a complete listing.

UNIVERSITY OF GEORGIA PRESS
706-369-6163
300 Research Dr
Athens GA 30605-2726
To the Manor Born: The Life of Gen. William H.T. Walker. First complete biography of the general. Available at bookstores or direct. $50. Many other titles.

UNIVERSITY OF ILLINOIS PRESS
800-545-4703
http://www.press.uillinois.edu
1325 S Oak St
Champaign IL 61820-6903
Titles include *The Civil War in Books: An Analytical Biography,* by David J. Eicher. Fully annotated bibliography of the 1,100 most important books on the CW.

UNIVERSITY OF IOWA PRESS
800-235-2665
Iowa City IA 52242
Titles include *Soldier Boy: CW Letters of Charles O. Musser, 29th Iowa* - 272 pp. $24.95.

UNIVERSITY OF MAINE PRESS
207-581-1408
51 Public Affairs Bldg • Univ. of Maine
Orono ME 04469-0150
Dear Friend Anna. Civil War letters from common soldier, home to his future wife - $21.95. Other titles.

UNIVERSITY OF MISSOURI PRESS
800-828-1894 • 573-882-0180
573-884-4498 Fax
http://www.system.missouri.edu/upress
2910 LeMone Blvd • Columbia MO 65201
Shades of Blue & Gray: Introductory Military History of the Civil War, by Herman Hattaway - 296 pp., $29.95. "... best clear, brief military history of the Civil War available..." (George Rable).

THE UNIVERSITY OF NEBRASKA PRESS
800-755-1105 • 402-472-3581
http://nebraskapress.unl.edu
press@unlinfo.unl.edu
312 N 14th St • Lincoln NE 68508-1623

UNIVERSITY OF NEW MEXICO PRESS
800-249-7737 • 800-622-8667 Fax
Bloody Valverde: A Civil War Battle on the Rio Grande, February 21, 1862, by John M. Taylor - 1st complete account of the largest battle in New Mexico. Hardcover, 200 pp. - $29.95.

THE UNIVERSITY OF NORTH CAROLINA PRESS
800-848-6224
800-272-6817 Fax
http://sunsite.unc.edu/uncpress/
Chapel Hill NC
The Darkest Days of the War: The Battles of Iuka & Corinth; *The Wilderness Campaign*; many more titles.

UNIVERSITY OF OKLAHOMA PRESS
800-627-7377
ldraper@uoknor.edu
Ms. Lennie Draper, Publicity Mgr.
1005 Asp Ave
Norman OK 73019-6050
Publisher of books about military history, including number of titles about the Civil War. Free catalogs.

UNIVERSITY OF SOUTH CAROLINA PRESS
800-768-2500 Orders • 800-868-0740 Fax
205 Pickens St
Columbia SC 29208-2911
Titles include *Lincoln's Abolitionist General* and *Confederate Hospitals on the Move.*

UNIVERSITY OF TENNESSEE PRESS
423-974-3321
http://www.lib.utk.edu/UTKgophers/UT-PRESS
293 Communications Bldg.
Knoxville TN 37996-0325
Voices of the Civil War series. *From Huntsville to Appomattox: R.T. Cole's History of the 4th Regiment, Alabama Volunteer Infantry, CSA* - 304 pp., hardcover, $32.95.

UNIVERSITY PRESS OF KANSAS
913-864-4155 • 913-864-4586 Fax
upkansas@kuhub.cc.ukans.edu
2501 W 15th St • Lawrence KS 66049
The Union Soldier in Battle: Enduring the Ordeal of Combat/Hess. *Stonewall of the West; Patrick Cleburne and the Civil War*/Symonds. Other Civil War & military titles. Free, complete listing available.

UNIVERSITY PRESS OF KENTUCKY
800-839-6855 Orders • 800-666-2211
800-870-4981 Fax
http://www.uky.edu/UniversityPress/
663 S Limestone St
Lexington KY 40508-4008
With Charity for All: Lincoln and the Restoration of the Union, by William C. Harris - 336 pp., hardcover, $37.95.

UNIVERSITY PRESS OF MISSISSIPPI
800-737-7788 • 601-982-6217 Fax
press@ihl.state.ms.us
Claudette Murphree
3825 Ridgewood Rd
Jackson MS 39211-6463
John Wilkes Booth - $20. *Tracing Your Mississippi Ancestors* - $14.95. *We Saw Lincoln Shot* - $17.95. *Pemberton* - $32.50. Other titles. Free catalog.

UNIVERSITY PRESS OF VIRGINIA
804-924-3469 • 804-982-2655 Fax
http://www.upress.virginia.edu/
upressva@virginia.edu
PO Box 3608
University Station
Charlottesville VA 22903-0608
Several books & studies on the Civil War including *Lee's Young Artillerist, Longstreet's Aide, Black Confederates & Afro-Yankees in CW Virginia*, etc.

URE PRESS
636 Piney Forest Rd
Danville VA 24540
Confederate Treasure in Danville -
documented, clues to 196,000 silver dollars
buried in Danville, Va. Hardcover -$26.07 ppd.

VANBERG PUBLISHING
800-799-0470
614-689-0471 Fax
http://www.vanberg-ent.com
PO Box 983
Lancaster OH 43130-0983
Annals of the 6th Pennsylvania Cavalry, by
Chaplain Samuel L. Gracey. "Rush's Lancers"
- $24.95. *History of the 9th Massachusetts
Battery*. "Bigelow's Battery" -$29.95. Add
$3.95 S&H.

WARWICK HOUSE PUBLISHING
804-846-1200
720 Court St
Lynchburg VA 24504
*Memoirs of Life in and out of the Army in
Virginia During the War Between the States* -
annotated letters from the Blackford family.
Leatherbound, 2 vol. set - $95 + $6 S&H.

WHITE MANE PUBLISHING CO.
888-WHT-MANE • 717-532-2237
717-532-7704 Fax
Harold Collier
PO Box 152
Shippensburg PA 17257-0152
America's Civil War publisher offers variety of
military history titles with special interest in the
Civil War. Free catalog.

WILLOW CREEK PRESS OF WASHINGTON
888-830-5612
PO Box 3730
Silverdale WA 98383
Kope's *Everything Civil War* - 304 pp.,
softcover. $19.95 + $2 S&H.

WRITE WAY PUBLISHING
800-680-1793
10555 E Dartmouth Ave Ste 210
Aurora CO 80013
Featuring such books as *The Sherman Letter*,
mixing history & mystery. Excellent reading.
$18.95. Call for a complete listing.

WSU PRESS
800-354-7360 • 509-335-3518
509-335-8568 Fax
http://www.publications.wsu.edu/wsupress
deweese@wsu.edu
Beth DeWeese
PO Box 645910
Pullman WA 99164-5910
*Confederate Raider in the North Pacific: The
Saga of the C.S.S.* Shenandoah, *1864-65.*
Reprint, 350-pp. paperback - $19.95 + $2.50
S&H. Other titles. Free catalog.

13TH VIRGINIA INFANTRY, CO. H
540-877-2483
Capt. David Melton
128 Susquehanna Trl • Winchester VA 22602
Members participate in battle reenactments, living history, camp & drill demonstrations, memorials/ceremonies/dedications & help preserve historical sites & Confederate battle flags. Recruits welcome & encouraged.

THE 17TH CONNECTICUT VOL. INFANTRY
407-295-7510
Maj. Jeff H. Grzelak
7214 Laurel Hill Rd • Orlando FL 32818-5233
Retrace the steps of the 17th Conn.; after 130 years, the regiment is on the march. Enlist today & see a part of U.S. history firsthand.

19TH ALABAMA INFANTRY REGT., ARMY OF TENN.
http://fly.hiwaay.net/~dsmart/index.html
Reenactment organization. Website provides many links to pages of related topics.

2ND MARYLAND INFANTRY, CO. A, CSA
410-531-3586
http://www.sutler.com/2ndMD/2ndMD.htm

4TH NORTH CAROLINA REGT., CSA, INC.
410-526-4927
Stephen Bockmiller, Recruiter
101 Fitz Ct Unit 204
Reisterstown MD 21136-3327
Infantry unit with members in Md., Va., & Pa. Living history emphasized. Reenactments, talks, displays, etc. Well- researched, uniform documentation. Nonprofit corp.

5TH NEW YORK, DURYEE'S ZOUAVES
http://www.zouave.org/index.html
PO Box 1601 • Alexandria VA 22313-1601
Enlist in the 5th NY for authentic living history & reenacting.

8TH REGT. NJ VOLUNTEER INFANTRY
609-654-5561 Days • 609-654-7168 Nights
Capt. Earl Aversano
226 Sunny Jim Dr • Medford NJ 08055
Honorary reactivated NJ unit which participates in reenactments & historical events throughout the eastern U.S.

AMERICAN CIVIL WAR ASSOCIATION
http://www.acwa.org
CSA contact: AdjCSAACWA@aol.com ;
Union contact: FedAdjACWA@aol.com
Arthur Henricks
PO Box 61075
Sunnyvale CA 94088-1075

Private, non-profit educational organization & reenactment society which uses living history to help the public gain better understanding of the Civil War. 350 current members. More info - send SASE.

AVALON FORGE
410-242-8431
John White, Owner
409 Gun Rd
Baltimore MD 21227-3824
Replica goods for 18th-century "living history." Items for military, farm & home. Catalog - $2.

BATTLE AT NARCOOSSEE MILL
John Holmes
PO Box 430178
Kissimmee FL 34743-0178
Annual event held on shores of East Lake Tohopeliga, east of St. Cloud, FL. Sponsored by SCV Camp 1516. Authentic CW reeanctors welcome.

BATTLE CRY
810 Gales Ave
Winston-Salem NC 27103
Multi-period reenacting publication covering Civil War & others. $8/yr. for 4 issues.

BATTLE OF AIKEN
803-642-2500
Barnard E. Bee Camp SCV
PO Box 1863
Aiken SC 29801-1863
Annual February reenactment of the battle against Sherman's invasion. Camps, cannon duels & cavalry charges. Period crafts, music & food. Dates for 1998 -Feb. 20-22.

BATTLE OF BLUE SPRINGS
423-638-4111
Greeneville/Greene Co. Chmbr of Commerce
115 Academy St
Greeneville TN 37743-5601
Battle scenarios with all branches, camp dance, church services. Annually - October. Spectator fee - $2, ages 12 & under free.

BATTLE OF CAMP WILDCAT & LIVING HISTORY ENCAMPMENT
606-878-6242
Fred Gillum
166 Middleground Way Apt 3
London KY 40744-8154
Reenactments, tacticals, ladies' tea, military demonstrations, pig roast, barn dance, fashion show, parade, review, & more. Registration $2. Annual April event.

BATTLE OF GRAND LAKE
419-586-5294
106 Haig St • Celina OH 45822-2708
Reenactment on shores of Lake St. Mary's.
Earthworks among best in OH. Artillery,
infantry, cavalry, medical, civilians. Battles,
tactical events, ladies' activities. Annually -
July.

BATTLE OF OLUSTEE (OCEAN POND)
904-397-2733
904-397-4262 Fax
Olustee Battlefield State Historic Site
PO Drawer G
White Springs FL 32096-0435
Reenactment with parade, skirmish & ball.
Full- & 3-quarter-scale artillery only. Open to
all authentic 1864 impressions as found in
actual battle. No fees. Annual event -
February.

BATTLE OF PALATKA
2171 Hoffman St
Jacksonville FL 32211-3217
Annual March reenactment on site at St.
Johns River Community College. Authentic
impressions welcome. Company drills, live
mortar fire, ladies' tea, military ball, living
history camps.

BATTLE OF PLEASANT HILL
Mason City Parks & Recreation
22 N Georgia Ave
Mason City IA 50401-3435
Battles, ladies' tea & fashion show, military
ball, children's presentation, period music,
competitions, ribbons. Annual event - June.

BATTLE OF POISON SPRING
501-685-2748
Annual March reenactment at Poison Spring
State Park, Arkansas.

BATTLE OF RESACA
PO Box 3336
Cumming GA 30128-6519
Annual May reenactment on 600 acres of
original battlefield. Battles, tactical, ladies' tea,
evening social with period music.

BILLIE CREEK VILLAGE REENACTMENT
765-569-3430
http://www.coveredbridges.com/bilcreek.htm
RR 2 Box 27
Rockville IN 47872-9503
Largest annual reenactment in IN. 30 historic
buildings to tour. Battles & military events;
extensive ladies', children's & medical events,
ball. Annual event - June.

BLUE & GRAY HERITAGE COMMITTEE
912-896-3258
Adel GA
Annual April reenactment & living history site.
Live-fire artillery, cavalry, & firearms
competitions. Memorial & worship services.
Proceeds benefit the non-profit committee's
fund for permanent living history site.

BRANDYWINE CREEK REENACTMENT
Jack Pickett
116 W Main St
Middletown DE 19709-1040
Annual May reenactment of the "Campaigns
of 1862." Tacticals, seminars, demonstrations,
night artillery firing. Authentic camping.

**BROOKSBY FARMS CIVIL WAR
ENCAMPMENT**
Edward Certusi
16 Maitland St
Milton MA 02186-4511
Battles, tours, lectures, displays, civilian
activities, CW dance. Annual event - July.

BROOKSVILLE RAID
352-683-3700
Greater Hernando Co. Chamber of Commerce
101 E Fort Dade Ave
Brooksville FL 34601
Florida's Best Event! Beautiful 1500-acre site.
Battle, ball. All units & branches welcome.
Annual event.

BROTHERS-IN-ARMS
52 Monarch Cir
Basking Ridge NJ 07920-3144
Reenactors, find out what units are local to
you. 100s of CSA/Union infantry, artillery, &
cavalry units. Men, women, children welcome.
3 units - $5 & SASE.

C & D COMMERCIAL PRODUCTIONS, INC.
800-600-6578
100 Dixie Ln
Wilmington DE 19804-2312
*A Call to Arms: Your Guide to Becoming a
CW Reenactor.* 52-min. video - excellent
recruiting tool. $19.95.

THE CALENDAR PEOPLE
800-758-2751
2083 Springwood Rd
PO Box 125
York PA 17403-0125
Civil War reenactment calendar featuring
pictures of 12 reenactment groups
(CSA/USA). $12 + S&H.

CAMP CHASE PUBLISHING
http://nemesis.cybergate.net/~civilwar
CampChase@compuserve.com
PO Box 707 • Marietta OH 45750-0707
How to Get Started in Civil War Reenacting -
36-pg. handbook, written by veteran
reenactor. Great tips. $5.

THE CANNONADE
PO Box 20601 • Rochester NY 14602-0601
*Nice Boom: The Amerian Civil War Artillery
Reenactor's Handbook,* Sean McAdoo, ed.
100+ pp., including drill, living history, tactics,
NCO training & more. $10.95 + $3 S&H.

CASTLE KEEP, LTD.
630-801-1696
630-801-1910 Fax
http://www.Reenact.com
ernie@Smartgate.com
Ernest Klapmeier
83 S LaSalle St
Aurora IL 60505
Reenactor supplies; clothing & equipment to
put man or woman into the field. Owner has
20 yrs. reenacting experience & understands
concept of authenticity.

CEDAR CREEK BATTLEFIELD FOUNDATION, INC.
540-869-2064
540-869-1438 Fax
http://www.winchesterva.com/cedarcreek
Suzanne Lewis
PO Box 229
Middletown VA 22645-0229
Visitors Center & bookshop overlooking
battlefield. October reenactment. Reference
library, large CW book selection, flags, prints,
maps & square foot certificates. All proceeds
go to preservation of battlefield.

CENTRAL GEORGIA CASTING
3445 Osborne Pl
Macon GA 31204-1843
Hand-painted/unpainted miniatures. Fast
service, custom work. Reenactor miniatures
from photograph. Sample infantry figure,
brochure & $5 credit - send $5.75 for 25 mm
or $9.75 for 54 mm. Brochure only - $2.

THE CITIZENS' COMPANION
614-373-1865
Camp Chase Publishing
PO Box 707
Marietta OH 45750
Magazine for civilian side of reenacting. Info.
on clothing, behavior, living history
impressions & more. $20/yr. for 6 issues.

CIVIL WAR ADVENTURES
800-624-4421
3-day encampments for all Civil War
enthusiasts. Come live the life of a Civil War
soldier. Free brochure.

CIVIL WAR LIVING HISTORY & BATTLES
860-526-4993
C. Quist
233 Main St • Deep River CT 06417-2055
Reenactment in Madison, NY. Shiloh
scenarios. Annual event - May.

CIVIL WAR LIVING HISTORY REENACTMENT
910-371-6613
Fort Anderson NC
Reenactment on grounds of Brunswick Town
State Historic Sites. Tours of earthwork fort
remains, small arms & military demonstra-
tions, civilian interpretations. Lectures/talks.
Annual event - February. No admission fee.

CIVIL WAR WEEK
803-722-2996
The Charleston Museum
360 Meeting St • Charleston SC 29403-6235
Harbor & land tours in historic Charleston, SC,
nationally recognized speakers, reenactors,
period music. Annual event - April. Brochure.

CIVIL WAR WEEKEND AT STOEVER'S DAM PARK
717-933-4294
Capt. Dennis R. Shirk
RR 3 Box 415A • Myerstown PA 17067-1644
Battles, tactical, living history, entertainment,
candlelight tours. Annual event, Lebanon, PA.
Contact for dates.

GENERAL NEWTON MARTIN CURTIS WEEKEND
David H. Ellis
81 Pleasant Valley Rd • Hammond NY 13646
Honors St. Lawrence County's contributions
to war effort & memory of Gen. Curtis. Period
encampment, skirmish, talks, living history.
Open to all CW enthusiasts. Annual event -
September.

DEPARTMENT OF THE SOUTH, INC.
352-394-7206
PO Box 680784 • Orlando FL 32868-0784
"Hilton Head Dispatch" - official newsletter for
reenactment community. Latest info. on
events, book reviews, battle reports, unit
history, life in trenches & on home front.
$17/yr. for 6 issues.

ENCAMPMENT AT LAUREL HILL
540-251-1833
J.E.B. Stuart Birthplace, Inc.
PO Box 240
Ararat VA 24053-0240
Encampment just outside Mt. Airy, NC, to
benefit the Stuart birthplace. Annual event -
June. Free registration.

FRONTIER DAYS CIVIL WAR
REENACTMENT
515-573-4231
http://jsp.org/fort/
thefort@fortdodge.ia.frontiercomm.net
David Parker
Fort Museum
PO Box 1798
Fort Dodge IA 50501-1798
Annual reenactments at Fort Museum & Fort
Dodge. Military ball, civilian impressions,
family activities. Call for dates.

GALLIA COUNTY FEDERAL ARMY
HOMECOMING
800-765-6482
Gallipolis OH 45631
Living history encampment at original army
campsite. Ladies' tea & workshops, period
entertainment. Authentic Union infantry,
artillery, medical, signal corps, engineering,
civilians, sutlers welcome. Annual event -April.

GIBBS SMITH, PUBLISHER
800-743-5439
http://www.gibbs-smith.com
info@gibbs-smith.com
PO Box 667
Layton UT 84041-0667
*Returning to the Civil War: Grand
Reenactments of an Anguished Time* - living
history at its best in full-color photography. 96
pp., softcover - $21.95. Free catalog.

GRANBURY CONVENTION & VISITORS
BUREAU
800-950-2212
100 N Crockett St
Granbury TX 76048-2127
Sponsors reenactments & other events.
Tourist info.

GRAND ANNAPOLIS CITY BALL
Stephen Bockmiller
101 Fitz Ct Apt 204
Reisterstown MD 21136-3327
Annual March ball with orchestral music &
refreshments. Period military or civilian attire
required. Attendance limited. Co-sponsored
by 4th NC Infantry & 5th US Cavalry.

HILTON HEAD DISPATCH
407-295-7510
7214 Laurel Hill Rd
Orlando FL 32818-5233
Publication indicating where to find reenactments, shows, & book fairs dealing in history.
Covering the Southeast. $15/yr. for 6 issues.

HISTORIC HAMPTON
800-800-2202 • 757-727-1102
http://www.hampton.va.us/tourism
710 Settlers Landing Rd
Hampton VA 23669-4035
Historic reenactments, world-class museums,
Chesapeake Bay seafood, Fort Wool,
Casemate Museum at Fort Monroe, new site
on the Va. Civil War Trail. Minutes from
Williamsburg. Free guide.

JACKSON'S FOOT CAVALRY
804-780-3373 • 800-833-5522
B. Brenner Wood
Now mustering "F" Company, 21st Regt.,
Virginia Volunteer Cavalry. We are historians
who interpret the Civil War by authentically
portraying the common soldier.

LAKE CHICOT STATE PARK CIVIL WAR
WEEKEND
800-264-2430
Don R. Simons
Lake Chicot State Park
2542 Highway 257
Lake Village AR 71653-9515
Reenactment of Battle of Ditch Bayou, camp
tours, living history demonstrations, tactical,
period ball. Annual event - October.

LIVING HISTORY & RAID OF QUEEN
ANNE'S RAILROAD
410-836-2642 John C. Houck
Lewes DE
2 train raids & battles. Candlelight camp tours.
All period impression welcome. Annual event -
August. Admission -$3 over age 12.

LIVING HISTORY ASSOCIATION, INC.
PO Box 1389
Wilmington VT 05363-1389
Reenactors' Liability Insurance. Multimillion
dollar policies available, covering
reenactments, encampments, black powder,
cavalry, artillery, etc. Info - $3.

LIVING HISTORY ENCAMPMENT
Larry S. Hoffman
3000 State Route 18
Hookstown PA 15050-1605

Annual May encampment includes Revolutionary War, Civil War, Lewis & Clark, the world wars, & modern armed forces. Daily drills, firing, crafts. Pioneer crafts & music.

MALTA ENCAMPMENT
Dr. Robert Richmond
4455 State Route 37 • Malta OH 43758-9756
Skirmish & battle, parade, ball, ladies' tea. Annual event - July. No fees.

MC LEAN COUNTY CIVIL WAR WEEKEND
309-827-5416
Ron Montgomery
711 E Wood • Bloomington IL 61701
Annual event. All branches of military & civilian welcome.

MISSISSIPPI (COLUMBUS) CONVENTION & VISITORS BUREAU
800-327-2686
Columbus MS
Annual February Battle of West Point & Prairie reenactment & authentic dance. Call for info. & dates.

NORTH-SOUTH SKIRMISH ASSOCIATION
http://mh004.infi.net/~nssa/
Phil Spaugy
501 N Dixie Dr • Vandalia OH 45377-2011
Team competition in high-level marksmanship with original or approved reproduction muskets, carbines, revolvers, & artillery at breakable targets in a timed match. Period regimental uniforms worn.

NORTHWEST REENACTMENTS
800-624-4421
Civil War Adventures, Inc.
1532 Lakeway Pl • Bellingham WA 98226
The ultimate Civil War experience. Reenactments, encampments for everyone. Call for info.

OGLEBAY PARK REENACTMENT
304-845-1893
Don McNabb
RR 1 Box 107A
Moundsville WV 26041-9801
Scored interactive tactical, ladies' tea, dance, children's activities. Annual event - June.

PIONEER VILLAGE REENACTMENT
319-355-0898
Bruce Kindig
3923 Forest Rd
Davenport IA 52807-2350
2 battles on 30-acre field, dance. Annual event - September.

REENACTOR'S JOURNAL
309-463-2123
309-463-2188 Fax
PO Box 1864
Varna IL 61375
For the "Who, what, where, when and how-to" of Civil War Reenacting. 12 issues - $24. Sample issue - $3.

REENACTOR'S WEB MALL
http://rampages.onramp.net/~lawsonda/mall
Links to directories of sutlers, basic 19th-century supplies, etc.

REENACTORS HOMEPAGE
http://www.cwreenactors.com
"Dedicated to the brave souls, North & South, who fought & died in the War Between the States."

SAMUELL FARM CIVIL WAR WEEKEND
Kevin Keim
380 Country Ln
Haslet TX 76052-4312
Annual March weekend near Dallas, featuring 3 battles, dance, period worship service. No reenactor fee.

KELLY SCHULTZ FARM REENACTMENT
716-839-3200 • 716-885-3755
Maj. Richard J. Rosche
840 W Delavan Ave
Buffalo NY 14209-1113
Battle of Five Forks reenactment & living history event, including trench warfare. Authentics only. Extensive civilian activities. Sutlers welcome. Annual event - June.

SHIP'S COMPANY, INC.
410-788-7264
Lawrence Bopp, Pres.
309 Roanoke Dr • Baltimore MD 21228
Official interpretive group of the USS *Constellation*, recruiting Federal sailors & marines for service aboard this 1855 war sloop - the last surviving warship to see Civil War action.

STONEWALL JACKSON MEMORIAL WEEKEND
540-972-7215
Bethel Baptist Church
10530 Beaver Ln • Spotsylvania VA 22553-3564
May reenactment where Pegram's artillery battalion encamped after Chancellorsville. Tacticals, church hospital, burials, auction, candlelight camp tour, recreation of 1863 memorial service held at church for Jackson.

STUHR MUSEUM LIVING HISTORY ENCAMPMENT
308-385-5316
308-385-5028 Fax
Gail Stoklasa
Nebraska
2 major battles, skirmishes, candlelight tours. All branches & units welcome. Encampment at Stuhr Museum of the Prairie Pioneer.

TOWN PARK LIVING HISTORY & REENACTMENT
410-836-2642
Maj. Gen. John C. Houck
402 Schucks Rd
Bel Air MD 21015-4916
Battles, demonstrations, camp life. Period music & dancing, memorial & church services. All branches & impressions welcome. Annual event - October. Admission - $3 over age 12.

USHER'S FERRY REENACTMENT
319-355-0898
Bruce Kindig
3923 Forest Rd
Davenport IA 52807-2350
3 battles, ball. Annual July reenactment of battle fought in 1860s town in Cedar Rapids.

VIDALIA REENACTMENT
912-537-7667
Vidalia GA
Annual March battle reenactment & living history encampment.

WINTER WEEKEND OF THE LIVING HISTORY SOCIETY
612-431-4760
ekatuin@compuserve.com
Elaine M. Katuin
7624 157th St W Apt 208
Apple Valley MN 55124-9166
Weekend gala featuring mid-19th-century dancing & civilian activities, workshops, ice skating & sledding. Period attire requested. Annual event - February.

YUMA CROSSING QM DEPOT HISTORIC SITE
520-329-0471
Wells Twombly
Yuma Crossing Foundation
PO Box 2768
Yuma AZ 85366-2768
Civil War encampment, 2 battles daily. Camping & some horses allowed. Ladies' fashion contest, lectures. No reenactor fee. Annual event - January.

HUDSON ALEXANDER
911 Velma Ln • Murfreesboro TN 37129-2367
Will research your soldier/unit from
Tennessee.

SIDNEY ALLINSON
660 Cairndale Road
Victoria • BC V9C 3L3 Canada
MILITARY PUBLICATIONS, INTER-
NATIONAL DIRECTORY helps you contact
over 600 specialist war journals worldwide.
10th ed. - $15.

ANTIQUE AMERICAN FIREARMS
847-304-GUNS
PO Box 1861 • Barrington IL 60011-1861
Civil War weapons search - match your
weapon's serial number with our database to
identify issuance. Annual membership.

BATTLEFIELDS REVISITED
BattRev@aol.com
Patricia Watt
PO Box 231 • New Cumberland PA 17070
Research Civil War soldiers, sailors - all
nationalities. Reports, records, histories.

BOOK HUNTERS
PO Box 7519
North Bergen NJ 07047-0519
Virtually any book located - no matter how old
or how long out of print. Title alone is
sufficient. Please inquire.

BRODERBUND
39500 Stevenson Pl Ste 204
Fremont CA 94539
Family Tree Maker CD-Rom - solid starting
point for genealogical research. PC
compatible with Windows programs, 386 or
higher, 4MB RAM (8MB recommended).

BROWN PUBLICATIONS
BrianB1578@aol.com
PO Box 25501
Little Rock AR 72221
In the Footsteps of the Blue & Gray - $24.95 +
$2 S&H. Describes CW-related research
sources in state archives, National Archives &
LDS collection. History of ea. corps &
hard-to-find technical information.

PAUL BUCHER
703-243-6654
PO Box 17304
Arlington VA 22216
Civil War military service records, Union &
Confederate, army & navy. 10-day
turnaround, reasonable fee.

CAVALIER HISTORY
Winston B. Wine, Jr.
921 Selma Blvd • Staunton VA 24401-2083
Freelance cavalry historian endorsed by
J.E.B. Stuart IV; advisor, Brandy Station
Foundation; speaking engagements,
research, tours, other services of Eastern
Theatre Cavalry. (See ad page 241)

THE CIVIL WAR GARRISON
PO Box 1681 • Springfield IL 62705-1681
Will research the veteran you designate &
write his personal story in the War Between
the States, or produce a Civil War plaque of
his experiences.

CIVIL WAR RESEARCH
219-483-0640
PO Box 8355 • Fort Wayne IN 46898-8355
Will research your Civil War soldier through
the official records. Provides brief report &
extracts from the official records - $34.95.

COLLECTORS' LIBRARY
541-937-3348
PO Box 263 • Eugene OR 97440-0263
THE publisher for key reference books on
accoutrements, guns, saddles, edged
weapons, etc., for pre-Civil War, Civil War,
Indian War & post-1900 period. Free illus.
catalog.

CONFEDERATE DESK
812-948-5057 • rebeldesk@aol.com
201 Virginia Ct • New Albany IN 47150-5076
New online research service. Most major
archives & manuscript depositories accessed
immediately. Call, write or access e-mail.

CONFEDERATE DIRECTORY
915-446-4439
David Martin
PO Box 61 • Roosevelt TX 76874-0061
Reference for vendors of Confederate
currency, books, tapes, flags, stationery,
memorabilia, reenactors' supplies, services,
memorials, etc.; includes COMPLETE
Confederate Constitution. $12 (ppd.).

CORTLAND COUNTY HISTORICAL
SOCIETY, INC.
607-756-6071
25 Homer Ave
Cortland NY 13045-2056
Hosts Suggett House Museum & Kellogg
Memorial Research Library. *A Regiment
Remembered: 157th New York Volunteers* -
Lt. William Saxton's diary, 157 pp. - $20 +
$3.40 S&H. NYS - add 8% sales tax.

COWLES HISTORY GROUP
http://www.thehistorynet.com
Attn: Military History Index
PO Box 3242 • Leesburg VA 20177-8111
Cross-referenced index of more than 3,000
entries, through 1000s of years of battle.
Every subject addressed in *Military History*
magazine's first decade of publication -$24.95.

CW BATTLES
1943 N Grimes Ste B229
Hobbs NM 88240
Handbook of 230 major Civil War battles;
when, where, who, what index. $9.95 + S&H.

R. DAMBRISI
1231 Ten Oaks Rd
Baltimore MD 21227
Search service; will locate & print text from
Official Records US/CS Army - $25/topic.

DELAWARE PUBLIC ARCHIVES
302-739-5318 • 302-739-3021
302-739-2578 Fax
http://del-aware.lib.de.us/archives
archives@state.de.us
Hall of Records
Dover DE 19901

JOHN EMOND
PO Box 44625
Washington DC 20026-4625
Will research military & pension records at
National Archives. Reasonable fees - no
charge until found.

GRAVE CONCERNS
PO Box 20094
Cincinnati OH 45220
Sell/trade photographs of burial sites of Civil
War generals blue & gray, politicians, spies,
notables - many hard to find. 5,000 photos on
hand; send SASE & needs. Catalog - SASE.

E. GREISSER
771D E Main St
Bridgewater NJ 08807-3339
Civil War soldiers from Philadelphia & New
Jersey. Pension, family & church records
when available.

W.D. GRISSOM, SR.
medals@cei.net
PO Box 59
Cabot AR 72023-0059
Medals, documents, related items.
Regimental research, reasonable price.
Specialist for US & foreign military medals.
Catalog - $1 (ref.).

JOHN GROSS
305-512-9542
PO Box 5645
Hialeah FL 33014-1645
Confederate research - info. on 1 million
soldiers! Speedy reply. $8/soldier. Unit
rosters, pensions, service records, etc. Send
SASE for more info.

H-BAR ENTERPRISES
800-432-7702
205-622-3040 Fax
http://www.hbar.com
hbar@oakman.tds.net
1422 Davidson Loop
Oakman AL 35579-5820
Official Records - every word indexed, both
reports & correspondence included. Custom
CDs available - choose your books. Create
own computer databases, add personal
notes. Call for info. (See ad page 239)

THE HANDLEY LIBRARY ARCHIVES
540-662-9041 x22
PO Box 58
Winchester VA 22604-0058
Contain numerous historical documents &
personal records.

HEIRLINES
800-570-4049
James W. Petty, Genealogist
PO Box 893
Salt Lake City UT 84110-0893
Will help you find your ancestors & begin
learning about your genealogy. Search
censuses, church, court, & land records,
military files, etc., in America & other countries.

HILL COLLEGE CONFEDERATE RESEARCH CENTER & MUSEUM
PO Box 619
Hillsboro TX 76645-0619
Civil War displays & exhibits; extensive
collection of research material.

HOFFMAN RESEARCH SERVICES
412-446-3374
http://www.abebooks.com/home/hoffsrch
hoffsrch@westol.com
Ralph Hoffman
PO Box 342
Rillton PA 15678-0342
Free international book search. Professional
bookfinders since 1965; members of Interloc,
Advanced Book Exchange & Virtual Book
Shop. Please send SASE w/ mail requests.

THE HORSE SOLDIER
717-334-0347 • 717-334-5016 Fax
http://www.bmark.com/horsesoldier.antiques
hsoldier@cvn.net
PO Box 184 • Cashtown PA 17310-0184
Buying, selling & appraising Civil War military
antiques: firearms, edged weapons,
photographs, documents, battlefield relics &
more! All items unconditionally guaranteed.
Soldier research service available.
Semi-annual catalog - $10/yr.

THE INDEX PROJECT, INC.
2525 N 10th St Apt 621
Arlington VA 22201
Non-profit group preparing computerized
index of 100,000 Union court-martials.

INFO CONCEPTS, INC.
800-747-1861 • 505-298-1528 Fax
11024 Montgomery Blvd NE Ste 284
Albuquerque NM 87111-3962
CW Regimental Info. System - computer-
based information source detailing 2,550
Confederate units, 50 orders of battle, 6,000
officers' names, maps, portraits, flags, etc.
$99.95 + $7 S&H. Call for info.

INKLINGS BOOKSHOP
804-845-BOOK
1206 Main St • Lynchburg VA 24504-1818
New & used books, out-of-print searches. Civil
War, South, Literature, History, Religion, etc.

INSTITUTE FOR CIVIL WAR RESEARCH
ICWRJohn@aol.com
7913 67th Dr • Middle Village NY 11379-2908
Histories of more than 7,500 Civil War units,
Union & Confederate. Organizational data,
engagement lists, maps, etc. $15/unit. Other
services.

JAMES RIVER PUBLICATIONS
804-220-4912
http://www.erols.com/jreb/civilwar.htm
102 Maple Ln
Williamsburg VA 23185-8106
*The Chronological Tracking of the American
Civil War per the Official Records*, 2nd ed.,
fully indexed, foreword by Dr. Arthur W.
Bergeron, Jr. The ultimate Civil War reference
manual - $39.95.

TED JONES, CIVIL WAR VETERANS
tedjones@epix.net
RR 1 Box 1317
Little Meadows PA 18830-9730
Let me find your Civil War ancestors. Write for
info.

RICHARD A. LA POSTA
860-828-0921
154 Robindale Dr
Kensington CT 06037-2054
Civil War books. Regimental histories. First
editions. Search service. Buy/sell/trade. Next
2 price lists - $1.

MAC MILLAN GENERAL REFERENCE
800-428-5331
201 W 103rd St • Indianapolis IN 46290-1093
The Atlas of the Civil War - puts the entire
Civil War at your fingertips. At bookstores or
order direct.

JAMES MEJDRICH
630-668-0384
128 N Knollwood Dr
Wheaton IL 60187-4731
Will check the register of Confederate graves
in Mississippi for $1/name & SASE.

MERIDIAN STREET USED BOOKS
317-482-4882
126 S Meridian St • Lebanon IN 46052
Buy/sell/trade used books on all subjects.
Search service.

MERTIN RESEARCH SERVICES
888-248-7166
PO Box 1323 • Summit NJ 07902-1323
Experienced genealogist will research Civil
War ancestors. Pensions, service records,
Union or Confederate.

JUDY MINGUS
30 Pleasant St • Methuen MA 01844-3119
Experienced researcher will research any
military records available in Washington, DC,
or regional material in Boston area. Send
SASE.

**GEORGE TYLER MOORE CENTER FOR
THE STUDY OF THE CIVIL WAR**
304-876-5399 • 304-876-5429
304-876-5079 Fax
Shepherd College
Shepherdstown WV 25443
For continuing study/education of the most
pivotal time in American History - the Civil
War. Research being compiled on CW
soldiers through a sophisticated database.

NATIONAL ARCHIVES & RECORDS ADMIN.
202-501-5400 • 202-501-5410
http://www.nara.gov
inquire@arch2.nara.gov
7th St & Pennsylvania Ave
Washington DC 20408

OUT-OF-STATE-BOOK-SERVICE
PO Box 3253 • San Clemente CA 92674-3253
Books located, out-of-print free search
service. No obligation.

PALMETTO HISTORICAL WORKS
803-699-6746
Tim Bradshaw
120 Branch Hill Dr • Elgin SC 29045-9383
Civil War researcher. Union & Confederate
letters, 6th East Tenn VI muster roll, tintypes.

PHOTOGRAPHY OF YESTERYEAR
423-510-9306
cwphotogpr@aol.com
Frank or Rita Harned
1 Pryor Dr • Chattanooga TN 37421-2278
Photograph birthplaces, churches,
cemeteries, landmarks. Photograph CW
battlefields of approximate location of your
ancestor's unit. Limited unit research available
for TN, GA, KY.

CLAUDE V. REICH, PhD
1516 N 14th St • Reading PA 19604
Open-ended database of more than 35,000
Pa. Volunteers at the Battle of Gettysburg.

RESEARCH DATABASE
http://www.civilwardata.com/acw
Don't miss the Civil War again! Visit the
largest, most in-depth, & fully searchable
research database of U.S. Civil War history.
See website for free demonstration.

DAVID B. ROBINSON
PO Box 35926
Richmond VA 23235-0926
Complete listing of every engagement in
Virginia referenced to the Official Records. 79
pp. - $12 ppd.

SAUERS HISTORY SHOP
800-510-1108
3531 Martha Custis Dr
Alexandria VA 22302-2002
Eagerly awaited research guide to Civil War
material in the *National Tribune*, 1877-1884.
$19.95 ppd. (In KY, $20.97).

PATRICK A. SCHROEDER PUBLICATIONS
804-376-1865
RR 2 Box 128
Brookneal VA 24528
Civil War books - myths about Lee's
surrender, Fighting Quakers, a Duryee
Zouave, record of North Carolina, diary of
Swedish officer. Archives research, prints,
notecards, postcards available. Free catalog.

S. SCHUMACHER
425-259-1641
103505.1733@compuserve.com
4027 Rucker Ave Ste 747
Everett WA 98201-4839
CW pension & bountyland packets
researched -$20/name. Send name, state
mustered in, wife's name, & regiment (if
known). Union soldier's burial place
researched; 200,000+ names - $10/name.
Send details & SASE.

D. SEADLER
3426 Queensborough Dr
Olney MD 20832-2552
Researches Official Records. Regiment, battle
reports pension, POW records - $10 for
search + first 10 xeroxed pages. 15¢/page
thereafter.

SEAWEED'S SHIPS OF HISTORY
800-SEA-WEED
304-652-1525 Fax
PO Box 154, Dept M
Sistersville WV 26175-0154
Histories of U.S. naval, army transports, most
Coast Guard, sunken ships, etc. $8 & up.

SOLDIER SEARCH
PO Box 1492
Culpeper VA 22701-1492
Pension & military records of individual
soldiers who fought in the Civil War. Records
are from the National Archives -
$49.95/soldier.

PAUL SPERLING
160 E 38th St #25 • New York NY 10016
Still looking for a book? Free search.

THE UNITED STATES CIVIL WAR CENTER
504-388-3156 • 504-388-4876 Fax
http://www.cwc.lsu.edu
David Madden, Director
Louisiana State University
Baton Rouge LA 70803-0001
Facilitates the creation of a database
encompassing *all* Civil War interests;
promotes CW studies from multiple
perspectives. Website: best comprehensive
index to historic & Civil War-related websites.

GEOFF WALDEN
35197 23 Mile Rd # 4
New Baltimore MI 48047-3639
Will research your ancestor who served with
the Kentucky Infantry or Artillery for $3/name.
Capsule unit histories for $8/regt. or battery.

JAMES & KAREN WARD
9906 Warson Ct
Richmond VA 23237-3908
Virginia Confederates. Photocopies of your
ancestors' military records from the Virginia
State Archives. Send soldier's name, county
or brigade & $40.

STEVEN J. WRIGHT
7644 Burholme Ave
Philadelphia PA 19111-2411
Civil War & Plains Indian Wars historian.

95TH ILLINOIS CIVIL WAR ROUND TABLE
Tom Steinkamp
1500 East Ave
Belvidere IL 61008-4563

ADIRONDAK CIVIL WAR ROUND TABLE
PO Box 2656
Glen Falls NY 12801-6656

ALABAMA CIVIL WAR ROUND TABLE
DPEACE6499@aol.com
Dan Peace
PO Box 531305
Birmingham AL 35253-1305

AMERICAN CIVIL WAR ROUND TABLE OF AUSTRALIA, INC.
http://www.health.latrobe.edu.au/hs/ss/cu/ACW
RTA/Home /cw1page
Barry Crompton, Pres.
14 Sunlight Crescent
East Brighton Victoria, 3187 AUSTRALIA

ANN ARBOR CIVIL WAR ROUND TABLE
http://www.izzy.net/~michaelg/aacwrt.htm
michaelg@izzy.net
Tom Nanzig
PO Box 995
Ann Arbor MI 48106-0995

ARIZONA CIVIL WAR COUNCIL
Georg Kuckworth
12602 N 20th Ave
Phoenix AZ 85029-2610

ASH COUNTY CIVIL WAR ROUND TABLE
Richard Waters
73 W Jefferson St
Jefferson OH 44047-1027

ATLANTA CIVIL WAR ROUND TABLE
devanetr@argold.com
Thomas R. Devaney
1358 Brawley Cir
Atlanta GA 30319-1709

AUGHWICK CIVIL WAR ROUND TABLE
PO Box 41
Three Springs PA 17264-0041

AUSTIN CIVIL WAR ROUND TABLE
110 Wild Basin Rd S Ste 290
Austin TX 78746-3337

BONNIE BALDWIN CIVIL WAR ROUND TABLE
7305 Inzer St
Springfield VA 22151-3007

BALTIMORE CIVIL WAR ROUND TABLE
410-661-4479
Don Macreadie
1809 Wendover Rd • Baltimore MD 21234
Meets 2nd Tuesday, 7:30 pm, Tall Cedars Hall, Putty Hill Shopping Center, Putty Hill Ave. & Old Harford Rd. Free newletter & other info. (incl. dues).

BATESVILLE AREA CIVIL WAR ROUND TABLE
Ken Spencer
7 Buckeye St • Batesville AR 72501-9198

BATON ROUGE CIVIL WAR ROUND TABLE
hildamax@intersurf.com
Charles Elliott
4025 Floyd Dr • Baton Rouge LA 70808-3724

BAY COUNTY CIVIL WAR ROUND TABLE
7th_nhrc@interoz.com
J.K. Lacey
PO Box 1331 • Youngstown FL 32466-1331

BENTON CIVIL WAR ROUND TABLE
http://www.civilwarbuff.org
Pam Ray • pamray@aol.com
520 Virginia St • Benton AR 72015

BLUE & GRAY CIVIL WAR ROUND TABLE OF PG COUNTY
John Wyrick
5608 Woodland Dr • Forest Hts MD 20745

BRANDYWINE VALLEY CIVIL WAR ROUND TABLE
131B Meadowlake Dr
Downingtown PA 19335-2137

BRYAN / COLLEGE STATION CIVIL WAR ROUND TABLE
Bill Vance
714 Encinas Pl
College Station TX 77840-6553

BUCKS COUNTY CIVIL WAR ROUND TABLE
PO Box 1868 • Doylestown PA 18901-0369

BULL RUN CIVIL WAR ROUND TABLE
703-330-1965
http://osf1.gmu.edu/~cgrymes/brcwrt/
brcwrthp.html
fit2prnt@erols.com
Karen Fojt
PO Box 196
Centreville VA 20122-0196
Lecture and discussion group devoted to the historical study of the years 1861-65.

DAN BUTTERFIELD CIVIL WAR ROUND TABLE
wh_ref@midyork.lib.ny.us
Cheryl Pula
57 New Hartford St
New York Mills NY 13417

CAMP OLDEN CIVIL WAR ROUND TABLE
609-275-0143
http://www.trenton.edu/~sirak/cocwrt/coindex.html
sirak@tcnj.edu
PO Box 11060 • Hamilton NJ 08620-0060

CAMP TIPPECANOE CIVIL WAR ROUND TABLE
http://www.dcwi.com/~yannerdr/ctcwrt.html
yannerdr@dcwi.com
Wells Cultural Center
7th & North Sts • Lafayette IN 47901

CAPE FEAR CIVIL WAR ROUND TABLE
blakedp@wilmington.net
PO Box 10535
Wilmington NC 28405-0535

CAPITAL DISTRICT CIVIL WAR ROUND TABLE
http://pages/prodigy.com/WNUW97A
WNUW97A@prodigy.com
PO Box 14871
Albany NY 12221-4871

CAPITOL AREA CIVIL WAR ROUND TABLE
David Finney
316 Thompson St
Howell MI 48843-1222

CAPITOL HILL CIVIL WAR ROUND TABLE
http://www.geocities.com/Athens/1799/
	cwrt9612.html
800 11th St NW # N415
Washington DC 20001-4514

CEDAR RAPIDS CIVIL WAR ROUND TABLE
graham.james@mcleod.net
205 Bernita Dr NW
Cedar Rapids IA 52405-4308

CENTRAL DELAWARE CIVIL WAR ROUND TABLE
PO Box 328
Odessa DE 19730-0328

CENTRAL OHIO CIVIL WAR ROUND TABLE
http://www.qn.net/~wittenberg/roundtable.html
ejwlaw@qn.net
Eric Wittenberg
923 E Broad St
Columbus OH 43205-1101

JOSHUA L. CHAMBERLAIN CIVIL WAR ROUND TABLE
PO Box 1046
Brunswick ME 04011-1046
Meets 7 PM 2nd Thursdays, Sept.-June at Junior High. Membership & monthly newsletter: reg. $20, family $30, non-resident associate $10. $50 members receive audiotapes of year's speakers.

CINCINNATI CIVIL WAR ROUND TABLE
http://members.aol.com/CintiCWRT/index.html
CintiCWRT@aol.com
PO Box 1336
Cincinnati OH 45201-1336

CIVIL WAR ROUND TABLE OF FORT MYERS
1821 LLewellyn Dr
Fort Myers FL 33901-5821

CIVIL WAR ROUND TABLE OF FREDERICKSBURG
PO Box 491
Fredericksburg VA 22404-0491

CIVIL WAR ROUND TABLE
RR 3 Box 135-60
Strafford MO 65757-9314

CIVIL WAR ROUND TABLE ASSOCIATES
501-255-3996
PO Box 7388
Little Rock AR 72217-7388
Est. 1968; oldest national CW battlefield preservation organization. Publishes *CWRT Digest*, newsletter devoted to news of contemporary activities, inspired by interest in CW history & historic preservation. $12.50/yr.

CIVIL WAR ROUND TABLE OF ALEXANDRIA / FORT WARD
4301 W Braddock Rd
Alexandria VA 22304-1007

CIVIL WAR ROUND TABLE OF ARKANSAS
PO Box 7281
Little Rock AR 72217-7281

CIVIL WAR ROUND TABLE OF BIRMINGHAM
3648 Kingshill Rd
Birmingham AL 35223-1424

CIVIL WAR ROUND TABLE OF BUFFALO
benedict@ns.moran.com
5559 Broadway
Lancaster NY 14086

CIVIL WAR ROUND TABLE OF CAPE MAY, NJ
http://www.jerseycape.com/users/cole/index.htm
billc@jerseycape.net
40 Secluded Ln
Rio Grande NJ 08242-1527

CIVIL WAR ROUND TABLE OF CENTRAL FLORIDA
Karl Eichorn
PO Box 255
Sharpes FL 32959-0255

CIVIL WAR ROUND TABLE OF CHARLOTTE
William Quinn
1018 Heather ln
Charlotte NC 28209-2540

CIVIL WAR ROUND TABLE OF COLORADO
1920 Bluebell Ave
Boulder CO 80302

CIVIL WAR ROUND TABLE OF D.C.
R. Warner
1550 Brookshire Ct
Reston VA 20190-4201

CIVIL WAR ROUND TABLE OF DALTON
PO Box 2316
Dalton GA 30722-2316

CIVIL WAR ROUND TABLE OF EASTERN PA
http://www.enter.net/~cwrt
holubowsky@mail.enter.net
Jayne Holubowsky
PO Box 333
Allentown PA 18105-0333

CIVIL WAR ROUND TABLE OF FAIRFIELD COUNTY
Guy Desmond
108 Diamondcrest Ln
Stamford CT 06903-4932

CIVIL WAR ROUND TABLE OF GREATER BOSTON
http://k12.oit.umass.edu/masag/1092o.html
Dr. Paul Griffel
14 Rolling Dr
Framingham MA 01701-3671
Monthly meetings on the last Friday of each month. Field trips. 37th year.

CIVIL WAR ROUND TABLE OF HAWAII
219 Kuuhale Pl
Kailua HI 96734-2943

CIVIL WAR ROUND TABLE OF KANSAS CITY
Richard Southall
5730 W 81st Ter
Shawnee Mission KS 66208-4807

CIVIL WAR ROUND TABLE OF KENTUCKY
Nicky Hughes
PO Box 1792
Frankfort KY 40602-1792

CIVIL WAR ROUND TABLE OF LAKE COUNTY
Tracy Cripps
101 N Grandview St Apt 312
Mount Dora FL 32757-5675

CIVIL WAR ROUND TABLE OF LOS ANGELES
Gordon Tifft
3796 Colonial Ave Apt 5
Los Angeles CA 90066-3656

CIVIL WAR ROUND TABLE OF MILWAUKEE
John H. Thompson
505 E Henry Clay St Apt 104
Milwaukee WI 53217-5656

CIVIL WAR ROUND TABLE OF MONTGOMERY COUNTY
Vicki Heiling
11843 Summer Oak Dr
Germantown MD 20874-1942

CIVIL WAR ROUND TABLE OF NAPLES
Mary Den Dooven
619 Binnacle Dr
Naples FL 34103-2725

CIVIL WAR ROUND TABLE OF NE ARKANSAS
Randy F. Philhours
414 W Court St
Paragould AR 72450-4246

CIVIL WAR ROUND TABLE OF NE OHIO
Tyrone Turning
1062 Douglas Dr
Wooster OH 44691-2771

CIVIL WAR ROUND TABLE OF NEBRASKA
John Higgins
4201 Fran Ave • Lincoln NE 68516-1705

CIVIL WAR ROUND TABLE OF NEW ALBANY
PO Box 1087
New Albany IN 47150-1087

CIVIL WAR ROUND TABLE OF NEW HAMPSHIRE
Barry Burnham
PO Box 369 • Epping NH 03042-0369

CIVIL WAR ROUND TABLE OF NEW ORLEANS
Charles J. Nunez
3220 Lake Trail Dr • Metairie LA 70003-3433

CIVIL WAR ROUND TABLE OF NEW YORK
217-677-2200
175 5th Ave # 2209
New York NY 10010-7703
Monthly Manhattan meetings, guest lecturers, battlefield tours. Dues $40/yr.

CIVIL WAR ROUND TABLE OF NORTHERN NEW JERSEY
Michael Mullins
29 Stagg Rd
Wayne NJ 07470-3944

CIVIL WAR ROUND TABLE OF NW ARKANSAS
http://www.tcac.com/~bunderdn/cwrt.htm
bunderdn@tcac.com
Bob Underdown
PO Box 2947
Fayetteville AR 72702-2947

CIVIL WAR ROUND TABLE OF OKLAHOMA CITY
James Caster
3401 NW 24th St
Oklahoma City OK 73107-1807

CIVIL WAR ROUND TABLE OF PHILADELPHIA
215-735-8196
Mike Cavanaugh
1805 Pine St
Philadelphia PA 19103-6601
Dedicated to preservation & fund-raising activities associated with the Civil War.

CIVIL WAR ROUND TABLE OF RACELAND
Jon Lowry
409 Highland Ave
Raceland KY 41169-1023

CIVIL WAR ROUND TABLE OF RICHMOND
1600 Westbrook Ave Apt 218
Richmond VA 23227-3327

CIVIL WAR ROUND TABLE OF SE OHIO
David Forman
1001 Beatty Ave
Cambridge OH 43725-1831

CIVIL WAR ROUND TABLE OF SOUTH CENTRAL CT
Albert S Redway
100 Woodlawn St
Hamden CT 06517-1339

CIVIL WAR ROUND TABLE OF SOUTH FLORIDA
Arlyn Austin Katims
6801 SW 79th Ave
Miami FL 33143-2637

CIVIL WAR ROUND TABLE OF SPRINGFIELD
David Preston
1314 N 2nd St
Springfield IL 62702-3834

CIVIL WAR ROUND TABLE OF ST AUGUSTINE
318 San Marco Ave
Saint Augustine FL 32084-1625

CIVIL WAR ROUND TABLE OF ST. LOUIS
http://home.stlnet.com/~cwrtstl
cwrtstl@stlnet.com
Hugh Johns
1783 Heffington
Chesterfield MO 63017-5424

CIVIL WAR ROUND TABLE OF STUTTGART
wolfgang.hochbruck@po.uni-stuttgart.de
Deutsch-Amerikanisches Zentrum
Charlottenplatz 17
D - 70173 Stuttgart GERMANY

CIVIL WAR ROUND TABLE OF THE NW CORNER
PO Box 35
Hotchkiss School
Lakeville CT 06039-0035

CIVIL WAR ROUND TABLE OF THE OZARKS
Rick Gorman
606 N 7th Ave
Ozark MO 65721-9320

CIVIL WAR ROUND TABLE OF VANDERBURGH COURTHOUSE
Robert Leach
PO Box 869
Evansville IN 47705-0869

CIVIL WAR ROUND TABLE OF WEST CENTRAL INDIANA
http://www.thnet.com/~liggetkw/cwrt/cwrtwci.htm
Emmaline Henry
404 Linwood Dr • Greencastle IN 46135-1137

CIVIL WARRIORS ROUND TABLE
818-224-2001
http://www.dentistry.com/cwrt
c/o Jeffrey L. Wissot, DDS
23067 Ventura Blvd Ste 101
Woodland Hills CA 91364-1113
Join this round table discussion group in the
West San Fernando Valley, Los Angeles, Calif.

CLAY COUNTY CIVIL WAR ROUND TABLE
Larry Kramer
RR 2
Flora IL 62839-9803

COOPERSTOWN CIVIL WAR ROUND TABLE
Thomas Malone
5 Susquehanna Ave
Cooperstown NY 13326-1220

COTEAU CIVIL WAR ROUND TABLE
David Rambow
113 S Hiawatha Ave
Pipestone MN 56164-1664

CUMBERLAND VALLEY CIVIL WAR ROUND TABLE
D Hartmann
PO Box 663
Chambersburg PA 17201-0663

CUYAHOGA VALLEY CIVIL WAR ROUND TABLE
Thomas L. Vince
49 E Main St
Hudson OH 44236-3003

DALLAS CIVIL WAR ROUND TABLE
214-368-6230
sdavis@why.net
Pax Glenn, President
3800 Lovers Ln
Dallas TX 75225-7101

DAYTON CIVIL WAR ROUND TABLE
http://www.infinet.com/~lstevens/a/ohcwrt.html
biggsk@aol.com
Karel Lea Biggs
106 Haig St
Celina OH 45822-2708

DC CIVIL WAR ROUND TABLE
1740 Bay St SE
Washington DC 20003

DECATUR CIVIL WAR ROUND TABLE
Sharon Lee
138 S Delmar Ave
Decatur IL 62522-2506

DELAWARE VALLEY CIVIL WAR ROUND TABLE
http://www.ourworld.compuserve.com/
homepages/paulag/ homepage.htm
PO Box 63006
Philadelphia PA 19114-0806

ELK GROVE CIVIL WAR ROUND TABLE
PO Box 1864
Elk Grove CA 95759-1864

FORT SMITH CIVIL WAR ROUND TABLE
Bob Vick
1102 Wofford Lake Rd
Fort Smith AR 72916-3611

FORT WAYNE CIVIL WAR ROUND TABLE
http://www.thnet.com/~liggetkw/cwrt/
ftwayne.cwrt.htm
dfboyle@juno.com
Robert Johnsonbaugh
6818 Woodcrest Dr
Fort Wayne IN 46815-5571

FORT WORTH CIVIL WAR ROUND TABLE
Jim Rosenthal
3952 Thistle Ln
Fort Worth TX 76109-3425

FREDERICK COUNTY CIVIL WAR ROUND TABLE
http://members.aol.com/Fredcocwrt/private/
index.htm
FredCoCWRT@aol.com
PO Box 4101
Frederick MD 21705-4101

CAPT. HENRY GALPIN CIVIL WAR CIVIL WAR ROUND TABLE
RR 1 Box 319
Little Falls NY 13365-9634

GENESSEE VALLEY CIVIL WAR ROUND TABLE
DTKTT@aol.com
Donna Payne
PO Box 451
Pavilion NY 14525-0451

GETTYSBURG CIVIL WAR ROUND TABLE
Barbara Angstadt
201 Hills Dr
Gettysburg PA 17325-2435

GLOVERSVILLE CIVIL WAR ROUND TABLE
James Morrison
95 Lincoln St
Gloversville NY 12078-2017

GRAND RAPIDS CIVIL WAR ROUND TABLE
Ron Farra
666 4 Mile Rd NE
Grand Rapids MI 49525-2106

GRANVILLE CIVIL WAR ROUND TABLE
http://www.infinet.com/~lstevens/a/ohcwrt.html
PO Box 129
Granville OH 43023-0129

GREATER TOLEDO CIVIL WAR ROUND TABLE
http://www.infinet.com/~lstevens/a/ohcwrt.html
http://www.netcom.com/~jobuford/CWRT/
     main.html
jobuford@ix.netcom.com
4325 Commonwealth Ave
Toledo OH 43612-2040

GREEN MOUNTAIN CIVIL WAR ROUND TABLE
http://members.aol.com/vtcw150/gmcwrt.htm
auntis@aol.com
PO Box 653
Woodstock VT 05091-0653

MAJ. ANDREW J. GROVER CIVIL WAR ROUND TABLE
41 Creamery Rd
Richford NY 13835-1001

HAMPTON ROADS CIVIL WAR ROUND TABLE
127 W Lorengo Ave
Norfolk VA 23503-4313

HARPERS FERRY CIVIL WAR ROUND TABLE
Dennis Frye
PO Box 355
Harpers Ferry WV 25425-0355
Meets 2nd Wed. of each month, Sept-June at
Camp Hill United Methodist Church, Harpers
Ferry, W.Va. Dues -$15/yr.

HARRISBURG CIVIL WAR ROUND TABLE
William Matter
3621 Brookridge Ter Apt 101
Harrisburg PA 17109-2131

HARTFORD CIVIL WAR ROUND TABLE
R D Wolff
105 Hedgehog Ln
West Simsbury CT 06092-2107

HAYWARD CIVIL WAR ROUND TABLE
2753 Meadowlark Dr
Union City CA 94587-3142

HOOSIER BLUE & GRAY CIVIL WAR ROUND TABLE
http://www.thnet.com/~liggetkw/cwrt/b&g.htm
James Gibson
PO Box 292
Cambridge City IN 47327-0292

HOUSTON CIVIL WAR ROUND TABLE
http://members.aol.com/Houstcwrt/index.html
reyork@ibm.net
Dean Letzring
PO Box 4215
Houston TX 77210-4215
Website: information, programs & schedule of
events.

IMPERIAL VALLEY CIVIL WAR ROUND TABLE
510 W Main St
El Centro CA 92243-2900

INDIANAPOLIS CIVIL WAR ROUND TABLE
http://www.thnet.com/~liggetkw/cwrt/indmain.htm
Beverly Roberts
10006 E Washington St Ste A
Indianapolis IN 46202-2624

INLAND EMPIRE CIVIL WAR ROUND TABLE
Don McCue
A.K. Smiley Public Library
125 W Vine St
Redlands CA 92373-4761

THE JACKSON CIVIL WAR ROUND TABLE
PO Box 3475
Jackson MS 39207

JEFFERSON COUNTY CIVIL WAR ROUND TABLE
http://www.thnet.com/~liggetkw/cwrt/jccwrt.htm
Eric Losey
3940 W Prall Ln
Scottsburg IN 47170-7811

KANAWHA VALLEY CIVIL WAR ROUND TABLE
888 S Washington St
Saint Albans WV 25177-3784

KNOXVILLE CIVIL WAR ROUND TABLE
PO Box 313
Knoxville TN 37901-0313

LAUREL HILL CIVIL WAR ROUND TABLE
Gary Birkett
PO Box 701
Stuart VA 24171-0701

ROBERT E. LEE CIVIL WAR ROUND TABLE
http://nj5.injersey.com/~mbwick
augn61a@prodigy.com or
mbwick@injersey.com
1162 Saint Georges Ave Ste 194
Avenel NJ 07001-1263

GEORGE W. LEE CIVIL WAR ROUND TABLE
Michael Yost
PO Box 500 • Howell MI 48844-0500

ABRAHAM LINCOLN CIVIL WAR ROUND TABLE OF MI
lstringer@ameritech.net
Liz Stringer, Pres.
23959 Brookplace Ct
Farmington Hills MI 48336-2728

LINCOLN CIVIL WAR SOCIETY
John Bloom
127 Mansfield Rd
Landsdowne PA 19050-1513

LINCOLN CLUB OF DELAWARE
David H. Burdash
1111 Bayview Rd
Middletown DE 19709-9625

LINCOLN GROUP OF BOSTON
Thomas Turner
27 Forest Trl
East Bridgewater MA 02333-1612

LITTLE FORT CIVIL WAR ROUND TABLE
Torlief Homes
2636 W Vermont Ave
Waukegan IL 60087-3648

LONG BEACH CIVIL WAR ROUND TABLE
9813 Via Sonoma
Cypress CA 90630-8680

LONG ISLAND CIVIL WAR ROUND TABLE
Richard Cashman
18 Dillmont St
Smithtown NY 11787-1602

LOUDOUN COUNTY CIVIL WAR ROUND TABLE
540-338-7550
PO Box 18
Lincoln VA 20160-0018
Meets monthly at Douglass Community
School, Route 7 E & Sycolin Rd., Leesburg.

LOUISVILLE CIVIL WAR ROUND TABLE
PO Box 1861
Louisville KY 40201-1861

MADISON COUNTY HISTORICAL SOCIETY CWRT
http://www.thnet.com/~liggetkw/cwrt/
mchscwrt.htm
Gerald Jones
2812 E 100 S • Anderson IN 46017-1802

MAHONING VALLEY CWRT
David Badger
RR 1 Box 389
New Galilee PA 16141-9619
Meets 2nd Tues., Sept-May.

MANITOWOC COUNTY CIVIL WAR ROUND TABLE
dmoore@lakefield.net
Dennis R Moore
1232 Arlington Ave
Manitowoc WI 54220-2628

MICHIGAN REGIMENTAL CIVIL WAR ROUND TABLE
junskimos@aol.com
John Moore
2119 Van Antwerp
Grosse Point Woods MI 48236

MID-ATLANTIC CONFERENCE OF CIVIL WAR ROUND TABLES
610-262-1614
CWRT of Eastern PA
PO Box 333 • Allentown PA 18105-0333
Special speakers. Annual conference - April.

MIDWEST CWRT CONFERENCE
Cincinnati CWRT
PO Box 1336
Cincinnati OH 45201-1336
Annual April conferences with several
speakers, book sales, raffles, tours.

MURFREESBORO CIVIL WAR ROUND TABLE
Pennie Jekot
2115 Shannon Dr • Murfreesboro TN 37129

NASSAU COUNTY CIVIL WAR ROUND TABLE
Walter Anthony
150 Lincoln Ave • Rockville Centre NY 11507

NATIONAL CONGRESS OF CWRTs
501-225-3996
CWRTA
PO Box 7388
Little Rock AR 72217-7388
Speakers & tours. Annual conference -
October.

NORTH CAROLINA CIVIL WAR ROUND TABLE
4109 Charles G Dr
Raleigh NC 27606-9237

NORTH COUNTY CIVIL WAR ROUND TABLE
slcha@northnet.org
St. Lawrence Co. Historical Assn.
PO Box 8 • Canton NY 13617-0008

NORTH LOUISIANA CIVIL WAR ROUND TABLE
http://www.prysm.net/~garyj/NLCWRT/nlcwrt.htm
garyj@prysm.net
Mary Margaret & Allan Richard / Garry Joiner
245 Forest Ave • Shreveport LA 71104-4506

NORWICH CIVIL WAR ROUND TABLE
Dave Manzer
594 Lyon Brook Rd
Norwich NY 13815-3427

OHIO VALLEY CIVIL WAR ROUND TABLE
Herb Parkinson
PO Box 164
Buffalo OH 43722-0164

OLD BALDY CWRT OF PHILADELPHIA
215-735-8196
609-829-4380
Civil War Library & Museum
1805 Pine St
Philadelphia PA 19103-6601
Monthly meetings, speakers, field trips,
heavily into preservation.

OLDE COLONY CIVIL WAR ROUND TABLE
David Kenney
43 Fairview St
Dedham MA 02026-3223

ONONDAGA CIVIL WAR ROUND TABLE
Tom Hunter
311 Montgomery St
Syracuse NY 13202-2009

ORLANDO CIVIL WAR ROUND TABLE
Hal K. Litchford
PO Box 1549
Orlando FL 32802-1549

OTTAWA NATIONAL CAPITAL CIVIL WAR ROUND TABLE
Mr. Cliff Forsythe
1002 Driftwood Cres
Gloucester, Ontario Canada K1C 2P1
Also Confederate Historical Association of
Canada. Monthly meetings.

PALM BEACH CIVIL WAR ROUND TABLE
James Roberts
829 Salem Ln
Lake Worth FL 33467-2764

WILLIAM DORSEY PENDER CIVIL WAR ROUND TABLE
John Derbyshire
PO Box 7828
Rocky Mount NC 27804-0828

PENINSULA CIVIL WAR ROUND TABLE
PO Box 1274
San Carlos CA 94070-1274

PENINSULA CIVIL WAR ROUND TABLE
PO Box 1794
Newport News VA 23601-1794

PENSACOLA CIVIL WAR ROUND TABLE
http://members.aol.com/PENCWRT/index.html
pencwrt@aol.com
Thomas R. Long, Jr.
4204 Rosebud Ct
Pensacola FL 32504-8448

PIEDMONT CIVIL WAR ROUND TABLE
William Stafford
150 Riley Forest Ct
Winston Salem NC 27127-7574

PLATTE VALLEY CIVIL WAR ROUND TABLE
Lawrence Lefler
1835 E Military Ave # 127
Fremont NE 68025-5465

PORTER COUNTY CIVIL WAR ROUND TABLE
Jeff Sandlin
103 E Mound St • Knox IN 46534-1133

PORTSMOUTH AREA CIVIL WAR ROUND TABLE
Jessie Hines
641 Mount Vernon Ave
Portsmouth VA 23707-2018

PUGET SOUND CIVIL WAR ROUND TABLE
D P Richardson
6614 NE Windermere Rd
Seattle WA 98115-7943

RANDOLPH COUNTY CIVIL WAR ROUND TABLE
http://www.thnet.com/~liggetkw/cwrt/
RCCWRT.htm
Meet at 101 W. Franklin St., Winchester,
Indiana.

RAPPAHANNOCK VALLEY CIVIL WAR ROUND TABLE
540-786-2470
Mwyckoff@pop.erols.com
Mac Wyckoff
PO Box 7632 • Fredericksburg VA 22404

RICHMOND CIVIL WAR ROUND TABLE
Sandra V. Parker, Sect.
PO Box 37052
Richmond VA 23234-7052
Meets 2nd Tuesday each month at Boulevard
Methodist Church, Boulevard & Stuart Ave.,
Richmond, Va., at 8 PM.

ROANOKE CIVIL WAR ROUND TABLE
Clive Rich
PO Box 11882
Roanoke VA 24022-1882

ROCHESTER CIVIL WAR ROUND TABLE
Jerry Poslusny
118 Burrows Hills Dr
Rochester NY 14625-2129

ROCKBRIDGE CIVIL WAR ROUND TABLE
PO Box 7
Brownsburg VA 24415-0007
Monthly meetings. Dues - $15. Bob Driver,
president.

ROCKLAND CIVIL WAR ROUND TABLE
Ken Dudonis
95 Hunt Ave
Pearl River NY 10965-1868

SACRAMENTO CIVIL WAR ROUND TABLE
7713 Las Lilas Ct
Citrus Heights CA 95621-1722

SAN ANTONIO CIVIL WAR ROUND TABLE
Rusy Mahan
13643 Princes Knls
San Antonio TX 78231-1948

SAN DIEGO CIVIL WAR ROUND TABLE
CWDAVE@aol.com
PO Box 22369
San Diego CA 92192-2369

SAN FRANCISCO CIVIL WAR ROUND TABLE
PO Box 2389
Livermore CA 94551-2389

SAN GABRIEL VALLEY CIVIL WAR ROUND TABLE
PO Box 80680
San Marino CA 91118-8680

SAN JOAQUIN VALLEY CIVIL WAR ROUND TABLE
8665 N Cedar Ave Unit 112
Fresno CA 93720-1823

SAVANNAH GRAYS CIVIL WAR ROUND TABLE
PO Box 15238
Savannah GA 31416-1938

SHENANDOAH VALLEY CIVIL WAR ROUND TABLE
George Hansbrough
209 F St
Shenandoah VA 22849-1126

SOUTH BAY CIVIL WAR ROUND TABLE
1475 S Bascom Ave Ste 204
Campbell CA 95008-0629

SOUTHERN MINNESOTA CIVIL WAR ROUND TABLE
1104 7th St SW
Rochester MN 55902-2005

SOUTHERN ONTARIO CIVIL WAR ROUND TABLE
quee@netrover.com
Dave Carney
28 James St
Georgetown Ontario, CANADA L7G 2H4

STILLWATER CIVIL WAR ROUND TABLE
http://www.infinet.com/~lstevens/a/ohcwrt.html
Dr. David R. Hayes
PO Box 366 • West Milton OH 45383-0366

SUFFOLK CIVIL WAR ROUND TABLE
Robert Hardy
5085 Indian Trl • Suffolk VA 23434-7322

TENNESSEE VALLEY CIVIL WAR ROUND TABLE
http://members.aol.com/TVCWRT/index.html
jfepperson@aol.com
Brian Hogan
11202 Suncrest Dr SE
Huntsville AL 35803-1620

TRI-VALLEY CIVIL WAR ROUND TABLE
PO Box 5076 • Pleasanton CA 94566

TWIN CITIES CIVIL WAR ROUNDTABLE
612-933-6696
Paul Olson
14699 Beacon Cir
Minnetonka MN 55345-4707
Meets monthly September-May for dinner &
guest speaker on Civil War topics.

TWIN TIER CIVIL WAR ROUND TABLE
Michael S. Winicki
PO Box 1108 • Olean NY 14760-1108
Sponsors of seminars, talks, presentations &
other Civil War activities. Supports
preservation efforts. Est. 1990.

ULSTER COUNTY CIVIL WAR ROUND TABLE
UCCWRT@mhv.net
PO Box 120 • Stone Ridge NY 12484-0120

VILLANOVA CIVIL WAR ROUND TABLE
International Studies
Villanova University
Villanova PA 19085

WACO CIVIL WAR ROUND TABLE
Jerry Powell
Baylor Univ Continuing Ed
Box 97288 • Waco TX 76798-7288

WATERTOWN CIVIL WAR ROUND TABLE
Richard Kraemer
871 LeRay
Watertown NY 13601

WEST CENTRAL OHIO CIVIL WAR ROUND TABLE
http://www.infinet.com/~lstevens/a/ohcwrt.html
302 N Wayne St
Van Wert OH 45891-1328

WESTCHESTER NY CIVIL WAR ROUND TABLE
PO Box 1861
Croton Falls NY 10519-1861

WESTERN OHIO CIVIL WAR ROUND TABLE
http://www.infinet.com/~lstevens/a/ohcwrt.html
PO Box 511
Celina OH 45822-0511

WESTMORELAND COUNTY CIVIL WAR ROUND TABLE
Jack Burger
323 N Maple Ave
Greensburg PA 15601-1818

WICHITA CIVIL WAR ROUND TABLE
pjhjr@juno.com
John Handley
PO Box 1654
Wichita KS 67201-1654

WICHITA FALLS CIVIL WAR ROUND TABLE
Bill Spears
PO Box 780
Wichita Falls TX 76307-0780

WILLIAMSBURG CIVIL WAR ROUND TABLE, INC.
757-838-1685
JPHA1982@aol.com
Peggy Vogtsberger
7 Carmel Ter
Hampton VA 23666-2807
Meets monthly, 2nd Thurs. 7:30 PM, Bruton
Parish Church Center, Duke of Gloucester St.,
Williamsburg. Excellent speakers, field trips.
Active in battlefield preservation & historical
interpretation. Dues - $20/yr.

WILMINGTON DE CIVIL WAR ROUND TABLE
Robert Widenor
2211 Beaumont Rd
Wilmington DE 19803-3016

WYOMING VALLEY CIVIL WAR ROUND TABLE
PO Box 613
Dallas PA 18612-0613

AIKEN LEE-JACKSON BANQUET
803-649-9475
SCV
PO Box 1863
Aiken SC 29802-1863
Annual January banquet. Hosted by Brig.
Gen. Banard E. Bee Camp #1575, SCV, to
benefit preservation.

ASHEVILLE MILITARY ANTIQUES SHOW
704-282-1339
Asheville NC
Arms & memorabilia of Civil War, Indian
Wars, world wars, etc. Annual September
event.

**CAPITAL OF THE CONFEDERACY CIVIL
WAR SHOW**
804-737-5827
Central VA Relic Hunters Assn
Richmond VA
More than 450 tables of original weapons,
uniforms, relics, currency, documents, &
personal soldier items. Hourly presentations
by Museum of the Confederacy. Annual event
- November.

CAROLINA TRADER PROMOTIONS
704-282-1339
http://www.trellis.net/carotrader
carotrader@trellis.net
Esther & Richard Shields
PO Box 769
Monroe NC 28111-0769
Promoters of military collectible shows.

CELEBRATE HISTORY
800-748-9901
http://www.celebratehistory.com
PO Box 70332
Port Richmond CA 94807-0332
Held annually every President's Day holiday
weekend (Feb. 13-15, 1998) at South San
Francisco Conference Center. Includes
complete Civil War round table & symposium.

CELEBRATION DINNER DANCE
616-349-6195
3330 S Rose St
Kalamazoo MI 49001-4723
Annual March dinner dance with period music,
dance instruction. Period dress optional.

**CENTRAL NC RELIC HUNTERS CIVIL WAR
SHOW**
704-463-5439 Terry Teff
704-289-4212 Mick Aderholdt
Salisbury NC
Civil War relics. Annual show - February.

CHRISTMAS AT THE FORT
334-861-6992
Fort Gaines Historic Site
PO Box 97
Dauphin Island AL 36528-0097
Annual living history weekend; 1998 dates -
December 5-6. Experience 1861 Christmas at
the fort with Confederate soldiers —
authenticity stressed. Candlelight tour, feast,
dance, drills, camp life, etc.

**CIVIL WAR MEMORABILIA, RELIC & BOOK
SHOW (SC)**
803-577-7766
Ray Davenport
Charleston SC
Hosted by Lowcountry CW Collectors Assn.
Display awards. Annual show - January.
Admission - $4 over age 12.

**CIVIL WAR MEMORABILIA, RELIC & BOOK
SHOW (VA)**
703-823-1958 John Graham
Northern Va. Relic Hunters Assn.
Fairfax VA
More than 275 tables of finest Civil War &
earlier military effects, memorabilia, relics &
books for sale or trade. Exhibitor awards.
Annual show - March. Admission - $4 over
age 12.

**CIVIL WAR SCULPTURE EXHIBITION &
SEMINAR**
800-438-5800
Grove Park Inn Resort
Asheville NC
Annual March exhibition. Vignettes, auctions,
discussions & more. Call for info. & free
brochure.

**COASTAL CAROLINA MILITARY
ANTIQUES SHOW**
704-282-1339
Wilmington NC
Arms & memorabilia of Civil War, Indian
Wars, world wars, etc. Annual event - July.

COHASCO, INC.
914-476-8500
914-476-8573 Fax
E. Snyder
Postal 821
Yonkers NY 10702
Semi-annual mail/phone auction catalogs
containing varied CW memorabilia: generals,
maps, letters, photos, ephemera, etc. Our
50th year in business. Catalog - $5.

CONFERENCE ON WOMEN & THE CIVIL WAR
800-473-3943
roslin@nfis.com
12728 Martin Rd • Smithsburg MD 21783
Through lectures on various topics, recognizes & honors the services performed by women for their country & its people during the 1860s.

EARLY AMERICAN HISTORY AUCTIONS
619-459-4159 • 800-473-5686
619-459-4373 Fax
http://www.cts.com/browse/ean
PO Box 3341 • La Jolia CA 92038
Mail bid auctions every two months; approx. 1,000 lots in each. Historic Americana & Civil War-related material. Always buying collections & accepting important consignments. Catalog - $36/yr. for 6 issues. Free on Internet.

FIREARMS SKIRMISH NATIONAL COMPETITION
North-South Skirmish Assn.
Winchester VA
More than 3,600 competitors on 200 teams competing with muskets, carbines, revolvers, mortars & cannon. Largest event of its kind. Sutlers, food, free admission. Annual event - May.

FORKS OF THE DELAWARE ANTIQUE & MODERN ARMS SHOWS
610-588-8305
Forks of the Delaware Historical Arms Society, Inc.
97 Johnson Rd • Bangor PA 18013-9274
Antique & modern arms, & related items. Presented 4 times/yr. $5 donation at door.

FREDERICK CIVIL WAR SHOW
301-253-4961
Ed Dishman
PO Box 246
Damascus MD 20872-0246
Annual April CW show, sponsored by Frederick Co., MD, CWRT & Central MD Heritage League. Admission - $4 over age 12.

GETTYSBURG BATTLEFIELD PRESERVATION ASSOCIATION
717-337-0031
Dr. Walter L. Powell, Pres.
PO Box 1863
Gettysburg PA 17325
Bi-annual newsletter "Battle Lines" (for $10 annual membership). Various Civil War books & prints available for donations. Annual Civil War Book Show.

GRAND ANNAPOLIS CITY BALL
Stephen Bockmiller
101 Fitz Ct Apt 204 • Reisterstown MD 21136
Annual March ball with orchestral music & refreshments. Period military or civilian attire required. Attendance limited. Co-sponsored by 4th NC Infantry & 5th US Cavalry.

GREATER BALTIMORE CIVIL WAR SHOW & SALE
410-465-6827
Courtney B. Wilson
8393 Court Ave • Ellicott City MD 21043
Civil War antiques & memorabilia. August show. Adult admission - $5.

HARRISBURG CIVIL WAR EXPOSITION & SEMINARS
717-780-2587
vlgentze@hacc01b.hacc.edu
Harrisburg Area Community College
1 HACC Dr • Harrisburg PA 17110-2903
Showcases reenactor demonstrations, living historians, historical societies' displays, merchants. Seminars, guest speakers. Advance registration required. Annual March-April event. Call for info.

HEART OF THE CONFEDERACY SPRING CIVIL WAR RELIC SHOW & SALE
707-477-8159
Steve E. Lister
PO Box 1014 • Jonesboro GA 30237-1014
Civil War relics. More than 300 tables. Annual event, south of Atlanta - March.

HILTON HEAD DISPATCH
407-295-7510
7214 Laurel Hill Rd • Orlando FL 32818-5233
Publication indicating where to find reenactments, shows, & book fairs dealing in history. Covering the Southeast. $15/yr. for 6 issues.

HISTORICAL COLLECTIBLE AUCTIONS
910-570-2803 • 910-570-2748 Fax
Holzman-Caren Associates
PO Box 975 • Burlington NC 27215-0975
Semi-annual auctions of Civil War collectibles. Consignments encouraged. Catalog - $18; next 3 for $45.

INTERNET CIVIL WAR EXPO
815-458-2029
http://www.bmark.com/cw.show
World's 1st Civil War Expo on the Internet, 24 hrs./day, 365 days/yr. Many major dealers. One month ads available for your extra relics, books, & other items.

KALAMAZOO ANTIQUE ARMS & PIONEER CRAFT SHOW
616-327-4557
Kalamazoo County Fair Grounds MI
Annual March show, featuring pre-1890
firearms, accoutrements, period fashions,
living history.

KENTUCKIANA ARMS COLLECTORS ASSN., INC.
PO Box 1776 • Louisville KY 40201-1776
Sponsors annual gun show in July; has
resurrected John Hunt Morgan show. 200
tables, weapons, relics, accoutrements,
displays, photos, memorabilia.

KERNSTOWN COMMEMORATION
540-678-8598 • 800-298-1861
Kernstown Battlefield Assn.
PO Box 1327 • Winchester VA 22604
Event scheduled for March 1998. Contact
KBA for details.

LEE/JACKSON BALL
757-421-7450 Aleta Carmody
757-421-7221 M.J. Forbes
L.A.M.B.S. & 15th Va. Cavalry
Hampton VA
Annual January ball with buffet, open bar,
period music & dance.

LEE/JACKSON CEREMONY
410-296-9235 Elliott Cummings
410-747-3271 Bob Lyons
Col. Harry W. Gilmor Camp #1388 SCV
Baltimore MD
Honors Lee & Jackson on their birthdays.
Reenactors, UDC, period civilians, spectators
invited. Held annually in January, at the
Lee/Jackson monument, Art Museum &
Wyman Park Drive, Baltimore.

LOWCOUNTRY CIVIL WAR SHOW
770-972-4904
Mike Kent
PO Box 336 • Grayson GA 30221-0336
Annual memorabilia, relic & book show, held
in Charleston, SC.

MARCH FOR GETTYSBURG
717-334-0772
717-334-3118 Fax
Friends of Natl. Parks at Gettysburg
10 Lincoln Sq • PO Box 4622
Gettysburg PA 17325-2205
Fundraiser for Land Acquisition Fund. March
follows route of Law's 15th Ala. Infantry to
Little Round Top. Prizes & seedlings.
Reenactors welcome. Annual event - April.

MID SOUTH CIVIL WAR SHOW
901-362-2874
James R. Chalmers Camp 1312, SCV
PO Box 161254 • Memphis TN 38186-1254
Annual Civil War show - February. Admission
- $4 age 13 & over; $2 ages 12 & under.

MIDWEST CIVIL WAR COLLECTOR SHOW
773-539-8432
Robert Nowak
3238 N Central Park Ave
Chicago IL 60618-5306
450 tables of American militaria to 1898.
Period uniforms & costumes welcome.
Non-profit annual event in Wheaton, IL -
September. Admission - $4 over age 12; $1
under 12.

MISSISSIPPI VALLEY CIVIL WAR SYMPOSIUM
800-298-1861
CW Education Assn.
PO Box 78 • Winchester VA 22604-0078
Special speakers. Annual event - September.

NATIONAL CIVIL WAR ARTILLERY & INFANTRY SCHOOL
315-483-9284
Frank Cutler
6343 Kelly Rd • Sodus NY 14551-9502
Training & classes in Youngstown, NY, under
top instructors from around the country. Live &
train inside historic fort. $6 fee. Annual event -
May.

NEW HOPE ANTIQUE ARMS FAIR
610-588-8853
New Hope PA
Semi-annual, invitational event featuring
firearms, swords, photos, uniforms, & more.
June & October. Admission - $5.

OCTOBER BLUE & GRAY CHAMPAGNE BRUNCH & AUCTION
215-735-8196
CW Library & Museum
1805 Pine St • Philadelphia PA 19103-6601
Auction of books, prints, art, relics. Proceeds
go to Civil War Library & Museum. Annual
event.

OHIO CIVIL WAR COLLECTORS & ARTILLERY SHOWS
419-289-3120
Mansfield OH
Annual May encampment, field hospital
scenarios, period music, sutlers, artillery
displays, firing demonstrations.

OLD DOMINION GUN SHOWS
540-238-1343
540-238-1453 Fax
PO Box 289
Woodlawn VA 24381-0289

OLDE AMERICAN COLLECTIBLES, INC.
13 Nathalie Ct
Peekskill NY 10566
Semi-annual auctions, mail/telephone.
Collections purchased outright or accepted on
consignment. Fully illus. catalog - $20 for
2-issue subscription.

OLE NORTH STATE MILITARY
COLLECTOR'S SHOW
704-786-8373
Carolina Hobby Expo
Raleigh NC
Annual January show of arms & memorabilia
of Civil War & other periods. Admission - $4.

POTOMAC ARMS COLLECTOR'S ASSN.
301-921-9673
PO Box 1812
Wheaton MD 20915-1812
Sponsors of annual October gun show,
Frederick, MD. Guns, knives, & related items.
Donation - $4.

RALLY FOR THE VALLEY
540-678-8598 • 800-298-1861
Kernstown Battlefield Assn.
PO Box 1327 • Winchester VA 22604
Event scheduled for July 1998. Contact KBA
for details.

RETURNING HEROES BALL
Patri & Barbara Pugliese
39 Capen St
Medford MA 02155-5824
Annual March ball featuring contra-dances,
quadrilles, waltzes, polkas, & schottisches.

SHARPSBURG HERITAGE FESTIVAL:
WHERE HISTORY COMES ALIVE
301-432-4065 Sid Gale
PO Box 456
Sharpsburg MD 21782-0456
Remembrance march, encampments,
scripted vignettes. Period camping on sites
Confederates held during battle. Barn dance
at Piper Farm. Annual event - September.

VICKSBURG CONVENTION & VISITORS
BUREAU
800-221-3536
601-636-4642 Hayes Latham
http://www.vicksburg.org/cvb
PO Box 110
Vicksburg MS 39181-0110
Annual March "Run Through History" through
Vicksburg NMP. 10K race, 5K walk, 1-mile
run. Refreshments, music.

WAR BETWEEN THE STATES
MEMORABILIA & ANTIQUE GUN SHOW
910-784-0301 Jerry Hart
Brig. Gen. Wm. R. Boggs Chapter, MOSB
Winston Salem NC
Memorabilia & guns. Annual event - March.
Admission -$4, children under 12 - $1.

97th REGIMENTAL STRING BAND
813-391-4565
PO Box 2208
Largo FL 33779-2208
Cassettes & CDs of the 80 most popular Civil War songs. Many vols. Coffee cups, T-shirts, & spoken history cassettes. Catalog - SASE.

ADDISON WORLDWIDE INC.
PO Box 3691
Pembroke NC 28372
"Don't blame me, I voted for Jefferson Davis." Bumper stickers - $3 ea., quantity discounts. T-shirts - $17.95 ea. (specify size).

AMERICAN AFGHAN COMPANY
410-744-5470
1074 Craftswood Rd
Baltimore MD 21228-1312
50" x 60" cotton weave Confederate battle flag afghan. For home, vehicle, or otherwise. $49.95 ea. Contact for other products.

AMERICANA SOUVENIRS & GIFTS
http://www.americanagifts.com
302 York St
Gettysburg PA 17325
Most complete line of Civil War souvenirs & memorabilia for both USA & CSA. Cannons, bullets, patches, toys, books, flags, videos, documents, insignias, & much more. (See ad page 242)

ANCIENT AMERICAN ART
601-566-2778 • 601-566-4925
http://www.pointsouth.com/aaa.htm
aaart@dixie-net.com
PO Box 1745
Verona MS 38879-1745
Handmade reproductions of battle & regimental flags of the Civil War. T-shirts $20. Prints $25. Wholesale discounts.

B.FORM CREATIVE MEDIA
908-846-5725
bform4@tribeca.ios.com
116 Park Pl
Highland Park NJ 08904-2202
Heavyweight, short-sleeve, hand screen-printed gray T-shirts. Image of Longstreet or Forrest in black. $11 + $3.50 S&H.

BARTLETT'S COLLECTIBLES
PO Box 545
Mechanicsburg PA 17055-0545
Civil War trading cards; superb photography, educational, collectible. Free sample card & catalog.

BATTLEZONE, LTD.
PO Box 266
Towaco NJ 07082-0266
Military patches, pins, decals, planes, books. 5,000+ items. Color catalog - $4.50 ppd. ($2 ref. w/ 1st order)

BELLE & BLADE
201-328-8488
201-442-0669 Fax
124 Penn Ave
Dover NJ 07801-5335
Send for catalog of war books, videos, toys, swords, knives, & gifts. Catalog - $3; free w/ order.

BLITZKRIEG PRESS
21 Meridian Cir
Newtown PA 18940-1742
Stationery, notepads, etc. For sutlers, Civil War enthusiasts; personal or business use. Any design you request or have. Send $1 for more info.

THE BLUE & GRAY SHOP
800-454-7104
531 Baltimore St
Gettysburg PA 17325-2606
Reasonably priced T-shirts of *The Killer Angels*, Gettysburg, etc. Videos, cassettes, CDs, calendars, etc.

BLUE MOON IMAGES
18 Washington St Ste 210
Canton MA 02021
Set of 8 Civil War watercolor notecards - 4 scenes. $8.95 ea. set + $2.50 S&H.

BOOKMARK
414-646-4499
414-646-4427 Fax
PO Box 335
Delafield WI 53018-0335
Mort Kuntsler's *Legends in Gray* calendars & notecards. $12.95 + $5 S&H. Catalog - $2.

THE BRADFORD EXCHANGE
9345 N Milwaukee Ave
Niles IL 60714-1393
The Heart of Plate Collecting. Limited edition collector's plates featuring historic events.

BRANDYWINE TEE
1099 Parkerville Rd
West Chester PA 19382-7036
Robert E. Lee, "Stonewall" Jackson, Colt pistols & powder flask T-shirts & mugs. Mugs - $3.50 ea. + $1 S&H.

BUFFALO ROBE TRADING POST
520-457-2322
George Henry
9 N 5th St
PO Box 741 • Tombstone AZ 85638-0741
Civil War, local history, American Indian,
western lawmen & outlaws. Gift shop,
artifacts, video & audio tapes. Historian in
attendance.

THE CALENDAR PEOPLE
800-758-2751
2083 Springwood Rd
PO Box 125 • York PA 17403-0125
Civil War reenactment calendar featuring
pictures of 12 reenactment groups
(CSA/USA). $12 + S&H.

CAVALIER SHOPPE
800-227-5491
Rex Jarrett, Owner
PO Box 511 • Bruce MS 38915-0511
Confederate flag apparel - 100% cotton.
Shirts, slacks, shorts, skirts, boxers, belts,
ties, watches, flags. Free catalog.

CHRIS & JACKIE'S
410-741-1909
PO Box 717 • Dunkirk MD 20754-0717
Civil War designs on decorative light switch
plates -$9.95-$14.95.

CIVIL WAR LABELS UNLIMITED
Paul Wilson
46 Sawmill Rd • Springfield MA 01118-1719
Personalized name/address labels,
bookplates, notecards & scratch pad
stationery - featuring your favorite CW
personalities (more than 220 available). Illus.
price list -$1.

COLUMBIA GAMES, INC.
800-636-3631
http://www.columbiagames.com/
questions@columbiagames.com
PO Box 3457 • Blaine WA 98231-3457
"Dixie" - a tactical CW card game consisting of
collectible cards - $7.95/deck of 60 random
cards. 1 for each regiment, battery & brigade
officer at Bull Run, Shiloh, Gettysburg. Free
catalog.

CONFEDERATE CALENDAR WORKS
PO Box 2084
Austin TX 78768-2084
Illustrated with previously unpublished &
researched photos of Confederate soldiers,
1861-65 events, etc. $11.95.

CONFEDERATE ENTERPRISES
800-996-8883
Flags, jackets, bumper stickers. Keep it flying!

CONFEDERATE GRAY
615-320-1715
615-320-3272 Fax
Meeks Booker
PO Box 121984
Nashville TN 37212-1984
Hand-carved music boxes that play "Dixie"
when opened; other tunes available. Named
for great Southern leaders or battles. Refer to
Source Book for 10% discount. Catalog - $2
(ref.).

CONFEDERATE MEMORIES
PO Box 261
Midlothian VA 23113-0261
Set of 12 Southern Christmas cards - 4
scenes, $11.95 + S&H. Illus. flier - SASE.

CONFEDERATE PRODUCTS
301-863-7870
PO Box 974
California MD 20619
10oz. coffee mug with imprint of Confederate
seal & flag -$6 ea. + $3 S&H.

CONFEDERATE SUPPLY CO.
PO Box 2012
Murfreesboro TN 37133-2012
Confederate flag souvenirs - bandanas,
license plates. Conf. battleflag - $15 + $2.50
S&H. Catalog - $1.

THE CORPORAL'S COLOURS
106 Haig St
Celina OH 45822-2708
Confederate Commemorative Series
Battleflag T-shirts. Designs based on solid
research. Portion of proceeds earmarked for
flag preservation. $15. Free list.

COTTON & CO.
800-994-5366
4 Penny Ct • Hendersonville NC 28739
Tapestries picturing Lee, with Lt. Col.
Marshal, leaving McLean House at
Appomattox CH. Choose wall hanging
($39.95) or afghan throw ($45). Machine
washable 100% cotton.

COWLES HISTORY GROUP CALENDARS
800-358-6327
PO Box 921
North Adams MA 01247-0921
1998 Civil War & Military History calendars.
Perfect gifts for history buffs - $14.95.

CROSSROADS COUNTRY STORE
540-433-2084
Shenandoah Heritage Farmer's Market
Route 11 S • VA
Shenandoah Valley's premier Civil War store;
books, flags, music, souvenirs, crafts, gifts,
jewelry. Part of the Shenandoah Heritage
Farmer's Market. Open Mon-Sat 10am-6pm.

W.S. DAVIS DESIGNER
205-851-0839
PO Box 143 • Clay AL 35048-0143
License tags - proudly display the Great Seal
& the Flags of the Confederacy. $8 (ppd.).
Dealer discounts.

DEERFIELD VALLEY WOOD CARVING
6 King Philip Ave
South Deerfield MA 01373
Historic wood carvings. Patriotic Civil War
themes, North & South; eagles, flags, etc.
Quality custom work. Free catalog.

DIXIE DEPOT
706-265-7533
706-265-3952 Fax
http://www.ilinks.net/~dixiegeneral
Dixie_Depot@stc.net
John Black
PO Box 1448 • 72 Keith Evans Rd
Dawsonville GA 30534
Pro-Southern educational products:
video/audio tapes, new/old books, bumper
stickers, flags, wearables, lapel pins,
exclusive Great Seal items. More than 600
items! Catalog. (See ad page 235)

THE EARLY AMERICAN HISTORY SHOPPE
603-772-7973
225 Water St
Exeter NH 03833-2417
Books (antiquarian & in-print), ephemera,
prints, antique memorabilia & collectibles,
T-shirts, CD-Rom, flags, games, tapes, maps,
mugs, miniatures, genealogies & more.
Specialize in the Civil War. Free catalogs.

EXCELSIOR PRESS
516-475-7069
516-874-2489 Fax
Don Roberts
PO Box 926
Bellport NY 11713-0926
Civil War Cabinet Cards. Color art prints of 24
famous regiments include period battle maps
& regimental histories. Boxed set - $23.95 +
$3.50 S&H (30-day money-back guarantee).
Catalog/brochure - $1 (ref. w/ purchase).

FREDERICKSBURG MONOGRAMMING & EMBROIDERY
540-373-3937
540-373-4006 Fax
604 Caroline St
Fredericksburg VA 22401-5902
Custom embroidery of favorite Civil War
designs. Casual clothing, fast delivery;
quantity orders/dealers welcomed. All work
on-site, from artwork to finished garment.

GETTYSBURG CIVIL WAR & ANTIQUE CENTER
717-337-1085
705 Old Harrisburg Pk
N Gettysburg Plaza
Gettysburg PA 17325
Multi-dealer complex in heart of antique
country. Civil War memorabilia, military art,
antiques & fine collectibles. Open 7 days/wk.
Free parking.

GOLDBENDERS
540-373-4573
110 Hanover St
Fredericksburg VA 22401-5929
Handmade Civil War rings, silver or gold.
Available with either Confederate or Union
flag.

GOSPEL TRUTH/CIVIL WAR ROOM
412-238-7991
228 W Main St • Ligonier PA 15658-1130
Full-service Christian bookstore & Civil War
room. Kunstler calendars, patterns, pewter
figurines, books, videos, music, hats,
accessories, shirts, Woolrich wool, much
more.

GRANNIE'S ATTIC SHURT HAUS
800-827-5127 • 717-337-8704
922 Johns Ave • Gettysburg PA 17325
Souvenirs, printed & embroidered T-shirts,
including Gnatek color portrait shirts. Flags &
accessories. 2nd shop located at 13
Steinwehr Ave., Gettysburg.

THE GREAT T-SHIRT CO.
717-334-8611
65 Steinwehr Ave • Gettysburg PA 17325
Souvenir T-shirts, sweatshirts & hats;
exclusive Civil War designs.

GREENBRIAR PRESS
PO Box 703 • Marietta GA 30061-0703
Notepads & notecards with envelopes. 2 color
notepads with Union or Confederate flag with
"From the desk of..." -8-1/2"x 5-1/2". Write for
details & prices.

RICHARDS GREGORY
PO Box 2342 • Lancaster SC 29721-2342
S.C.A.R.Y. (Southern Citizens Advocating Relocation of Yankees). 100% cotton T-shirts (L & XL) - $12. + $3.50 S&H. South Carolina flag on front.

HALLOWED GROUND
717-337-0010
PO Box 3983 • Gettysburg PA 17325-0983
T-shirts - Army of Northern Virginia, Army of Potomac, Forrest, Lee's Lts, Iron Brigade, Cleburne, Stonewall Brigade, etc. 100% cotton. $14.50 ppd.

THE HAMILTON COLLECTION
4810 Executive Park Ct
PO Box 44051 • Jacksonville FL 32231-4051
Collectible plates, featuring Civil War Generals.

CARL A. HEDIN
3562 Antarctic Cir • Naples FL 34112-5041
3 Civil War bookmarks (U.S. commemorative stamps). Battles, generals. Laminated. 2-3/4"x8-1/2". $3.50 ea. or 3 for $9.95 ppd.

HERITAGE BOOKS
Dale Curry
313 Woodlawn Ave • Zanesville OH 43701
Civil War books & gifts. Free catalog.

HERITAGE EMBROIDERY
402-488-7913 • 402-488-8167 Fax
http://WWW.CivilWarMall.com/Image.htm
Heritage@navix.net
Tom & Dorothy Rivett
PO Box 22424
Lincoln NE 68542-2424
Exclusive Mort Kunstler art images embroidered on quality American-made garments. Personalization available for reenactors, round tables, museums & galleries. Visit our online catalog.

HISTORIC IMPRESSIONS
8394 Creek St
Jonesboro GA 30236
T-shirts & caps. Quality shirts, 8 selections - $15 ea. ppd. Caps, 3 selections - $19 ea.

HISTORIC SPORTSWEAR
615-754-4334
611 Oakwood Ter
Mount Juliet TN 37122-2107
Beautiful silk necktie! Show your pride with Southern Banners, crafted with Southern pride of the finest silk. Free brochure & dealer list.

HISTORICAL IMPRESSIONS
888-603-0100
970-256-0157 Fax
lskaf@iti2.net
PO Box 60323
Grand Junction CO 81506-0323
PC & Mac standard & multimedia Civil War screensavers for Union, South or mixed versions. Limited ed. art, posters, bookmarks, magnets, postcards. Dealer inquiries welcome. Catalog. (See ad page 233)

HUMMEL PRINTING
610-286-0399
PO Box 171
Geigertown PA 19523-0171
12 Civil War-theme Christmas cards (4 dif. styles) with envelopes - $8 + $1.50 S&H. Special occasion & ladies' notecards, Civil War-theme writing paper & envelopes. Catalog - $1.

INDY SCREEN PRINT
800-344-9899
1700 Georgetown Rd
Speedway IN 46224
"Heroes in Blue & Gray" - American Anthem Collector's Series #1, 100% cotton T-shirt. S-XL - $14.95 ea. + $5 S&H. XXL/XXXL - add $2.

IRISH BRIGADE GIFT SHOP
504 Baltimore St
Gettysburg PA 17325
T-shirts, sweatshirts, jackets, books, flags, recruiting posters, photos, pins, stationery, prints, figurines & more - all relating to the Irish Civil War service. Detailed item list -send business-size SASE.

J.J.B. LTD.
PO Box 507
Shamokin PA 17872-0507
Civil War print/calendar of the year 1861. Day-to-day events. 20"x17-1/2" - $29.95.

W. E. JACKSON & COMPANY
401-232-3570 Fax
PO Box 3842
North Providence RI 02911-0042
Civil War engravings, awards. Series of 3D embossed notecards from handcut dies. Lee, Jackson, Meade, artillery action, etc. 10 cards & envelopes per box.

JKG HANDCRAFTS
PO Box 667
Glade Spring VA 24340-0667

Handmade Confederate battle flag quilts - $150-$350. Others flag quilts available - send SASE for descriptions.

JM COMICS
PO Box 56982 • Jacksonville FL 32241-6982
First & only historically accurate Civil War comic series. "Southern Blood" takes you from Fort Sumter to Appomattox. 1 yr/12 issues - $22.50.

KATE GALLERY
652 Great Plain Ave
Needham MA 02192-3305
18th-20th century architecture, furniture & decorative art prints. Framed & unframed. Fine notecards. Illus. catalog -$2.

LANG GRAPHICS
414-646-2211
PO Box 99
Delafield WI 53018-0099
Mort Kunstler's new Civil War calendar & notecards. Beautifully done, fully illustrated. $12.95 + $5 S&H. Catalog - $2.

LEGACY TIE WORKS
888-851-1122 Orders
635 Bonnie Pl
Franklin TN 37064-2954
"The Five Flags of the Confederacy Collection" ties -100% Italian silk, jacquard weave. $34.50 ea. ppd.

MAGNOLIA T-SHIRT LTD.
PO Box 121
Malvern PA 19355-0121
Gettysburg T-shirt; 1st in Civil War Battles series, using victor's colors, names of commanding generals, dates & more. M/L - $17.95 ppd.; XL/XXL - $19.95 ppd.

TY MAWR CLASSICS, INC.
800-998-7051
PO Box 4221
Martinsville VA 24115-4221
Civil War coverlet by artists at Ty Mawr Classics. 100% cotton throw, triple weave, multi-color. 50"x70" - made in USA. $53.95.

DON MEREDITH'S CIVIL WAR ART
813-962-1225
PO Box 370020
Tampa FL 33697-0020
Ordinary photos turn into extraordinary CW-era portraits, with strict attention to detail. Prices vary from $75. Discounts for photos showing proper uniform, gear, pose, etc. Free color brochure.

MHR & SONS
7387 Bethany Ridge Rd
Guysville OH 45735
Personalized bookplates. CW theme: 50 for $14, 100 for $24. Add 10% S&H.

MOUNTAIN MIKE'S TRADING POST
717-741-0369
Michael Taylor
2083 Springwood Rd
PO Box 195
York PA 17403-0195
Olde style stogies. Marsh Wheeling, America's oldest cigar manufacturer. Box of 25 - $25 + $5 S&H.

NEWFIELD PUBLICATIONS
PO Box 16613
Columbus OH 43272-2388
Set of Civil War cards. Many scenes, incl. *Battle of Gettysburg: Pickett's Charge*, by Mort Kunstler.

OHIO SILVER
301-834-5389
PO Box 124
Brunswick MD 21716-0124
Silver bullet key chains & necklaces. Minie bullet replicas (.575 cal.) on key ring or sterling silver chain.

OLD GUARD, INC.
215-572-7913
7511 Sycamore Ave • Elkins Park PA 19027
Gettysburg generals on 100% cotton T-shirts. Pickett, Hood, Longstreet, Armistead, McLaws, etc. $12. Catalog -$3.

OLDE SOUTH, LTD.
T. R. Meetze
PO Box 11302 • Columbia SC 29211-1302
Classic check design - Confederate flag background. Send void check & deposit slip with $13.95 (incl. S&H) for 200. Script lettering & personal message available.

PEPPERELL STAMP WORKS
800-752-4656
Bradford PA 16701-0527
Collectible rubber stamps. Offering learning with stamping. Current sets include Victorian Flowers, Civil War, Sailing Ships, Endangered Species, Railroads. $4.95/stamp + $3.50 S&H.

PIXELCHROME PROFESSIONAL
4304 Standridge Dr • The Colony TX 75056
Gettysburg commemorative posters - 11"x17" - full color. Art prints of the Penn. & Va. monuments. Both posters -$15 + $3.95 S&H.

PORKCHOP & HAMBURGER HILL
PO Box 191
Honeoye Falls NY 14472-0191
Civil War license frames - $9.95-$29.95 +
$4.95 S&H for 1st frame, $1 ea. add'l. Frame
includes: regiment, 1 year, USA or CSA flag,
& blue/gray force decal. 120-pg. military
catalog - $2.95.

PYRAMID AMERICA
901-452-1323 • 800-737-1323
Quality USA, Texas or Confederate flags &
flag apparel. Jackets, shorts, T-shirts,
bandanas, backpacks, knives, framed/
unframed prints, more. Call for more info.

RAINBOW CARD CO.
800-473-5213 • 516-367-6790
516-367-3063 Fax
717 E Jericho Tpke Ste 315
Huntington Station NY 11746-7502
Official Currier & Ives "Civil War" card set.
Limited edition (5,000 sets), individually serial
numbered, 16 full-color cards - $14.95/set.
Catalog - $1.

RBM ENTERPRISES
502-893-5057
PO Box 6374, Dept A
Louisville KY 40206-0374
Updated version of our classic necktie.
Confederate battle flags with red stripes on
navy or gray background -$18.50.

THE REBEL CO.
770-947-1863
PO Box 15191
Atlanta GA 30333-0191
Ships more than 30 traditionally Southern
Rebel products. Delicious syrups, preserves,
dressings, honey, sauces, relish, jams,
chutney, peanuts, pecans & more. Free
catalog.

REGIMENTAL FLAG & BANNER
919-496-2888
919-496-7720 Fax
rebelflags@aol.com
1909 Seven Path Rd
Louisburg NC 27549
Flags - historical to modern. Civil War theme
shirts, caps. Free catalog.

RIENZI PRESS
802-888-3439
Brad & Sue Limage
RR 2 Box 630
Morrisville VT 05661-9802

"Vermont Soldiers in the Civil War" - calendar
printed annually with large prints of Vermont
brigades, CDUs, letter excerpts & battles on
corresponding dates. $10 + S&H.

RIVERDALE DECORATIVE PRODUCTS
PO Box 4959
1920 S Court St
Montgomery AL 36103-4959
Civil War battle scene pillows by Mort
Kunstler. From $15.

RUFFIN FLAG COMPANY
706-456-2111
706-456-2112 Fax
http://www.mindspring.com/~micromgt/ruffin.htm
241 Alexander St NW
Crawfordville GA 30631-2804
Auto tags, bumper stickers, books, T-shirts,
crew sweatshirts, polo shirts, regulation battle
flags, etc. Jeff Davis, Dixie's Pride, N.B.
Forrest, etc. Retail/wholesale. Catalog - $1.

SARAH ADAMS PRODUCTIONS
717-432-2752
717-432-8820 Fax
Civil War wrapping paper - photographic
scenes of Manassas, Shiloh, Gettysburg,
Antietam & others. 2 sizes. Coordinating
ribbon also available.

SCENIC EFFECTS, INC.
510-235-1955
510-235-9901 Fax
Wendy Schuldt
PO Box 332
Point Richmond CA 94807-0332
Ltd. ed. of historically accurate buildings, ea.
handmade. Some include figures & are
hand-painted; unpainted available.
Catalog/listing - send SASE.

SCHOOLHOUSE ANTIQUES
717-334-4564
Gettysburg PA 17325
Antique guns, relics, swords, uniforms,
souvenirs. Close to battlefield - 5 mi. on
Business Rt. 15 South.

PATRICK A. SCHROEDER PUBLICATIONS
804-376-1865
RR 2 Box 128
Brookneal VA 24528
Civil War books - myths about Lee's
surrender, Fighting Quakers, a Duryee
Zouave, record of North Carolina, diary of
Swedish officer. Archives research, prints,
notecards, postcards available. Free catalog.

SCREEN PRINT IMAGE
9302 S Mooreland Rd
Richmond VA 23229-8126
Lee, Jackson, Stuart, Mosby, Forrest, Flags of
the Confederacy, other multicolor designs on
first quality T-shirts, sweatshirts. From $12.

SCRIBNER'S
800-303-8337
907 4th St SE • Roanoke VA 24013
Confederate T-shirt with flag & inscription, "It's
a Southern Thing, You Wouldn't Understand."
Prices vary by size, $11.95-15.95 + $3 S&H.

SENECA RIDGE GALLERY
412-828-0240
426 Allegheny River Blvd
Oakmont PA 15139-1725
Civil War & 18th-century art, books, videos,
games, music, more!

SILVERWOOD INDUSTRIES, INC.
813-662-1075
11756 Browning Rd # 300
Lithia FL 33547
Personalized unit wall plaques with your
photo, name & unit. 6"x5", walnut grain, gold
lettering & stars. $19.95 (ppd.). 10% discount
on 6 or more.

SOUTHERN HERITAGE PRINTS
205-539-3358
George Mahoney, Jr.
PO Box 503 • Huntsville AL 35804-0503
Civil War flags, memo pads, envelopes,
bookmarks, paperweights, chronology
chart/map, prints. *Last Charge at Brandy
Station*, ltd. ed. print by C.E. Monroe, Jr. -
$135 inc. S&H. Portion of proceeds goes to
APCWS. (See ad page 234)

STARMASTER
http://www.iboutique.com/starmaster/index.html
2500 Laurelhill Ln
Fort Worth TX 76133-8112
Playing cards featuring Civil War generals,
battles, armaments & trivia. 3 decks - $18.
Free catalog.

STARS & BARS GIFT SHOP AT BEAUVOIR
601-388-9074 • 601-388-1313
2244 Beach Blvd
Biloxi MS 39531-5002

STRATFORD'S NOVELTY, LTD
803-797-8040
Kent Stratford
PO Box 1860
Goose Creek SC 29445-1860

Civil War-related novelties & gifts.
Confederate flag imprinted products &
merchandise. You name it—we have it in the
souvenir and/or novelty line. Free list.

STRICKLAND ENTERPRISES, INC.
800-454-7104 • 717-334-2472
531 Baltimore St
Gettysburg PA 17325-2606
Shirts, hats, clothing. Outfitters of popular Civil
War culture. Novelty slogans. Custom
embroidering. Free catalog.

TARA HALL, INC.
800-205-0069 Phone & Fax
http://www.ncweb.com/biz/blackhawk
tarahall@earthlink.net
Vic Olney
PO Box 2069
Beach Haven NJ 08008-0109
Meagher's Irish Brigade, Fighting 69th,
Corcoran's Irish Legion memorabilia, shirts,
jackets, hats, sweaters, steins, pins, flags,
books, miniatures, poster, belt buckles,
NINAs, etc. Free catalog. (See ad page 232)

THE TEE SHIRT GUY
609-547-9486 Phone & Fax
1225 Keswick Ave
Haddon Heights NJ 08035
Custom-printed T-shirts, sweatshirts, hats,
jackets, bumper stickers. Designs include
armies of the Potomac & Northern Virginia,
69th Irish Brigade, Jackson, Lee, Longstreet,
Chamberlain. M/L/XL - $13 ppd. XXL - $15.

TL SPECIALTIES
RR 4 Box 336B • Wynantskill NY 12198
Civil War clocks & plaques. Reproduced prints
from *Leslies* and *Harpers* magazines of
1860s. Walnut/burnt wood stain. Free
brochure - SASE.

THE TURNING POINT
800-454-7104
240 Steinwehr Ave
Gettysburg PA 17325-2814
Reasonably priced T-shirts of *The Killer
Angels*, Gettysburg, etc. Full color & one
color. Videos, cassettes, CDs, calendars, etc.

U.S. SURPLUS SALES
888-794-6296
http://www.dixienet.org/ads/commercial/
    us_surplus_sales/ usss.html
1184 W Highway 436
Forest City FL 32714
Confederate T-shirts, sure to inspire friends of
the South everywhere. Free flier.

THE VILLAGE SHOPPE
800-454-7104
Old Gettysburg Village
Gettysburg PA 17325
T-shirts reasonably priced of *The Killer Angels*, Gettysburg, etc. Full color & one color. Videos, cassettes, CDs, calendars, etc.

VILLAGE SURPLUS
PO Box 530931
Mountain Brook AL 35253-0931
Confederate flag magnets - $5 ppd.

VIRGINIA STEREOSCOPIC EMPORIUM,
PO Box 1718 • Stafford VA 22555-1718
Civil War Stereoscopic cards. Beautiful 3D image when viewed through stereo viewer. Set of 6 cards - $19.95 + S&H. Catalog - $2.

N. WASSERMAN & CO.
800-USPS-492
490 City Park Ave
Columbus OH 43215-5780
1995 CW postage stamps come to life on 5 beautifully decorated 11 oz. porcelain coffee mugs - "The Women," "The Battles," "The Union," "The Confederate," & "War Heroes." $9.95 ea. + $1.50 S&H.

X FACTOR PUBLISHING
511 Alondra Dr
Huntington Beach CA 92648-3711
Series 1-100 high gloss, color, 3.75" sq. collectors cards of "Great Battles of History" - $24.95.

ZANGRONIZ PHOTOGRAPHY
301-924-2539
4011 Muncaster Mill Rd Ste 101
Rockville MD 20853-1426
U.S. Civil War reenactment postcards. First of series. Images of actual events. 4 cards in each set. 4 sets @ $1.50/set + $2 S&H. (See ad page 230)

BLACKJACK TRADING COMPANY
Chuck Hanselmann
PO Box 707 • Blythewood SC 29016-0707
Buyer of family Confederate paper, stamps, letters, autographs, currency, slave documents, slave tags, & estates.

BOGG & LAURENCE PUBLISHING CO., INC.
800-345-5595 • 305-866-3600
305-866-8040 Fax
1007 Kane Concourse
Bay Harbor Islands FL 33154-2105
The new *Dietz Confederate States Catalog and Handbook*, 2nd printing. Most comprehensive treatment of Confederate stamps & postal history; reorganized & expanded for easier use. Hardcover, 300 pp. - $75.

CIVIL WAR STORE
504-522-3328
212 Chartres St • New Orleans LA 70130
Mail order catalog - weapons, currency, bonds, stamps, letters, diaries, CDVs, prints, slave broadsides & bills of sale, autographs, photos. Catalog - $4.

CONFEDERATE POSTMASTER
PO Box 1864
Middletown CT 06457-1864
Repro stamps, 60 different envelopes. Regimental envelopes on special order. 2 stamps, stationery available to match: U.S. Corps w/ division stationery; framed C.S. stamps. Finest quality now available. Catalog - $2 (credit on order); send SASE. (See ad page 234)

FLEETWOOD
800-443-3232
800-628-3123 Fax
http://www.unicover.com/fleetwoo.htm
James A. Williams
1 Unicover Ctr
Cheyenne WY 82007-2109
First-day Civil War covers (20). U.S. Postal Service's "Classic Collection" series. Stamps, cancellation marks, & custom envelopes. $51.45 - 1st edition.

BRIAN & MARIA GREEN, INC.
910-993-5100 • 910-993-1801 Fax
http://www.collectorsnet.com/bmg/index.shtml
bmgcivilwar@webtv.net
PO Box 1816J
Kernersville NC 27285-1816
Civil War autographs, letters, documents, diaries, CSA stamps, covers, currency, etc. Catalog - $5/yr for 4 issues.

CARL A. HEDIN
3562 Antarctic Cir
Naples FL 34112-5041
3 Civil War bookmarks (U.S. commemorative stamps). Battles, generals. Laminated. 2-3/4"x8-1/2". $3.50 ea. or 3 for $9.95 ppd.

HARDIE MALONEY
504-522-3328
212 Chartres St • New Orleans LA 70130
Civil War store. Confederate currency, bonds, stamps, covers, CDVs, letters, diaries, documents, autographs, pistols & swords.

MYSTIC STAMP CO.
Camden NY 13316
Giant grabbag of more than 200 U.S. stamps includes obsolete issues - $2. Adults only, limit 1 per address. Price lists.

HOWARD L. NORTON
PO Box 22821
Little Rock AR 72221-2821
Buy/sell/appraise. Autographs, Civil War items, Americana, historical documents, photographs, coins, currency, stamps, postal history. All transactions confidential. Catalog.

OSBORNE-KAUFMANN
800-WE DO BUY (933-6289)
Trish@webuystamps.com
522 Old State Rd
Lincoln DE 19960
Buy/sell collectible Confederate stamps & envelopes.

PINE BARREN STAMPS
609-978-0373
PO Box 779 • Barnegat NJ 08005-0779
Est. 1954. Genuine mint Confederate stamps, Civil War Centenary stamps, Union stamps. Deluxe price list - $5.

POSTAL COMMEMORATIVE SOCIETY
47 Richards Ln
Norwalk CT 06851-3422
Civil War Stamp Collection & art print of *Sheridan's Men* by Mort Kunstler. Limited edition.

STAMP OF APPROVAL
800-808-0567
10 Kendall Green Dr
PO Box 2157
Milford CT 06460-3068
Original Battle of Gettysburg decorated envelope, postmarked the first day the Gettysburg stamp was issued - 7/1/1963. Call for details.

TARGET AUCTIONS
816-761-8259 Orders
http://www.usbusiness.com/target/us.htm
PO Box 17841
Kansas City MO 64134
"Tattered Flags" - the most fun you'll ever
have fighting the Civil War! Original game for
the PC, $14.95 + $3 S&H. Other Civil War
games, stamps.

TWO COLONELS ENTERPRISES
330-745-2888 Phone & Fax
http://www.webchamps.com/twocolonels
twocolonels@webchamps.com
Daniel P Sens
1287E Sevilla Ave
Akron OH 44314-1457
Patriotic reproduction stamps & stationery.
Many designs. Union & Confederate. Genuine
stamps, covers, & paper. Prices on request.
Free wholesale & retail catalogs.

N. WASSERMAN & CO.
800-USPS-492
490 City Park Ave
Columbus OH 43215-5780
1995 CW postage stamps come to life on 5
beautifully decorated 11 oz. porcelain coffee
mugs - "The Women," "The Battles," "The
Union," "The Confederate," & "War Heroes."
$9.95 ea. + $1.50 S&H.

AMAZON DRY GOODS
319-322-6800 • 319-322-4138
319-322-4003 Fax
J. Burgess, Pres.
407 Brady St • Davenport IA 52801-1510
Victorian apparel & accessories. Corsets,
bonnets, hoop skirts, fans & snoods, hats,
paper dolls, flags, books, patterns, shoes &
boots. Sutlers' wholesale catalog. Retail
catalogs (pattern, shoe, & general) - all 3 for
$15.

ARROWHEAD FORGE
605-938-4814
RR 1 Box 25 • Wilmot SD 57279-9718
Tools, fire irons, candleholders, grills, eating
utensils, tomahawks, & much more. Catalog -
$3.

AVALON FORGE
410-242-8431
John White, Owner
409 Gun Rd
Baltimore MD 21227-3824
Replica goods for 18th-century "living history."
Items for military, farm & home. Catalog - $2.

THE BAG MAN
615-859-9658
Patrick Strickland
588 Dividing Ridge Rd
Goodlettsville TN 37072
Best possible reproductions. Knapsacks - $50
& up; S&K copper or tin canteens - $39 & $55.

BENCKENDORF PIPES
515-255-0838
PO Box 30062
Des Moines IA 50310-3330
Finest reproduction & collectible pipes &
smoking accoutrements. Free catalog.

BERMAN LEATHER
617-426-0870
617-357-8564 Fax
Robert S. Berman
25 Melcher St
Boston MA 02210-1516
Leather hides like CW era for belts, straps,
clothing, bags, even footwear. Full catalog of
hardware, tools, buckles & kits - $3 (ref.).

THE BLOCKADE RUNNER
615-389-6153
http://www.blockaderunner.com
brunner@tsixroads.com
103 Blackman Blvd
Wartrace TN 37183
18th-19th c. goods.

BONNET BRIGADE
Pat Wullenjohn
PO Box 28 • Fremont CA 94537-0028
Civil War-period clothing, equipment,
weapons, accoutrements, & camping
equipment. Catalog - $3.

BOOKS & COMPANY
PO Box 1046 • Dunkirk NY 14048-1046
Historical recipes & cooking info. from CW
era. Recipes from notable figures & soldiers.
History of some classic recipes. $7 ppd.

BORDER STATES LEATHERWORKS
501-361-2642
501-361-2851 Fax
1158 Apple Blossom Ln
Springdale AR 72762-9762
Civil War collectibles, original weapons &
equipment. Reproduction cavalry saddles &
equipment. Custom hand-forged bits.

WILLIAM H. BOYDEN
198 W Plumstead Ave
Lansdowne PA 19050-1307
Hand-rolled & tied cartridge tubes made from
Frankford Arsenal pattern; paper matches
close to original color. 20 tubes - $5 + $2 S&H.

KEN BROWN
614-498-8379
17261 Sligo Rd • Kimbolton OH 43749
Quality, handmade, reproduction cavalry tack,
equipment & accoutrements. Free brochure.

C & C SUTLERY
208-388-0973 • 208-384-9523 Fax
CLOX@RMCI.NET
HC 33 Box 3330 • Boise ID 83706
Full-service Civil War supplier. Uniforms, etc.

C & D JARNAGIN
601-287-4977 • 601-287-6033 Fax
http://www.jarnaginco.com
PO Box 1860
Corinth MS 38835-1860
Military & historical outfitters. Research,
develop, & manufacture high quality uniforms,
leather gear, footwear, & tinware for American
troops, 1750-1865. 18th-century & CW
catalogs - $3 each. (See ad page 239)

C & H SUTLERY
10619 W Atlantic Blvd # 145
Coral Springs FL 33071-5610
Authentic, all natural, no perfume, hypo-
allergenic, homemade lye soap. Great for
reenactors, naturalists. 3 bars - $5.98.

THE CARRIAGE HOUSE
918-367-6425
PO Box 8
Slick OK 74071-0008
Wooden wheels for cannon, old auto, carriage & decor.

CARRICO'S LEATHERWORKS
316-922-7222
316-922-3311 Fax
David Carrico
811 5000 Rd
Edna KS 67342
Authentic reproduction Civil War cavalry equipment & accoutrements. Saddles, bridles, holsters, belts, etc. Free price list.

CARTRIDGES UNLIMITED
314-664-4332
Mike Watson
4320 Hartford St # A
Saint Louis MO 63116-1917
Cartridges - blank, dummy & live; tubes; labels; trapezoids for rifle, carbine & pistol. Authentically rolled. Catalog - free w/ SASE.

CASTLE KEEP, LTD.
630-801-1696
630-801-1910 Fax
http://www.Reenact.com
ernie@Smartgate.com
Ernest Klapmeier
83 S LaSalle St • Aurora IL 60505
Reenactor supplies; clothing & equipment to put man or woman into the field. Owner has 20 yrs. reenacting experience & understands concept of authenticity.

CHILE-N-CRACKER'S
702-267-4072 Phone & Fax
Lindy Dubner, Jim Miller
PO Box 2865 • Carson City NV 89702
Exclusive line of quality replica calico buttons & clothing patterns. Unique reproduction toys & sundries of mid-19th century. Dealer inquiries welcome. Brochure - send SASE.
(See ad page 231)

CIVIL WAR EMPORIUM, INC.
408 Mill St • Occoquan VA 22125
From harmonicas to working cannons. Working repros. Decorator models. Consignments welcome. Buy/sell.

CONFEDERATE GRAY
615-320-1715 • 615-320-3272 Fax
Meeks Booker
PO Box 121984
Nashville TN 37212-1984

Hand-carved music boxes that play "Dixie" when opened; other tunes available. Named for great Southern leaders or battles. Refer to Source Book for 10% discount. Catalog - $2 (ref.).

COON CREEK
602-886-8273
601 S Desert Steppes
Tucson AZ 85716

CRANE MERCANTILE & MFG. CO.
314-231-4163
1212 Allen Ave
Saint Louis MO 63104-3914
Purveyor of finest cavalry saddle hardware. Iron frame coat strap buckles. McClellan saddle kit, tree & all hardware. Brochure - $2.

CRESCENT CITY SUTLER
812-983-4217
17810 Highway 57
Evansville IN 47711-9318
Reproduction & original Civil War uniforms & equipment. Catalog - $3.

DEAD HORSE FORGE
1220 Price Station Rd
Church Hill MD 21623-1315
All types of knives, Hawks & other ironware, powder horns & gourd canteens. Brochure - send SASE.

DIXIE FASHIONS
804-527-2028
George Dunn
11300 Cedar Hill Ct
Richmond VA 23233-1847
Confederate & Union exact reproduction uniforms, made to fit, museum-quality work, including all leather accessories, shell jackets, sashes, frocks, trousers, Kepis, shirts. Catalog - $3.

DIXIE GUN WORKS, INC.
800-238-6785 Orders only • 901-885-0700
901-885-0440 Fax
PO Box 130
Union City TN 38261-0130
The source for firearms, parts, shooting supplies, leather goods, uniforms, books, patterns & cannons. 600-pg catalog with more than 8,000 items - $5.

THE DIXIE SUTLER
PO Box 5162
Mobile AL 36605
Specializing in Civil War-period supplies & collectibles for the reenactor or collector.

DONNA'S STITCHES BACK IN TIME
800-808-7685
We stitch for sutlers. High-quality muslin shirts - $13.50 wholesale. Also sell retail. Price list on request.

THE EMPORIUM
417-683-2764
Ed & Maryln Peterka
RR 1 Box 363
Ava MO 65608
Supplies for the muzzleloader & living history participant. Patterns, hosiery, ladies' straw hats. Catalog - $3 (ref.).

FAIR OAKS SUTLER, INC.
540-972-7744 Noon-9 PM
540-972-3256 24-hr Fax
9905 Kershaw Ct
Spotsylvania PA 22553-3768
High-quality replica Civil War uniforms, accoutrements, equipment & muskets; Kepi & bummer caps our specialty. Satisfaction guaranteed. Catalog - 2 stamps.

FALL CREEK SUTTLERY
765-482-1861
765-482-1848 Fax
http://fcsutler.com
AJF5577@aol.com or fcsutler@aol.com
Andy Fulks
PO Box 92
Whitestown IN 46075-0092
Authentic reproduction Civil War & mid-19th-century uniforms, leather goods, weapons, shoes, tents, insignia, reference books & more. 32-pg catalog - $3. (See ad pg 242)

FAMILY HEIRLOOM WEAVERS
717-246-2431 Phone & Fax
familyheirloom@mindspring.com
775 Meadowview Dr
Red Lion PA 17356-8608
Reproduction fabrics - historically accurate ingrain carpets & jacquard coverlets. Uniforms, shirtings, etc. Brochure & swatches - $4.

FOUR SEASONS TENTMASTERS
517-436-6245
4221 Livesay Rd
Sand Creek MI 49729
Est. 1968. Hand-crafted tent dwellings for Civil War & other time periods. Full line of accoutrements from ground up - poles, stakes, ropes, transport bags. Guide & catalog - $2.

FRAZER BROTHERS' 17TH REGIMENT
214-696-1865
214-426-4230 Fax
5641 Yale Blvd Ste 125
Dallas TX 75206-5026
Uniforms & equipment, artillery hardware, & side arms. Civilian clothing (men only). Handmade leather goods. Large supply of tinware. Boots. American products.

FRENCH'S STORE & TRADING COMPANY
717-530-5037
PO Box 454
Shippensburg PA 17257-0454
Authentic Civil War reproductions of trade goods, 17th-19th century. Cavalry & leather goods & saddles. Catalog - $1.

FRONTIER SADDLE
941-322-2560
Gabriel Libraty
5530 Juel Gill Rd
Myakka City FL 34251
Replica saddles of the Old West & military; from mountain man to Civil War to classic Western saddles. Free catalog.

GDR ENTERPRISES
803-889-6360
PO Box 807 • Hollywood SC 29449-0807
Wooden ammunition crates; shipping containers, chests, officer's desk, & more. Handcrafted reproductions for military historians since 1982. Photo-illus. catalog - $2.

CARL GIORDANO, TINSMITH
330-336-7270
tinsnip@newreach.net
PO Box 74 • Wadsworth OH 44282-0074
18th- & 19th-century reproductions. Hand-wrought, custom work. Brochure - send SASE.

GREAT CIRCLE FORGE
PO Box 9040 • Lexington OH 44904-9040
Hand-forged ironwork: tent stakes, tripods, potted plant stands, coat racks, decorative hooks, trammel hooks, & more. Catalog - $1.50.

GREY OWL INDIAN CRAFT SALES CORP.
718-341-4000 • 718-527-6000 Fax
Wes Cochrane
13205 Merrick Blvd
PO Box 340468
Jamaica NY 11434-0468
Green River knives, powder flasks, military buttons, buckskin, leathers, dags, strikers, books, tapes, videos, recordings, etc. 200 custom kits/4000+ items. Catalog - $3.

THE HAVERSACK DEPOT
210-620-5192
1236 River Acres Dr
New Braunfels TX 78130
Museum-quality products at reasonable
prices, incl. US haversack, CS cartridge box
sling & CS leather belt with Ga. frame brass
buckle. Satisfaction guaranteed.

HEARTLAND HOUSE
540-672-9267 Phone & Fax
Nick Nichols
Old Blue Ridge Tpke • Rochelle VA 22738
Troiani calls us "the *Stradivarius* of historical
leather craftsmen." Full line of Victorian-era
saddlery, tack & equestriana (U.S., C.S.,
British military, & civilian). Illus. catalog - $4
(ref.).

HILLBILLY SPORTS, INC.
410-378-4533
PO Box 70 • Conowingo MD 21918-0070
Leather goods, period firearms, uniform items,
camp items & much more. Catalog - $3.

HIS LADY & THE SOLDIER SUTLERY
517-435-3518 Summer • 352-583-4627 Winter
851 Kaypat Dr
Hope MI 48628-9615
Period hair goods & accessories for the lady &
gentleman reenactor. Catalog - $2.

HISTORICAL SUPPLY CO.
802-464-0535
PO Box 12
Wilmington VT 05363-0012
Authentic brass camp candlesticks perfect for
19th-century impression. Set of 2 - $12.95 +
$3 S&H.

HOOP & HAVERSACK SUTLERY
517-643-5368
PO Box 415
Merrill IL 48637-0415

THE HOUSE OF TIMES PAST
864-834-0061
634 W Darby Rd
Greenville SC 29609
Period shop with authentic clothing, rifles,
muzzleloading supplies & accessories for
living historians & reenactors. Catalog - $2.

HUSS MACHINE WORKS
RR 3 Box 216
San Augustine TX 75972
Iron reproduction of camping, cooking & other
blacksmithed gear for the Civil War reenactor.
Catalog - $2.

J & J WAGONS
PO Box 363
Orlando FL 32802-0363
Authentic wagons for reenactments, living
history/special events. QM Wagons, Reg. AO
Wagons, & U.S. Grant-style wagons. All for
rent in the Southeast.

J.K. LEATHER
540-955-0301
Dave Allen
RR 2 Box 3026
Berryville VA 22611
Repairs & restoration of all leather goods,
esp. antique saddles & tack. Custom-made
leather products. Handmade saddles.

JAMES COUNTRY MERCANTILE
816-781-9473 • 816-781-1470 Fax
JAMESCNTRY@aol.com
Del Warren or Michael Gooch
111 N Main St • Liberty MO 64068-1639
For your military & civilian reenacting needs -
weapons, accoutrements, clothing, patterns.
Illus. catalog - $6 ppd.

GORDON WILSON JENKS & CO.
800-835-7933
Goex black powder - all granulations, incl.
authentic new cartridge powder.

K & P WEAVER
Ken & Paula Weaver
PO Box 1131 • Orange CT 06477-7131
Historically accurate repro men's clothing for
military or civilian impression. Custom-made
with handsewn buttonholes. Quality
accessories; cherry dominoes, checkers with
canvas board. Catalog with swatches - $1.

LEVI LEDBETTER, SUTLER
704-485-4746 Orders
Frank Lanning, Prop.
7032 Mineral Springs Rd
Oakboro NC 28129-8855
Uniforms are our specialty. Tentage,
knapsacks, accoutrements, canteens, tinware,
blankets, buttons, buckles & brogans. Price
list - send long SASE.

LOG CABIN SHOP
800-837-1082 • 330-948-1082
330-948-4307 Fax
http://www.logcabinshop.com
logcabin@logcabinshop.com
8010 Lafayette Rd
PO Box 275
Lodi OH 44254-0275

Full line of muzzleloading guns, kits, components, supplies, accessories, books, cookware, blankets, etc. 200-pp. catalog - $5.

HEIDI MARSH PATTERNS
3494 N Valley Rd
Greenville CA 95947-9604
Authentic patterns & how-to books of the CW era (1855-1865) for all ages. Ballgowns, blouses, undergarments, hoops, boning, etc. Playing cards & other sundries; books. Catalog - $3.

TY MAWR CLASSICS, INC.
800-998-7051
PO Box 4221 • Martinsville VA 24115-4221
Civil War coverlet by artists at Ty Mawr Classics. 100% cotton throw, triple weave, multi-color. 50"x70" - made in USA. $53.95.

MECHANICAL BAKING COMPANY
309-353-2414
http://www.mtco.com/~slogsdon/mbc.html
jlarkin@mtco.com
Jeanie Larkin
PO Box 513P • Pekin IL 61555-0513
Bakers of army-style hardtack. Great for reenactors & living histories. Edible teeth dullers. Price list & sample -$1.50. 4-6 weeks for delivery.

MENDELSON'S LEATHER
501 Short St • Grants Pass OR 97527-5443
Master leather craftsman makes moccasin boots, full spectrum of custom goods you can't find anywhere else.

MERCURY SUPPLY CO.
409-327-3707
101 Lee St
Livingston TX 77351
Civil War uniforms, reproduction equipment, tents, accoutrements, leather goods, firearms military & civilian. Catalog - $2.

MOUNTAIN MIKE'S TRADING POST
717-741-0369
Michael Taylor
2083 Springwood Rd
PO Box 195
York PA 17403-0195
Olde style stogies. Marsh Wheeling, America's oldest cigar manufacturer. Box of 25 - $25 + $5 S&H.

NASHVILLE DEPOT
615-833-2275
141 Neese Dr • 500 Zodiac Bldg
Nashville TN 37211

Authentically reproduced carpetbag in colorful period designs. Lined interior with pockets & enclosed rigid bottom. Leather handles & straps. 18"Lx18"Dx"8"W -$79.50 + $6.75 S&H.

NINETEENTH CENTURY MERCANTILE
508-398-1888 Phone & Fax
Barbara A. Amster
2 N Main St • South Yarmouth MA 02664
Hard-to-find goods recreated in ca.1800s fashion. Housewares, dry goods, toiletries, remedies, hardware, fashion accessories, etc. All presented in 19th-century mercantile atmosphere. Hundreds of items.

THE NORTHWOOD SUTLERY
715-381-0288
Phillip Cudd
415B Wisconsin St N • Hudson WI 54016
Sales of original & reproduction Civil War-era military & civilian equipment & supplies. Specialize in medical items. Free catalog.

OLD SUTLER JOHN
607-775-4434 Phone & Fax
Westview Station
PO Box 174 • Binghamton NY 13905-0174
Full line of quality reproduction Civil War guns, bayonets, swords, uniforms, leather items, & other collectibles. Catalog - $3. (See ad page 236)

PANTHER LODGES
304-462-7718 • 304-462-7755 Fax
PO Box 32-CB
Normantown WV 25267-0032
Famous for Civil War tentage & gear for reenactors. Our A-frames, wall tents, & sibleys set the standard for quality tentage. Catalog - $2 (ref. w/ 1st order).

R & K SUTLERY
217-732-8844
1015 1200th St
Lincoln IL 62656-5047
Complete line of military uniforms & civilian clothing for both men & women; coats, pants, skirts, blouses, dresses, etc. Top quality tents, Officer's Wall, A-frames, dog tents & sibley. Catalog - send SASE.

RARE BOOK REPUBLISHERS
703-573-5116 • 703-573-5897 Fax
http://www.raredocs.com
paconose@erols.com
PO Box 3202
Merrifield VA 22116-3202
The Cook's Own Book (1832), premier cooking reference used by families on both

sides of the Civil War. More than 2,500 recipes. Hardcover - $28.95 + $3.50 S&H.

REB'S TRADING POST
3608 Alta Vista Dr
Waco TX 76706-3741
Canvas goods, lodges, tents, flys, bags, etc. Blanket rifle sheaths, antler products, leather products, belt blanks, holsters, etc. Catalog - $1.

THE REBEL CO.
770-947-1863
PO Box 15191
Atlanta GA 30333-0191
Ships more than 30 traditionally Southern Rebel products. Delicious syrups, preserves, dressings, honey, sauces, relish, jams, chutney, peanuts, pecans & more. Free catalog.

RED WILLOW CANVAS COMPANY
319-628-4815
John Honn
131 W Main • PO Box 188
Oxford LA 52322-0188
Makers of quality authentic shelters for reenactors including common shelters, officers' tents & guards' tents. Catalog - $1.

THE REGIMENTAL QUARTERMASTER
215-672-6891
215-672-9020 Fax
PO Box 553
Hatboro PA 19040-0553
CW repro muskets, carbines, revolvers, swords, uniforms, shoes, boots, buckles, buttons, tents, tapes, tinware, equipment, accoutrements, accessories. Catalog - $2 ($1 ref.).

RICHMONVILLE TINWARE
800-501-1675 • 541-678-1675
PO Box 407 • 21328 Highway 99E
Aurora OR 97002-0407
Highest quality, historically correct tinware obtainable. Custom orders welcome. Catalog - $3.

S & S FIREARMS
718-497-1100
718-497-1105 Fax
7411 Myrtle Ave
Glendale NY 11385-7433
Military Americana. Antique gun parts, carbines, Enfield, buttons, insignia, books, equipment, appendages, headdress, etc. Reenactor supplies. Original & reproduction. Photo-illus. catalog - $3.

S & S SUTLER OF GETTYSBURG
717-677-7580
717-337-0438 Fax
Tim Sheads
PO Box 218
Bendersville PA 17306-0218
Reproduction Civil War uniforms, leather goods, insignia, tinware, & more. Free catalog.

SANTA FE SALES
Edward Benrock or Marion Webb
1 Ranch Club Rd Ste 3-402-O
Silver City NM 88061
Replicas. Relive American History through us for hard-to-find historical accessories, books, reprints, tinware, numerous historical items. Catalog - $3.

SARAH ADAMS PRODUCTIONS
717-432-2752
717-432-8820 Fax
Civil War wrapping paper - photographic scenes of Manassas, Shiloh, Gettysburg, Antietam & others. 2 sizes. Coordinating ribbon also available.

EDWARD SEMMELROTH
517-278-2214
415 Fleming Rd
Tekonsha MI 49092
Antique iron sales, restoration & reproductions, incl. 1820s-1870s style kitchen cookstove. Custom casting & restoration in any medal; no job too big or small.

TOM SMITH
716-337-0181
12101 New Oregon Rd
Springville NY 14141
US Cavalry Horse Equipment, 1859-1917. Custom work. Correct hardware & leather spec's (no harness leather). Color catalog - $7.

STALEY'S SUNDRIES
540-899-6464
540-373-2469 Fax
710 Caroline St
Fredericksburg VA 22401-5904
Largest collection of Civil War music anywhere. Military insignia, flags, hats, clothing, patterns, buttons, buckles, miniatures, books, magazines & gift items.

SUTLERS OF THE SIXTEEN
905-338-9427
Lorne & Nancy Weller
1359 White Oaks Blvd #906
Oakville Ontario L6H 2R8 CANADA

Period footwear, 19th-century historical clothing, pine boxes & more.

SUTLERS WAGON
Stamatelos Bros, Prop.
PO Box 390005
Cambridge MA 02139-0001
Fine quality American military items, 1775-1900. Civil War uniforms, headgear, accoutrements, buckles, tack, photos, swords, documents. Buy/sell.

SWAMP FOX SUTLERY
816-364-2150
Craig Pierce, Prop.
3906 Seneca
Saint Joseph MO 64507
Civil War reenactor supply, original & reproduction.

T5 ENTERPRISES
208-788-3348
Larry & Wende Thornton
4 Freedom Loop
Bellevue ID 83313
Buy/sell/trade U.S. cavalry & horse-related equipment (1833-1943).

TARA HALL, INC.
800-205-0069 Phone & Fax
http://www.ncweb.com/biz/blackhawk
tarahall@earthlink.net
Vic Olney
PO Box 2069
Beach Haven NJ 08008-0109
Meagher's Irish Brigade, Fighting 69th, Corcoran's Irish Legion memorabilia, shirts, jackets, hats, sweaters, steins, pins, flags, books, miniatures, poster, belt buckles, NINAs, etc. Free catalog. (See ad page 232)

TENTSMITHS
603-447-2344
603-447-1777 Fax
PO Box 1748
Conway NH 03818-1748
Authentic period tentage of unsurpassed quality. Each tent made to your specifications by people who care.

TIMELESS TEXTILES
717-930-0201
Mary Harkless
321 N Union St
Middletown PA 17057-1442
Historically correct fabric, retail & wholesale, for reenactors of all eras. Carry both civilian & military, ladies' & men's fabrics.

TIPPECANOE FRONTIER TRADING CO.
937-667-1816
114 E Main St
Tipp City OH 45371-1962
Thousands of items serving reenactors, hunters, history buffs. Gunsmith for restorations, information, minor repairs (1700s-1900s). Long-range shooting supplies. Catalog - $4.

JAMES TOWNSEND & SON, INC.
219-594-5852
http://www.jastown.com/
PO Box 415
Pierceton IN 46562-0415
Large selections of reenactment supplies, 1740-1840. Clothing, blankets, eyeglasses, cookware, trade silver, shoes, hats, lanterns, tentage, knives, kegs, etc. Catalog - $2.

TURKEY FOOT TRADING CO.
419-832-1109
Allen & Colleen Schroll
PO Box 58
Grand Rapids OH 43522-0058
18th- & 19th-century merchandise: beads, clothing, iron work, tinware, more. Catalog.

TWIN OAKS SADDLERY
407-790-2461
11580 46th Pl N
Royal Palm Beach FL 33411
American-made Civil War goods/ reproductions. Cartridge box plates, carbine box, cap box, sword belts, sashes, holsters, saddlebags, saddles & parts, belts & buckles, tinware. Catalog - $2.

UPPER MISSISSIPPI VALLEY MERCANTILE CO
319-322-0896
319-383-5549 Fax
1607 Washington St
Davenport IA 52804-3613
Top quality goods & supplies for Civil War reenactors; uniforms, tinware, tents, leather goods, muskets, books, weapons, patterns, more. 100-pp., illus. catalog - $3.

V.C.R.
675-794-4652 • 888-794-4652
RR 5 Box 77
Crawfordsville IN 47933
Quality handmade chairs for all occasions. Free brochure.

VILLAGE TINSMITHING WORKS
330-325-9101
Bill & Judy Hoover
PO Box 189
Randolph OH 44265-0189
Quality reproduction & period items. Lead-free solder on potable items. More than 80 items. Custom orders. Catalog - free w/ long SASE.

THE WINCHESTER SUTLER, INC.
540-888-3595
540-888-4632 Fax
270 Shadow Brook Ln
Winchester VA 22603-2071
Reproduction Civil War firearms, uniforms, camp gear, accessories, shoes, boots, hats, etc. Catalog - $4.

WORLD EXONUMIA
815-226-0771
Rich Hartzog
PO Box 4143BWX
Rockford IL 61110-0643
Civil War & sutler tokens, medals, slave tags, Civil War dogtags, corps badges, sutler paper, GAR reunion badges, etc. Buy/sell; mail bid sales. Publisher of *Sutler Paper Money*. (See ad pg 231)

20TH MAINE, INC.
207-865-4340 • 207-865-9575 Fax
Patricia Hodgdon
49 West St • Freeport ME 04032-1127
Specialized bookstore devoted to Civil War
with new & old books, art, music, videos,
antiques & much more.

AMERICAN HERITAGE MARKETING GROUP, INC.
5904 Welborn Dr
Bethesda MD 20816
Longstreet! Civil War video on the war's most
controversial general; in-studio film version of
live stage play - $29.95 + $4.95 S&H.

THE AMERICAN LISTENERS' THEATRE
888-283-4695
PO Box 50056
Austin TX 78763-0056
Listen to the Civil War tales of Ambrose
Bierce. 2 cassette set, 3 hrs. $22.50 (ppd.).

AMERICANA SOUVENIRS & GIFTS
http://www.americanagifts.com
302 York St
Gettysburg PA 17325
Most complete line of Civil War souvenirs &
memorabilia for both USA & CSA. Cannons,
bullets, patches, toys, books, flags, videos,
documents, insignias, & much more. (See ad
page 242)

BATTLEFIELD VIDEO PRODUCTIONS
6374 Larch Ln
Macungie PA 18062-9380
Civil War guns video. 47-min. video of the
guns of the Civil War, their makers, & those
who used them. Live fire demonstration.
$29.95 ppd.

BELLE & BLADE
201-328-8488
201-442-0669 Fax
124 Penn Ave
Dover NJ 07801-5335
Send for catalog of war books, videos, toys,
swords, knives, & gifts. Catalog - $3; free w/
order.

BELLE GROVE PUBLISHING CO.
800-861-1861
PO Box 483
Kearny NJ 07032-0483
Titles include *History of the 57th
Pennsylvania, Four Years Campaigning in the
Army of the Potomac.* Videos of "lost" films
from silent movie era - *CW Cinema* Vols I-III.
Call/write for more info.

BETWEEN THE BULLET & THE BATTLEFIELD
814-695-9893
PO Box 511 • Hollidaysburg PA 16648-0511
Historically correct video presents the "Truth &
Myths of CW Medicine." Visit actual aid
stations & field hospitals in Gettysburg &
Antietam. $21.95 + $3 S&H.

BLACKSTONE AUDIO BOOKS
800-729-2665
PO Box 969
Ashland OR 97520-0033
More than 600 titles, rentals by mail,
unabridged recordings. Free catalog.

THE BLUE & GRAY SHOP
800-454-7104
531 Baltimore St
Gettysburg PA 17325-2606
Reasonably priced T-shirts of *The Killer
Angels*, Gettysburg, etc. Videos, cassettes,
CDs, calendars, etc.

BOOKCASSETTE SALES
800-222-3225
1704 Eaton St • PO Box 887
Grand Haven MI 49417-0887
Fragments of the Ark, by Louise Meriwether -
audiocassette, unabridged. Peter Mango
delivered the stolen gunboat *Swanee* to the
U.S. navy & brought with him a group of
runaways united by love & painful histories.
ISBN 1-56100-556-8, $23.95.

BOOKS ON TAPE
Ed Mauss, Dir. of Publication
123 Briarwood Ln • Aliso Viejo CA 92656
Unabridged audiobooks for rental or
purchase. Large selection of Civil War
accounts & biographies, acclaimed authors.
Catalog - $5 (ref.).

BRIGADE BUGLER
609-589-3901
George Rabbai
PO Box 165 • Pitman NJ 08071-0165
Civil War infantry bugle calls, book & cassette,
$19.95 ppd. for set. *Teach Yourself How to
Play the Bugle* - for all levels of buglers,
includes exercises, tonguing & lip flexibility. $8
ppd.

BUFFALO ROBE TRADING POST
520-457-2322
George Henry
9 N 5th St • PO Box 741
Tombstone AZ 85638-0741

Civil War, local history, American Indian, western lawmen & outlaws. Gift shop, artifacts, video & audio tapes. Historian in attendance.

C & D COMMERCIAL PRODUCTIONS, INC.
800-600-6578
100 Dixie Ln • Wilmington DE 19804-2312
A Call to Arms: Your Guide to Becoming a CW Reenactor. 52-min. video - excellent recruiting tool. $19.95.

CAROLINA VIDEO PRODUCTIONS, INC.
PO Box 751
Isle of Palms SC 29451-0751
Video on Fort Sumter. 1-hour documentary of authentic photos & full-color action. Historian narrated. Unusual facts & opinions. $24.95.

CATHEDRAL AUDIO BOOKS, INC.
800-479-0099
Steven Kalb
341 Beirut Ave
Pacific Palisades CA 90272-4625
The Killer Angels, classic novel by Michael Shaara, on 9 audiocassettes with selected music soundtracks from the film *Gettysburg*. Must-have for *Gettysburg* buffs - $49.95.

CLASSIC IMAGES
800-888-5359
Jack Foley
PO Box 2399 • Columbia MD 21045-1399
Video series; live-action footage with archival photos, animated maps, narration, & music. Includes Shiloh, Manassas, Vicksburg. Free catalog.

COLLECTING THE CIVIL WAR
800-440-8478
PO Box 18844 • Denver CO 80218-0844
2 videotapes - "Collecting the Union Soldier" vol. 1, & "... Confederate Soldier" vol. 2. Expert descriptions, close-up color photography. 100s of items. $19.95 ea.; set $29.95. Add $4 S&H.

COMMAND POST
201-627-6272
201-627-6627 Fax
PO Box 1015 • Denville NJ 07834-0615
Books & videos on the Civil War, including the role of women. Free catalog.

COMMUTERS LIBRARY
800-643-0295 • 703-827-8937 Fax
commlib@aol.com
Joseph Langenfeld
PO Box 3168 • Falls Church VA 22043-0168

Superb narrations of Lincoln's writings. *Lincoln's Letters* ("audio best of the year" - Publishers Weekly). *Lincoln's Prose* (includes Gettysburg Address). Beautiful editions - 2 cass. $16.95 ea. Free catalog.

THE CONFLICT BOOKSHOP
800-847-0911
EPETE1731@aol.com
213 Steinwehr Ave • Gettysburg PA 17325
Latest in Civil War titles, as well as fine collection of used & rare books, audio & video tapes & other memorabilia. Free flyer.

CRITTENDEN SCHMITT ARCHIVES
http://www.erols.com/tyrannus/archives/
     csavideo.html
PO Box 4253 • Courthouse Station
Rockville MD 20850
Technical & historical books & videotapes relating to weapons & ammunition of all types & eras.

CW ASSOCIATES
900-443-9854 x0019 ($1.29/min.)
PO Box 8545
New Haven CT 06531-0545
"The War Between the States Day by Day." Call now to hear what significant events occurred today in the CW (1861-1865). Average call - 3 min., $3.87. Must be 18 yrs. old or have parental permission.

DIXIE DEPOT
706-265-7533 • 706-265-3952 Fax
http://www.ilinks.net/~dixiegeneral
Dixie_Depot@stc.net
John Black
PO Box 1448 • 72 Keith Evans Rd
Dawsonville GA 30534
Pro-Southern educational products: video/audio tapes, new/old books, bumper stickers, flags, wearables, lapel pins, exclusive Great Seal items. More than 600 items! Catalog. (See ad page 235)

DONALD DREW
PO Box 422 • Stillwater MN 55082-0422
Basic training video for the beginner. Directly from Harde's. Professional production. All facings, rifle movements, load/fire procedure, etc. VHS - $27 ppd.

THE FLAG GUYS
914-562-0088 x305
http://www.flagguys.com
Flagguys@aol.com
283 Windsor Hwy Dept 305
New Windsor NY 12553-6909

Flags of all types & sizes. Books, Kepis, accessories, swords, cassettes, CDs, novelties. Free catalog.

FUSION VIDEO
800-959-0061
100 Fusion Way • Country Club Hills IL 60478
Videos on the Civil War & American history. Contact for complete listing.

GARRETT PRODUCTIONS
800-870-9626
Thomas A. Garrett
185A Newberry Commons
Etters PA 17319-9362
Insight to the Battle of Gettysburg, 28-pg book. Great for first-timers or refresher - $10.97 ppd. *The Monuments of Gettysburg* 40-min. videotape - $32 ppd.

GETTYSBURG NMP BOOKSTORE
800-JULY 3 1863
717-334-1891 Fax
Robert Housch
Visitor Center - Electric Map
95 Taneytown Rd • Gettysburg PA 17325
Complete Civil War bookstore specializing in books, tapes, CDs & videos. Free catalog.

GREY OWL INDIAN CRAFT SALES CORP.
718-341-4000
718-527-6000 Fax
Wes Cochrane
13205 Merrick Blvd
PO Box 340468
Jamaica NY 11434-0468
Green River knives, powder flasks, military buttons, buckskin, leathers, dags, strikers, books, tapes, videos, recordings, etc. 200 custom kits/4000+ items. Catalog -$3.

GREYSTONE'S HISTORY EMPORIUM & GALLERY
717-338-0631
717-338-0851 Fax
http://www.GreystoneOnline.com
461 Baltimore St
Gettysburg PA 17325-2623
Producers of *CW Journal* have created a store, gallery & museum. Military miniatures, books, videos, collectibles, art, exhibits, story theatre. Unique merchandise.

INDEPENDENT PUBLISHERS
3535 E Coast Hwy
Corona del Mar CA 92625-2404
War & Warriors series. Books, videos, audiotapes. Men, machines, strategies, battles, & politics of war. Catalog -send SASE.

INSTITUTE FOR PUBLIC AFFAIRS
217-786-6799
217-786-6542 Fax
University of Illinois at Springfield
Springfield IL 62794
The Lincolns of Springfield, Illinois, a video documentary distributed nationally by PBS - $24.95.

T.R. KOBA & COMPANY
419-588-2938
11918 Berlin Rd
Berlin Heights OH 44814-9667
Rebel Fire/Yankee Ice, The Johnson's Island Story, video documentary featuring the music of Bobby Horton. VHS. $28.45. The story of the Confederate POW camp.

THE LEXINGTON CIVIL WAR COMPANY
540-464-1100
Lexington, Virginia: Auto Tape Guide to Civil War Sites. Drive at your own pace. Featuring music by Bobby Horton.

MAJOR VISTA MEDIA, INC.
800-554-3108
111 S Monroe St
Monroe MI 48161
Custer's Monroe - narrated 30-min. video tour around hometown of George & Libbie Custer, featuring homes, sites & photos. $29.95 + $4 S&H.

MARILL PRODUCTIONS
PO Box 460820
San Francisco CA 94146-0820
Video documentaries on Colt revolvers (1836-1869) & Bowie knives (1820-1870), in-depth, exquisite. $29.95 ea. or both for $45.

MARY LOU PRODUCTIONS
800-774-8511
PO Box 17233
Minneapolis MN 55417-0233
"Gift of Heritage" - how-to video showing you the process of creating your own family documentary, including tips on researching, organizing, & combining info. - $32.95. Call for more info.

MEDIA MAGIC
517-393-3100
517-393-3338 Fax
3120 Pine Tree Rd
Lansing MI 48911
3 new feature-length Civil War video programs - *School of the Soldier, The Battle of the Wilderness,* & *The Battle of Fort Stedman.*

MODEL EXPO, INC.
Mount Pocono Industrl Park
PO Box 1000
Tobyhanna PA 18466-1000
Video catalog of historic ship model kits.
Video & color catalog - $5.

JOHN S. MOSBY HERITAGE AREA
540-687-6681
PO Box 1178
Middleburg VA 20118-1178
Maps of Mosby Heritage Area - $20.
Audiotape driving tour "Prelude to Gettysburg"
- $17. Free "Drive Through History" brochure.

MOVIETECH
2590 NE 201st St
Miami FL 33180-1910
Relive the Battle of Olustee & the 20th annual
reenactment with video narrated by Luke
Halpin. Reenactor interviews. Captures the
solemnity & excitement of the 3-day event.
$19.95 + $4 S&H.

MUSEUM OF HISTORIC NATCHITOCHES
318-357-0070
840 Washington St
Natchitoches LA 71457-4728
*The Forgotten March: the Red River
Campaign.* Video documenting the largest
campaign west of the Mississippi. $22.50 ppd.
(Proceeds benefit museum)

PRESERVATION ENTERPRISES
412-285-6995
228 E Pearl St
Butler PA 16001-4472
A Visit from a Civil War Soldier - video.
Extraordinary one-man show based on Pvt.
Hinchberger's diary & recollections. Color,
VHS, 50 min. $22.95 ppd.

RECORDED BOOKS, INC.
800-638-1304
http://www.RecordedBooks.com
RecordedBooks@RecordedBooks.com
270 Skipjack Rd
Prince Frederick MD 20678-3410
More than 1,800 titles narrated by experts.
Unabridged, studio recordings. Free brochure.
Call for info. on special discounts.

S. B. PRODUCTIONS
509-682-2616
PO Box 548
Chelan WA 98816-0548
Full hour of the soldier's story from camp life
to first battle to letters home. Written &
narrated by Scott Brundage. Tape - $14.95.

SANGAMON STATE UNIVERSITY
217-786-6799 • 217-786-6542 Fax
Springfield IL 62794
The Lincolns of Springfield, Illinois, a video
documentary distributed by PBS. Not the
myth, but the midwestern, middle-class, &
victorian. $24.95.

THE SCHOLAR'S BOOKSHELF
609-395-6933 • 609-395-0755 Fax
http://www.scholarsbookshelf.com
books@scholarsbookshelf.com
110 Melrich Rd
Cranbury NJ 08512-3511
A major book catalog company that produces
three 88-pp. Military History catalogs each
year. Catalogs feature a substantial variety of
Civil War books & videos. Free catalog.

THE SOUTHERN ARMY ALBUM!
John Mills Bigham
4833 Arcadia Rd
Columbia SC 29206-1307
Christopher Memminger's homeplace. 4
families share Confederate oral histories &
images. Military headstones 1776+ recorded
in 3 antebellum churchyards. Lasting regional
1992 video production. $21.95.

**TEXAS A&M UNIVERSITY PRESS
CONSORTIUM**
800-826-8911 • 409-847-8752 Fax
FDL@tampress.tamu.edu
Gayla Christiansen
PO Box C
College Station TX 77843-0001
*Mighty Stonewall, Make Me a Map of the
Valley, Fallen Guidon, Confederate General of
the Southwest.* From $12.95 to $35. Also
Voices of Valor (audio) $10.95 cassette,
$17.95 CD. Free catalog.

THOMAS PUBLICATIONS
800-840-6782 • 717-334-1921
717-334-8440 Fax
Dean S. Thomas
353 Buford Ave
Gettysburg PA 17325-1138
Publishers of Civil War books. Many titles.
Ghosts of Gettysburg series videos. Free
catalog.

TIME-LIFE VIDEO
800-843-1199
PO Box 85571
Richmond VA 23285-5571
Civil War Journal - video cassettes of the
critically acclaimed series, from $9.99 to
$19.99.

TN RELEASING CO.
800-289-6682
400 S Farrell Dr Ste B205
Palm Springs CA 92262-7960
Out of the Wilderness and *Black Easter* -
video documentaries of Abraham Lincoln's life
& assassination. 75 min. & 50 min. - $29.95
ea.; both for $54.95.

THE TURNING POINT
800-454-7104
240 Steinwehr Ave
Gettysburg PA 17325-2814
Reasonably priced T-shirts of *The Killer
Angels*, Gettysburg, etc. Full color & one
color. Videos, cassettes, CDs, calendars, etc.

VIDEO PORTRAITS
800-378-8764
PO Box 108
Vinton IA 52349-0108
New Market video. Largest assembly of
troops, cavalry & artillery since the original
1864 battle. 90-min., professional produced -
$19.95 ppd.

THE VILLAGE SHOPPE
800-454-7104
Old Gettysburg Village
Gettysburg PA 17325
T-shirts reasonably priced of *The Killer
Angels*, Gettysburg, etc. Full color & one
color. Videos, cassettes, CDs, calendars, etc.

VOYAGER VIDEO, INC.
800-786-9248
PO Box 1122
Darien CT 06820-1122
Video catalog designed specifically for
educational enrichment. History, world culture,
African Americans, etc. Catalog.

STEVE WARREN
1612 S 126th Ave E
Tulsa OK 74128
Last Raid at Cabin Creek - 90-min.
documentary of South's greatest victory in the
Indian nations. $15.99 ppd.

ALABAMA BUREAU OF TOURISM & TRAVEL
800-ALABAMA • 334-242-4554 Fax
http://www.state.al.us
alabamat@mont.mindspring.com
Russell A. Nolen
401 Adams Ave • PO Box 4927
Montgomery AL 36103-4927
Birthplace of the most dramatic chapter in American history. Site of historic battles, parks, politics, & much more. Free travel guide.

AMERICANA TOURS
800-220-7609
http://www.telepath.com/amtour
amtour@telepath.com
Les Rodman
Visit historical sites of the CW: Gettysburg, Fredericksburg, Manassas, Virginia Capitol, White House of the Confederacy, & others. Notebook containing historical narrative provided.

BATTLEFIELD TOURS
800-972-5858
4638 N Ravenswood Ave Ste 204
Chicago IL 60640
In-depth, slow-paced Civil War walking tours.

BELLE GROVE PLANTATION
540-869-2028
PO Box 727 • 336 Belle Grove Rd
Middletown VA 22645-0727

BILLIE CREEK VILLAGE REENACTMENT
765-569-3430
http://www.coveredbridges.com/bilcreek.htm
RR 2 Box 27
Rockville IN 47872-9503
Largest annual reenactment in IN. 30 historic buildings to tour. Battles & military events; extensive ladies', children's & medical events, ball. Annual event - June.

BLUE & GRAY EDUCATION SOCIETY
804-797-4535
416 Beck St • Norfolk VA 23503
Non-profit organization which interprets battlefields for public visitation. North Anna is most recent achievement. More than 600 members via tax-exempt donation. Seminars, tours, symposiums & debates.

CAMP MOORE CONFEDERATE MUSEUM & CEMETERY
504-229-2438
70640 Camp Moore Rd • PO Box 25
Tangipahoa LA 70465

440 of Camp Moores soldiers buried in cemetery. Museum contains artifacts from the camp, which was destroyed by Union forces in 1864. Walking tours offered.

CAMPAIGN TOURS
800-343-6768
508-750-9692 Fax
Brian Crowley
435 Newbury St
Danvers MA 01923-1065
Many fascinating Civil War tours: Shenandoah Valley, Atlanta & Vicksburg campaigns. Call/write for info. Free catalog.

CAVALIER HISTORY
Winston B. Wine, Jr.
921 Selma Blvd
Staunton VA 24401-2083
Freelance cavalry historian endorsed by J.E.B. Stuart IV; advisor, Brandy Station Foundation; speaking engagements, research, tours, other services of Eastern Theatre Cavalry. (See ad page 241)

CENTER STATE 29
800-732-5821
"Virginia's Civil War Connection." Follow Highway 29 to sample sites rich in Civil War heritage & history. Call for free brochure.

CHARLES COUNTY
800-766-3386
PO Box B
La Plata MD 20646
Historic inn with visitors like John Wilkes Booth. Dr. S.A. Mudd's house. Rolling meadows, forests, coastline, & Maryland seafood. Bird watching guide available.

THE CHARLESTON MUSEUM
803-722-2996
360 Meeting St
Charleston SC 29403-6297
Harbor & land tours, reenactments. Nationally recognized speakers. Period music. Call or write for upcoming events, exhibits, tours, & more. Free brochure.

CHRISTMAS AT THE FORT
334-861-6992
Fort Gaines Historic Site
PO Box 97
Dauphin Island AL 36528-0097
Annual living history weekend; 1998 dates - December 5-6. Experience 1861 Christmas at the fort with Confederate soldiers—authenticity stressed. Candlelight tour, feast, dance, drills, camp life, etc.

CIVIL WAR EDUCATION ASSOCIATION
800-298-1861 • 540-667-2339 Fax
21 N Loudoun St
Winchester VA 22601-4715
Non-profit organization presenting the finest
seminars, symposia, & tours. Develops
educational materials, publishes/distributes
Civil War books. Contact for extensive
calendar of events.

**CIVIL WAR LIVING HISTORY
REENACTMENT**
910-371-6613
Fort Anderson NC
Reenactment on grounds of Brunswick Town
State Historic Sites. Tours of earthwork fort
remains, small arms & military demonstra-
tions, civilian interpretations. Lectures/talks.
Annual event - February. No admission fee.

CIVIL WAR SOCIETY
800-247-6253 • 540-955-1176
540-955-2321 Fax
cwmag@mnsinc.com
PO Box 770
Berryville VA 22611-0770
Membership includes award-winning *Civil War
Magazine*, calendar, newsletters, membership
cert., preservation & education activities,
ancestors research guide, tours, seminars,
discounts & camaraderie. Call for brochure.

CIVIL WAR TOURS, INC.
770-908-8410 • 888-678-8942
Deaj95@aol.com
Tour battlefields of the Atlanta Campaign with
an historian. Stand in trenches, see
Soldier-Life Demonstrations of either side.
Step-on-guide service/group rates available.
Mon-Sat., 1/2 or full day.

CIVIL WAR TOURS OF TENNESSEE, INC.
615-356-7537
Stuart M. Moore, President
PO Box 1298
Fairview TN 37062-1298
Daily tours of Confederate invasion of
Tennessee in 1864, culminating in battle of
Franklin & Nashville. Free brochure.

CIVIL WAR WEEK
803-722-2996
The Charleston Museum
360 Meeting St
Charleston SC 29403-6235
Harbor & land tours in historic Charleston, SC,
nationally recognized speakers, reenactors,
period music. Annual event - April. Brochure.

CLASSIC QUESTS
800-458-5394
2 Federal St
Saint Albans VT 05478-2035
Escorted tours, many with multi-night stays in
fine hotels/inns. Quality historic & scenic
tours. Escorted rail tours. Free catalog.

CONFEDERATE HISTORICAL INSTITUTE
501-225-3996
PO Box 7388
Little Rock AR 72217-7388
Est. 1979 to promote study of Confederate
history. Speakers & tours, annual institute -
April. Newsletter. Membership - $20/yr.

THE CORINTH CIVIL WAR CENTER
601-287-9501
http://www.corinth.org/
civilwar@tsixroads.com
PO Box 45
Corinth MS 38835-0045
Offers 12-minute video of Corinth's role in the
Civil War. Walking/driving tour maps
available. Small gift shop.

DAVIS CREEK CAMP
406-342-5423 • 406-665-3538
Sarpy Route
Hysham MT 59038
Ride the actual trails of Custer. Authentic
equipment. Tours ride through Custer's Last
Stand reenactment, Reno Creek & Little Big
Horn (all on horseback).

THE DELTA QUEEN STEAMBOAT CO.
800-347-4318
30 Robin St Wharf
New Orleans LA 70130-1890
Civil War Vacations - special cruises aboard
an authentic paddlewheeler explore the war's
strategies & turning points on the mighty
rivers with special guest historians, authors, &
CW experts. Call for more info.

DIXIANA
800-272-3589
Private Southern Pride Airline club for
weekend getaways. Affordable air
transportation for members only. Call for more
info. on membership requirements &
application.

EDGERTON'S TRAVEL SERVICE, INC.
800-643-4604
Civil War cruise - relax & enjoy the beautiful
Tennessee & Cumberland rivers on the
Mississippi Queen. Visit Shiloh, Florence,

Paducah, Decatur, Dover, & famous battlefields. Noted lecturers. Free brochure.

FARNSWORTH HOUSE INN
717-334-8838
401 Baltimore St • Gettysburg PA 17325-2623
"Showplace of the Civil War." Daily house tours, fine dining. Bed & breakfast - Victorian elegance, private baths. Tavern, bookstore.

GETTYSBURG ADDRESS VISITOR'S GUIDE
717-334-6296
http://www.gettysburgaddress.com
gbtours@mail.cvn.net
778 Baltimore St • Gettysburg PA 17325
"Where History Comes Alive." The center of everything & all within walking distance. Package & group plans available.

GETTYSBURG CONVENTION & VISITORS BUREAU
717-334-6274
717-334-1616 Fax
http://www.gettysburg.com
35 Carlisle St • Gettysburg PA 17325
Helps promote various events such as collectors' shows, Civil War book shows, etc. Contact for a complete listing of all yearly events.

GETTYSBURG GROUP RESERVATIONS
717-334-6020 • 800-447-8788
grpres@mail.cvn.net
200 Steinwehr Ave • Gettysburg PA 17325
Offer years of service & professionals to arrange tours your group will long remember & cherish. Tours planned for Gettysburg & surrounding areas.

GETTYSBURG ONLINE
717-334-0090
http://138.234.80.3/~s000057/main.html
shoffman@cvn.net
Seth Hoffman
397 Village Dr
Gettysburg PA 17325
Complete tourist guide to Gettysburg, showing B&Bs, specialty shops, activities for kids, etc., on the Internet.

GETTYSBURG SCENIC RAIL TOURS
717-334-6932
106 N Washington St
Gettysburg PA 17325
Ride into history, April-October. Special events include Civil War train raids, Lincoln weekend, fall foliage trips, dinner trips, & Santa trains. Group rates available.

GETTYSBURG TOUR GUIDES
717-334-1124
Gettysburg National Military Park
97 Taneytown Rd
Gettysburg PA 17325-2804
Licensed battlefield guides, tested & licensed by Natl. Park Service to ensure quality/accuracy. Personal tour in your car; short/long tours. Over 75 years experience.

GRANBURY CONVENTION & VISITORS BUREAU
800-950-2212
100 N Crockett St
Granbury TX 76048-2127
Sponsors reenactments & other events. Tourist info.

GULFSTREAM VANGUARD
804-288-9700 • 804-288-0916 Fax
Richmond VA 23232
Follow the route of the "Final Campaign." Limousines, sedans, 14 passenger vans.

HISTORIC AIR TOURS, INC.
800-VA BY AIR
Williamsburg-Jamestown Airport
PO Box 681 • Williamsburg VA 23187-0681
See the battlefields on historic air tours. See the Lower Peninsula, Richmond, Petersburg, etc. Reasonable & reliable. Expert commentary.

HISTORIC HAMPTON
800-800-2202 • 757-727-1102
http://www.hampton.va.us/tourism
710 Settlers Landing Rd
Hampton VA 23669-4035
Historic reenactments, world-class museums, Chesapeake Bay seafood, Fort Wool, Casemate Museum
at Fort Monroe, new site on the Va. Civil War Trail. Minutes from Williamsburg. Free guide.

HISTORIC HAUNTS OF WINCHESTER
540-662-3424 Phone & Fax
Mac Rutherford / Keith Toney
PO Box 1415
Winchester VA 22604-1415
Ghost & history walking tours in Winchester, Va.; 7 PM Sat. from Cork St. Tavern, April-Oct. Adults $8, Children 6-12 $4. Info. on Gettysburg & Antietam historic tours.

HISTORIC TRAVELER MAGAZINE
717-657-9555
102430.410@compuserve.com
6405 Flank Dr
Harrisburg PA 17112

Bi-monthly magazine guide to historic sites. Travel, routes, background, etc. $11.97/yr.

HISTORY AMERICA TOURS
800-628-8542 • 972-713-7173 Fax
PO Box 797687
Dallas TX 75379-7687
Specializing in Civil War tours & cruises, accompanied by historians. From motor coach to clipper ship. Call for details & free brochure.

CRAIG HOWELL
chowell@erols.com
1825 T St NW
Washington DC 20009
Eastern battlefield guide for individuals or groups, single or multiple day. Custom-tailored tours for battlefields of your choice.

HUNT-PHELAN HOME
901-344-3166 • 800-350-9009
533 Beale St
Memphis TN 38103
Discover a Civil War treasure. Built in the 1800s; filled with the family's original furnishings & documents. Free brochure.

JEFFERSON DAVIS STATE HISTORIC SITE
912-831-2335 • 912-831-2060 Fax
338 Jeff Davis Park Rd
Fitzgerald GA 31750
Confederate memorial & museum, containing relics from a Ga. battle flag to rare uniforms. Davis family's capture at this site on May 10, 1865, marked official end of the Confederacy.

KENNESAW MOUNTAIN NATL BATTLEFIELD PARK
770-422-3696
900 Kennesaw Mountain Dr
Kennesaw GA 30152

KENTUCKY HERITAGE TOUR GUIDE
800-225-TRIP
Capital Plaza Tower
500 Mero St Fl 22
Frankfort KY 40601-1957
Contains all the info. you'll need to conduct your own visit to Kentucky. Civil War battle reenactments, historic outdoor dramas, driving tours. Free guide.

KURTZ CULTURAL CENTER
2 N Cameron St
Winchester VA 22601-4728
Welcome center for historic Winchester Civil War Information Center, Patsy Cline display, rotating exhibits. Open daily. (See ad page 229)

THE LEXINGTON CIVIL WAR COMPANY
540-464-1100
Lexington, Virginia: Auto Tape Guide to Civil War Sites. Drive at your own pace. Featuring music by Bobby Horton.

THE MADISON HOUSE B&B
800-828-6422 • 804-528-1503
Dale & Irene Smith
413 Madison St
Lynchburg VA 24504-2435
Lee surrendered here. Longstreet recuperated here. Early, Dearing, Garland, Rodes buried here. Elegant accommodations. "Dedicated to Yesterday's Charm with Today's Convenience." Civil War Library. Tour packets.

MAJOR VISTA MEDIA, INC.
800-554-3108
111 S Monroe St
Monroe MI 48161
Custer's Monroe - narrated 30-min. video tour around hometown of George & Libbie Custer, featuring homes, sites & photos. $29.95 + $4 S&H.

MANSFIELD PLANTATION
800-355-3223
1776 Mansfield Rd
Georgetown SC 29440-9500
Historic bed & breakfast combining the best of the old & the new South. $75-$95/night, double occupancy. Guided tours for groups of 12 or more with advance registration - $6/person.

PATRICK MC DONALD
912-748-6286
PO Box 366
Pooler GA 31322-0366
Civil War tours of the low country, battlefields, skirmish sites, forts, historic homes, etc. of Savannah, Ga., Beaufort, S.C., Hilton Head Is., Ridgeland, S,C., & environs. Long/short tours. Licensed guide.

MISSISSIPPI (COLUMBUS) CONVENTION & VISITORS BUREAU
800-327-2686
Columbus MS
Annual February Battle of West Point & Prairie reenactment & authentic dance. Call for info. & dates.

MISSISSIPPI TOURISM
800-WARMEST
PO Box 1705
Ocean Springs MS 39566-1705

Free Civil War guide to the battlegrounds & other historic places of Mississippi.

MISSOURI DIVISION OF TOURISM
800-777-0068
Convention & Visitors Bureau
Cape Girardeau MO
"Hearts of Blue & Grey" Civil War sites - Fort D, Union Monument & fountain, Confederate War memorial, CW hospital.

MONOCACY BATTLEFIELD & BOOKSTORE
301-662-3515
Parks & History Association
4801 Urbana Pike # B
Frederick MD 21704

JOHN S. MOSBY HERITAGE AREA
540-687-6681
PO Box 1178
Middleburg VA 20118-1178
Maps of Mosby Heritage Area - $20. Audiotape driving tour "Prelude to Gettysburg" - $17. Free "Drive Through History" brochure.

NEWPORT NEWS, VA
888-493-7386
Battlefield tours, historic houses, harbor tours, museum exhibits & living history events. Free visitor guide & Civil War tour brochure.

OATLANDS PLANTATION & GIFT SHOP
703-777-3174
20850 Oatlands Plantation Ln
Leesburg VA 20175

PAGE ONE
PO Box 4232
Richmond VA 23220
Guide to Virginia Civil War - all the Civil War trail sites.

PAMPLIN PARK CW SITE
804-861-2408
http://www.pamplinpark.org
6523 Duncan Rd • Petersburg VA 23803
Battlefield where in April 1865 Grant's forces "broke through" Confederate defenses, ending longest siege in US history. Pathways along original Confederate fortifications, interactive games. Tour a plantation house.

PARKERSBURG/WOOD CO. VISITORS & CONVENTION BUREAU
800-752-4982
http://wvweb.com/www/parkersburg.html
350 7th St
Parkersburg WV 26101-4610

Uncover wonderful, unexpected surprises in Greater Parkersburg, W.Va. Historic Victorian-style homes, river of intrigue.

JOHN PELHAM HISTORICAL ASSN, INC.
757-838-1685
http://members.aol.com/JPHA1982
JPHA1982@aol.com
Peggy Vogtsberger
7 Carmel Ter
Hampton VA 23666-2807
Bi-monthly newsletter, "The Cannoneer." Annual convention & tour of Fredericksburg; commemorative ceremony at Kelly's Ford. Supports preservation; active in erecting monuments. Archives located at Jacksonville Public Library, Jacksonville, Ala.

PENN STATE ALUMNI ASSN.
814-865-7679
Mary Jane Stout
105 Old Main • Pennsylvania State University
University Park PA 16802-1501
Penn State-sanctioned lecturers & battlefield walking tours by leading historians/authors. Also available over the Internet. A continuing & distance education service.

PENNSYLVANIA
800-VISIT-PA x606
Full color guide to all the sites & attractions of historic Pennsylvania.

TIMOTHY J. REESE
301-834-6261
118 E Main St • PO Box 458
Burkittsville MD 21718
Crampton's Gap & South Mountain Battlefield tours -customized, individual or group, by author, historian & professional tour guide. Also tour sites peripheral to 1862 MD Campaign.

RICHMOND NEWSPAPERS SUPPLEMENTARY PUBLICATIONS
800-422-4434
PO Box 85333
Richmond VA 23293-5333
The Insider's Guide to the Civil War (Eastern Theater), Travel Guide - $9.95.

ROOTS & WINGS EXCURSIONS
800-722-9005
Walk in the footsteps of Civil War heroes. See the war's most important sites with expert guides. Gettysburg, Antietam, Richmond, more.

SCHRIVER HOUSE
717-337-2800
309 Baltimore St
Gettysburg PA 17325
Civil War House Tour of George Washington
Schriver's private residence built in 1860.
Presents civilian point of view.

SELBY HOUSE
540-373-7037
226 Princess Anne St
Fredericksburg VA 22401-6039
Four spacious rooms, private bath, full
breakfasts. Official tour guide for battles of
Fredericksburg, Chancellorsville, Wilderness,
and Spotsylvania Court House. Member of
APCWS.

STEAMBOATIN' VACATIONS
800-214-2579
Travel America's rivers on 3-14 night
steamboating cruise. Free brochure.

STONEWALL JACKSON HOUSE
540-463-2552 • 540-463-4088 Fax
Michael A. Lynn
8 E Washington St.
Lexington VA 24450-2529
The Confederate general's only home with
restored garden & museum shop. Tours every
half hour Mon-Sat 9-5, Sun 1-5; last tour
begins at 4:30PM. Open until 6PM
June-August. Closed major holidays.

SURRATT HOUSE MUSEUM & GIFT SHOP
301-868-1121
301-868-8177 Fax
http://www.engr.umd.edu/~clwspoon/surratt.html
Laurie Verge, Director
PO Box 427 • 9118 Brandywine Rd
Clinton MD 20735-0427
1852 home of the Surratt family. Served also
as a tavern, hostelry, post office & link in the
Confederate spy network. Played role in
Lincoln assassination. (See ad page 236)

TIME TRAVELERS ANTIQUES
717-337-0011
312 Baltimore St
Gettysburg PA 17325
Fine general line of quality Americana,
collectibles & decorative arts in ca.1901
Victorian house. Costumed Civil War walking
tours of Old Baltimore Street sites.

M. TRACEY TODD
803-571-6036
mttodd@mindspring.com

Walk Charleston, SC - the "cradle of
secession" - with local historian & museum
administrator.

TRAVEL AMERICA, INC.
800-225-2553
131 Dodge St Ste 5
Beverly MA 01915-1861
Seminars & trips on such topics as the
American Revolution, the Old West, the Civil
War, American History. Contact for info.

VALENTINE RIVERSIDE
800-365-7272
550 E Marshall St
Richmond VA 23219-1852
Richmond's innovative history park at the falls
of the James River. Civil War tours,
sound/light show, vintage carousel, high-tech
exhibits, African-American history/tours,
archeological digs, living history.

VICKSBURG CONVENTION & VISITORS BUREAU
800-221-3536
601-636-4642 Hayes Latham
http://www.vicksburg.org/cvb
PO Box 110
Vicksburg MS 39181-0110
Annual March "Run Through History" through
Vicksburg NMP. 10K race, 5K walk, 1-mile
run. Refreshments, music.

VIRGINIA DIVISION OF TOURISM
800-321-1865 • 804-371-8164
804-786-1919 Fax
http://www.VIRGINIA.org
901 E Byrd St
Richmond VA 23219-4069
Call for free Civil War brochure, "Virginia Is for
Lovers" travel guide & state highway map.

WAYFARING TRAVELERS
410-666-7456
http://www.gorp.com/wayfaring
Elizabeth Coxe
27 Sunnyview Dr
Phoenix MD 21131-2036
Walking tours along the backroads & hidden
corners of historic Shenandoah Valley &
colonial Virginia.

WINCHESTER-FREDERICK CO. VISITORS CENTER
540-662-4135
1360 S Pleasant Valley Rd
Winchester VA 22601-4447

**YANKEE DRY TORTUGAS NATIONAL
PARK FERRY**
800-634-0939 • 305-294-7009
PO Box 5903
Key West FL 33040
8 AM sailings. Galley on board for breakfast &
lunch -snacks. Guided tour of Fort Jefferson
by on-board guide. Year-round schedule.
Fare - $79 adults; $69 seniors; $49 children.

7TH REGIMENT, TEXAS VOL. BRIGADE
303-221-3099
Capt. E. Roy Jordan
300 E Harmony Rd • Fort Collins CO 80525
Civil War gun club to promote family fun
through black powder shooting & safety.

THE AMERICAN HISTORICAL FOUNDATION
800-368-8080 • 804-353-1812
804-359-4895 Fax
http://www.ahfrichmond.com
1142 W Grace St
Richmond VA 23220-3613
Firing reproductions of Lee's 1851 Navy
Revolver (Limited). Colt's 34d Model Dragoon
Revolvers, Jackson LeMat, JEB Stuart Le
Mat, Lee/Grant Henry Rifles, etc.

DALE C. ANDERSON CO.
4 W Confederate Ave • Gettysburg PA 17325
Firearms, edged weapons, uniforms,
accoutrements, & 1000s of other objects
touching all periods & significant events,
1776-1945. Emphasis on Civil War era. Our
37th year. Photo-illus. militaria catalog issued
bi-monthly - $12/yr.

ANDERSONVILLE ANTIQUES
912-924-2558 • 912-924-1044
Peggy & Fred Sheppard
PO Box 26 • Andersonville GA 31711
Authentic Civil War guns, swords, buttons,
documents; books on the Civil War.

ANTIQUE AMERICAN FIREARMS
847-304-GUNS
PO Box 1861 • Barrington IL 60011-1861
Civil War weapons search - match your
weapon's serial number with our database to
identify issuance. Annual membership.

THE ARTILLERYMAN
800-777-1862 • 802-889-3500
802-889-5627 Fax
firetec@firetec.com attn.artilleryman
RR 1 Box 36, Monarch Hill Rd
Tunbridge VT 05077-9707
Quarterly magazine dealing with artillery,
1750-1898. Safety, places to visit, history,
workshops, & more. $18/yr. Sample - $2.

ATLANTA ARSENAL
5750 Pebblebrook Trl
Gainesville GA 30506-6595
Reproduction Confederate painted canvas
accoutrements, copy from originals, incl.
cartridge boxes, cap boxes, bayonet
scabbards, slings, belts. Free price list.

AUTAUGA ARMS, INC.
800-262-9563 • 331-361-2950
331-361-2931 Fax
817 S Memorial Dr
Prattville AL 36067-5734
Brass tube scope, 6x15 magnification. Scope
length 382 mm. $149.95 + $10.95 S&H
includes mounts.

BATON ROUGE ARSENAL
504-667-1861
PO Box 40512
Baton Rouge LA 70835-0512
Manufacturers of steel cannon tubes,
cartridges, & limbers. 1841 six-pounder field
gun, 2.6" Wiard rifle, 12-pounder field
howitzer, breech-loaders, etc. Pricelist -SASE.

BATTLEFIELD VIDEO PRODUCTIONS
6374 Larch Ln
Macungie PA 18062-9380
Civil War guns video. 47-min. video of the
guns of the Civil War, their makers, & those
who used them. Live fire demonstration.
$29.95 ppd.

ROBERT L. BAXTER
1207 Nettie Dr
Miamisburg OH 45342-3428
New muzzleloader brass castings, parts, &
supplies. Dealer inquiries invited. Catalog - $2.

BELL CONSULTING, INC.
352-753-0219
Ted & Pat Bell
PO Box 579
Lady Lake FL 32158-0579
Antique handguns, Bowie knives, cartridge
belts & holsters, rifles, deringers, swords.
Buy/sell/trade. Catalog - send #10 SASE.

BELLINGER'S MILITARY ANTIQUES
770-992-5574
Bill Bellinger
PO Box 76371-SB • Atlanta GA 30358-1371
FULL-TIME DEALER of antique firearms,
edged weapons, belt plates, leather goods,
books & miscellaneous from the 17th-19th
century. Civil War a specialty. Catalog - $3; 4
issues - $10 (overseas - $20).

BLACK CREEK GUN SHOP
540-888-3349
193 Myers Ln
Winchester VA 22603-2859
Black powder & percussion caps at huge
savings. Musket caps, pistol caps, rifle &
cannon powder. Can be shipped through the
mail with certain limitations.

BLACKSWORD ARMOURY, INC.
352-495-9967
11717 SW 99th Ave
Gainesville FL 32608-5800
Replicas of historical weapons & armor from
ancient to Civil War. Catalog - $3.

THE BLADESMITH
George M. Sweeney
171 Dean St
Mansfield MA 02048-2421
Handcrafted frontier & Native American
knives. Copper-bladed knives, battlefield
daggers, custom Bowies, Civil War Bowies, all
with sheaths - $90-$200. For more info, send
$1 & SASE.

BORDER STATES LEATHERWORKS
501-361-2642
501-361-2851 Fax
1158 Apple Blossom Ln
Springdale AR 72762-9762
Civil War collectibles, original weapons &
equipment. Reproduction cavalry saddles &
equipment. Custom hand-forged bits.

BOWDOIN EXPLOSIVES, INC.
207-737-2630
RR 1 Box 1799
Litchfield ME 04350-9601
Elephant black powder - now 10% faster
burning with easy pour tin spouts. Supply your
event with the best. Call for pricing.

BOXER GALLERY & FRAME CO.
330-494-2348 Phone & Fax
PO Box 2362
North Canton OH 44720-0362
Prints by Troiani, Kunstler, Strain. Mounted
officers (15"H) & other Gettysburg figures
(9"H) in full color. Free list of swords,
bayonets, belts, buckles, insignia.

WILLIAM H. BOYDEN
198 W Plumstead Ave
Lansdowne PA 19050-1307
Hand-rolled & tied cartridge tubes made from
Frankford Arsenal pattern; paper matches
close to original color. 20 tubes - $5 + $2 S&H.

WALTER BUDD
3109 Eubanks Rd
Durham NC 27707-3622
Finest selection of US military antiques,
firearms, swords, uniforms, head gear, cavalry
equipment, McClellan saddles, mess gear,
horse-drawn army wagons & rolling stock, etc.
Subscription rate - $5 for 8 issues.

CALDWELL & CO. COLLECTIBLES
765-482-6280
civilwr@in-motion.net
816 Pleasant St
Lebanon IN 46052
Edged weapons, firearms, Civil War items &
general antiques. Buy/sell. Free catalog.

KEITH CANGELOSI
4201 Frenchman St
New Orleans LA 70122
Civil War military antiques. Longarms,
carbines, handguns, edged weapons. List - $2.

CANNON, LTD.
614-667-6896
http://www.florentine.com/cannonltd
2414 Bethel Church Rd • Coolville OH 45723
1/8 through full-scale cannons - 150 firing
models, bronze & steel-lined ductiles & solid
steel barrels. Museum kiln-dried oak
carriages. Video & catalog - $12.

THE CANNONADE
PO Box 20601
Rochester NY 14602-0601
*Nice Boom: The Amerian Civil War Artillery
Reenactor's Handbook*, Sean McAdoo, ed.
100+ pp., including drill, living history, tactics,
NCO training & more. $10.95 + $3 S&H.

CARTRIDGES UNLIMITED
314-664-4332
Mike Watson
4320 Hartford St # A
Saint Louis MO 63116-1917
Cartridges - blank, dummy & live; tubes;
labels; trapezoids for rifle, carbine & pistol.
Authentically rolled. Catalog -free w/ SASE.

CHATTAHOOCHEE B.P.S. CO.
770-889-6738
PO Box 2543 • Cumming GA 30128-6506
Colt muskets! N-SSA approved.

CIVIL WAR ANTIQUES
419-878-8355 • 419-882-5547
David W. Taylor
PO Box 87 • Sylvania OH 43560-0087
Pedigreed Civil War antiques, guns, swords,
uniforms, buckles, flags, drums, letters,
diaries, etc. Bought/sold. Catalog - $10.

CIVIL WAR EMPORIUM, INC.
408 Mill St
Occoquan VA 22125
From harmonicas to working cannons.
Working repros. Decorator models.
Consignments welcome. Buy/sell.

CIVIL WAR STORE
504-522-3328
212 Chartres St • New Orleans LA 70130
Mail order catalog - weapons, currency,
bonds, stamps, letters, diaries, CDVs, prints,
slave broadsides & bills of sale, autographs,
photos. Catalog - $4.

COLLECTOR'S ARMOURY
800-544-3456 x515 • 703-684-6111
703-683-5486 Fax
James W. Hernly
PO Box 59, Dept CWB • Alexandria VA 22313
Full line of "non-firing" reproduction pistols,
rifles, cannons, Civil War swords, knives,
bayonets, canteens, cap boxes, bugles &
flags. Free catalog. (See ad page 242)

COLLECTORS HERITAGE, INC.
PO Box 355
Bernardsville NJ 07924-0355
Reproduction museum-quality military swords,
knives, & bayonets. Catalog - $5 (ref.).

COLT BLACKPOWDER ARMS CO.
718-499-4678 • 718-768-8056 Fax
5 Centre Market Pl
New York NY 10013-3239
Genuine Colt percussion arms. 1851 Navy,
1860 Army, Walker, 49' Pocket, 61' Musket &
Artillery, many more plus Colt accessories.
Free 12-pg catalog.

COLUMBUS ARMORY
706-327-1424 Phone & Fax
David S. Brady
1104 Broadway • Columbus GA 31901-2429
Complete Civil War store featuring books,
relics, art, muskets & supplies. Buy/sell/trade.
Free price list. (See ad page 236)

COMPANY QUARTERMASTER
716-693-3239 • 716-693-3237 Fax
Terry Schultz
258 Zimmerman St
North Tonawanda NY 14120-4509
Enfield 3-band, bright barrel, lock & bands,
Italian markings removed, 1860s proofs, 1862
TOWER lock, BSAT stock cartouch, stock
darkened, square-eared screw escutcheons &
more. $455 + $10 S&H.

DAVID CONDON, INC.
540-687-5642 • 800-364-8416 Orders only
540-687-5649 Fax
PO Box 7 • Middleburg VA 20118-0007
Dealing in fine antique firearms since 1957.
Store located at 109 E Washington St (Route
50), Middleburg, Va.

THE CONESTOGA CO., INC.
800-987-BANG (2264)
PO Box 405
Bethlehem PA 18016-0405
Carbide cannons from 9" to 25", starting at
$49.95 ppd. Free catalog.

CONFEDERATE STATES ARSENAL
910-960-2466
Robert M. Schaber
1305 Spring Ave
Spring Lake NC 28390-2239
Antique artillery reproductions, sights,
accessories, parts. Full-scale only.
Restorations, work on original cannons. Free
catalog.

CRITTENDEN SCHMITT ARCHIVES
http://www.erols.com/tyrannus/archives/
csavideo.html
PO Box 4253 • Courthouse Station
Rockville MD 20850
Technical & historical books & videotapes
relating to weapons & ammunition of all types
& eras.

DEAD HORSE FORGE
1220 Price Station Rd
Church Hill MD 21623-1315
All types of knives, Hawks & other ironware,
powder horns & gourd canteens. Brochure -
send SASE.

DR. K. DIETRICH
PO Box 994 • Stockbridge MA 01262-0994
Buy/sell Civil War memorabilia, soldiers'
letters, weapons & accoutrements, images.
Listing - 2 stamps.

DIXIE GUN WORKS, INC.
800-238-6785 Orders only • 901-885-0700
901-885-0440 Fax
PO Box 130 • Union City TN 38261-0130
The source for firearms, parts, shooting
supplies, leather goods, uniforms, books,
patterns & cannons. 600-pg catalog with more
than 8,000 items - $5.

DIXIE LEATHER WORKS
502-442-1058 • 800-888-5183 Orders only
502-448-1049 Fax
PO Box 8221
Paducah KY 42002-8221
Military & civilian museum-quality repros. 60+
hard-to-find leather items. Documents, maps,
printed labels & stationery. Swords, firearms,
& hats. Handmade chairs, desks; leather
medical cases & bottle roll-up kits. Photo-illus.
catalog - $6.

R. STEPHEN DORSEY ANTIQUE MILITARIA
541-937-3348
PO Box 263 • Eugene OR 97440-0263
Largest western dealer in pre- & post-Civil
War, Civil War, & post-1900 U.S. militaria.
Guns, accoutrements, edged weapons, etc.
Catalog - $8 for 4 issues.

DONALD DREW
PO Box 422 • Stillwater MN 55082-0422
Basic training video for the beginner. Directly
from Harde's. Professional production. All
facings, rifle movements, load/fire procedure,
etc. VHS - $27 ppd.

DRUMMER BOY AMERICAN MILITARIA
717-296-7611
Christian Hill Rd
RR 4 Box 7198
Milford PA 18337-9702
Civil War repro goods: uniforms, buttons,
leather goods, insignia, firearms, tinware,
canteens, flags, books, blankets, sabers, etc.
Catalog - $1.

DYNAMIT NOBEL-RWS, INC.
81 Ruckman Rd
Closter NJ 07624-2102
Caps for muzzleloaders. Ignites black powder
& substitutes non-corrosive, non-erosive,
non-mercuric, & non-toxic. A cap to fit any
blackpowder gun.

EITNIER RIFLES
317-798-3525
Jerry Eitnier
PO Box 125
Hillsboro IN 47949-0125
Iron-mounted Southern guns.

ELF HOLLOW FORGE
910-763-7903
504 Woodlawn Ave
Wilmington NC 28401-7226
Hand-forged knives & tomahawks. Replica &
original design. Color photo brochure - $2.

FALL CREEK SUTTLERY
765-482-1861
765-482-1848 Fax
http://fcsutler.com
AJF5577@aol.com or fcsutler@aol.com
Andy Fulks
PO Box 92
Whitestown IN 46075-0092
Authentic reproduction Civil War & mid-19th-
century uniforms, leather goods, weapons,
shoes, tents, insignia, reference books &
more. 32-pg catalog - $3. (See ad pg 242)

FIREARMS SKIRMISH NATIONAL COMPETITION
North-South Skirmish Assn.
Winchester VA
More than 3,600 competitors on 200 teams
competing with muskets, carbines, revolvers,
mortars & cannon. Largest event of its kind.
Sutlers, food, free admission. Annual May
event.

N. FLAYDERMAN & CO., INC.
305-761-8855
PO Box 2446
Fort Lauderdale FL 33303-2446
Antique guns, swords, & knives. Nautical,
western & military collectibles from
Revolutionary through Spanish-American
wars. Catalog - $15.

THE FLINTLOCK ROOM
201-543-1861
201-543-1865 Fax
http://www.flintlockroom.com
6 Hilltop Rd
Mendham NJ 07945
Collectibles for Connoisseurs - classic
firearms, fine cigars, military figurines, prints &
militaria, Victorian miniatures.

FRAZER BROTHERS' 17TH REGIMENT
214-696-1865 • 214-426-4230 Fax
5641 Yale Blvd Ste 125
Dallas TX 75206-5026
Uniforms & equipment, artillery hardware, &
side arms. Civilian clothing (men only).
Handmade leather goods. Large supply of
tinware. Boots. American products.

GOEX, INC. (BELIN PLANT)
717-457-6724
1002 Springbrook Ave
Moosic PA 18507-1814
Last American manufacturer of authentic
black powder for reenactors, target shooters,
hunting & competition. Goex black powder
(FFg). Quality & consistency to make every
shot your best shot.

WILL GORGES CIVIL WAR MILITARIA
919-636-3039
919-637-1862 Fax
http://www.collectorsnet.com/gorges/index.htm
rebel!@abaco.coastalnet.com
2100 Trent Blvd
New Bern NC 28560-5326
Largest active inventory of authentic items in
the Southeast. Fine quality uniforms &
weapons our specialty. Buy/sell/appraise/
broker. Catalog - $10.

GREY OWL INDIAN CRAFT SALES CORP.
718-341-4000 • 718-527-6000 Fax
Wes Cochrane
13205 Merrick Blvd • PO Box 340468
Jamaica NY 11434-0468
Green River knives, powder flasks, military
buttons, buckskin, leathers, dags, strikers,
books, tapes, videos, recordings, etc. 200
custom kits/4000+ items. Catalog - $3.

THE GUN REPORT
309-582-5311 • 309-582-5555 Fax
John Mullen
PO Box 38
Aledo IL 61231-0038
The new *Gun Report Index* - your guide to 35
years of collectible firearm history. 128 pp.,
$24.95 + $3.50 S&H.

DENNIS HEATH
919-569-8781
RR 1 Box 55A
Deep Run NC 28525-9703
Civil War weapons, relics, accoutrements.
Catalog - $7/yr.

HILLBILLY SPORTS, INC.
410-378-4533
PO Box 70
Conowingo MD 21918-0070
Leather goods, period firearms, uniform items,
camp items & much more. Catalog - $3.

HISTORIC FRAMING & COLLECTIBLES
410-465-0549
Joe Parr
8344 Main St
Ellicott City MD 21043-4653
Civil War weaponry & assorted items. Military
art by all major artists, including aviation &
WWII. True conservation-quality framing.

THE HORSE SOLDIER
717-334-0347 • 717-334-5016 Fax
http://www.bmark.com/horsesoldier.antiques
hsoldier@cvn.net
PO Box 184
Cashtown PA 17310-0184
Buying, selling & appraising Civil War military
antiques: firearms, edged weapons, photographs, documents, battlefield relics & more!
All items unconditionally guaranteed. Soldier
research service available. Semi-annual
catalog - $10/yr.

THE HOUSE OF TIMES PAST
864-834-0061
634 W Darby Rd
Greenville SC 29609

Period shop with authentic clothing, rifles,
muzzleloading supplies & accessories for
living historians & reenactors. Catalog - $2.

HUNTERDON IMPORTING CO.
304-728-7730
PO Box 187 • 192 High St
Harpers Ferry WV 25425-0187
Engraved swords - US Foot Officer's & CSA
Cavalry Officer's.

JACQUES NOEL JACOBSEN, JR.
718-981-0973
60 Manor Rd
Staten Island NY 10310-2626
Antiques & military collectibles, insignia,
weapons, medals, uniforms, Kepis, relics,
photos, paintings, & band instruments.
Catalog - $12 for 3 issues. $15 overseas.

JAMES COUNTRY MERCANTILE
816-781-9473
816-781-1470 Fax
JAMESCNTRY@aol.com
Del Warren or Michael Gooch
111 N Main St
Liberty MO 64068-1639
For your military & civilian reenacting needs -
weapons, accoutrements, clothing, patterns.
Illus. catalog - $6 ppd.

GORDON WILSON JENKS & CO.
800-835-7933
Goex black powder - all granulations, incl.
authentic new cartridge powder.

JOHN'S RELICS
803-549-7751
John Steele
227 Robertson Blvd
Walterboro SC 29488-2752
Civil War & colonial relics, arms
accoutrements, veteran memorabilia,
newspapers, books, CW tokens, photography,
buttons & related memorabilia. Catalog - $1
(ref. w/ purchase).

KAWARTHA MARKETING COMPANY
705-639-2572
705-639-1809 Fax
RR 1 Station W
Norwood Ontario, KOL 2VO Canada
Firearms, cannons, knives, helmets,
bayonets, daggers, swords, surplus, uniforms,
etc. Including originals that have seen battle.
Catalog - $4 (ref. w/ order).

KINGSTON MILITARY ANTIQUES
770-336-9354
Jerelhook@aol.com
Jere Hook
PO Box 217 • Kingston GA 30145-0217
Buy/sell/trade pre-1898 militaria, mostly Civil
War. By appt. only. Catalog - 32¢.

L & G EARLY ARMS
2049 Clermont Laurel Rd
New Richmond OH 45157-9557
Authentic Civil War guns. Free list w/
business-size SASE.

GEORGE LAYMAN
55 Littleton Rd Apt 24F
Ayer MA 01432-1762
1866 Peabody Breech-Loading Rifle Catalog,
new repro. *Rolling Block Rifle; A Guide to the
Maynard Breech Loader.* Single shot books.

LEGEND PRODUCTS CORPORATION
21218 Saint Andrews Blvd
Boca Raton FL 33433-2435
"Black Canyon Powder" solves the problem of
sulfur corrosion & fouling. Direct
weight-for-weight replacement for black
powder.

LEGENDARY ARMS, INC.
800-528-2767 • 908-788-7330
908-788-8522 Fax
PO Box 479 • Three Bridges NJ 08887-0479
Museum-quality, authentic duplication. Finest
repros: swords, knives, battle axe, & bugle,
uniforms of the Civil War.

LEGENDARY ARMS, INC.
800-875-7967 • 212-532-ARMS
Greeley Square Station
PO Box 20198 • New York NY 10001-9992
High-quality reproduction swords, sabers,
spurs, entrenching tools, bayonets, cutlasses.
Officers', Cav., NCOs, etc. Call for price list.

LODGEWOOD MFG.
414-473-5444 • 414-473-8970 Fax
William V. Osborne II
494 Ventura Ln • Whitewater WI 53190-1500
Civil War guns & parts. United States martial
arms 1780-1898.

LOG CABIN SHOP
800-837-1082 • 330-948-1082
330-948-4307 Fax
http://www.logcabinshop.com
logcabin@logcabinshop.com
8010 Lafayette Rd • PO Box 275
Lodi OH 44254-0275

Full line of muzzleloading guns, kits,
components, supplies, accessories, books,
cookware, blankets, etc. 200-pp. catalog - $5.

HARDIE MALONEY
504-522-3328
212 Chartres St
New Orleans LA 70130-2215
Civil War store. Confederate currency, bonds,
stamps, covers, CDV.s, letters, diaries,
documents, autographs, pistols & swords.

MARILL PRODUCTIONS
PO Box 460820
San Francisco CA 94146-0820
Video documentaries on Colt revolvers
(1836-1869) & Bowie knives (1820-1870),
in-depth, exquisite. $29.95 ea. or both for $45.

JOSEPH L. MARTIN
770-428-1966
PO Box 603
Smyrna GA 30081-0603
Buying, selling, trading fine Civil War swords,
guns, uniforms, flags, etc. Over 35 yrs of
experience in dealing military items.
Competent appraisals available.

MATUSZEK'S
847-253-4685
Frank Matuszek
126 E Wing St # 210 • Arlington Hts IL 60004
Civil War & Indian War firearms, swords,
uniforms & other collectibles. Sample catalog
- $2. Mention the Civil War Source Book!

MERCURY SUPPLY CO.
409-327-3707
101 Lee St • Livingston TX 77351
Civil War uniforms, reproduction equipment,
tents, accoutrements, leather goods, firearms
military & civilian. Catalog - $2.

MILES OF HISTORY
423-337-2540
http://www.collectorsnet.com/miles
huskey@usit.net
Miles Huskey
PO Box 599 • Sweetwater TN 37874-0599
Buy/sell/trade Civil War items. Images,
buttons, weapons, documents, personal
items, & authentic period jewelry available
through internet auction on website.

THE MILITARY COLLECTION
PO Box 830970M • Miami FL 33283-0970
Helmets, uniforms, field gear, awards,
medals, flags, weapons, swords, photos, etc.
Catalog - $8.

MORGAN'S CIVIL WAR MEMORABILIA
7864 Pullbridge Ct
West Chester OH 45069-1687
Buys/sells/trades buttons, relics, documents, weapons. Catalog - free w/ SASE.

MOUNTAIN STATE MUZZLELOADING SUPPLIES, INC.
800-445-1776 • 304-375-7842
304-375-3737 Fax
Terry Lambert
RR 2 Box 154-1 Dept CW
Williamstown WV 26187-9540
Everything for muzzleloading hunters, shooters, & builders. Guns, parts, shooting/cleaning supplies, casting supplies, books, bags, etc. Catalog - $4 (ref.).

MUSEUM OF AMERICAN CAVALRY
540-740-3959
Peter & Jane Comtois
298 Old Cross Rd
New Market VA 22844-9511
History of the Horse Soldier from colonial times through Vietnam & modern times. Gift shop with books, flags, weapons, relics, other items. Formerly Indian Hollow Antiques.

MUSEUM OF HISTORICAL ARMS, INC.
2750 Coral Way Ste 204
Miami FL 33145-3200
Catalog-reference book contains more than 1600 imported items for sale. Firearms & edged weapons, all periods. Catalog - $10.

MUSEUM REPLICAS LIMITED
PO Box 840
Conyers GA 30207-0840
Reproductions of authentic museum quality, historically accurate replicas of weapons & period battle wear. Catalog - $1.

NAVY ARMS CO.
201-945-2500
689 Bergen Blvd
Ridgefield NJ 07657-1499
Finest in quality replica firearms. Revolvers, Sharps rifles & carbines, Enfields, leather goods.

NESHANIC DEPOT
610-847-5627
610-847-8618 Fax
283 Durham Rd • PO Box 367
Ottsville PA 18942-0367
Historic artifacts, muzzleloading guns & supplies, originals, reproductions, & historic flags.

NMC ENTERPRISES
800-591-2999 (24 hrs.)
913 18th St Ste 2
Santa Monica CA 90403
Civil War blackpowder accessories; fine, hand-crafted leather. Holsters, belts, pouches, bags, buckles. Free catalog.

THE NOBEL COLLECTION
800-806-6253
PO Box 3444 • Merrifield VA 22116-3444
Historic reproductions & collectible swords. From King Arthur to Samurai. Free catalog.

OLD SOUTH MILITARY ANTIQUES
919-523-7181
Dennis Heath
403A E Newbern Rd
Kinston NC 28501
Full line of Civil War muskets, swords, accoutrements & artifacts at reasonable prices. Shop open Mon-Sat. Catalog - $7/yr.

OLD SUTLER JOHN
607-775-4434 Phone & Fax
Westview Station • PO Box 174
Binghamton NY 13905-0174
Full line of quality reproduction Civil War guns, bayonets, swords, uniforms, leather items, & other collectibles. Catalog - $3. (See ad page 236)

OSAGE PRESS
800-200-4792
PO Box 5082
Rockford IL 61125-0082
Repro of 1860 Spencer Repeating Rifle Patent Drawings -start at $13.95. Free catalog.

PALADIN PRESS
800-392-2400
http://www.paladin-press.com
pala@rmii.com
Tina Mills
PO Box 1307
Boulder CO 80306-1307
American Swords and Sword Makers.
Definitive book for all edged weapons. Collectors, dealers, etc. 664 pp. -$79.95. Catalog - $2.

PAULSON BROS. ORDINANCE CORP.
715-263-3300
715-263-3301 Fax
PO Box 121
Clear Lake WI 54005-0121
Limber & chest parts.

PENINSULA FIREARMS
813-547-6471 • 813-547-6175 Fax
7116 78th St N
Pinellas Park FL 33781
Civil War reproduction muskets, revolvers &
accessories. Catalog - $3.

PETRO-EXPLO, INC.
800-588-8282 • 817-478-8888
817-478-8891 Fax
http://www.fastlane.net/~petro
petro@fastlane.net
7650 US Hwy 287 #100
Arlington TX 76017
Elephant black powder for use in
Flintlock/Caplock rifles & shotguns. Performs
excellently in rifles & shotguns in all weather
conditions.

THE PICKET POST
540-371-7703
Tim Garrett & Bill Henderson
602 Caroline St
Fredericksburg VA 22401-5902
Civil War military antiques: canteens, buttons,
swords, guns, images, buckles, uniforms.
Buys/sells. Photo-illus. catalog - $10 for 3
issues.

PLAINESMAN GUN SHOP
RR 1 Box 199 • Tomah WI 54660-9736
Civil War & Indian War rifles & carbines. No
mail order, so stop in & see the Plainesman
Gun Shop.

POWDER HORNS
PO Box 397
Fletcher OH 45326-0397
Make powder horns from start to finish,
including engraving them for your use, gifts,
display, or sale -$12.95.

R & R BOOKS
716-346-2577
3020 E Lake Rd
Livonia NY 14487
Books on weapons, featuring *The British
Soldier's Firearm, Spencer Repeating
Firearms, Confederate Edged Weapons*, etc.

RAPINE BULLET MANUFACTURING CO.
215-679-5413
9503 Landis Ln
East Greenville PA 18041-2541
Civil War bullet molds. Catalog - $2.

THE REGIMENTAL QUARTERMASTER
215-672-6891 • 215-672-9020 Fax
PO Box 553 • Hatboro PA 19040-0553

Civil War repro muskets, carbines, revolvers,
swords, uniforms, shoes, boots, buckles,
buttons, tents, tapes, tinware, accoutrements,
accessories. Catalog - $2 ($1 ref.).

RICHMOND ARSENAL
804-272-4570 Phone & Fax
7605 Midlothian Tpke
Richmond VA 23235-5223
100% authentic Civil War antiques, from
common bullets & buttons to museum quality
weapons, accoutrements, uniforms, drums &
flags. Photo-illus. catalog - $10 for 3 issues.

L. ROMANO'S RIFLE CO.
315-695-2066
551 Stewarts Corners Rd
Pennellville NY 13132
Quality reproduction Spencers rifle & carbine
1860 models, 56/50 cal. Machined action &
parts made in NY. Free catalog.

S & S FIREARMS
718-497-1100
718-497-1105 Fax
7411 Myrtle Ave
Glendale NY 11385-7433
Military Americana. Antique gun parts,
carbines, Enfield, buttons, insignia, books,
equipment, appendages, headdress, etc.
Reenactor supplies. Original & reproduction.
Photo-illus. catalog - $3.

SCHNEIDER ENTERPRISES
414-534-6813
1252 N Browns Lake Dr
Burlington WI 53105-9794
Lowest prices, high quality on Civil War field &
naval-style cannons, & Gatling guns.
Brochure - $2.

SCHOOLHOUSE ANTIQUES
717-334-4564
Gettysburg PA 17325
Antique guns, relics, swords, uniforms,
souvenirs. Close to battlefield - 5 mi. on
Business Rt. 15 South.

SHARPSBURG ARSENAL
301-432-7700
301-432-7440 Fax
101 W Main St • PO Box 568
Sharpsburg MD 21782-0568
Purveyors of fine Civil War militaria; firearms,
edged weapons, buttons, bullets, leather
accoutrements, battlefield relics, books, flags,
personal & camp items, paper, letters, framed
prints. Buy/sell.

THE SINGLE SHOT EXCHANGE MAGAZINE
803-628-5326 Phone & Fax
singleshotex@earthlink.net
Dept B • PO Box 1055
York SC 29745-1055
Monthly magazine for black powder cartridge,
silhouette & Schuetzen shooters, & antique
gun collectors. Buy/sell/trade, historical &
how-to articles. Antique & classic firearms
only - $27.50/yr. V/MC accepted.

DALE S. SNAIR
816-747-0341
904 Deer Run Apt C
Warrensburg MO 64093
Civil War images, paper items, weapons,
accoutrements. $4 for next 4 price lists.

SOUTH BEND REPLICAS, INC.
219-289-4500
61650 Oak Rd • South Bend IN 46614-9345
Antique ordnance replicas since 1972. Solid
cast, machine bored, sleeved & lathe turned.
128-pg., 1200-photo catalog - $7. Brochure
only - SASE.

STAFFORD WHEEL & CARRIAGE
610-486-0567
Jeff Stafford
1019 Lieds Rd • Coatesville PA 19320-4837
Restoration & reproduction of Civil War
cannon carriages, wheels, & rolling stock.

STARS & BARS MILITARY ANTIQUES
540-972-1863
9832 Plank Rd • Spotsylvania VA 22553-4243
Civil War militaria: edged weapons, uniforms,
accoutrements, medals, weaponry, prints, etc.
On Chancellorsville battlefield, est. 1976.

STEEN CANNONS
606-329-2477
http://206.152.255.5/steen
steencannons@wwd.net
10730 Midland Trail Rd
Ashland KY 41102-9679
Authentic, full-scale reproductions. All barrels
cast solid, machine bored, sleeved, & lathe-
turned. Several models from which to choose.
Manufacturer of cannon carriages, limbers &
cannon & limber hardware.

STONE EAGLE PRESS
209-661-4030
PO Box 838
Madera CA 93639-0838
Manual of arms for the rifle & musket, from
original text (*U.S. Infantry & Rifle Tactics,
1861*) - $10.25.

STONEMAN TREASURERS
PO Box 15309
Philadelphia PA 19111
Musket & trapdoor Springfield parts.
Affordable historical collectibles, incl.
bayonets, swords, tools, relics, etc. 6-pg. list -
$1 + stamp.

SWORD & SABER
717-334-0205
2159 Baltimore Pike
Gettysburg PA 17325-7015
Specializing in original Confederate & Union
documents, framed items, relics, weapons &
swords. 5 illus. catalogs -$10.

THEME PRINTS, LTD.
800-CIVL WAR • 718-225-4067
PO Box 610123 • Bayside NY 11361-0123
Books, antique arms, historic documents,
photographs, letters & autographs from
Revolutionary era to early Hollywood.
Includes Civil War memorabilia. Fully illus.
catalog - $5, or $12/yr. (5 issues).

TIPPECANOE FRONTIER TRADING CO.
937-667-1816
114 E Main St • Tipp City OH 45371-1962
Thousands of items serving reenactors,
hunters, history buffs. Gunsmith for
restorations, information, minor repairs
(1700s-1900s). Long-range shooting supplies.
Catalog -$4.

**UPPER MISSISSIPPI VALLEY
MERCANTILE CO**
319-322-0896
319-383-5549 Fax
1607 Washington St
Davenport IA 52804-3613
Top quality goods & supplies for Civil War
reenactors; uniforms, tinware, tents, leather
goods, muskets, books, weapons, patterns,
more. 100-pp., illus. catalog - $3.

W.M.B. BLACK POWDER REPLICAS
314-631-1514
PO Box 6952
Saint Louis MO 63123-0252
The Yorktown Mortar Kit, 1/10th scale replica,
barrel is 3" long with 1" bore. Walnut wood
with brass hardware - $50. Catalog - $2.

WARNER LIMITED
800-371-9373
19 Seekonk Rd
Great Barrington MA 01230-1562
"Genovese: Civil War Gun series" prints. All
prints shipped flat.

WHITACRE'S MACHINE SHOP
540-877-1468
519 Turtle Meadow Dr
Winchester VA 22602-1986
Civil War rifle barrels. Fit original stocks.
1842, 1855-1863 Spring, 2-Band, Carbine.
Enfield barrels - Parkerhale style, Mississippi
& Zouave barrels. 3-land groove, tapered
depth rifling. N-SSA approved.

WILDMAN'S CIVIL WAR SURPLUS
770-422-1785
2879 S Main St
Kennesaw GA 30144-5624
Rare & antique guns, books, & other Civil War
collectibles. Price list - $2. (See ad page 233)

THE WINCHESTER SUTLER, INC.
540-888-3595
540-888-4632 Fax
270 Shadow Brook Ln
Winchester VA 22603-2071
Reproduction Civil War firearms, uniforms,
camp gear, accessories, shoes, boots, hats,
etc. Catalog - $4.

WISE CUSTOM KNIVES
910-353-1311
Michael Wise, Knifemaker
197 Charles Rd # 6
Jacksonville NC 28546
Custom-made knives.

YE OLDE POST OFFICE
334-928-0108
17070 Scenic Hwy 98 • PO Box 9
Point Clear AL 36564-0009
Dealer in antique & military collectibles, guns,
swords, uniforms, books, etc.

YESTERYEAR
615-893-3470
Larry W. Hicklen
3511 Old Nashville Hwy
Murfreesboro TN 37129-3094
Quality dug & non-dug Civil War artifacts of all
types. Buckles, buttons, swords, guns, paper,
leather, etc. Mail order subscription - $5/yr.

JOHN G. ZIMMERMAN
304-535-2558
PO Box 1351 • 1195 Washington St
Harpers Ferry WV 25425-1351
Master gunsmith; custom-made Civil War
muskets. Price on request.

NOTES

NOTES

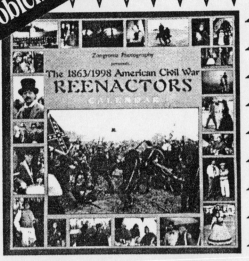

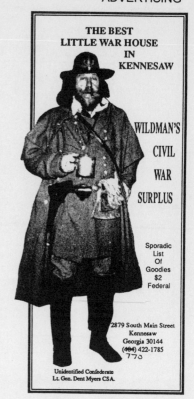

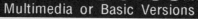

ACROSS THE DARK RIVER

The Odyssey of the 56th NC Infantry in the American Civil War
by Clyde H. Ray

In this novel, Ray recreates a period of American history in the words and experiences of the men and women who lived it. Almost every character actually existed, and almost every incident actually occurred. *Our State* magazine says: "Two features set this book apart from the average, run-of-the-mill battlefield Civil War novel. First, the descriptions of 1860s military life and tactics are highly accurate. Second, the soldiers in this book actually existed. A haunting look at North Carolinians at war."

Across the Dark River is available from:
Parkway Publishers, Inc., Box 3678, Boone, NC 28607
Cost: $18.95; S/H $3.00. NC Residents Add 6% sales tax.

ELM TREE
COLLECTIBLES, INC.

GENERAL ROBERT E. LEE

GENERAL U.S. GRANT

Custom developed 8" x 10" Grant or Lee photograph
$39.95 + $4 S&H each.

We are the archival source for rare Civil War photographs.
requests taken and items located.
No catalog. VISA, MasterCard, checks accepted.
Immediate Shipping
17 Parkstone Court • Stone Mountain, GA 30087
1-800-639-9886
http://www.elmtree-collectibles.com
elmtree@mindspring.com

Always Buying

Rockbridge Publishing
Civil War • Virginiana • Ghosts

NEW BOOKS
Our Own Fine Titles and More
FREE CATALOG

(800) 473-3943
P.O. Box 351 • Berryville, VA 22611

Our complete catalog on line (see ad page 244)
http://rockbpubl.com
cwpub@visuallink.com

Do you have a favorite Civil War business or site or product that is not included in this edition?

Use this form to make sure they're included in the 1999 edition of Jack Burd's Civil War Source Book.

I'd like to recommend the following for inclusion in the next edition. (Please give us as much information as you can .... at least a phone number so we can follow up!)

Company name _____

Contact _____

Address _____

City _____ State_____ Zip+4_____ - _____

Phone_____ Fax _____

e-mail_____ home page _____

Description of product or services _____

_____

_____

_____

_____

Your name (optional) _____

Your address _____

Your City/State & Zip _____

Thanks for Helping Make the Source Book Even More Helpful!

Rockbridge Publishing Company
P.O. Box 351 • Berryville, VA 22611
(800) 473-3943 • (540) 955-3980 • cwpub@visuallink.com